REFLECTIONS ON THE REVOLUTION OF OUR TIME

REFLECTIONS ON THE REVOLUTION OF OUR TIME

HAROLD J. LASKI

REPRINTS OF ECONOMIC CLASSICS

Augustus M. Kelley, Bookseller
New York 1968

Published by
FRANK CASS AND COMPANY LIMITED
67 Great Russell Street, London WC1
by arrangement with George Allen & Unwin Ltd.

Published in the U.S.A. by A. M. Kelley,
24 East 22nd Street, New York, U.S.A.

First edition	1943
New impression	1968

Library of Congress Catalog Card No. 68—14931

Printed in Holland by
N. V. Grafische Industrie Haarlem

TO MY FRIENDS

E. R. MURROW AND LANHAM TITCHENER

WITH AFFECTION

CONTENTS

PREFACE

This book owes an immense debt to my friends, especially to those endless debates at 17 Clarkson Road where my fellow evacuees and I have discussed its problems term after term, since war began, until, with the midnight news, we turned from analysis of principle to speculation upon the event. It owes much, too, to my students who, in the seminars at the London School of Economics and Political Science, have insisted on trying to understand both what they are fighting for and how they can free future generations of students from the curse of war. Much of it has been shaped by the questions and criticisms put to me at Labour Party conferences all over the country, and in those lectures in camp and aerodrome where the determined heckling of soldiers and airmen has taught me how Cromwell's Ironsides became that unbeatable instrument, a thinking army. I add that no small part of its doctrine is the outcome of the pride every citizen of this country is bound to have in the amazing heroism and endurance in the common people he has witnessed day by day during the blitz, and by the majestic spectacle of Russian resistance in the face of a threat which seemed almost to have civilization by the throat. I have, too, been naturally influenced by watching the skill with which President Roosevelt taught the American people the lesson that they can only belong to themselves as they give their service to freedom, and I hope I have not missed the significance of the opposition he so superbly fought until Japan, at Pearl Harbour, made the nature of the issue unmistakable.

I cannot but place on record how much I have learned from the writings of Professor E. H. Carr, especially from his *Conditions of Peace*, from those of Professor Max Lerner, Leonard Woolf and Kingsley Martin; and from talk with my friends Louis Lévy, André Labarthe, and Félix Gouin, I have learned not a little of the causes which led to the betrayal of France and of the spirit by which she will renovate that civilized tradition her people have so largely helped to shape.

I finished this book, begun in the second month of the war, just as Parliament began to discuss the issues of reconstruction, and Sir William Beveridge's *Report* on the Social Services provided at least one fundamental test by which we can judge how far the British government is really prepared to make the Four Freedoms part of the heritage of the next generation. To what is written in the pages that follow I need only add that the whole burden of Sir William's remarkable analysis seems to me to reinforce the conclusion there reached, that it is in the months between now and our victory that we have to take those vital decisions upon which depends our power to use it for great purposes. If we wait beyond the victory before we make our choice, we shall throw away one of the supreme opportunities of history.

I have dedicated this book to two friends with whom I have shared many hours of both grief and happiness in these years. Mr. Titchener, I know, will not mind my saying with special emphasis that our country owes an immense debt to Mr. E. R. Murrow. Day and night since before the war began he has done everything that courage and integrity can do to make events in this country a living reality to his fellow citizens of the United States. I am only one of the many Englishmen who have found in his faith and trust in our people a new power to endure and hope.

Lastly, as always, I could not have written this book had not all that has gone to its making been shared with my wife. I say no more than this because she would not permit me to say more. But at least I can put on record my knowledge that danger shared is affection deepened.

HAROLD J. LASKI

MANOR COTTAGE
LITTLE BARDFIELD, ESSEX

November 27, 1942

Chapter I

ON THE SPIRIT OF THE AGE

I

WE are in the midst of a period of revolutionary change that is likely to be as profound as any in the modern history of the human race. We shall not understand its inner nature unless we recognize it to be as significant in its essentials as that which saw the fall of the Roman empire, the birth, with the Reformation, of capitalist society, or, as in 1789, the final chapter in the dramatic rise of the middle class to power.

It is not a revolution made by thinkers, though some of them have foreseen its coming, and even shaped the large outlines of its direction. It is not a revolution, either, which any group of statesmen has deliberately brought about, even though some of them, consciously or unconsciously, have hastened its advent and increased its momentum. Its nature lies, as its inevitability will be found, in all that goes to give its present character to our society. We can, of course, recognize its advent and prepare for it; in that event, we might build a civilization richer and more secure than any of which we so far have knowledge. Or we may choose to resist its onset; in which case, it will appear to some future generation that our age has sought rather to sweep back the tides of the ocean than to oppose the decrees of men.

As always in a period of revolution, the drive to fundamental change is accompanied by disintegration and conflict; and, as always also, these are attributed to the wanton choice of evil men instead of to those deeper and impersonal causes which they are powerless to control and of which they are no more than transient symbols. As always, also, we seek less to discover those impersonal causes than to find some easy and partial remedy which will effect, at least for our own time, a passing obscuration of the obvious and more painful symptoms of the disease. *Après nous le déluge* has been the motto of every British Prime Minister from the Peace of Versailles until September 3, 1939. He has been content to chant some magic slogan where he ought at least to have attempted ruthless diagnosis. For only as we are aware of the nature of our disease can we embark upon the serious task of cure.

We are told that what is wrong with our age is its persistence in clinging to the outworn principle of national sovereignty; if the unit of political organization were to correspond with the unit of economic production, we should enter the promised land. Or the cure is found in a reformed education; and we are told that we train our people for a world that is dying instead of seeking to discipline their minds to the world that is struggling to be born. Could we but make men aware of the meaning of their inheritance, a newer and a better spirit would, we are informed, preside over the destinies of mankind. Others find the root of our malady in the decay of the religious spirit. Without the recovery of faith, they affirm, there is no sanction for those canons of civilized behaviour which alone make possible the preservation of a civilized purpose among men. Others, again, would find our salvation in the famous maxim *ne pas trop gouverner*; it is in the excessive zeal of statesmen to control every nook and cranny of the body politic that the source of our ills is to be found. Let government restore once again freedom of enterprise to business men, and we could enter upon a new era of creativeness from which war and insecurity could be abolished.

There is, of course, a sense in which each of these remedies has a hint of truth, even if it be partial and fragmentary. It is true enough that the sovereign national state is strategically incompatible with the world-market; for it is compelled, in order to safeguard itself, to narrow the potentialities of material benefit which that world-market offers us by its own inherent nature. The sovereign national state has, on the economic plane, compelled us to rethink ourselves into most of the cruder fallacies of the mercantilist age, and, thereby, to plan for restriction when the immanent logic of our machines demand that we plan for plenty. But so to plan for restriction is to pursue a policy necessarily detrimental to our neighbours. Inevitably, they resist its impact; and inevitably also, if they have the power, they take the means to minimize its influence. But, in the context of sovereignty, if they have the power the means involved are the threat, or the reality, of war; and it follows that those who connect the principle of national sovereignty with war have a strong case on their side.

Yet it is a partial case only. For even if the external strains upon our productive system were removed by the abrogation of national sovereignty, the histories of Rome and the United States make it clear that, in the absence of other fundamental changes, internal strains would still remain from which profound and violent conflict would be born. It is not necessary to deny that a world free from the poison of the sovereign state would be, on every plane, a better world than ours. But it would still not have solved the central problems we confront. It would still have to decide upon the purposes to which its power was to be devoted.

We need more education, better adapted to the character of our time. No person with even a fragment of civic sense is likely to deny this need. The main body of our population is untouched, in any profound way, by our cultural heritage. It goes through life mainly unaware of the forces which shape its destiny, the easy prey, in crisis, of any loudly proclaimed nostrum, quick to fall upon anyone, individual or group, to whom it is persuaded to attribute its ills. It has barely been trained to make its needs articulate. It has bewilderment without philosophy, and the abyss which normally separates its mental habits from those who rule over it means that, for the most part, neither can penetrate the mind of the other.

But a new spirit in education is not a factor independent of the material environment. Men cannot will its coming in a vacuum. They must be prepared to admit the evils caused by its absence; the changes its presence would secure must be assured of welcome. It halts in coming because there are doubts precisely upon these two heads. There is a vested interest in the perpetuation of ignorance which is endemic in our civilization. We cannot get rid of ignorance save as we are willing to attack that vested interest; and the signs are clear that it will bitterly defend itself if we move to the attack.

The decay of the religious spirit is widespread. But if we seek for a religious revival, we must be careful to define our terms with some precision. If, thereby, we mean a revival of faith in the supernatural, the evidence is clear that, especially in any of the historically dogmatic forms, it is unlikely; for their power to offer rational proof of their title to acceptance dwindles with every advance in the scientific understanding of the universe. There is, moreover, no form of cruelty in human experience to which the religious spirit has not been able to accommodate itself; there is a grim truth in the accusation that its votaries have been content, for the most part, to see it operate as the opium of the people. There is, again, no great advance in human knowledge of which the classic religions have not been the uncompromising opponents until its truth was so obvious that some shamefaced accommodation had to be sought. If by the religious spirit we mean the power of some system of theological dogma to influence the social behaviour of ordinary men, the answer to its claims is the simple one that their conduct, as believers, has been no better, if no worse, than that of the average in the given age.

But if by the religious spirit we mean an insistent call to devote oneself to an end beyond the private satisfaction of personality, the answer surely is that all the great movements of our time have commanded the power to invoke in their service a quality of effort in which the essence is the religious spirit. Whether we examine the history of socialism, or that of the nationalist movements which have revivified China and India, Republican Spain and Czechoslovakia, the root of their being has been their capacity, amid all their blunders, and even crimes, to win from men a passionate devotion, an ultimate selflessness, which has been the secret of all successful religions. In any other sense than this, the decay of the religious spirit is the natural outcome of historical causes it is now impossible to reverse upon any serious scale.

Unless, indeed, the world reverts to something like a chaos of competing barbarisms. It may possibly do so; and it might then well be that little bands of devotees would find escape from the ills of such a world in a variety of esoteric mysticisms the truth of which would be perceived only by those who had personally experienced their meaning. But if we are granted a world capable of planning for itself an ordered and rational life, the problem is to discover how to harness the emotional energies the great religions have been able to release to the purposes that ordered and rational life seeks to fulfil. The decay, in a word, recognized by the votaries of the historic faiths is the result, and not the cause, of the revolution that is proceeding.

All government arises because men move in opposed ways to their objectives; no one but an anarchist would deny that its existence is, under any circumstances we can foresee, a necessary condition of peaceful social relations. But the argument that, especially in the economic sphere, we are over-governed, is not one with which it is easy to have patience. Less government only means more liberty in a society about the foundations of which men are agreed and in which adequate economic security is general; in a society where there is grave divergence of view about those foundations, and where there is the economic insecurity exemplified by mass-unemployment, it means liberty only for those who control the sources of economic power.

It is too often forgotten by those who attack the intervention of government in the economic sphere that this has been primarily due to experience of its absence. The controls we know, whether of labour-conditions, of the issue of securities on the stock exchange, or of the right to build, have all been the outcome of a social experience that the unregulated competition of private interests has never resulted in a well-ordered society. This may be concealed for a considerable period, as when the vast resources of the American continent were being exploited for the first time by machine-technology; but when the society reaches maturity, there, as elsewhere, the land of opportunity becomes, literally for millions, the land of frustration, unless the acquisitive impulse can be harnessed to an agreed social purpose. The business man had a whole epoch in which to exercise his power for social ends; even to-day, outside the Soviet Union, he is still predominantly master of the machinery of the state. Yet in that epoch, his power to convince his fellows that the liberty from governmental control he demands is in their interest has visibly shrunk all over the world.

Business men have never complained of government intervention intended to protect their interests; tariffs, subsidies, bounties on export, special credit facilities, these, to take examples only, they have rarely failed to applaud. The intervention to which they have objected is that which has sought either the consumers' protection or that of the under-privileged in the labour-market. Against it, they have invoked those "economic laws" which, in their devotion to freedom, they have identified with the laws of nature. But they have forgotten that the "laws" of economics are, in fact, for the most part mere exercises in deduction from the logic of an abstract society only dimly patterned upon the world we know. That abstract society is one in which competition is always perfect and labour always mobile; an unemployed miner, in this happy world of concepts, can become to-morrow a tapesizer in a cotton-mill at the behest of that market of whose operations he and his employer alike have always perfect knowledge.

The economics upon which business men have relied were essentially a fighting creed made for them by men who were seeking, on their behalf, to state the case against the defenders of a decaying feudal society. They assumed, as it was made, the validity of certain assumptions which the main body of economists from Adam Smith to John Stuart Mill would have thought it madness to doubt: that private property in the instruments of production is sacred, that whatever is done by government agency must be less well done than if attempted by private enterprise, that the law-making power operates in the common interest, that each man knows his own interest best, and is in the best position to advance it.

It was an economics largely made in an epoch of advancing horizons, of growing optimism, of confident belief in the inescapable beneficence of the "invisible hand." It saw the new men advance so rapidly to power that it rarely stayed to investigate the social cost of their advance. It knew little of the impact of inherited wealth, less of monopoly, less still of the mysteries of company-finance or of that money-power which, in our own time, has come to dominate the economic scene. It accepted the inescapable validity of the gold standard; it assumed the power of the ordinary investor to have access to that esoteric knowledge which is, in fact, the private possession of a privileged few. It announced proudly that its system meant the sovereignty of the consumer without enquiring into the degree to which its method of distribution was socially beneficent. It even declared that, such was the magic of the system, each participant was able to secure from the pile of wealth exactly what he was "worth."

Yet, through it all, the simple difficulty remained that while its argument convinced the successful, it could not convince those who were excluded from the benefits of the system. So long as its power to produce profitably expanded, it imposed its faith without undue difficulty; the concessions statesmen were driven to make limited the volume of expressed and active discontent. When that power began to contract, and the policy of concession threatened the privileges of the successful, the discontent began to widen to revolutionary proportions. Those excluded from benefit then attacked, not the volume of the concessions conferred, but the system itself upon which the concessions depended. They saw society rather as "Pigeon" Paley saw it, than as a harmony miraculously produced by an invisible hand.

To argue, before this situation, that we should return to a world free from economic interventionism is like arguing to the exponents of expanding capitalism in the mid-nineteenth century that Britain should go back to the principles of a feudal economy. History does not permit men the luxury of escaping their inheritance. The business men will not return to their mastery of the state upon their own terms for the simple reason that no one has any longer confidence in them except themselves. All their assumptions broke down by all the vital tests of verifiable experience. When they had the chance of reform, they demanded "recovery" instead. But by "recovery" they meant a return to exactly those conditions which resulted in the need for reform. It could not be forgotten that they were the makers of the slums, that their system required the maintenance of an army of permanent unemployed, that they had opposed, at their inception, every one of those social changes which have come to be regarded as an integral part of the civilized tradition.

It is irrelevant that they were sincere in their conviction that *ne pas trop gouverner* was a maxim of universal well-being; every man believes in the doctrines by which he is sheltered from the blasts of life. The business men had a century's space in which to prove the social validity of their philosophy. At the end, it could be written down, for all its early conquests, only as a grim failure which enslaved whole continents to the rapacious service of private profit. It is sufficient commentary on the claims of the business men to rule unfettered in the economic domain to say that, in the United States, the richest country in the world, twelve million citizens were in 1939 dependent upon relief for their means of life, and that in Great Britain, the second richest country, one out of every four children was undernourished. Only violent conflict ending in utter defeat would persuade the masses in either society to entrust their fortunes once again to the Bounderbys and Gradgrinds of a new Coketown.

Upon one other specific for our ills it is worth while to spend a little time. The crisis of our time, says an eminent historian, is due to the breakdown of the rule of law. "The present danger," he has written,[1] "is despotism. It must be prevented, and by legal limitations on government. . . . We must preserve and strengthen those bounds beyond which no free government ought ever to go, and make them limits beyond which no government can ever legally go. We must make *ultra vires* all exorbitant acts of government."

No rational person will disagree with this desire. But we are not told why the rule of law, whether in domestic or international affairs, has broken down. We are not told how we are to place legal limitations on government. We are given no definition of those "limits beyond which no government whatever can ever legally go." We are not provided with a list of those "exorbitant acts of government" which are to be made *ultra vires*, nor of the methods by which this end can be achieved.

Those who speak of restoring the rule of law forget that respect for law is the condition of its restoration. And respect for law is at least as much a function of what law does as of its formal source.

[1] *Foreign Affairs* (N.Y. 1935), and see *Constitutionalism, Ancient and Modern* (1940), especially the last chapter, where Professor C. H. McIlwain makes the same point with characteristic grace and learning.

Men break the law not out of an anarchistic hatred for law as such, but because certain ends they deem fundamental cannot be attained within the framework of an existing system of laws. To restore the rule of law means creating the psychological conditions which make men yield allegiance to the law. No limitations upon government can be maintained when society is so insecure that great numbers deny the validity of the very foundations upon which it is based.

The problem of restoring the rule of law is a twofold one. It is, first, the problem of discovering why it has broken down; and it is, next, the problem of finding such a new social equilibrium as will remedy the defects thus discovered. We can all agree that a world in which treaties are broken at the whim of their makers is an evil world, or that we seem to live in a nightmare when an eminent jurist can equate the night of June 30, 1934, with the quintessence of justice. But we shall not go far towards the restoration of respect for law merely by mournfully proclaiming the tragedy of its destruction.

At the back of the minds of those who find the source of our ills in the breakdown of the rule of law is the notion of certain fundamental procedures which condition the validity of all particular acts of law. It is important to remember that no procedures are regarded as fundamental in an age when men are battling about the purposes to which they should be devoted. Legal forms are respected when men feel that they have the great ends of life in common. The outstanding characteristic of our age is exactly the suspension of that agreement. We have reached a period when the very premisses of social life are called into question. In such periods, the ability to maintain the rule of law is always minimal. It is restored as men find the conditions upon which they can agree once more to the ultimate premisses. But ages like our own have always been ruthlessly careless of procedural values when what is in debate is the ends those values are to serve. In the struggle for power the rules are at a discount when life itself is at stake. They recover their prestige only as it becomes clear that there is room for accommodation between the parties to the conflict.

II

In a general way, our period has no historical uniqueness about it. The qualities it reveals have been characteristic of every other period in which a social system has entered decisively upon its final phase of decline. They are evident as the middle ages drew to their close, and, again, in the forty years which preceded the outbreak of the French Revolution. They pervade the major part of Russian literature in the half-century before the fall of the Czarist régime. There is nothing mysterious about them, not even our inability to detect their significance; for it is the habit of every social system in decline to emphasize to itself the glories of its past rather than the possibilities of its future.

The main feature of such times is the absence of security. The old routines have gone; traditional habits seem outmoded; men are afraid of what the morrow may bring forth. This is not a sudden condition in our civilization, the inevitable outcome of the war of 1914. For the war of 1914 was itself the outcome of insecurity; and its coming was only the expression of other tensions, besides that in the international sphere, the volume of which had alarmed men of insight in the decade before 1914. In England, for example, the inability of the older political parties to adjust themselves to the demands of labour was already a significant portent; and it was similarly significant that the normal processes of political discussion could find no adequate way of dealing with the Irish question. Looking back, we can see now that it was a half-conscious sense of the bankruptcy of an old order which persuaded Mr. Lloyd George to make his suggestion of a coalition government to Sir Austen Chamberlain in 1910.

The absence of security, above all in the years after 1918, brought profound consequences in its train. Men live by their routines; when these are called into question, they lose all power of normal judgment. They become uncertain of the criteria by which behaviour is to be judged. Discussion becomes a challenge; new ideas seem to be a threat. They become gripped by fear, and fear, by its nature, is the enemy of thought. So that where men are too fearful to understand they move to suppress because they dare not stay to examine. By clinging with passion to their wonted routines, they insist that the challenge to it is blasphemy. They will not hear the voice of reason which tells them that courage only can meet, because courage only can understand, the implications of a challenge. The plea of reason then seems to them a demand for surrender. Invited to experiment, they act like children who are terrified of the dark. Each item of change called for becomes transformed for them into an assault upon their most cherished values. They must give away nothing, they insist, lest they be called upon to surrender all. In this atmosphere, not only are they deaf to reason; they are even unresponsive to the leadership which gropes for reason. They will listen to nothing save the echo of their own voices; all else becomes dangerous thoughts. They assure themselves that the heart of the people is sound. It is misled by agitators and intellectuals; as if these ever got an audience unless it was out of their power to respond to something deeply felt in the popular consciousness.

They are afraid, and they do not know the causes of their fear. They see all their familiar values called into question. The men of letters give them a picture of their society which dismays them by its rejection of their traditional outlook. They feel acutely the stress of class-division, the antagonism which divides youth from age. They sense everywhere the presence of frustration; they are even frustrated themselves because their traditional wisdom is at a discount. Those whom they have been accustomed to lead are frustrated because, increasingly, they see no meaning in the worship of the older gods.

All civilizations in decline bemoan the lack of faith; by which they mean the lack of faith in their traditional faith. Their rulers become *laudatores temporis acti*; the golden days are transferred, in ever-increasing measure, to the past. The demands they encounter they find it an effort even to understand; men, they say, were so much more reasonable in their own younger days. They are accustomed to the exercise of power. They hardly know, they rarely consider, the minds and feelings of those excluded from its authority. But, because they are afraid, they fail to remember that the secret of power lies in its capacity continually to adapt itself to new needs, and to recognize that new men are continually necessary to effect the adaptation. For, in a period of new needs, their very novelty presents itself to them, in their fear, as a threat to their power.

Fear is the parent of revolution, for it inhibits that temper of accommodation which is the essence of successful politics. Fear does this is many ways. It is not merely that it stands in the way of recognizing necessary social change. It is not merely, either, that it is hostile to ideas. It resents the men, both in politics and in thought, who are capable of vision. It feels safe only with mediocrity, for that is fashioned in the image of the routine to which it clings. It is not accident, for example, that from 1920 until 1932, the United States had a succession of mediocre Presidents; men shaken out of their routine by the war of 1914 were eager, at all costs, to escape from the dangers of novelty and experiment. Nor is it accident that when, in 1932, catastrophe induced the United States to elect an experimental President, his policies, most of them the commonplaces of every mature civilization, should have been greeted by the timid as though he had merged Washington with Moscow.

As with the United States, so with Great Britain and France before 1939. In each case, the experience of a government of moderate reform was sufficient to send the "safe and sound" men into a panic of dismay. They had, no doubt, a moment of amused expectation as they watched the new men struggling with the reins of power. But they rapidly became convinced that they alone could safely drive the coach. Exactly as the ancient régime found the moderate programme of Turgot meat too strong for its digestion, so the owners of property in Britain and France were dismayed at the cost of the modest reforms of the MacDonald and Blum governments. Since it was upon their confidence that such governments necessarily depended, their fears were sufficient to drive the new men from power. Their places were taken by those who set their compass firmly by the old maxims in which the "safe and sound" men could place confidence. They believed that they had thus conquered the need for fear.

They had their own men in power; but nothing else was changed. All the new problems remained, with the same insistent emphasis as before. They could not renew faith in the fundamentals of the régime; they dare not, granted the constituency upon which they depended, do more than tinker with its incidentals. To the observer they seemed, as systems, to have lost the secret of their dynamic. The graver the issue they confronted, the more carefully they concealed its dimensions from themselves; and the more angry they grew at the insistence of their critics that they did not see the issue in its full perspective.

That was above all the case, I suggest, with Britain after 1931. On the internal side, nothing was done of major proportions. Unemployment, the depressed areas, housing, nutrition, education, on all of these the central outlines of the problems remained as they were before the government took office. It handled the crucial problem of India with the same graceless inability to grasp its new horizons as its predecessors had shown in handling America in the eighteenth century and Ireland in the nineteenth. There seemed nothing it could cope with audaciously or imaginatively. It was perhaps symptomatic of its general temper that, as the war of 1939 began, it abandoned a very modest instalment of penal reform because a proposal to abolish flogging might have jeopardized its majority in the House of Commons.

This fear of tackling boldly the internal aspects of policy was more than matched by timidity in the international sphere. British statesmen were confronted with novelties they shrank from handling either with assurance or courage. On the one hand was the Soviet Union, conscious of growing strength, and built upon foundations which, right or wrong, were at the opposite pole from British experience and British faith; but a Soviet Union whose primary interest, because its primary necessity, was peace. On the other were Germany and Italy, both of which had overthrown democracy, both of which were burning to alter the map of the world, by negotiation, if possible, by force if need be. The rulers of Germany and Italy were driven to the need for that alteration partly in the hope that conquest abroad would prove, after the ancient pattern, compensation to their people for despotism at home, and partly to avenge the humiliation of defeat and disappointed hopes in the war of 1914.

Hitler and Mussolini at once began a policy of challenge to the powers whose interest was the maintenance of peace. They announced what they wanted; as soon as they discovered an unequal opponent, they took what they wanted. Each step in their activities found the British government timid and uncertain in the face of one wanton aggression after another. It sacrificed Abyssinia and Albania to Italy. It allowed Republican Spain to become the victim of the Fascist dictators. It offered up the democracy of Czechoslovakia upon the altar of Hitler's ambition, even pretending, in this instance, that a decision on the part of Czechoslovakia to defend itself from extinction would be a threat to the peace of Europe for which that state would be wholly responsible.

To the plea that only a technique of collective security would save Europe from being eaten, leaf by leaf like an artichoke, by the dictators, it paid no heed. It convinced the Soviet Union that Great Britain no longer had the will to resist aggression. The outcome of the British government's inability to make up its mind about its policy was the conclusion of a non-aggression pact between Germany and the Soviet Union. The one thing that might have deterred Hitler from risking a war for European domination was the fear of being attacked on two fronts; the agreement with the Soviet Union removed this fear. He made largely impossible demands upon Poland which, after the destruction of Czechoslovakia, had been guaranteed by Britain against aggression. On August 31, 1939, Hitler moved against Poland; two days later, Britain and France declared war on Germany. All the years of "appeasement" thus ended in the very catastrophe they were intended to avoid.

It is vital to ask why, in the six years of Hitler's rule especially, the British Government never developed any consistent line of action likely to deter the aggressor. Something at least must be attributed to its leaders' natural horror of any policy which led, by its implicit threat, to the prospect of war. Whatever is to be said against Mr. Chamberlain, he had the important defence that he clung to peace longer even than it was reasonably possible to look for peace. But, when that is said, the indictment of British statesmen in the years after 1931 is a very heavy one. They condoned Japanese aggression in Manchuria and after. They condoned each item of Italian aggression; they even loaded its author with fulsome praise, while they remained completely silent before the grim excesses of his internal régime. They condoned, also, each item of German aggression, even conniving at the dismemberment of Czechoslovakia. The so-called policy of non-intervention in Spain inevitably destroyed a nascent democracy whose friendliness would have been vital to British strategic interests in the Mediterranean. They deliberately cold-shouldered the Soviet Union in the five years in which it could readily have been mobilized for the peace Great Britain was anxious to preserve. In those years, they made it obvious that if they would not welcome, at least they would be indifferent to, a German attack upon the Soviet Union; they thus aroused there the natural suspicion that they would view its destruction with equanimity. It is impossible not to compare the indifference of the British government to the fate of two democracies, both destroyed with either its active or its passive consent, with their solemn guarantees to semi-fascist states like Poland, Rumania and Greece.

Let us grant to the British government the fullest credit for their hatred of war. It was yet obvious, at least from 1935, that they were dealing with states which did not share their aversion, and were prepared, whenever the gamble seemed legitimate, to use war as a deliberate instrument of state-policy. There was only one way, in those years, to prevent the coming of war. That was to take a definite stand against its use as a method of change the moment it reared its head. Had that been done, whether over Manchuria or over Abyssinia, the ruin of the aggressor was certain; and his ruin would have had profound repercussions upon his later partner. There was a point, clearly, at which Mr. Chamberlain and his colleagues were not prepared for further "appeasement." But the logic of their attitude implied that, before this point was reached, they must organize a threat to aggression so formidable that the aggressor was not only made aware of the risks he ran, but was left with the knowledge that the threat was not an empty one.

To hesitate, to leave the gamble open, to court the dictators was, above all with a Fascist power, to convey the impression of weakness and uncertainty. In the complex game of power-politics that Mr. Chamberlain and his colleagues were playing, weakness and uncertainty are the cardinal sins. Nothing other than these could have been inferred in Rome and Berlin from the dismissal of Mr. Eden and Sir Robert Vansittart, and the ostentatious exclusion of Mr. Churchill from office in favour of a curious series of half-known mediocrities. And it was not that Mr. Chamberlain was not warned, hardly less from the benches of his own party than from those of the Opposition. His policy, as he was well aware also, aroused deep suspicion and resentment in the United States. It led directly to the abandonment of an active foreign policy by the Scandinavian powers, by Holland, and by Belgium who watched the worsening panorama with no hope but that of evading a catastrophe from which they had, in fact, never a chance of immunity. It resulted in the utter destruction even of the moral prestige of the League of Nations.

It was a policy condemned from the outset to complete frustration. Why was it adopted? The only answer, I think, lies in the fear felt by Mr. Chamberlain and his colleagues at the possible consequences, as they envisaged them, of the alternative policy of collective security. For the pivot of that policy must have been a partnership in defence with the Soviet Union. Their whole outlook on life was built upon hatred of its philosophy. They may well have regretted the more brutal habits of Hitler and Mussolini. But the Fascist dictators had left untouched the class-structure of their societies. To risk their overthrow—which was what the alternative policy meant—was to risk revolutionary upheaval, perhaps Communist upheaval, in Italy and Germany. If peace was a major objective of Mr. Chamberlain, so, also, was the avoidance of any policy which might further the coming of socialism; and so long as no British interest seemed directly threatened, there seemed hardly any sacrifice of others he was not prepared to make. Had Hitler halted at Munich, had he been prepared, even, to take his pound of flesh from Poland by negotiation instead of war, there is little reason not to suppose that an Anglo-German accommodation could have been arranged. On the very eve of war, the British Ambassador in Berlin was assuring Hitler of this prospect. War did not come because of Mr. Chamberlain's hatred of the "evil things" in Germany. He saw their malign influence extended to area after area with but little more than formal protest; even the final rape of Czechoslovakia aroused in him only a belated protest. He came to condemn them as evil only when he was compelled to understand that they were an integral part of a technique of conquest which included the defeat of Britain within the sphere of its hopes.

Mr. Chamberlain, in fact, was playing power-politics from the moment he assumed office without any grasp of the fact that the basis of power-politics is fear. He was anxious for two things from the outset incompatible with each other. He was anxious to maintain the vested interests of Great Britain in all their historic amplitude; and he was anxious for peace with exactly the men who could not survive as dictators if those vested interests were maintained. The only way in which he could have driven them to peace was by forming a coalition against them so overwhelming in its contingent force that they would not have dared to take the risks of breaking it. But he could not bring himself to form that coalition for two reasons. He feared the consequences of their downfall, on the one hand; he feared an increase in the prestige of the Soviet Union on the other. Out of fear, he made the worst of both worlds. He lost the possibility of peace; and he helped to drive the Soviet Union into a position difficult to distinguish from that of benevolent neutrality to the dictators. The leaders of the Soviet Union, indeed, were wrong in their conviction that there was no aggression at the expense of another state to which Mr. Chamberlain was not prepared to accommodate himself. They were wrong because they misunderstood—a natural misunderstanding in men unaccustomed to the relationships of a political democracy—the temper of the British people, and its power to compel attention to its views. But they did not profoundly misinterpret the temper of a British Prime Minister who could watch without regret the destruction of Czech democracy, but could hasten to guarantee the integrity of semi-fascist Poland which had eagerly played the jackal to Hitler at Munich.

The real trouble with men like Mr. Chamberlain is one with which the historian is familiar in a revolutionary period like our own. They have a deep sense that something is wrong; they feel profoundly insecure because they have that sense. But they have made their bargain with fate, and their only conception of policy is, out of fear, blindly to defend what is because they shrink from attempting experiment with the unknown. Even the collectivism which war-organization forces upon them, they pursue timidly and half-heartedly. They hardly dare to state the kind of world they want because, for them, the forces which are shaping a new world produce in them only fear and doubt. They have, one need not hesitate to emphasize, a deep sense of responsibility about policy. But they see their environment, with its challenge and danger, not as an opportunity for reconstruction; they see it as a warning to preserve all that may be of the *status quo*. Fear of the unknown is the mainspring of their stark immobility. They have no imaginative insight into the new world that is being shaped for us.

For them, and for their kind, the Russian Revolution has played in this epoch practically the same part as the French Revolution played a century and a half ago. Instead of seeing it as, in part, the inevitable outcome of long years of grim misgovernment, and, in part also, as the logical intellectual outcome of two hundred years of industrial, and three hundred of scientific, revolution, they see only the crimes and follies that have accompanied it, and the fact that the main burden of these has been borne by men of the same class as themselves. They seek to draw a *cordon sanitaire* around the Russian Revolution exactly as their ancestors did with that in France in 1789. They cannot understand that this produces Stalin in our own day as surely as it produced Robespierre in 1789, that no one, as yet, has ever been able to draw a *cordon sanitaire* about ideas. To the threat of revolution, there is, historically, only one answer: the reforms that give hope and exhilaration to those to whom, otherwise, the revolutionaries make an irresistible appeal.

But men who are afraid cannot embark upon wholesale reform. Their timidity is incapable of the temper large experiment requires. They suffer, as no other men suffer, from the delusion that to concede something is to lose everything. They listen to the protest of every petty interest in their ranks which insists that to yield here is to open the floodgates. They devote all their energies to turning away from the obvious direction of events. They insist upon relying on past experience at a time when reliance upon past experience has brought them to exactly the difficulties in which they find themselves. They are afraid of new ideas, bewildered at the new temper, astonished that the wonted way of life can be called into question. Their attitude to the changes they observe is like nothing so much as the amazement of Louis XVI in the famous conversation with the Duc de Rochefoucauld. They are, as of course they insist, fully prepared for necessary changes; it only happens that all the main changes which are demanded do not appear to them to be necessary. They are convinced, as their ancestors were convinced in 1789, that the main outlines of our social system have been permanently laid. They are prepared to see alterations in the detail of its framework. But they view with angry apprehension changes which go to the foundations of the social structure.

Any men who, as a class, have long been accustomed to rule fear the consequences of change which may displace or limit their authority. It was so with Charles I; it was so with Louis XVI and his court; it was so, again, with Nicholas II and his advisers. They have been schooled to a routine which they have come to identify with right; they cannot imagine that the world can grow away from their routine. At first, they are mainly amused when their routine is called into question; the new radicalism may even make some sort of fashionable appeal. But, as scepticism grows militant, they become more apprehensive; and the apprehension quickly takes the form of anger. But their anger does not still the doubts; on the contrary, they are more eagerly pressed. So that the anger which, in its first beginnings, may stoop to argument, is transformed by fear partly into suppression, and partly into a nostalgia for that past where doubt was unthinkable. At that point, almost any proposal of change awakens anger, even when, like the social legislation of President Roosevelt, for example, there is not a tincture of radicalism about it. For in a mood of fear, every innovation is a portent. It is the thin end of the wedge. It is necessary to remember what lies behind. The apparent moderation conceals darker purposes which, if this proposal succeeds, will shortly see the light of day. Action, it is argued, must be taken now, lest it be too late to-morrow. Fear, in this atmosphere, becomes the permanent counsellor of those who hold the keys of power.

This fear may reveal itself less in the positive sense of active hostility to change than in the negative sense of an inert awaiting upon events. This was, for example, the dominant temper in the United States from 1920 to 1932, and in Britain during the Premiership of Lord Baldwin. The assumption was that things right themselves if left alone, that, if we refuse to recognize the uncomfortable, it is bound, in the long run, to perish from inattention. We stave off the coal problem with a subsidy; but we do not tackle the coal problem. We prohibit general strikes by law; but we do nothing to deal with the conditions which lead to a general strike. Neither President Coolidge nor President Hoover made plans, in the epoch of prosperity, to deal with the slump which was persistently predicted; they preferred to listen to the siren voices which assured them, in Mr. Hoover's words, that America in March, 1929, had "solved the problem of poverty."

The theory of passive acquiescence is born partly of satisfaction with things as they are and partly of fear of experiment. Its result is always evasion of the need for positive action, and concealment, if possible, of all that creates the need. The long silence of Lord Baldwin over the British need for re-armament is a supreme example of the price that has later to be paid for this sort of evasion. By giving Hitlerite Germany over two years' start in the process of re-armament, even apart from its scale, he gave it, almost by definition under a system of power-politics, at least two years' right to agression. When his successor turned to the handling of his inheritance, he was called upon to deal, although he did not know it, with a deterioration it was already too late to arrest.

My argument is the simple one that fear blinds men to the realities of political relations; and it is always at its maximum at periods when, like our own, it is most necessary to see clearly. Once there is fear, reason has little chance to influence men's minds. For when they are afraid, they seek comfort and not criticism; they collect those about them who can be relied upon not to dissent. They are then led, by a dreadful logic, to refuse even those changes which their hearts urge them to admit, lest this be interpreted as weakness. Men swept by panic are always more ruthless than men who can stay to argue. They lose, thereby, that power to compromise which is of the essence of successful politics. Had the Conservative Party accepted Mr. Gladstone's Home Rule Bill of 1886, there would not have been a neutral and suspicious Eire in September, 1939. Had the Liberal Party, after 1874, recognized the right of working men to a full share of places in the House of Commons, it would not now have shrunk to a pale ghost of its former self. Had the Weimar Republic tackled the Nazi movement with courage in its early days it would not have fallen with the ignominy heaped upon it. History gives men their opportunity to act with foresight. But their self-interest is shrouded in fear; so that, when the opportunity comes, fear blinds their eyes, and it passes unrecognized.

One final instance of the tragic consequences of fear is worth examining since it illustrates my argument from a different angle. Ever since its foundation in 1917, the Soviet Union has been afraid of an attack from some alliance of capitalist states. The civil war, and the grim years of intervention, of course, gave it good reason for this fear. Its policy, accordingly, was built upon the assumption that its safety lay in the division of its enemies. From 1919 to 1934, therefore, it mainly concentrated its attention upon friendship with those powers, especially Germany, which regarded themselves as victims of the war of 1914; if it was attacked it could hope, if not for assistance, at least for neutrality from them. After 1934, when Germany proclaimed itself the spearhead of the anti-Soviet forces, the U.S.S.R. completely changed its diplomatic orientation. It joined the League of Nations—which it had previously denounced as a union of robber-states—and became the leader of those who sought to organize collective security against aggression. After Munich, it began to be clear that the Soviet conception of collective security had little hope of success. The Soviet government made a final effort to make terms with Britain and France. Convinced by the negotiations that neither had any firm will to agreement, the Soviet Union turned to that Germany of which for six years it had been the outstanding critic and made terms with Hitler which assured it, at least temporarily, of neutrality from that quarter. The Soviet Union, in search of security, thus abandoned the leadership of the anti-Fascist forces which it had assumed ever since Hitler's advent to power.

Treaties, in these days, have an inconstant air of fragility about them. The Soviet Union, therefore, used its power, intensified by the war, to insure itself against attack beyond anything that the treaty implied. It obtained, first, strategic outposts in Esthonia, Latvia and Lithuania, and then, by forcing the resignation of their governments, secured their incorporation in the Soviet Union. It occupied the ruins of Poland, roughly along the Curzon line of 1920; and, under threat of war, it compelled Rumania to return the province of Bessarabia which itself it had been compelled to surrender in 1918. All this was achieved by a diplomacy behind which, at each stage, was the naked threat of force. None of the states involved was in a position to resist. The Soviet Union, therefore, was able to return to the Russian frontiers of Czarist days in these regions without, practically, striking a blow.

Its experience with Finland was different. From this state, as from the Baltic provinces it was later to absorb, the Soviet Union sought strategic outposts. Finland yielded to most, though not to all, of the Soviet demands. After a brief delay, the Soviet Government produced, in the well-known Hitler manner, a series of frontier incidents and provocations. It refused the Finnish offer of investigation and mediation. It announced that the Finnish attitude was a threat to Soviet security. A puppet government, mainly consisting of Finnish exiles who had not been in their country for twenty years, was recognized; and, in its name, the Soviet Government proceeded to make war on Finland. It insisted, of course, that it was not making war, since it was acting in the name of the pseudo-government it had created, even though it was obvious that the authority of that pseudo-government extended only so far as the Soviet troops advanced. When, after three months' heroic resistance, Finland capitulated, the pseudo-government disappeared into obscurity, and the Soviet Union proceeded to enforce something rather more drastic than its original demands upon its beaten foe.

It is, I think, a reasonable assumption that a nation of four millions cannot be a serious threat to a nation of one hundred and eighty millions. What induced the Soviet Union which, ever since its inception, had been one of the foremost protagonists of international peace, to embark upon the annihilation of a state with which it had a treaty of non-aggression until the very outbreak of hostilities, and upon whose advance to socialism it had offered congratulations but a few months before? Every item in the Soviet adventure in Finland coincided in character with that Fascist technique of aggression upon which, for six years, the Soviet Government had been foremost in heaping execration. There was the same manufacture of frontier incidents; there was the same denunciation of the constituted government as a band of robbers and reactionaries; there was the same insistence that a peaceful and friendly people constituted a threat of outrage. When Finland resisted, there was the same insistence that, behind its defiance, were the manœuvres of the Soviet Union's enemies. There was the same refusal either of direct negotiation, or of mediation, after hostilities began. There was even the same assurance to the Russian people, as Hitler was accustomed to make to Germany, that the action was hardly more than a police operation to which no serious importance need be attached.

The Finnish adventure of the Soviet Union can be defended only on one or more of four grounds. It can be defended on the ground that might is right; it can be defended on the ground that the Soviet Union can do no wrong; it can be defended on the ground that those who share in the benefits of the Soviet system are, like the citizens of Rousseau's utopia, "forced to be free"; or it can be defended on the ground that the strategic necessities of the Soviet Union made it imperative to close a loophole in the Baltic through which Leningrad might easily be overwhelmed by a powerful enemy.

Only the last of these grounds even deserves discussion, though it should be said that Soviet enthusiasts have taken their stand upon all of them. It is the proof of how persistent has been the fear of invasion ever since 1917, and how little even the immense growth in the power of the Soviet Union has diminished that fear. It is reflected, also, in the outpourings of denunciation upon the Finnish government; we hate none so deeply as those whom we have grievously wronged. It proves how little reliance the Soviet government really placed upon the treaty with Hitler; for a strong Germany was the only power capable of using Finland as a base from which to attack the Soviet Union. The policy, therefore, was either an insurance against a German victory, and its consequences, or was born of the fear that after some patched-up peace in Western Europe, the capitalist powers might again concert an alliance against the Soviet Union, perhaps using a Germany with which they had made peace as the spearhead of the attack.

Fear drove Stalin and his associates into exactly that cynical policy of brute force they had, for long years, been foremost in denouncing. No power had gained so deep a hold on progressive opinion as the Soviet Union by its firm condemnation of aggression; the attack on Finland gravely jeopardized that hold. The substance of the case for it made by its friends was that action is permitted to the Soviet Union which that power may denounce when any other state attempts it. That is not a defence an honest observer will be inclined to make. It provided its enemies, in fact, with the case for an attack upon it, and the narrowness with which the collision was avoided was very small. Up to the attack on Finland, working-class opinion of the Soviet Union would have made it difficult for any democratic government to join in, or be passive before, a coalition against the Soviet Union; exactly as that opinion compelled the end of intervention in 1920, so it would have prevented it again. But the policy of Stalin, between the Finnish attack and Hitler's assault on Russia, went a long way towards dividing and confusing working-class opinion in the democracies. The contrast between the peaceful cession upon which Lenin insisted, and the demand for vassalage which Stalin enforced, was too glaring to be defensible to any save those for whom all Soviet action has the character of a religious dogma it is unnecessary to defend. Nor is the contrast made more palatable to socialists when it is accompanied by a vituperative hypocrisy which, had Hitler before the Russo-German treaty been its author, Stalin would have been the first to condemn in phrases that would have been obediently echoed by Communist parties all over the world. And none of this is less true because, when Hitler attacked Russia, Finland became his ally. For it is at least arguable that the support necessary to enable Mannerheim and the Finnish reactionaries to adopt that policy was organized for them by Stalin when he launched his attack on Finland. Those who congratulated him on the far-sighted wisdom of his Finnish policy forget that, without it, there might well have been resistance to Mannerheim in Finland, and that the attack risked that goodwill among the workers which has been one of the most important Russian assets ever since 1917.

I have dwelt at length upon this instance because it shows how far men will go beyond their avowed purposes when they are in the grip of fear. Nothing is so fatal to critical analysis because nothing so paralyses the faculty of rational judgment. Once the rulers of a society become afraid, reason itself seems to become their enemy. Those who judge their policy mistaken at once become identified with their enemies; even a failure to applaud leads to the suspicion of ill-will. And the deeper the fear, the greater the brutality it breeds. The rulers are driven, by an insane logic, into ever greater cruelty in order to suppress the memory of their first errors. They dare not stay to think; to do so is to make their obsession suspect. They become blind to their difficulties, and deaf to any warnings about them. A time even comes when they can abide no messenger of evil news. So that they become the prey of sycophants who aid them to build a ghost-world from which reality is excluded. As they brood in their prison, only complete victory and utter defeat seem possible. Having banished reason, they have lost the clue to the middle way since they realize that the worst may happen, they are driven to take precautions against it, and politics becomes a Borgian conspiracy in which he only is safe who strikes first. Life is then subdued to the medium of the informer and the secret police; and these ultimately shape the contours of policy. Thought, in such an atmosphere, ceases to have meaning in politics; tolerance is taken as proof either of ill-will or weakness. Those come to prosper only in whose counsel the leaders hear the echo of their own illusions.

Action taken under the impulse of fear can know no law save its own will. Its source hides any power to distinguish between categories of right and wrong. In such a régime, principle becomes futile, since success is the only criterion of good. The need to conceal one's mind, lest penalty follow upon its open expression, puts a premium on skilful insincerity. Ordinary citizens cease to have a public character; they are driven to conceal themselves in the routine of private relations. The fanatic and the bully take charge; and they use the hypocrite and the time-server as their instruments. Their habits, of course, provoke an antagonism which, because it is denied the means of overt self-expression, is driven into conspiracy. But conspiracy, when a government is afraid, is an invitation to reprisal which inevitably reaches far beyond the ranks of the conspirators. It provides a ground for making terror a permanent instrument of policy; and, since terror is bound to provoke hate, as Robespierre and Stalin have both discovered, it becomes ever more difficult to modify its operation.

A government built upon fear is driven into tyranny; nearly twenty-five centuries have passed since Aristotle, with his customary precision, noted its traits in detail. It is this kind of fear which haunts our age, and sets its perspective. It is a contagious fear, for, in the community of nations, sane men must seek to deal with madmen, if these be the rulers of states. And because they must so deal, they will find that the madness fear has inspired infects some of their own citizens; there are Englishmen to whom Hitler has become a hero upon whose habits they model their own ambitions. Fear, in a word, is the parent of madness. It is bound to persecute, whether its persecution take the form of terrorism within or war without; and the protests of its victims lead it on to a tempo of ever-increasing brutality. That can be seen in the German treatment of the Jews; it is hardly less evident in the savage assault upon the countries Hitler has ravished. Men who begin with violence as a technique for securing power move, as rulers, to the concentration-camp and the machine-gun. They do not know how to govern even in a state of siege.

III

The fear that surrounds our civilization is the outcome of a situation in which a growing proportion of citizens feel that it is unjust in its principles. We can see the same phenomenon in each of the ages that has a similar revolutionary character. In each, also, the way to the removal of the fear was either the attainment of a new social equilibrium upon which men were agreed or, alternatively, such a new access of prosperity under the old order as persuaded men to accept unrevised foundations for a further period. Anyone, for example, who examines the impact of Puritanism on the rulers of Britain three centuries ago, or that of the Chartists in the nineteenth century, can see much the same mood in rulers and ruled alike. The first are fearful about the mood of the masses, and see in it a challenge to law and order; the second demand profound political reconstruction which they can only be persuaded to forgo when a new tide of prosperity offers them new opportunities of well-being.

These instances can be put in a more generalized form. A government can always keep the allegiance of the multitude so long as it can satisfy their established expectations. Granted this ability, the wide contrast between the lives of the rich and poor will matter comparatively little over a narrow period. There will be hate and envy, and the alarm these breed in the mind; but they will, as a rule, lack both the volume and the organization that make them a serious threat. The failure to satisfy them gives rise to grievance; and grievance becomes a philosophy of dissent unless the social order in which it operates is both swift and wise in making concessions to it. For a philosophy of dissent is bound to drive towards the basis of the social order against which it is a protest. It fastens upon the irrationalities of that order as the causes of its frustration. Unless those who benefit from them are able to prove their validity, a philosophy of dissent becomes, pretty quickly, an attack upon the constitutive principle of the social order in which the discontent has arisen.

That was remarkably the case with seventeenth-century Puritanism. Cartwright and his successors prepared the road on which Lilburne and Winstanley marched. A criticism of ecclesiastical forms became an attack upon social principles; and men like John Goodwin found that the way to spiritual salvation was through a political gate.[1] And in a political democracy like ours, this is bound to be particularly the case. For in such a form of organized society, the power to choose the rulers rests, formally, with the masses; and there is a constant need in any government to satisfy their established expectations lest they suffer the penalty of loss of power.

This situation has become increasingly general in countries like Great Britain, France and the Germany of the Weimar régime. There, the fundamental basis of party-structure has been economic, and a growing working-class party, whose *raison d'être* has been, essentially, the inadequacy of distribution, has competed with its rivals for working-class suffrages. In the mature political democracies of the West, this was bound to mean, short of war and revolution, the electoral triumph of the working-class party unless its rivals were able to provide such increasing material benefit to the masses that there did not appear any special need for that triumph.

That need will, in fact, be felt in every democracy which has

[1] Cf. his *Right and Might Well Met* (1649); and cf. A. P. Woodehouse, *Puritanism and Liberty* (1938), pp. 89–90.

attained economic maturity. Once that stage comes, there are, invariably, not only stagnation of opportunity, but also the demand, because of that stagnation, that the power of the state be used to mitigate the consequences of social inequality. We can see this situation developing in, and transforming, the United States before our eyes. What has there been the dramatic product of a decade of intense depression has, with ourselves, been more evenly distributed over an effort of nearly forty years.

But the driving force is the same. The state is changed from a *laissez-faire* state to a social service state; and those only can effectively operate its power who are willing to use it for this end. But this they can only do upon two conditions, at least successfully. The drain of positive action by the state must not disturb the owners of property in the society; and it must not affect the power to market commodities at a profit. For our economic system lives by the confidence of owners in their power to make profit; and if this confidence be disturbed, that psychological atmosphere is absent in which men easily consent to the cost of great social reforms. A situation then emerges in which the contrast between rich and poor, the difference, also, between their ways of thought, becomes of momentous significance. The rich are called upon to justify the privileges they enjoy; and the arguments by which they defend them do not appear adequate to those excluded from the privileges. It then becomes necessary for those who deny this adequacy to attack the basis upon which those privileges rest.

They seek, therefore, the foundations of a new economic order; and the nearer they come to producing conviction among the masses, the less able are the privileged to maintain confidence in their position. This decline in confidence, moreover, so strikingly manifest in America during the Roosevelt régime, itself diminishes the ability of the economic system to provide the means of satisfying mass-expectation. Investment halts; unemployment increases; there may even be something like a "strike" of capital. The contradiction between the political sovereignty of numbers and the economic sovereignty of the privileged threatens the foundations of law and order. This is the atmosphere in which fear drives men to extra-constitutional action.

It is a fear intensified in the older civilizations—though less so in the new world—by the deep social cleavage between classes. They live so differently that they think differently too. They rarely exchange ideas. They have few organized and continuous opportunities to penetrate each other's thoughts and hopes. For the major part of their lives, they might almost belong to different species, so fragile and interstitial are the threads which connect them. In Britain, for example, they go to different schools; in large part, also, they go to different universities. The main permanent positions in Church and State are the appanage of a single class for the most part trained separately from its poorer neighbours for the places in them. An eminent statesman, like the late Lord Balfour, for example, was in the political life of his country for over fifty years; yet the only recorded contact with the working-class of which his biographer has to tell is with his valet and his chauffeur. The Trades Union Congress is nearly seventy years old; but when its chairman is presented to the King it is an event striking enough to be commemorated by leading articles in the press. The depth of our inequality, in fact, has been so little touched by the progress of political democracy in the last forty years that it is not an exaggeration to say that the two nations into which Britain is still divided hardly possess a common culture. And the faith of the rich in political democracy is pretty strictly conditioned by the unstated assumption that its principles are not applicable in the economic realm.

Historically, in fact, political democracy, throughout Western civilization, is the price the middle class had to pay for the support of the masses in its struggle with the feudal aristocracy for power. It welcomed that support until victory was certain; it has been doubtful of its consequences ever since. Everywhere, after its victory, it made an alliance with the class it had defeated; everywhere, also, it used its victory to make laws which would safeguard their joint hold upon the vital centres of power. The history of political democracy in the period since the French Revolution is the history of its acceptance so long as the masses do not seek to extend it to the planes of economic and social life. On those planes, the attempt of democratic principles to make their way has been resisted with the same firmness as the feudal aristocracy showed in its struggle with the rising middle class. On the evidence, the fact is so far inescapable that if those who live by owning have to choose between the continuance of their ownership, and the continuance of democracy, they will choose the continuance of ownership. They will even insist, with obvious sincerity, that they do so in the interest of the whole community.

It is because we are being driven to the point at which that choice has to be made that the atmosphere of our generation is tinged with fear. For property, as Madison said, is by far the most durable source of faction; and over its constitution men will kill and be killed without mercy or constraint. We have learned that from the French and Russian Revolutions; we have learned it, also, from the use to which Hitler has put the possession of power. If it be said that these are abnormal instances, in which a new equilibrium is establishing itself, one has only to examine the struggle between capital and labour to see that revolutionary violence differs quantitatively rather than qualitatively from the limits to which men will go when they are fearful for their property. Peaceful possession of property is characteristic only of those epochs when the established expectations of men are satisfied. As soon as dissatisfaction is widespread, there is fear; and, with the coming of fear, once again there is danger to the prospect that men can argue rationally about concepts of change.

There is thus nothing mysterious about the central source of our differences at the present time. What has broken down is the equilibrium established by the French Revolution when it brought the middle class to power. Its rule was, in many ways, a government of great qualities, active, industrious, moderate and even tolerant. It was rarely imaginative government, for imagination is not the characteristic quality of the middle class. It has also been, for the most part, timid government; its main concern has been evasion of the need to make great decisions, since these disturb that sense of security, that maintenance of the tried routine, which are the middle-class criteria of successful rule. It thinks of the habits by which it conducts its private affairs as those by which the public business is to be carried on; even the imperial mission of the middle class was conceived essentially as though it was a vast trading enterprise. The power to project its mind beyond itself, the power, even more, to build a relation of affection between itself and those whom it controls, have been characteristics of which the middle-class government is increasingly incapable. It thinks almost wholly, even in the context of the arts, in terms of what Carlyle called the cash-nexus. It has failed to realize that relations so built can only endure when the security and opportunities for wealth, which are its own aims, are extended continually to the poorer sections of the population.

Since the last war generally, and since the great depression in particular, it has been widely understood that, especially in the context of political democracy, the cash-nexus provides no assured basis upon which to build the hope of continued power. The contradictions of the régime have been profound. There have been many ambitions and few places. The old have found little room or sympathy for the aspirations of the young. The workers have not merely been unemployed in vast numbers; they have been educated to the point where they resent their unemployment as a proof of inadequacy in the social process. There is a great increase in political scepticism, and that at a time when the range and intensity of our problems call for the unity of an agreed and deeply held political faith. The government of the middle class continues; but it is not able to command any profound confidence. There is the sense everywhere that the men are not equal to the issues, that the mountain labours with no product proportionate to its travail. If there has been, at least in Britain, little actual disorder, there is the fact that the idea of disorder has entered deeply into men's minds. Two wars, and the complex phenomenon of which, so far, the Russian Revolution is merely the chief incident, have thrown into the melting pot the traditional values and the traditional techniques which middle-class government erected into a system. The gale of fundamental change is in the air; and the rule of the middle class rests upon a fragile and uneasy equipoise.

For the middle class does not seem to understand what, in a period like our own, it is essential for it to realize: that the conditions have called into question the basic character of our social constitution. When the workers are deeply convinced that the present distribution of wealth is unjust; when, organized as a major political party, they pronounce the present system of private ownership not merely inequitable but, also, incompatible with the potential wealth in which they might share; when, all over western civilization, they are growingly convinced that the poverty from which they suffered is at once unnecessary and caused by the present economic system; when the subject-peoples of empire are increasingly disinclined to accept that subjection upon which a good deal of middle-class supremacy depends; when the workers urge that they have tried to reorganize the form and spirit of all political institutions without being able to rationalize social conditions; when, by no means least, the decay of religious faith prevents them from hoping for benefits in the next world that will compensate for the deficiencies of their present situation; then, it may be argued, the stage is set for one of those fundamental revolutions of which the Reformation is the supreme example in the modern time.

But there enters here the tragic result of that defect of imagination in the middle class which I have already noted. It cannot appreciate the mind of its critics. It attributes to envy what is due to disbelief.

Able, on its own premisses, to show that its balance-sheet does not permit of large concessions, it exhibits that characteristic weakness of a challenged order, the inability to know what or when to yield. It is afraid itself to inaugurate fundamental change partly because, like every class long accustomed to rule, it believes that the final bargain with history has been made, and partly because, again like such a class, fear of the unknown inhibits in it the power to reason generously. The result is that at the very moment when its own safety calls it to lead the nation beyond the boundaries it has been wont to regard as secure, it becomes determined to insist upon remaining within them, to identify them, indeed, with the well-being of all classes. It cannot conceive, that is, of security except upon its own terms; and not even the fate of the middle class in Russia, Germany and France, makes it understand that security upon its own terms is no longer available to it.

For to maintain that security, it must do one of three things. It must be able to achieve recovery upon a scale which removes the disbelief in its capacity to govern successfully; that the condition of the system no longer permits it to do. Or it must destroy the democracy which has been the main form of its political expression in order to attack the historic institutions of the working class through which the disbelief in its capacity to rule is organized into action. Or, again, it must itself inaugurate fundamental changes which permit the adaptation of the relations of production to the forces of production. It must, that is to say, inaugurate that rarest of historical phenomena, a revolution by consent.

So far, as in Italy and Germany and France, it is to the second of these methods that the middle class has turned. To do so, it has allied itself with the kind of party of which Hitler and Mussolini are the leaders. But when it has elevated them to power, it finds that it is no longer master in its own house. For Hitler and Mussolini, who represent the outlaw-forces of Society, having come to power, wish to retain it; and they adapt the state-apparatus to the needs that retention requires. They have, whether they will or no, at once to satisfy their followers, and, sooner or later, to satisfy those masses whom they have at once wooed and attacked in their march to power. The first need involves the kind of gangster-rule we associate with fascism, and this, very rapidly, creates exactly the conditions of insecurity the alliance was intended to avoid. The second, as we have grimly learned, involves a policy of international aggression which, in the end, means war. But since war on the modern scale is the inevitable parent of violent social change, it produces exactly the internal disruption the alliance sought to prevent.

The result is the unmistakable one that, everywhere, a species of behaviour is becoming prevalent peculiar to times of profound disorder in history. It is not merely the outcome of war, though the war intensifies it; for the war itself is the outcome of the temper of which I am speaking. What is breaking down is respect for the idea of law itself because the laws made by the middle class can no longer contain the purposes which the masses believe to be socially valid. We are at one of those turning-points in history where what is required is, so to say, a diet of great reforms. But because such a diet is a threat to the middle-class conception of security, that class is afraid of its results on the social digestion. It thinks, therefore, as very notably in the United States, in terms of recovery as the antithesis of reform; and it grows more afraid the more insistently the physicians diagnose the depth of the disease. Fear, as I have insisted, leads to intolerance, which is bound, at some stage, to lead to suppression. We become involved in a vicious circle where fundamental change is at once demanded and refused by men who do not examine, and are ever less able to appreciate, the meaning of each other's premisses. That is a position in which violent conflict between them is certain unless they realize the imminence of the catastrophe in time.

We confront, in a word, the need not for a law here, or a law there, but for a vital change in the whole spirit of government. Either that must come with the co-operation of those who now rule, or the objective facts will compel a violent change in the principles of the society they govern. I do not pretend, for reasons I shall examine later, that it will be a change for the better; as in Germany those may be brought to power who will take our community into a new dark age. But, even were that to be the case, the new rulers would confront the same central problem and be as unable as their predecessors to solve it in terms of peace. For the new Germany has solved none of the problems the Weimar Republic failed to solve; and it has only prepared a terrible revenge for its rulers by reason of the methods through which they have evaded them.

"It is not the mechanism of laws that produces great events," Tocqueville told the French Chamber two days before the overthrow of Louis Philippe, "but the inner spirit of government." All over Western Europe and America that inner spirit of government refuses adaptation to the demands of a new time. It has broken down, exactly as the rule of the feudal aristocracy broke down, because, within the terms of its principles, it cannot exploit the potentialities of production. It is compelled to suppress invention; it is driven to every device of restriction its ingenuity can think out; it imposes, at the same time, growing technological unemployment. We have reached a situation in which three things are outstanding. The commercial aristocracy of our age at once impoverishes and degrades the men who serve it, and then abandons them to the charity of the public. The power to distribute fails everywhere in our civilization to keep pace with the power to produce that is at our disposal; and business men are compelled to ask the aid of the state in restricting, in the interest of their profits, the supplies which men so badly need. The character of our class-relations makes scientific discovery on the one hand the enemy of the worker it displaces, and, on the other, of the producer whose plant it renders obsolete; and it thus frustrates the central implication of science which is the extraction of abundance by human power over nature. To these must be added the further consequence that our system of education produces, in this situation, large numbers whose opportunities are disproportionate to their ambitions and who are, therefore, transformed by legitimate disappointment into the enemies of society.

None of these problems is met, and all of them are exacerbated, by the abandonment of democracy as a framework for the state. For that abandonment, as we have seen, means the refusal of free discussion, and that refusal is ultimately inimical to the spirit which scientific discovery requires. A civilization at once so complex and so fragile as ours must postulate the need for scientific discovery as a primary condition of its survival. On these terms, a social order built upon the denial of democracy is bound rapidly to deteriorate unless it learns, with equal rapidity, how to transform its processes of coercion into processes of consent. But, to do so, it must learn to placate grievance, and the only way to its placation lies through the highroad of free discussion. Free discussion, as I have said, is born of security, and security, in its turn, comes only when the great majority of men feel that they have the great ends of life in common. They do not feel that now; that is why our society is poised on the abyss of so immense a convulsion. As always in such a time, when the superficial occasions of that convulsion are removed, the basic fact emerges that the curse of our social order is its irrational inequalities. Either we must find ourselves able to co-operate in their removal, or we shall move rapidly to conflict about them. Either, that is, the middle class must co-operate with the workers in essential revisions, as the aristocracy was wise enough to do, even if at the eleventh hour, a century ago over the Reform Bill, or violent revolution will be unleashed by means that may well transform the ends either party to the conflict has in view. This is the ultimate choice that lies before us. Let us at least approach it with the knowledge that we are compelled to choose.

Chapter II

THE RUSSIAN REVOLUTION

I

THE Russian Revolution stands to the twentieth century in the same historical relation as the French Revolution stands to the nineteenth. Each had been prepared by long ideological analysis in which the supporters of those who held the reins of power were unable to answer the challenge of those who denied the validity of its operation. Each was the outcome of a long epoch of misgovernment in which the inefficiency of the rulers was almost more striking than their oppressiveness. Each began in a mood of optimism and exhilaration which seemed to offer the prospect of wide horizons of freedom. But each rapidly encountered, upon the issue of the disposition of property-rights, antagonisms so profound that internal dissension provoked dictatorship. In each case, also, dissension over property produced abroad the fear of infection; foreign governments therefore intervened in order, for the protection of their own social systems, to put a term to the novelties they feared. In each case, again, two profound consequences followed upon revolutionary change. The psychological outlook of the under-privileged was permanently affected; and the privileged everywhere had to adjust their claims to a recognition of that new outlook. The adjustment, however, was passionately resisted after 1790; and only after a generation of war did it begin, in a fundamental way, to enter into the everyday habits of government. When it did so enter, it became clear that, despite the heavy price men paid for its admission, it raised in a remarkable way the level of satisfaction at which response is made to the claims of ordinary men.

We are, at present, in the period of reaction from the ideology of the Russian Revolution; so that our power to judge it with any detachment suffers from the passionate emotions it has aroused. To some, its benefits are so clear, its achievements so immense, that they are unable even to consider their cost; while to others, that cost has been so ugly and so overwhelming that the very notion of either benefit or achievement is dismissed as unthinkable. Extremism of either kind is as foolish and as dangerous with the Russian Revolution as with that of France, or its true precursor, the Reformation.

Our business, as we examine its nature, is to recognize the causes which have given to it the forms it has assumed. That its follies and blunders and even crimes, have been immense, no one has recognized more freely than Lenin, its supreme architect. That many of them were, in great part, the outcome of the policy adopted by its enemies, external not less than internal, is, on the evidence, painfully clear. We can only understand the Russian Revolution in the degree that we recognize it as the first stage in a fundamental transformation of the social principles of Western civilization. If we regard it as less than this, we shall wholly mistake its nature.

It is not, of course, even as the first stage, a transformation wrought rapidly, or wrought by Russians alone. In a sense, the whole movement of ideas we call modern history went to its making. It could not have been what it is without the scientific revolution of the sixteenth and seventeenth centuries; and it could not have been what it is without the impact of the so-called industrial revolution of the eighteenth. Hobbes and Locke, Rousseau and Hegel, that socialist tradition in which Marx is the outstanding name, shaped the slow affirmation of the ideas and the methods in which it culminated. But let us remember, too, that the men who sowed the Bolshevik seed were the lineal descendants of the Jacobin representatives on mission, and that these join hands, through the correspondence Committees of the American Revolution, with the Agitators of Cromwell's army who, in their turn, owe an immense debt to the habits of the itinerant Puritan preachers of the age. The Russian Revolution, despite its appearance in a nation widely dispersed over Asia as well as Europe, is above all an European revolution. It happened first in Russia because the opposition there to its central principles was too weak, in the background of military defeat, to organize resistance to their claims. But the causes from which it was born affect, if in different ways, the whole of Western civilization, and its momentum will not end until those causes have been tackled by remedies proportionate to their profundity.

A long tradition of misgovernment; an inability, out of that tradition, to recognize the validity of substantial grievance; a determination, therefore, on the part of those who ruled to deal with grievance rather by suppressing than by remedying it; when suppression failed, an insistence upon intensifying its rigours rather than a search for comprehensive accommodation; the dissipation of the common man's faith in the capacity and goodwill of his rulers by bankruptcy and corrupt cruelty at home, and defeat abroad; these are the terms in which the stage for the Russian adventure was set. Moderate men were driven to despair by the ineptitude of the régime; extremists were driven to desperation. Those who profited by the system were so few, in proportion to those who suffered from it, that when the magic of their traditional authority was dissipated, they had no means by which they could retain their power. Let us remember that in Russia in 1917, as in France in 1789, the moral foundations of potential power had been sapped long before the revolutionaries took over the possession of the state. Political power was reorganized when it had, as it were, no longer a spiritual principle to clothe it with respectability.

For the rulers of Czarist Russia had been so long estranged from their subjects that they did not know their needs even when they encountered their expression. The aristocracy, like that of France, was probably the most cultivated in Europe; but, like that of France, also, long years of discussion separated from the obligation to take decisions had paralysed their wills, so that when the crisis came, they did not know how to formulate a policy, much less to compel its execution. Naturally they yielded place to the men who, like Lenin, had the wisdom to plan, and the resourcefulness to act, who, even more, had built their planning upon a philosophic insight into the structure and functioning of the civilization of which they were set on becoming masters. The Bolshevik Party triumphed in the Revolution because, in a period of virtual anarchy, it alone knew how to wrest from it the certitude of direction and the firmness of control a government necessarily requires in order to be a government. Their opponents had nothing to which to appeal save a traditional habit of obedience which had broken down, and an historic patriotism which previous outrage had dissolved. The Bolsheviks knew how to restore both. They offered order for chaos, and hope for fear. They restored a routine of habit to men who had become panic-stricken by uncertainty and breakdown. They drew public opinion to their side partly by the skill with which they diagnosed popular wants and partly by the vigour they infused into their exercise of power.

No doubt the Bolsheviks had great opportunities on their side. The machinery of government had largely ceased to function; maltreatment and defeat had made the defence forces of the state no longer loyal to the legal rulers; there was, over all of Russia, that widespread revolutionary discontent which, though it had in fact been long preparing—as 1905 made evident—seemed to dissipate at a stroke the traditional habit of obedience. The Bolsheviks were a party of iron discipline, schooled by the genius of Lenin to watch with care the minutest movements of public opinion. They only knew what the masses wanted. They only had the insight to go to the masses offering them what they wanted. They obtained their support because they meant, as no other party meant, the prospect of peace and bread. They met opponents divided in interest and uncertain of direction. While these debated, they were able to act. They seized power because they only, among those who struggled for it, had a consistent view both of the way to attain it and the ends for which it could be used.

It is, of course, one thing to seize power; it is another, and a quite different thing, to maintain its possession. No one who reads the grim history of civil war and intervention in the Soviet Union can fail to be impressed by the achievement the Bolshevik retention of power represents on any showing. They had to improvise an administration; they had to build and organize an army; they had to deal with widespread famine and disease; over vast areas of their territory the very means of communication had broken down; everywhere, too, nations which had suffered oppression from Great Russia, asserted their right to a separate existence. They had to contend with Germany; while the erstwhile allies of the Czar occupied territory and armed and financed their internal opponents. Foreign trade largely disappeared; and a rigorous blockade was enforced against the new state-power. In those early months of the régime, the capacity to retain power must have seemed minimal above all to those who were in charge of its destinies.

Yet they succeeded; and it may be suggested that they succeeded, essentially, for three reasons. They succeeded first and foremost, because they brought to the common people of Russia the first hope, in a century of misgovernment, of power over their own lives. No one can analyse the decrees of the Bolshevik government in that first momentous year of its history without something akin to awe for its leaders. It is not only the depth of the insight they displayed into the wants of the governed; it is not only the largeness of the conceptions with which they operated. It is, even more, the width of the avenues they opened to talent—here the resemblance to 1789 is remarkable—and the genius with which they appealed, again as in 1789, to the highest creative impulses they encountered. They did not seem apart and aloof from those over whom they ruled; they were one with and of them. They had the insight to associate with their adventure those *nouvelles couches sociales*, the workers and the peasants, who in field and factory, in army and in soviet, both learned responsibility for the exercise of power and acquired an interest in the régime from participation to its governance. The break-up of the large landed estates, moreover, and the wholesale expropriation of the capitalist class, gave peasants and workers a sense of mastery over their fate they had never previously possessed. Amid all the ruin of civil war and famine in the early period of the October Revolution, it is noteworthy that observers consistently report an immense exhilaration among the people. They feel that they are living in a great epoch; they feel they are dying for great ends. Not even the coming of dictatorship, after the attempted assassination of Lenin, seems to have deprived them of the conviction that a new and wider freedom was theirs.

That, I think, was the first reason for the Bolshevik retention of power. The second reason was foreign intervention. It may be doubted whether it ever, in fact, reached proportions likely to have resulted in the overthrow of the régime; and this is significant in itself, because the cause of that inadequacy, above all in Britain, was undoubtedly the deep and growing volume of resistance to it on the part of the organized workers. They viewed with intense distrust an assault upon the first effective socialist revolution in the world by statesmen whose primary motive was defence of private property. The speedy accumulation by the Soviet government of a fund of goodwill among the workers which only its own errors could dissipate, is a factor which every capitalist government, especially the democratic, had consistently to take into account; for no foreign government has ever aroused among workers in other countries anything like the same interest or the same enthusiasm. And foreign intervention immensely aided the Bolsheviks because it aroused among the Russian people, even among many who were dubious or hostile, that deep sense of national exclusiveness, the emotion of patriotism which the idea of a government imposed by the foreigner seems almost instinctively to arouse. It is probable that, even without foreign intervention, the Bolsheviks would have held their ground. When it came upon a scale that was irritating, without being decisive, it was a help, and not a hindrance, to them.

The third factor in Bolshevik success was the character of the agents of Russian counter-revolution. To the genius of Lenin and his colleagues, the dying society could only oppose a series of sorry adventurers who had no programme to offer save the restitution, in some form, of the régime against which the Revolution was so magistral a protest, and no method of implementing that restitution save brutal pogrom and savage bloodshed. Wherever they went, they inoculated the population with hate against what they represented; and, over massive areas of the country, their habits created the passionate conviction that the Bolsheviks were deliverers from their ugly vengeance. The Bolsheviks might stand for a Red Terror; but that was associated with big and creative purposes the common sense of the masses was able to appreciate. The White Terror seemed to have little purpose save terror itself. The vista its possible permanence unfolded was that of a return to a previous condition of servitude in which literally millions would pay dearly for their brief hour of freedom. Not even during the worst moments of the French Revolution has reaction seemed so brutal or so ugly as during the Russian civil wars. The progress of the adventurers was as hideous as the revenge wreaked upon the citizens of Paris by Thiers and Gallifet, after the Commune of 1871, and upon an immensely larger scale. The Whites conveyed by their own policies the conviction that the Revolution was indeed a popular one. They contributed to it an emotional drive which enabled it to transcend all the chaos and famine and disease which accompanied its evolution to victory.

II

The history of the Russian Revolution, after the close of the Civil Wars, divides itself naturally into three periods. There is the period, which ends in 1924 with the death of Lenin, during which he, above all, provided it with the means of its consolidation. There is the period from 1924 to 1927 during which effective progress halted while the Bolsheviks were convulsed by the factional fight for power between Stalin and Trotsky. There is the period, finally, since 1927, in which, with the centralization of effective power in Stalin's hands, the Soviet Union has begun the fulfilment of an immense programme of collectivization and industrialization at a pace, and upon a scale, which no other society has previously known. Nothing, indeed, like the rate of change in these years has been seen save in the opening up of the immense resources of the North American Continent.

We must avoid the temptation to compare these stages with those in the history of previous revolutions; the conditions of the Revolution in Russia makes its character unique. To deal with an immense population, most of whom were illiterate, and unaccustomed to the technology of the machine; to weld into an effective unity a congeries of different nationalities, many of whom did not even suspect the meaning of Western civilization; to build up great defence forces which would counter any effort on the part of hostile powers to take advantage of the society's weakness; rapidly to proceed with the discovery and exploitation of Russian resources, without inviting dependence upon foreign capital for their development; to retain the loyalty of the masses to the régime without permitting them the continuous certainty of that level of consumption to which even the Czarist epoch had accustomed them; to persuade them, that is, to postpone present satisfactions by producing the deep conviction of great future benefits; to break down, especially among a deeply individualist peasant population, the ingrained habits of an acquisitive society; constantly to innovate and experiment upon a scale where possible error left the narrowest margins of safety; all the time to thread its way amid the complexities of diplomatic relations which, at the best, were unfriendly, and, at the worst, actively hostile; to convince, by reason of those dangers, the working-class of a large part of the world that the interests of the Russian Revolution were something that they, too, must defend; to build an administrative apparatus for the new state in which confidence was possible; to evoke and train the talent proportionate to the scale of the adventure; to secure from that talent, as it was trained, the loyalty and devotion which would fit it to found the new civilization inherent in the principles of Bolshevism; here, on any showing, were gigantic tasks. Their fundamental architecture could only have been conceived by a man of Lenin's boldness of conception, fertility of resource, and dominating courage of will. On any showing, too, what was achieved in his lifetime represented as much as any revolutionary statesman has ever been able to wrest of fulfilment of his dreams. It gives him an unquestionable title to be regarded as one of the supreme figures of modern history.

The experiment of the Russian Revolution has, I think, demonstrated certain things beyond any shadow of doubt. Some of them, of course, were historically known before that Revolution; and its experience has merely confirmed them; others are new, and it may well be that their novelty constitutes the real significance of the Revolution. It is a reaffirmation of previous experience that a Revolution opens up an immense reservoir of new talent, which would, otherwise, have no opportunity of effective expression. Just as, without the Civil Wars of the seventeenth century, Cromwell and Ireton, Lilburne and Winstanley, would hardly have emerged even into the footnotes of history, so, without the Revolution, Lenin and Trotsky would have been rather dreary exiles, wandering between the different capitals of Europe, and Stalin an obscure conspirator, worth half an inch of newspaper for a bold offence against the laws of property.

But more than this. The Revolution not only revealed wide capacity for leadership among hitherto unknown men; that is a commonplace of revolutions. Far more important was its revelation, again a vital confirmation of previous experience, that a change which broadens the basis of power in society offers at once the evidence that a far greater number of the population is capable of creative activity than the previous relations of production had led men to suppose. Since 1917, it has become evident that there is in the Soviet Union, as no doubt in every people, a power in opportunity of service to evoke a massive capacity of response which is apparently inexhaustible so long as the opportunity remains. In the generation since 1917, there is literally hardly a village in the Soviet Union which has not produced, in the context of its special need, its local Hampden capable of arousing it to efforts of which it had not previously known that it was capable. And this capacity for response is not limited to any special line of life. The more widely it is evoked, the more fully is it displayed.

For, indeed, the sense of wide horizons opening to a population hitherto confined to narrow perspectives of opportunity is bound to evoke what is best in the spirit of a people. That this has taken place on an immense scale in the Soviet Union does not permit of serious denial. That, alongside its evocation, there has gone the deliberate organization of channels through which new opportunities have made themselves felt both to the humblest citizen, and in the most backward areas, there is ample evidence to prove. The scale, for example, upon which education has been organized has given to millions not only a sense of that cultural heritage to which, previously, they had been denied access; it has given them, also, a power to make themselves articulate, an ability to explain the wants they have, which is of the essence of freedom. And that educational effort, it is notable, has been extended to nations, as in the Caucasus and the Arctic Circle, who had not previously known even the benefit of a written language. Nothing in the history of colonial administration even begins to compare with the Soviet achievement in this field; the effort of Great Britain in India where for over a century, a similar opportunity has presented itself, is a mean and poor thing by comparison. Nor can the difference be explained except by the argument that the social philosophy of the Bolsheviks gave them a direct interest in the elevation of the backward peoples they controlled, while the social philosophy of British imperialism made it suspect each cultural advance in India as an implicit challenge to its own authority as an alien power there.

Nothing in modern times even approximates to the scale or the rapidity of the Soviet advance in the field of education. It took over a century to build the modern structure of the British educational system; and its advanced stages are still confined to a very small section of the population. Yet the British evidence is clear that a far greater proportion of the nation's children could profit from a more advanced education than are able to attain it; and it is important that nothing debars them from it save the economic and social implications of the British property system. From those implications, the Soviet outlook upon education is wholly free; and it is, I think, legitimate to argue that, some dozen states of the American Union apart, the educational opportunities of Russia are now better than those of any other country in the world. They mean not only a greater power to evoke talent which may be harnessed to social achievement. They mean, also, a far smaller proportion of frustrated lives. And they imply an anxiety on the part of the rulers of the Soviet Union both to train and to utilize ability which goes far beyond that exhibited in any other state in modern times.

That educational achievement has gone hand in hand with important achievements in other social spheres. The liberation of women from an inferior status has been accomplished upon a remarkable scale. Care for the health, sanitation and safety of the workers in field and factory does not, it is probable, surpass in quality what, at its best, has been done in the most advanced Western states; but what has been done not only compares favourably with that quality, but has, further, been done at a pace which would have been unthinkable in any capitalist society. There, it is probable, each stage of the development would have been fought as the Factory Acts were fought in Great Britain, as the abolition of child labour is still fought in the United States of America; and professors and other learned men would have exhausted their ingenuity to prove either that the achievement was undesirable in itself, or that, though desirable, the economic situation made it impracticable to embark upon so large an experiment.

The planning of production for community consumption has had further remarkable results. It has proceeded under special conditions both of advantage and of disadvantage. The expropriation of landlord and capitalist meant that the vested interests known to the capitalist world did not stand in the way of access to the forces of production; and this has meant a rate of exploitation with which nothing compares save the opening up of the American continent. That expropriation, moreover, has made possible the ending of social dependence upon the profit-making motive as a stimulus to productive effort.

The outcome of this freedom has been, unquestionably, of immense social advantage. It has meant that, in the planning of the productive effort, attention can be concentrated not upon effective demand but upon social need. With all the limitations of so immense an experiment, it is true to say that, as a consequence, in the economic development of the Soviet Union first things have come first. Manufacture is not conditioned to that prospect of risk-taking which is able to attract the cupidity of the owner of private capital. Men are not important merely in terms of the property they own. It is certainly not true to say that, in the famous socialist phrase, the power over men has been replaced by the administration over things. But it is true to say that, in the narrow economic sphere, there is a more genuine basis for economic freedom for the masses in the Soviet Union than they have elsewhere previously enjoyed.

The reason for this is twofold. In part, it is due to the fact that the rate at which the country's resources are being exploited has removed the haunting fear of unemployment from the lives of men and women; at a time when, in capitalist civilization, literally millions dread this omnipresent fear, not only is it absent from the Soviet Union, but there is no reason to suppose, on grounds of theory, that it need ever again become a factor of which account must be taken. The second reason, I suggest, why there is this widespread sense is the sense that millions, in every field and factory, help to make the conditions under which they live; in an important sense unknown in capitalist countries, there are the effective beginnings of constitutional government in industry. The rules of an enterprise are not made at the discretion of an employer who owns it, and who can run it, subject only to the limits of trade union can impose, in his own way and for his own purposes. The rules are genuinely the outcome of a real discussion in which men and management participate. And the absence of the profit-making motive, in the ordinary acceptance of that term, has the undoubted effect of making discussion far more a mutual search for a common satisfaction, the kind of compromise which gives men the sense of freedom because they find their own wills represented both in the solutions arrived at, and in the procedure by which they are reached than is the case with industrial negotiations even in the advanced capitalist countries. The Soviet motive for arriving at an agreed solution of difference is far greater than it is, say, in differences in industry or agriculture in Great Britain or in the United States, in the relation between management and men in the coal-mining industry of the first, or among the workers in the Imperial Valley of California.

The Soviet government may make one further claim in this field. In the classic sense, the profit-making motive has gone; even though there are great disparities of wages, these are a return to function, and not to ownership. But it is legitimate to argue that the absence of the profit-making motive has been more than compensated for by those which have replaced it. In part, this is achieved by a wage-return strictly proportioned to function and output; in part, it is the outcome of a new and significant appreciation of the dignity of labour; in part, again, it is due to the fact that performance of distinction in agriculture and industry is an important highroad to political power. In a capitalist economy, wealth is so overwhelmingly the measure of power that those are small in number who can be attracted by opportunities of a different kind. In the Soviet Union, wealth has to compete, as a source of satisfaction and authority, with at least half a dozen other avenues to power to which at least equal attraction attaches; with the result that the effort necessary to the maintenance of the social purpose can be evoked without such a stratification of society as is inherent in every mature capitalist economy.

Certain other advantages of the system must be emphasized. On any showing, there is nothing like that frustration of science which is characteristic of the capitalist economies in their phase of contraction. The Soviet system, whatever its limitations, is able to plan for plenty and not for restriction; it does not have, at each stage of production, to think in terms of profit for individual owners who have an interest apart from, sometimes antagonistic to, that of the community as a whole. Even if we allow for the fact that new experience of its possibilities among the general public has given its prospects something of that status of awe which they possessed in the Europe of the seventeenth century, it is still, I think, true to say that the social function of science, its rôle as the indispensable servant of mankind, is more fully realized in the Soviet Union is, proportionately, given greater scope, than is, or even can be, the case in capitalist societies. For the worker does not feel that technological advance is a threat to his security, and he lacks, accordingly, that hostility to new invention which is endemic in a capitalist society. Nor is there that interest in the suppression of scientific discovery which the entrepreneur who lives by profit is bound to feel. The evidence of encouragement to the scientist is widespread; and the career offered to him is on a scale, and of a significance, that it would be difficult to rival in capitalist countries.

To one other aspect of Soviet conditions it is worth while to refer. No one who has examined at first hand the Soviet administration of justice (the sphere of political offences apart) can doubt that in experimentalism, on the one hand, and in quality of humane approach, on the other, it is on a level superior to that of most other countries. If, as I believe, the administration of courts and prisons is a vital index to the quality of a civilization, this is of the first importance.

What the Soviet Union has done is to relate crime, in all its phases, to the economic environment of which it is so largely the expression. That has enabled it to deal with the criminal less as the enemy of society than as its victim, to embark upon prison reforms of a magnitude which, in their social results, are far beyond anything in the older civilizations. A person convicted of one of the ordinary criminal offences in the Soviet Union has a larger chance of returning to normal life normally than is the case anywhere else; and the historic demand for equality before the law is, political offences again apart, more substantially realized there than in any other country with which I am acquainted. Bench and bar alike have a far more active and sustained interest in the improvement of legal procedure than anyone has displayed in Western Europe since Jeremy Bentham. In this field, it is no exaggeration to say that the rest of the world must go to school to the Soviet Union.

III

On any showing, I think, these are immense achievements; and we gain nothing by denying them. Their proper appreciation is, indeed, imperative if we are at once to see the Russian Revolution in its proper perspective and, not less important, to understand the reasons for the deep hold it has won over the working-class in other countries. An immense price, no doubt, has had to be paid for them; and I shall consider the nature and consequences of that price. But if this is to be set in its background, the fact of immense achievement must be recognized. Without it, it is, I think, pretty certain that the régime would not have been able to maintain itself in the face of its internal and external difficulties.

For it is broadly true to say that the worst errors and crimes of the régime have not persuaded the masses to abandon two convictions. They believe, first, that they live under a system the central principle of which is superior to that of older civilizations. They believe, second, that they are entitled to optimism about its future. The importance of these convictions is obvious, not least because of their resemblance to the analogous mood in England and France after their revolutions. For they mean, I suggest, that whatever may be the habits or the fate of individual Soviet leaders, the long end of the Revolution has crystallized into a permanent part of the established expectations of the masses; and whoever may come to the leadership of the Soviet Union will have to take full account of those expectations. So the social and economic purposes of the Cromwellian Revolution survived the collapse, at the Restoration, of his political system. So, also, no French régime, after 1794, could have hoped for permanence which did not in considerable degree satisfy the claims of the Jacobin tradition.

To see the price that the Soviet Union has had to pay for its achievement, we must be clear about the conditions its makers confronted. They were dealing with a barely literate and semi-Westernized country, accustomed only to a half-Byzantine, half-Oriental despotism. The industrial middle class was a tiny fragment of the population; and the urban proletariat was only a small proportion of the vast peasant mass which was its overwhelming majority. Czarist Russia was only beginning its industrial revolution; and no small part of its knowledge of technology was dependent upon foreign direction and control.

Those who made the Revolution intended to apply Marxist principles. They assumed a necessary period, on the Marxist model, of iron dictatorship. But they believed that this was to be a workers' dictatorship against the owning, especially the capitalist, class, and they were confident that the necessity of dictatorship would be transitional only; as social ownership became firmly established, a workers' democracy would naturally emerge. Not less important is the fact of their profound conviction that revolutions on their own pattern were impending in the West. Their emergence would not only strengthen the foundations of the Soviet Union; the security they implied would ease, as no other factor would ease, the birth-pangs of the new order. They assumed a unified psychology of the workers of the world which would issue in unified action.

It is important to realize, also, in how considerable a degree the Bolshevik leaders were alien in their approach and habits from the socialist leaders of the West, how steeped, also, from the necessities of their position, in the conspirational tradition. Lenin and Trotsky were known to the executive committee of the Second International; but they were dim figures in its Congresses who never even remotely approached the power to command a majority there. Many of the Bolshevik leaders, and notably Stalin, had no acquaintance at all with European socialism of the West, and no realization of what a movement built within a constitutional tradition might mean. Few of them had ever grasped the importance of political democracy simply because its impact, whether for theory or practice, had never impinged in any profound way upon the experience with which they were directly concerned. They saw it only from the outside, and, as very obviously with Lenin, they saw it most clearly in terms of the bitter disappointments Marx and Engels had suffered, as their expectations of imminent revolution had been constantly defeated. Not least, they were unaware, as Marx and Engels were unaware, of the vitality and importance of the habit of self-government. They tended throughout to see the socialist movement in Western Europe generally, and in England in particular, in terms of a Russian experience largely alien from it.

That experience was fundamental to the Bolshevik technique. It led them to rely, not upon democratic ways of party-organization, but upon the effective control of their movement by a professional group of highly disciplined revolutionaries whose lives were spent in conspiracy. They rarely operated in public; their lives were a long battle with the secret police. They combined an intense will to power with an intense suspicion of any outlook which deviated by a hair's breadth from their own. They were accustomed to instant obedience; and they regarded intellecual error as a grave crime. No determination is more omnipresent in their writings than their understanding that they must not repeat the mistakes of the Paris Commune, the failure of which they attributed, above all, to democratic weakness. They were the general staff of a revolutionary army; the business of the ranks they commanded was to obey.

It must be said that, in the context of Tsarist Russia, they had profound justification for their views. They were dealing with a people unaccustomed to self-government. They were fighting men, as the history of the Civil Wars makes clear, who would have treated them without mercy had they faltered for a moment. They were, I think, compelled either to abandon the idea of a socialist revolution or to abandon dictatorship. Their central problem, in 1917, was less the seizure of power than its consolidation. For that, above all with Lenin, they trusted to a European Revolution which did not come. Its failure to arrive had immense results. It encouraged all the forces in Russia itself to which they were opposed; and it therefore added immensely to the task of economic rebuilding. The failure of European Revolution to arrive led to their breach with the socialist movement of the West. It encouraged their "splitting tactics"; since they could not rely on the socialist leaders, they would make a movement of their own. Their doctrine and strategy had proved itself by success; the leaders of Socialist democracy, by failing to adopt them, betrayed Marxism and thus became, in their view, the objective supporters of capitalism. They therefore created separate Communist parties everywhere, which fought against the historic Socialist parties, and even, as in pre-Hitlerite Germany, assisted the enemies of socialism in the belief that they would be the residuary legatees of the latter. After the creation of the Communist International, they imposed upon the parties they had created the same strict orthodoxy in doctrine and rigidity in behaviour which had characterized their own rise to power. Fearful of capitalist intervention in the Soviet Union, they made those parties a nightmare to capitalist states, especially in countries in which economic and psychological conditions were favourable to their growth. It is probable enough that, in the first months of the Revolution, the Bolsheviks definitely looked forward to the introduction of political democracy. It seems pretty clear that, after the attempt on Lenin's life in 1918, the transformation of Soviet dictatorship into democracy was never, save, perhaps for a brief moment in 1936, when the new constitution was promulgated, really seriously considered. The emphasis of Bolshevism was always on the sham character of Western democracy, never upon the merits that it possessed.

Why is this? The answer, I think, is a complicated one. Partly, it was the result of the failure of socialist leaders in the West, and especially in Germany, to use their opportunities, as the Bolsheviks judged they could have been used, at the end of 1918. This persuaded them of the need to isolate the Soviet Union from contamination by a world in which even avowed Marxists were corrupted. Partly, it was the outcome of their view of themselves as the vanguard of a history which it was their obligation to impose. Partly, once more, it was the prestige they gained among the more advanced socialists which persuaded them that Lenin's adaptations of Marxism were the universal recipe of socialist success. And this view, naturally enough, became ever more profound as they watched the growth of Fascism in Europe, and the weakness of the democracies before its growth.

But the real reason lies, I think, in the internal history of the Soviet Union. Its isolation, in considerable part, imposed by the capitalist powers, meant that the Soviet government had to depend upon itself for economic development; and it had either to go on with the New Economic Policy of 1921, which meant, in all probability, a return to capitalism on a large scale, or to abandon that policy and set about the wholesale industrialization of Russia upon a modern basis. But, if it was to follow the second course, logic demanded, in a vast country mostly peopled by illiterate peasants, the imposition of a discipline upon the population which only a dictatorship could achieve. That dictatorship was the more inevitable since the price of industrialization if it was to be achieved without dependence upon foreign capital, was the grim restriction of consumption-goods, and the collectivization of agriculture since, without this last, the restriction of consumption goods could not have been maintained. A large Kulak class would, in the course of a decade, have been fatal to the policy of industrialization since it would not have accepted the limitations this imposed. And these necessities were sharpened at every point by the need to develop defence-forces upon a scale which gave assurance against the possibility of foreign attack. This need, in its turn, increased both the tempo and the scale of industrialization. It required that limitation upon the power to produce consumers' goods which has been one of the first things to impress any foreign visitor to the Soviet Union.

It has been an effort, in short, to compress into less than a generation a period of development which, even in the United States, has taken a century and a half, and been assisted there by the wholesale investment of foreign capital. It has been an effort made with a population in large degree untrained for the purpose undertaken, a population, it is highly probable, which would not, among the peasantry at least, have accepted the implications of immense present sacrifice for assumed future gain, had these been presented to them for free choice. I do not think that any government but a dictatorship would have dared to make the attempt, and then only a dictatorship actuated by an intense religious faith in the absolute rightness of its convictions. Anyone who remembers how heavy was the price paid by Western Europe for the necessary discipline required by the Industrial Revolution, and has read the passionate literature of protest that change evoked, can begin to imagine something of the scale of the experiment the Soviet leaders have attempted. Granted the initial decision to attempt it, I do not think it could have been carried out by democratic means. For any government which submitted itself to popular re-election upon the basis of the sacrifices exacted by the Bolsheviks, would, it is difficult not to believe, have been overwhelmingly swept from power.

Granted, therefore, the aim set, internal grounds alone required a dictatorship; and there were external reasons also which I shall discuss later. The dictatorship was, again of necessity, that of the Communist Party; for, granted the aim set, only those who accepted it could, in the conditions, have been allowed to share in the exercise of supreme power. This it is which explains why the soviets, in the early years of the system a quasi-independent source of authority, have, as time has passed, become no more than an organ of registration for the will of the Communist Party. For had they been permitted a genuine independence, the fundamental aim would, at the best, have been jeopardized; and, at the worst, there might have been an antithesis between Soviet purpose and Communist purpose which would have drifted, especially in a crisis like that of the liquidation of the Kulaks, into civil war.

The dictatorship of the proletariat, in fact, became necessarily the dictatorship of the Communist Party; for every serious purpose, the party has been identical with the apparatus of the state. But the dictatorship of the party has not meant the dictatorship of its rank and file. As in all political organizations, the official apparatus of the party would have carried immense weight. But in the Communist Party of the Soviet Union it has been an oligarchy superimposed in ever more intense measure upon a party-democracy. For disputes between its members and those who disagreed with its views have taken the place of the ordinary party struggles in a parliamentary democracy. And, still more important, the struggle between factions in the Communist Party over some principle or detail of economic policy had the vital consequence that those who won were, for all effective purposes, the state.

Differences in view, therefore, were, inevitably, a struggle for the possession of the state. Defeat meant, often enough, as in Stalin's struggle with Trotsky or in that between him and Bukharin, a conflict for the right to use the state-power for a fundamentally different emphasis. The defeated faction was inevitably expelled because, in threatening the unity of the party, it threatened also, by the facts of the case, the unity of the state; and no state, by the inherent logic of its nature, will permit any threat to its unity. A leader who was beaten, therefore, had either to disappear from the political scene, or to fight against the party which had a monopoly of power. What, in fact, was a breach of discipline in a democracy became an act of treason in the Soviet Union. The ends which turned upon victory or defeat in the internal struggles of the party were too vital to permit it to be otherwise.

This is, I suggest, the root of the explanation of those purges and executions in the Soviet Union which have so bewildered its friends in the democratic countries. The defeated faction must either submit or conspire; the system leaves them no middle path. And because, even after submission, they are always a threat, whether open or secret, to the victors' hold on power, the temptation of the victors to deprive them of the opportunity to be influential is enormous. No monoparty dictatorship can afford democratic habits even within itself, for the critics of its majority have then too open an avenue to power. The majority will, accordingly, use every instrument at its disposal to intensify its hold on power. It monopolizes the instruments of propaganda. The plebiscite—historically the characteristic weapon of dictators—is invoked at intervals to offer confirmation of its popularity. Because it is driven to suppress those who differ from it, it is bound to extend the use of the secret police; and, as is always the case with such a body, they will not seldom foment or invent what they are unable to discover. Those in power must see to it that their rivals are hated or despised. Because so much is at stake, they must either hold no elections at all or win all elections. Prestige usually demands the latter. They must, therefore, see to it that all candidates chosen are persons of whom they can approve; and this means organizing the party membership from persons who will support them. They must prevent all discussion which they do not believe they can afford. In the long run, the logical outcome of this development is the domination of the state by a small circle who have the power and the skill to manipulate and control the apparatus of the party. So long as they control its membership, and the armed forces of the state are on their side, only wholesale and organized disaffection among the masses can deprive them of their power. And, granted the gigantic influence of propaganda, especially in a population which has only recently attained literacy, granted, also, that the main function of the secret police is to prevent organized disaffection, to break the hold on power of a determined minority is only possible in the most extreme circumstances such as defeat in war.

To this internal result must be added the vital influence of the foreign situation. Ever since its victory in 1917, the Bolshevik Party has been convinced that foreign capitalists were determined upon the destruction of the Revolutionary experiment. Intervention and the civil wars gave them substantial ground for their view; and at constant intervals since they have had reason to believe that it would be verified. But this has also meant a suspicion of foreigners in the Soviet Union, markedly illustrated by the difficulties its government has presented both to the visitor and the would-be emigrant, even if the latter was seeking merely to attend a scientific congress abroad. The first fear of any criticism evoked by its policy has always been lest it be linked to, or the precursor of, foreign intervention. Nothing is more feared in the Soviet Union; and that fear has been used by the dominant faction of the Bolsheviks for two ends. In the first place, it has been used to evoke a narrow and intense patriotism among the masses, the sense that they have in the Revolution a possession of which all foreign powers are profoundly jealous, which, therefore, they must defend at all costs. Arising out of that patriotism, in the second place, there has been the deliberate use of this fear as a weapon with which to attack the critic; everyone who does not follow the party line is presumed to have contacts with, even, like Trotsky, to be the actual agents of, a foreign enemy.

Since such contacts are, by their very nature, akin to treason, the internecine conflicts of the party have been even more intense, especially since 1936, than those of the French Revolution. For an opposition that sought to organize itself seriously was, quite literally, gambling for its head. Not only was this the case. The members of the opposition were often the heroes of the Revolution whom the populace, as with Trotsky, had been taught to venerate. Until the moment of their fall, they had immense prestige. Any government, therefore, which accused them of treachery, could not afford, for fear of popular clamour, not to secure a conviction. The result was not only the need for espionage on a vast scale, so that the very thoughts of men were under surveillance. It was also the growth of the secret police into something like a state within a state. In protecting the party line, as this was defined by the dominant faction, from attack, it was preventing the government of the state from being overthrown. It became, therefore, a pivotal instrument in the hands of that dominant faction for maintaining its power. No doubt there was always sufficient reality in foreign hostility to the Soviet

Union to make it an essential instrument. But what increased its authority to literally stupendous proportions was the fact that it was the instrument of one section of a single party which identified itself with the state and permitted no rival party even to criticize its identification.

From this angle, I suggest, three things emerge which do much to explain the internal, and even external, habits of the Soviet Union. The decision to industrialize at so swift a tempo meant immense sacrifices from the people; it meant, also, the collectivization of the peasants by compulsion; and it meant that no normal methods of opposition could be allowed since these would delay, and, therefore, jeopardize, the process of industrialization. When to these are added the fear of foreign invasion, the necessity, therefore, for gigantic armaments to repel its possible onset, the ever more rapid tempo of industrialization which armaments required, it is, I think, clear that no procedures capable of frustrating the decision which Stalin took when he secured agreement to the experiment of socialism in a single country were possible. To that experiment he was bound to adapt every item of policy. No foreign connections could be permitted unless they strengthened it. No domestic criticism could be allowed unless it enhanced the prospect of success. Any other connections, and any other criticism, were bound, *a priori*, to seem counter-revolutionary in essence; for, given rein, they were certain to impede the fulfilment of the central idea upon which the whole structure depended. More, there was always the risk, most notable in the historic conflict between Stalin and Trotsky, that, if criticism made headway, it might result in driving the dominant faction from power.

Upon this hypothesis, we can understand the swift turns and changes in Soviet policy. The government is separated from the party and from the masses simply because it has taken an initial decision which has prevented it from risking free discussion with either. It has been driven, therefore, to rely more and more upon holding the army, and using the secret police, as its essential instruments, though its ability to make concessions now to one, and now to another section of the population has been important; for it thereby safeguarded itself against a combination of the discontented which might have wrecked it. The party, as a whole, which was a real democracy in Lenin's day, is now little more than an organ of formal registration for the will of its inner bureaucracy. Nothing exists like the vivid debate which resulted in Brest-Litovsk, or the adoption of the New Economic Policy; a situation in which the victor and vanquished share a sufficient volume of common opinion to continue co-operation. Their struggle is for the exclusive manipulation of the state-power. And this struggle has had to be dramatized upon a plane where the sacrifices it exacted were intelligible to a vast population which was beginning for the first time both to enjoy literacy, and to interest itself in the process of politics.

It is, I think, the effort to explain these issues to the masses which explains the passionate intensity of Soviet politics. Everything has to be over-simplified and over-dramatized. Every leader must be either a hero or a scoundrel. And since industrialization is the essence of politics, every economic issue is always a political question. An inefficient manager jeopardizes the plan; is his inefficiency technical or political; is it incapacity or sabotage? A collection of sulky peasants may infect a whole neighbourhood. Is their sulkiness intense enough to be regarded as counter-revolutionary? A soldier's staff view of armament problems may raise questions of industrial machines which go to the heart of foreign policy; and his view may anticipate a turn of direction for which the inner controllers are not prepared. Confronted by problems of this kind, Stalin and his colleagues have been compelled not merely to make every issue a political issue; they have been compelled, further, to make every critic an enemy. The great trials and purges have been, from this angle, so many victories offered to a people whose training in politics is still on a primitive level, but who can understand and appreciate "victories" against the "enemy" because the enemy is counter-revolution, which it associates with the old and evil régime from which it was freed in 1917.

Such a technique, it must be added, has demanded its victims wholesale; the army and the ranks of management have above all suffered from them. And since a strong army and an efficient management are inherently urgent for the success of the system, every purge has necessarily meant something like an economic upheaval, and has interfered, thereby, with the smooth working of the plan. In all this, the encouragement to orthodoxy of outlook is obviously immense; doubt of the government's policy may so easily become "counter-revolution." Doubt, moreover, must continuously be made more difficult. Hence there emerge the extravagant emphasis upon the government's infallibility, the eulogies of Stalin in terms more fitted to a god than to a man. The emphasis and the eulogies particularly when, as with Radek, one has shared in making them, render a return to a critical temper ever more difficult, since the critic then runs the risk of having his original agreement charged to his account as deliberate deception. They add what is nothing so much as the atmosphere of religious emotion to the relation of the masses to their rulers. The deeper that emotion, the more secure is the rulers' hold upon the allegiance of their subjects; the more difficult, accordingly, it becomes to ask for an objective analysis of their claims.

Nor is this view weakened, I suggest, by the fact that there is an immense volume of "self-criticism" in the Soviet Union, even, on a vast scale, confessions both of omission and commission from the humblest worker to the central figures in the great treason trials. At the base, that self-criticism is invaluable to the régime. It serves to inform its rulers of defects in minor aspects of the administration which do not jeopardize their hold upon the government and may well, as they are rectified, strengthen it; while, at the apex, by the admission of conspiracy, they convey the conviction of the widespread dangers the régime confronts, the skill and pertinacity of its enemies, the need for instant and continuous alertness on the part of its friends. The whole process reveals the fact, and strengthens the belief, that, lurking in the most innocent-seeming doubts, there may be concealed profound counter-revolutionary sentiments, and that there must be unceasing vigilance against their growth. These sentiments may appear in an exhibition of Ukrainian paintings which do not paint the peasants and their houses in an atmosphere of appropriate joy. "This entire collection," wrote *Pravda*, "cannot be regarded as other than an insolent attack of Ukrainian bourgeois nationalists." So, also, in 1936, the music of the eminent composer Shostakovitch was denounced for a "left stress on ugliness." Mr. and Mrs. Webb have shown how fantastic can be the range of this "disease of orthodoxy."

This atmosphere, of course, squares ill with the large promises of democracy authorized by the Soviet Constitution of 1936. One of the sources which explains its character was the emphasis of Soviet foreign policy at the time of its promulgation. The history of Soviet policy is clearly divisible into four periods, each marked by a dual aim. From 1917 to the end of Lenin's leadership, one of its aims was to provoke world-revolution. From 1924 to 1934, its main purpose was to prevent a combination of the capitalist powers against it; for this reason its weight was thrown on the side of the weaker European states like Germany. After 1934, and until the Russo-German Pact of 1939, its object was the cultivation of the democracies in the effort to find security against the menace of Nazi and, possibly, Japanese aggression. From the conclusion of the Russo-

German pact, the foreign policy of the Soviet Union has been mainly an effort to utilize the war for the protection of its strategic interests, if necessary, as in Poland and Finland, by force of arms.

In each of these periods, this is to say, the Soviet Union, like any great state concerned for its integrity and interests, has largely played power-politics. But, in each of these periods, there has been, though with diminishing tempo, a secondary motive which derives from the original inspiration of the Revolution, and of which the Communist International has been the essential instrument. The Russian Revolution was a socialist revolution, conceived in the belief that it would be followed rapidly by revolutions elsewhere. Their onset was postponed, it was believed, by the treachery of social democratic leaders, and the Communist International was founded to assist their coming in foreign countries. By founding and assisting Communist parties there, the Communist International was to be the general staff of the world-revolution. It was to weaken the enemies of the working class everywhere; it was to promote that mass-will to revolution which Lenin considered the social democratic leaders had betrayed.

But by about 1924 it was clear that the impulse to world-revolution was, at least for the time, exhausted. The Communist International quickly settled down into the position, increasingly emphasized, of a secondary department of the Soviet Foreign Office. It had its importance, partly because it served to announce the continued faith of the Soviet leaders in world-revolution, and partly because, through its agency, they were able to exercise an influence, sometimes even a considerable influence, upon the working class in foreign countries. And it was particularly important to them, as the war of 1939 has revealed, because it has enabled them to control the national communist parties in the interests of Soviet foreign policy. It is this control alone which can explain the remarkable changes in the personnel of those parties, most notably in Germany; and this only can be offered as a serious explanation of Communist policy in France and Britain, after September 3, 1939, and Communist policy in Germany. There, as elsewhere, the nature of Soviet evolution, after Stalin's assumption of full leadership, necessitated men who would follow without undue hesitation the line of policy he laid down.

The period which makes this clear is that from 1934 to 1939. In that period, the main need of the Soviet Union was protection from the contingent threat of Hitler. It was that need which led it to join the League of Nations which, until then, it had denounced as a union of bandit states. It was that need, further, which led it to assume the direction of the anti-Fascist forces of the world, and to protest against any attempt to appease them; for it saw, rightly enough, that an agreement between Hitler and the West would be followed by a Nazi attack on the Soviet Union. It was as the leader of the anti-Fascist forces that it assisted, if with a certain economy, the Republican government in Spain. It was the need for protection from Fascism, also, which led the Communist International not only to impose the "Popular Front" policy upon Communist parties everywhere, and to attack the historic tendency of socialists to a pacifist outlook; everyone remembers how urgently the Soviet Ambassador in London "lobbied" the British Labour Party to vote for a programme of increased armaments after 1936.

The purpose of this policy was to unite all progressive opinion against any increase in Fascist power which threatened the security of the Soviet Union. There is no reason to doubt the sincerity of this turn in outlook. The main interest of the Soviet Union was peace; and, could it be secured, a strong and united League, prepared to meet aggression, seemed to offer the best prospect of peace. But certainly Great Britain and, for the main part of this period, France preferred, if possible, the appeasement of Hitler to the prospect of challenging him, especially since that prospect might well imply social revolution in at least Central and South-Eastern Europe. It was not until after March 1939, when it became clear that they could not appease Hitler save by accepting his domination, that Britain and France became anxious for an alliance with the Soviet Union; and, even as late as that summer, it is probable that had Hitler been willing to direct his ambitions to a conquest of Soviet territory, they would have offered no objection. But, so soon as Britain and France sought seriously for this alliance, it became less desirable to Stalin and his colleagues. For, first, the Franco-British guarantee to Poland was, in effect, the certainty that, if war came, its major impact would be on the West; it was, therefore, an indirect guarantee of Soviet frontiers. And, second, it gave Stalin the superb bargaining counter with Hitler that he could free the latter from the danger of a war on two fronts, on the model of 1914; he clearly learned early that he would be paid highly for that freedom. He had no sense of obligation to the principle of collective security; he was as much entitled to use it as a convenience as were Mr. Chamberlain and M. Daladier. He was convinced, on good evidence, that neither bore him goodwill; had he doubted it the contemptuous character of the Anglo-Soviet negotiations in the summer of 1939 would have convinced him of it. The conclusion of a pact with Hitler, moreover, offered him two great advantages, absent if he made an alliance with Britain and France. It allowed him—a vital Soviet need—to contract, at least for a time, out of a major war, with all that this meant for the orderly evolution of his domestic policy; and it enabled him to exact a price, which neither the French nor the British were in a position to pay, for his neutrality.

He therefore made his terms with Hitler. The latter embarked upon a policy of which war was the certain outcome; and in both Poland and the Baltic countries, and, later, in South-Eastern Europe, Stalin got, or took, his price. How far his attitude was due to his inner conviction that Britain and France contemplated a super-Munich at the expense of the Soviet Union, it is difficult to say; the secrecy of his operations, which were, for example, quite certainly unknown to the Soviet Ambassador in London until their results were published, makes any estimate of his inner views pure guess-work. The *volte face* is illuminating for its impact upon the national communist parties, and reveals the degree to which, as I have said, the Communist International had become a mere department of the Soviet Foreign Office. For those parties had become so accustomed, in the previous five years, to recognize, rightly indeed, in Hitler the chief enemy of the working-class, that their leaders, while explaining their hostility to bourgeois governments in Great Britain and France, pledged their support with enthusiasm to the defeat of Hitler.

But Stalin did not want a major war. No one could say where and how it would develop; no one could estimate the strains it might impose upon the Soviet Union. Its preservation from danger was, naturally enough, his main preoccupation. Within a month, therefore, of September 1939, all the national communist parties completely changed their outlook. The war became an "imperialist" war; it made no difference to the workers whether Hitler or his opponents were successful. The only interest of the workers was in peace. Even the attack on Finland, so precisely comparable in character to Hitler's aggressions, was defended by Communists with passion. It was essential to the safety of the Soviet Union; it was, therefore, obviously justified.

Objectively, this is to say, Stalin transformed the national Communist parties into the defenders of Hitler for no other reason than his own need for peace, on the one hand, and his own requirements in strategic defence on the other. He had made them announce that one standard of international behaviour applied to the Soviet

Union, and another to all other powers. From parties fiercely demanding that Fascist aggression be resisted at all costs, they became, in answer to his need, parties insisting that Fascist aggression be appeased at any price. There is really no rational way of explaining this remarkable somersault except by its relation to the needs of the Soviet Union. They accepted as a religious principle the doctrine that whatever the Soviet Union did served the needs of socialism. They were thus able to believe that a peace between the main enemy of Bolshevism and the Soviet Union, even when made at the risk of a world war, and the subjection of Western Europe to Hitler was, in some mysterious fashion, in the interest of the workers of the world.

I shall discuss later in this book the astonishing implications of this view. Here, it is only necessary to say that this use of the Communist International to serve the interests of the Soviet Union, without regard to further consequences, followed logically from the decision to build socialism there without regard to the economic development of other countries. For if the Soviet Union were to become involved in a major war, the strain on its economy would certainly be serious, and, possibly, disastrous. It is not only that all the emphasis of its industrial production would have to be reorientated, with all the repercussions this would have upon its agriculture as the ability to supply the peasants with consumers' goods diminished in the strain of war; it is also that defeat would work ruin to the present holders of power. Stalin, therefore, had to effect his own Munich in 1939, even though he could exact a price for it. For he could not take either the economic or the psychological risks involved in the retention of leadership in the world-struggle with Fascism.

IV

It is in these terms, I think, that the meaning of the Russian Revolution can best be approached. On any showing, it represents important gains; but it is useless to deny that it represents immense gains at an immense price. It is, of course, obvious that the Bolshevik seizure of power could not have been followed by any rapid achievement of democratic forms of government; both the aims of the Bolsheviks and the nature of their inheritance made this impossible. To have admitted the classic freedom of opposition to elements which were prepared to wage civil war upon those aims, to have given them freedom of speech and association, would have presented the Revolution to its enemies; the history of the Weimar régime is sufficient proof of that. Dictatorship was a necessary consequence of the conditions the Bolsheviks confronted. Without it, quite certainly, there would have been a return to capitalism.

The real problem, I suggest, is of a different kind. I cannot share the view of those who think that, as soon as the Bolsheviks had restored law and order, it was their business to establish the classic procedures of democracy; that is, I think, to make these procedures absolutes, instead of relating their possibility to special historical circumstances. And the special character of the Russian circumstances is surely beyond dispute. An economically backward country, in which the urban proletariat was a fragment only of the population; an immense and mainly illiterate peasantry, profoundly individualist in outlook; a congeries of half-savage peoples, massively superstitious, and with no training in political procedures; a nation, in any case, with no experience at all of the democratic process, and ringed round with enemies which had already sought the overthrow of its government; the notion that such a people should have been left free to determine its ways of life in the sense that so highly developed a political people as the British or the French could have done, that notion, I think, makes nonsense of the meaning of historic tradition and experience. A people, as every profound revolution has gone to show, must grow into the use of political freedom. It cannot plunge into its full employment directly after long immersion, amid manifold disasters, in a semi-barbaric and wholly reactionary despotism.

But that is not to say that the continuous deepening of democratic experience was not essential; Lenin, it may be suggested, saw that when he emphasized, time and again, the importance of giving an ever-widening circle the exercise of actual responsibility Two things handicapped the evolution away from dictatorship. The first was the isolation of the Soviet Union—for which the capitalist powers have a heavy responsibility—and the second was the development, which had begun in Lenin's last years, and grew rapidly after his death, of the dictatorship of the Bolshevik party into the dictatorship of its bureaucratic apparatus. After 1924, and particularly after 1927, Stalin and his associates, but, above all, Stalin, acquired a vested interest in power which they were not prepared to surrender. To that vested interest there have been sacrificed both democracy in the party, and the greater democracy beyond to which it would gradually have led. To it, also, have been sacrificed much in Germany, in China, and in Spain, that would have made for that very world-revolution upon which the rapid success of the Russian Revolution depended.

One has only to compare the atmosphere of the Communist Party under Lenin with the atmosphere under Stalin's leadership to see that this is the case. Lenin did not easily brook opposition; but there was vital discussion of his views in his lifetime, and his critics within the party were neither exiled nor executed for opposition to him. But, after Stalin wrested the leadership from his rivals, the whole temper of the party changed. Dissent from Stalin's views became of itself the expression of counter-revolutionary opinion. There were mass-purges, mass-exiles, and mass-executions. Despite the pledges of the Constitution of 1936, there is no freedom of speech, except for Stalin's adherents, no freedom of the press or assembly. Everyone knows that the elections are a farce; no candidatures are possible which reject the party line, and even the ballot-papers for them read like a hymn to Stalin. Freedom of movement is gravely restricted. Contact with foreigners is looked upon with suspicion. There is arbitrary arrest; there is long imprisonment, and even execution, without trial. It is difficult to obtain foreign literature, especially newspapers, except under official sanction. There is rigorous censorship of foreign journalists in the Soviet Union, and though this was abolished for some months in 1939, it was on the understanding that despatches hostile to the reputation of the Soviet Union might result in expulsion. Citizens cannot travel abroad without the permission of the government; and anyone who has seen a Soviet delegation at a scientific congress must have had the impression that he was watching a regimental detail assisting at the obsequies of "bourgeois" science. Though the right of asylum is granted by the Constitution to foreigners persecuted for service to the working-class, few Communists fleeing from Fascist terror abroad have been permitted to take advantage of it; and many of those who have done so have had bitter cause to regret it. Most political offences, and their possible ambit is wide, are tried in secret; there is no writ of *habeas corpus*, no right to subpoena witnesses, no right to a professional defence, with ample time to rebut the charges, in the case of alleged political crime. The death-penalty may be imposed for injury to, or theft of, collective property; and even "teasing, mocking, or persecuting" a shock-worker may, under Article 58 of the Criminal Code, become "wrecking," and so punishable with death. How vast and how terrible are the powers of the secret police emerged in 1938 at the trial of Yagoda who had been its head until his arrest. The system of hostages has been used; and relatively young children have been encouraged and eulogized for the denunciation of their parents.

I know no justification of these things which seems to me rationally based. It can only be justified for those in whose eyes the rulers of the Soviet Union can do no wrong. And they can take that view only by applying to the Soviet Union criteria of judgment which they would refuse to apply to other countries, to the Germany of Hitler, for instance, or to the Italy of Mussolini, where similar repressions exist. A socialist need not hesitate to admit that there are periods in which the suspension of the rule of law is inevitable; he cannot honourably defend the range and intensity of the bureaucratic dictatorship Stalin has established except by the argument that the means, however terrible, justify the end. But if he does so argue, he is confronted by the problem of whether the use of such means does not drive those who employ them to lose sight of the end. Certainly it is difficult not to feel that the range and intensity of the Soviet dictatorship has for its objective less the achievement of its socialist end than the maintenance of Stalin and his chosen associates in power at all costs. It is difficult, otherwise, to explain the price that has been imposed for dissent from his views; it is difficult otherwise to explain the Oriental eulogies that are so exhaustively lavished upon him. The cult of Stalin, indeed, has become a veritable religion, with the Politbureau as a college of Cardinals, and the secret police acting as inquisitors for a Bolshevik Pope. Deviation from orthodoxy is, as in a militant religion, punished by imprisonment or death.

The main emphasis of this temper had originated during the defeat of Trotsky between 1924 and 1927; and it is customary to refer to that defeat as the Thermidor of the Russian Revolution. The truth is that all such analogies are out of place. The dictatorship is the maintenance of personal power by a small group of men. But I think there is no real evidence to show, despite many and grave errors, that they maintain personal power for its own sake merely. The great end of the Revolution remains in being; the ugly twist its control has taken is due to reasons which need separate exploration. And it is proper to note that the habits of the dictatorship appear to seem far less evil to millions of Soviet citizens than they do to the outside observer. Partly, that is the outcome of the fact that the Russian people has never known the psychological implications of constitutional and democratic government; partly, too, it is the outcome of the fact that, as I have noted, there are important realms in which the achievement of the dictatorship is very great and, rightly, recognized as such by the masses; partly, in the third place, the alternative to it might so easily be the restoration of a régime the evil habits of which have been driven into the bones of the present Soviet generation by almost twenty-five years of unceasing propaganda. There is a national pride in what the Soviet government has done which only profound disaster, perhaps only disaster from without, could destroy, at least until it is commonly accepted by the average citizen that the régime is secure from attack. And I do not think he yet believes in its security.

For he has been educated, both by experience and propaganda, to think of the Soviet Union as the land of the socialist revolution, beset by enemies, internal and external, on all sides. He believes in its achievement and its prospects as firmly as the early Christians believed in the certainty of the Second Coming. Support of the régime is, for the masses, a sacred trust; to betray it is as difficult as for an early Christian to put his pinch of incense upon the altar of the pagan gods. Faith in the régime is not only the assurance of salvation for himself; it is holding high its standard on behalf of the unemancipated masses elsewhere. For him, most of the criticism of the régime comes from those whose ill-will to it can be shown; and when the rest comes from those whose treachery will be proved by such organized drama as the mass-trials, it is likely to be equally discounted. And when the ordinary citizen finds that he can himself criticize with a good deal of freedom the matters which concern his daily life, the conditions, for instance, of his job; when he sees about him, too, the endless possibilities of improving his position; he is tempted to believe that there is enough substance in the Revolution to justify his faith in its ultimate fulfilment. The times are hard; but when have they not been hard? The dictatorship is stern and unbending; but if it were relaxed, might not the capitalist and the landlord come back? Tolerance, constitutionalism, free discussion, these are memories that perish easily in a passionate time; and they are less likely to be born easily in a society that has never known them. We have to remember that it took one hundred and fifty years to acclimatize in England the idea of religious toleration; and its achievement was only the outcome of a long and difficult struggle. We must not judge the history of the Soviet Union by standards derived from our political maturity only.

I do not seek to defend either the range or the intensity of the Soviet dictatorship, for I believe that both of them are utterly disproportionate to the problems out of which they have arisen. I believe it to be not less true of Stalin and his associates than of any other dictators that they are profoundly corrupted by the exercise of absolute power. But I think we have got to explain that range and that intensity, and I think the explanation is more complicated than is usually supposed. Partly, as I have sought to show, it is the outcome of the decision to establish socialism in the Soviet Union only, without regard to economic evolution elsewhere. That decision meant that every difference in the party was, in the nature of things, a struggle for the state; it was bound, therefore, to sharpen the dictatorship. Partly, it was the outcome of the international insecurity of the Soviet Union; that meant a great increase in the necessary pace of Soviet industrialization which, in its turn, sharpened the significance of party-difference, and, therefore, the struggle for power. Partly, again, it was the outcome of an industrialization imposed rapidly upon a people unaccustomed to the discipline of the machine. Unless the response to machine-technology could have been imposed ruthlessly, the organization of its benefits could not be looked for in the time that Stalin and his associates conceived themselves to possess. We who can read of the iron age of our own industrial revolution must be careful here in our judgments; and an American commentator who remembers Heeren and Gastonia, the grim revelations of the La Follette Committee on civil liberties, the unforgettable picture Mr. Steinbeck has drawn of the Joad family will at least hesitate in the ease of his condemnation.

No doubt all of this must be read in the context of the personal psychology of Stalin and his associates, and this, in its turn, in the context of Bolshevist philosophy. We are dealing with men who have, rightly or wrongly, a conviction that is religious in its profundity that they are bringing the inevitable future to the birth. They have a vision of its character. They are convinced that it is infinitely precious. They believe that no sacrifices are too great for its attainment. Intelligibly enough, they set the price they must impose upon this generation against the final liberation of its successors they believe themselves to be organizing. They believe that the only sin is weakness, that error is as profound a threat to victory as was heresy to the Christian of an earlier age. Their effort has for them all the elements of a crusade. To grasp their temper we must try to realize the inner compulsions which, given the postulates of action, drives relentlessly forward all the great revolutionaries of history, Mahomet, Luther, Calvin, Cromwell. For them, whatever jeopardizes their concept of the Revolution is as hateful and as morally wrong as was Rome to the Puritan of England and Scotland, and of the American emigration. To suggest toleration to them is like suggesting to a Puritan accommodation with Rome. They have the truth, and they will die rather than fail to impose it.

I do not think anyone in England or America can fully understand the spirit of Bolshevism who has not studied with some particularity the literature of seventeenth-century Puritanism on its more militant side. There is the same consciousness of election, the same realization of the infinite worth of grace, the same contempt for the normal habits of human nature, a good deal, too, of the Puritan's conviction that whatever denies his central truth is error from the devil the infection from which cannot be destroyed too early. The Bolshevik, not less than the Puritan, is guided by his inner light, and that drives him inescapably to his goal even if, on his pilgrimage, he is seen to break the heart of half the world in his own radiant confidence, in his zeal for personal confession out of an intimate experience which has freed him from the weight of traditional error, in his glad knowledge that the ultimate victory is certain, in his power to suffer all earthly torment on behalf of the vision, in his conviction of the utter worthlessness of all insights not derived from his own postulates of thought, in the belief, perhaps above all, that he is the forerunner of what is inevitably ordained, his resemblance to the seventeenth-century Puritan is a remarkable one. No one who has seen a Bolshevik Congress at work but can recognize there the historic hopes of the earlier movement; a meeting of the Praesidium at Moscow must have its psychological affinities with those Putney Debates of Cromwell's Ironsides the Clarke Papers have so happily preserved for us. Even the Bolshevik contempt for "bourgeois" learning is exactly paralleled by the suspicion of secular learning with which the "mechanick preachers" are filled; and the Bolshevik reliance upon their texts from Marx and Lenin and Stalin is identical with the Puritan dependence upon citations from the Scriptures.

No portrait of a Bolshevik is complete without its emphasis upon his immersion in a tradition of persecution and conspiracy in which he learns contempt of personal danger and pride in martyrdom. The reader, for example, of Demitroff's testimony at the Reichstag Fire Trial in 1934 could easily imagine that he was listening to the witness John Bunyan felt himself compelled to bear. Both types, alike, are schooled by grim experience to an iron discipline of which the lesson is that what matters is the victory of the gospel and that only in fidelity to its claims can the individual find the highroad to his salvation. It is noteworthy, too, that the strategy of the Puritan to a hostile government resembles that of the Bolshevik in a marked degree. He is foremost in his denunciation of an intolerance directed against himself; as he achieves power, he can be equally emphatic in his denial of tolerance for others. Convinced of the possession of truth, they believe that it involves the obligation to compel uniformity. They see in the variations of doctrine an inevitable source of intellectual error, and, therefore, of confusion in behaviour; for when men refuse to accept necessary truth, they are a menace to order and society. The Puritan enthusiast sought to compel men to grace as individuals; the Bolshevik seems to compel a collective salvation. But in each there are the three vital qualities, humility, penitence and the conviction of an awaiting glory, which provides the faith that its professor's mission is to transform the character of human behaviour that it may be prepared for a higher station in the universe. That the Puritan's mission came, as he believed, from the grace of God, while that of the Bolshevik comes from his grasp, as he insists, of the laws of history, makes little difference to the identity of impact the inspiration makes.

It is, I think, too, of pivotal importance to the grasp of this outlook, that the Bolshevik has the same impatient contempt as the Puritan for the exponent of half-measures. Just as to Pascal with his Jansenist sense of infinite degradation, the luminous moderation of Montaigne imperils salvation; just as Prynne could find in the "unlovelinesse of lovelocke's" the highroad to damnation; so the Bolshevik finds in the minutest deviation from the stream of party doctrine the prospect of counter-revolution which, for him, is what damnation is to the Puritan. Each must be all or nothing. Each refuses to see any aspect of life save in the context of his supreme aim. Each finds it more difficult to forgive the half-friend than the open enemy. Each lavishes upon his opponents a wealth of abuse which, for the faithful, is a completely effective substitute for the objective analysis of doctrine. Nothing less than a complete regeneration of society is the object at which each aims; and it is easy to see that any faltering in this objective can be equated with an absence of grace. The Bolshevik handles his opponent with the same armoury of sacred text and scurrilous abuse as the Puritan; what the Roman Church is to one, so is bourgeois society to another. Prynne, after all, handled Archbishop Laud in much the same way as Lenin handled Kautsky; and the Puritan's citations of Scripture are the precise equivalent of the Bolshevik's citations of Marx. Each, too, as the Church Book of the Bunyan meeting, and the confessional experiences of a Communist Party group, make evident, is living a life each item in the behaviour of which is responsible to, and judged by, the fellowship in whom he is united in his search for salvation. And in the same vital way as Puritanism succeeded as it became a movement able to bring hope and exhilaration, the promise of a future share in the true riches of life, to the disinherited, so has the appeal of Bolshevism been built upon its pledge of election to the proletariat. And because the power to withhold salvation from its aspirants evokes fear in those who yearn to share in its wealth, so Bolshevism, like Puritanism before, while it has bred the hero and the saint, has bred in so many, too, the sycophant and the hypocrite. Fear is an essential instrument in its purposes. But fear alone does not explain its power. Fear could no more have won to Puritan doctrine the allegiance of Milton and Cromwell, of Lilburne and Bunyan, than fear could have brought Lenin and Trotsky, Stalin and Voroshilov to the service of the Bolshevik cause.

I do not think, therefore, that the erosion of dictatorship in the Soviet Union is a simple matter; certainly its disappearance cannot be effected by a simple act of will on the part of Stalin and his colleagues. That could not be the case simply because so abrupt a transition would jeopardize the whole foundations of not merely the Stalin régime, but even of the Soviet Union. It would mean the devotion to the struggle for power of energy and purposes that are now harnessed to the economic effort of the Union, and could not, without paralysis, be harnessed elsewhere. That is part of the price paid for the change of a party dictatorship which admitted democracy within its ranks to the dictatorship of a narrow bureaucracy which has stifled all initiative not regarded by itself as orthodox. Clearly, for example, if the process of industrialization were to be hampered by the kind of debate which occurred during the fight for control between Stalin and Trotsky, the production of capital and consumption goods would be checked at every turn. For that fight would mean doubt of the faith; and it is the hold of the faith which confers the power to impose the continual fulfilment of orders. Dictatorship is more likely to be followed by anarchy than by freedom unless it is able to offer the prospect of security, internal and external, as freedom is sought for and conceded.

I believe, therefore, that the decline of dictatorship in the Soviet Union is, above all, dependent upon the growth of a wide popular faith in its security. And that is a matter which depends at least as much upon events without as upon events within the Union. So long as there is a widespread conviction that the capitalist powers are prepared to attack the Soviet Union, so long the dictatorship will persist; for so long it will be able to utilize national sentiment on its own behalf. So long, also, as the possibility of that attack exists, all dissident opinion in the Soviet Union will look expectantly to foreign assistance for aid; and there is good reason to accept the Soviet view that such expectations have rarely been disappointed. The people of the Soviet Union will not feel secure until they see that the power of a great state to act aggressively is curbed so far as organization can curb it. When they have that confidence, the demand for democratic concessions from the dictatorship will follow rapidly. But I am confident that an atmosphere of international security is the necessary prelude to its coming.

For, as it comes, no dictatorship can impose over a long period the controls that are necessary to its permanence. Given external security, it is impossible, in the modern conditions of communication, to build a Chinese wall about a whole civilization. The growth of education, even the impact of industrialization itself, these make, by nature, for demands no dictatorship can safely refuse. Were it to do so, it would invite internal disruption. For it would involve a sullen discontent among men and women increasingly conscious of the frustration of their powers, and increasingly suspicious of the motives of those who frustrated them. At present, Stalin and his associates have a powerful reply to any such resentment. They can say that the admission of the classic principles of democracy provides the enemies of the Soviet Union, as they provided the enemies of the Weimar Republic, with exactly the opportunity and procedures for which they are looking. They can insist that every régime in danger has been compelled to assume vast powers of protection against their abuse. If this is the case in a political democracy in which, as in Great Britain, the parliamentary system has been unchallenged for over two and one half centuries, it is not surprising that a régime which is attempting to build something like a new way of civilized life should feel insecure after less than a generation of experience in which foreign and civil war have defined the habits of thought.

The argument is a powerful one, I think, on any showing. It is useless not to remember that, apart from the working-class, there have been few who have not displayed to the Russian Revolution a hatred even more vitriolic than our ancestors displayed to the French Revolution. It is useless, either, to forget that in the critical years from 1933 to 1939 the statesmen of the European democracies exhausted all their ingenuity in evading the proffered alliance of the Soviet Union, and that, even on the very eve of war, the British Ambassador in Berlin could see no reason against an Anglo-German alliance if the Polish problem could be peacefully solved. It is, too, of clearly immense importance that, the moment Stalin made the grave error of attacking Finland, there were wide circles of opinion in favour of accommodation with Germany in order to begin the psychologically more satisfactory process of attacking the Soviet Union as a joint effort in the name of "Christian" civilization. We have constantly to remember, in short, that in the degree that the Soviet Union conducts its experiment successfully, it thereby threatens the whole social and economic structure of the existing capitalist order. The anxiety for its breakdown, the fear of its success, have been among the most considerable influences of our time in social thought; economists have even found an audience for the argument that it was bound to break down on *a priori* grounds, without even the pretence of examining what it had achieved.

The ugliness in it, and the cruelty, which have been both immense, and its blunders, must not blind us to the fact that it is yet the most colossal event in history since the Reformation. For it coincides, like the latter, with a total crisis in civilization. And if, as it proceeds, it is able to show that the private ownership of the means of production is unnecessary to the efficient organization of economic life; if, further, it can demonstrate that there is an adequate substitute for the profit-making motive which, as it works, makes unemployment unnecessary; if it is able to show that the heritage of culture can be made accessible to the mass of a nation, and that the impact of science on industrial technique is not a continuous threat to the economic security of the worker; obviously, then, the Russian Revolution will have opened a new and creative epoch in human experience as vital as any in our knowledge. It is, of course, clear that these prospects are all contingencies. But no one who fails to note their existence can adequately measure the implications of the Revolution.

But, very definitely, they are as yet contingencies merely. They may be shattered by war; for the diversion, over time, of any considerable effort to its cost might easily destroy popular faith in the purpose of the Revolution, quite apart from the possibility that war might entail defeat. Quite clearly, also, the sacrifices the purposes entail are likely to be far more prolonged in an industrially backward country like the Soviet Union than they would be in an advanced one like the United States of America; the colossal figures of increased volume of production do not conceal the fact that output per worker in the Soviet Union is still far lower than in the more advanced capitalist countries, and the ultimate test lies in the capacity of the Soviet worker to out-distance the worker in a capitalist society. If these contingencies can be met, the impact of the Russian Revolution will, clearly enough, compel the rapid transformation of capitalism. It will, everywhere, have to adjust itself to the new way of life just as feudalism was compelled to adjust itself to the immensely greater potentialities of individualistic capitalism after the sixteenth century.

That, at any rate, was the history of the French Revolution; it compelled, all over the world, an adjustment both of ideas and of institutions to the purposes it embodied. It did so despite its blunders and its crimes; it did so despite the wars that were waged against it; and it did so despite the fact that, to the main men of property in that generation, its ideas seemed the incarnation of original sin. The effect of the French Revolution was, for half a century after its occurrence, to set the decisive context of European history. It awakened in thousands of humble men hopes and aspirations they did not know themselves to possess; and these came to shape new criteria of social judgment to which, increasingly, the governing class had to adjust its mind. It staked the claim of a *nouvelle couche sociale* to a place in the sun; and the Europe of the nineteenth century had to find room for it in the calculations of statesmen.

I see no reason to suppose that the effect of the Russian Revolution may not be similar in character. It is, above all, a challenge to the foundations of middle-class civilization, an assertion that a man may not be excluded from the essential goods that civilization has achieved simply because he is not an owner of the instruments of production. That assertion has already won widespread welcome all over the world, not merely in the constituency to which it has been directly addressed. Indeed, its acceptance is the logical outcome of any system of representative government that is based upon a universal and equal franchise.

For in an unequal society, where what is most impressive is the contrast between riches and poverty, it is inevitable that men should seek to use their political power to redress the balance implied in that contrast. They will seek to do so as soon as they become convinced that a policy of concessions merely from the rich to the poor does not satisfy their established expectations. And as soon as they seek to do so either there must be inaugurated a series of massive social and economic reforms which prove that the balance is being consciously and continuously redressed, or there will be an attempt forcibly to change the character of the state. Either, that is, classes must co-operate to change the foundations, or the abyss between them will grow so wide that conflict is inevitable.

It is the fact that this conception has been given so vivid an actuality in the Russian Revolution which provides it with its dynamic, even explosive, character. It intensifies so suddenly and so sharply the challenge to the existing order that it induces both excessive hopes and excessive fears. Excessive hopes, because the comparative ease with which the Bolsheviks seized power tempts extremists everywhere to underestimate both the strength of the resistance they will encounter and the complexities of the problem of consolidating power if and when it is won; and because revolutionary optimism always exaggerates the ease with which deep-seated habits can be changed. Excessive fears, because all those whose interests are jeopardized by infection from the Russian Revolution tend to infer from it not the desirability of reforming while there is yet time, but the necessity of safeguarding themselves from the danger of infection. The result, handled unwisely, is to widen the gulf between classes; and the more profound the faith the Revolution evokes, the more conscious do men become of the width of the gulf. This makes the temper of possible accommodation more difficult of access; and it also gives an undue influence to the extremist voices on either side.

The Russian Revolution, in fact, like its French predecessor, has become a subject upon which very few men can speculate calmly, so immense are the hopes and fears built upon its outcome. The hopes tempt those who hold them to insist that nothing the leaders of the Soviet Union do can be wrong; and the fears tempt its enemies to argue that not even its most obvious achievements are real. Hope that is deaf to reason, and ignorant of the power of prescription, always exacerbates every conflict of ideas within a society; just as fear, in the same case, shuts men's ears to the most obvious call for necessary change. The most urgent problem of the Russian Revolution is not the praise or blame it should exact, but the need for its understanding; and nothing is so rare. For where understanding of so immense an event halts, it may easily lead to the protagonists of either side arming themselves to ensure the victory of their outlook.

It is this possible outcome of the fear and hope aroused by the Russian Revolution which has made two decisions of Moscow since 1917 such disastrous decisions. The first was the decision of Lenin to split the working-class forces of the world by founding the Communist International and, therewith, the national Communist Parties; the second was the decision of the Soviet Union to enforce upon its constituents everywhere a view of the war of 1939 which made them the exponents of revolutionary defeatism in the states opposed to Hitler and Mussolini. The first was a disastrous decision for a number of reasons. It turned the mind of each Communist party into a conspiratorial direction. It gave the status of rigid orthodoxy to a strategy or revolution the validity of which was built almost wholly on the assumption that the unique experience of Russia was a pattern for peoples with a century of quite different history behind them. It turned the Communist parties outside the Soviet Union into narrow sects the tempo of whose activity was set, not by the situations they confronted, but by the international requirements of the Soviet Union. It also gave a pretext to Fascist parties to pose as the representatives of patriotism and order which, though it had no substance in fact, gave them access to alliances they would not otherwise have possessed. And the fact that the organization of the Communist parties had the right centralism, ever-increasing in tightness, of their Russian model, gave them a contempt for ordinary men. They worked, no doubt, for the future of an abstract proletarian, but they were rarely acquainted with the realities of human nature.

That centralism is natural enough in the historic circumstances which the Russian Revolution confronted; without it, the discipline and élan of the Bolsheviks would not have been attained. But, first it required the genius of Lenin to give it the requisite adaptability of manœuvre on the field of battle; and, second, it accorded ill with the habits of states accustomed over a long period to representative democracy in the political field. Its origins, indeed, go further back than Lenin. Part of it, I think, is directly traceable to Rousseau's idea of the legislator who is to bring the ideal state into being by imposing his purpose on a people not yet ready for its acceptance. That view, natural in the offspring of Calvin's Geneva, with his profound conviction that men have been corrupted by social institutions, passed from him to Babeuf and his fellow-conspirators. They saw their hopes in France broken by evil men; and they thought of a conspiratorial dictatorship as a process of compulsion to virtue. From Babeuf, through Buonarroti and the secret societies of nascent European democracy in the first forty years of the nineteenth century, the idea passed to Marx and the socialist movement; and it is easy to see how, in the bitterness of his exile, he transformed it into that proletarian dictatorship which, on the analogy of Rousseau's legislator, was to "force men to be free." Mixed with the dubious metaphysics of the Hegelian dialectic, it enabled, less the party as the whole, than its bureaucratic apparatus, so to speak, as they could urge, with the authentic voice of history. What they urged was what the "real will" of the proletariat would demand could it but know what was best for itself; it enabled the party to transcend those temporary and immediate, even irrational, interests which obscured for the masses the truths to which the parties had access. It involved, indeed, the denial that what a proletariat seemed to want was what it wanted at all, whenever what it seemed to want went counter to what the party decided was good for it. And if other parties of a proletarian complexion refused to accept the superior insight of the Communist party, it meant that they must be denounced as objectively the enemies of the working-class.

The dialectic, indeed, was the ideal philosophy for an extremist group convinced of its possession of eternal truth, and certain that all its enemies or critics were always wrong. It gave them an unbreakable faith; and it gave them the fanatic's contempt for all who did not see, as they saw it, the priceless importance of the end. But it led them to the use of tactics which seemed outrageous to those not wholly convinced that the end was as certain as they made it. It made them contemptuous of any who hesitated to go the whole way with them; and from contempt they could pass easily to the belief that the destruction of all socialist influence they could not control was the necessary prelude to their own victory. They were even prepared to combine with their avowed enemies for this purpose, convinced that, in the end, they were bound to be the residuary legatees of power. In fact, of course, the real result of their manœuvres was to create a monumental confusion in the world-proletariat to the profit not of the workers but of their enemies. Only zealots for a doctrine which ignored reality could have preferred the prospects of the workers under Hitler to their prospects under the Weimar Republic. I think it probable that, had Lenin not precipitated the fatal split in the working-class forces implied in the foundation of the Communist International, certainly not Hitler, and perhaps not Mussolini, would have attained to power. But the preliminary condition of their success was that, through Communist fanaticism, the organized forces of the working class were divided and hesitant when they could have been united and strong.

The second disastrous decision was that which, after October 1939, resulted in the growth of revolutionary defeatism among the Communist parties of the democracies. I have already explained why the Soviet Union, for very good reasons, was led to adopt a policy of neutrality in this war. There is no doubt that this policy was a profound shock to the constituent parties of the Communist International. The *volte face* had to be explained; and it had so to be explained that the Communist parties did not appear, within the democracies, to wish or work for a Fascist victory. The only way to do this was to insist that this was an "imperialist" war, on the model of 1914, the results of which were indifferent to the true interests of the worker; and thence to argue, as Lenin argued in 1914, that the class-conscious proletarian would work for the overthrow of his "bourgeois" government and its replacement by a government of the masses. The elaborate and unedifying casuistry by which this view was defended can hardly, I suspect, have deceived the realists in the Kremlin, whatever its hold abroad. It was the outcome of Soviet fear of Germany, and, objectively, is unintelligible except on the basis of that fear. Partly, I think, it must be attributed to the impact upon Stalin and his associates of the poison of unlimited power.

For they have rid themselves of any outside their own circle who could speak to them on equal terms. They have ceased to submit vital decisions to criticism. They have come to expect that whatever they announce shall be received with unlimited and punctual applause, to equate, indeed, criticism of their decisions with counter-revolutionary sentiment. The situation of men who have made themselves immune from the need to consider any opinion but their own is bound to result in grave mistakes; and it makes no difference in what kind of state that situation is found. It creates in them the fatal illusion of infallibility than which there is no myth more dangerous; and that myth leads on, still more fatally, to persecution of those who are unable to accept its implications. When that stage is reached, everything that makes for peaceful relations between men is menaced, simply because those who have the illusion of infallibility cease to regard themselves as men, and, even worse, cease to regard their subjects as ends not less than instruments.

Here, I suggest, the Communist parties outside the Soviet Union have served Stalin ill. They can, of course, argue that they were ignorant of each stage of its development until it was operative, and that it was impossible for any of them to take a line which would have meant an attack on the Soviet Union. But the answer surely is that a world-movement which seeks for world-influence ought not to allow one of its constituent parties to get into the position where its decisions are beyond criticism; and, further, that the Soviet government would never have sought to impose the line those parties have followed had not their past supineness given it the right to anticipate that it would be supported in whatever policy it might adopt.

That abdication from the duty of critical judgment is the real sin against the light which all dictatorship imposes upon its subjects; and it is also the source of the immense risks which all dictatorships, whether of the Left or the Right, necessarily run. For abdication from the duty of critical judgment on the part of its subjects, even more of its devotees, necessarily means that it becomes rapidly separated from the mind of the masses whom it controls. It must, therefore, at all costs maintain its prestige; and this consists either in carrying forward every policy to success, or finding a plausible scapegoat if it fails. It was necessary, therefore, for Stalin to throw overboard not only the policy, and its implications, Litvinov had followed from 1934, but also the praise which had been lavished upon the advance of Finnish democracy since 1936; and this catastrophic reversal of attitude had necessarily to be accepted as the insight of genius. But I think the real consequence of the change in all who are not vowed to the myth of Bolshevik infallibility has been to create the first profound doubts since 1917 of the identity of Soviet interest with those of the world-proletariat. Granted the victory of Great Britain, the result of that doubt is bound to be the need for Stalin to arrive at some *modus vivendi* with the victor which will be destructive of the legend of his own infallibility.

It is this kind of catastrophic change that a dictatorship should, at all costs, avoid. Lenin did so because of two things. He always permitted vital criticism without resentment; and he always avoided laying the foundations for mass-antagonism from those upon whose support he could reasonably count. That was why he could accept a defeat like that of Brest-Litovsk without humiliation; that, also, is why he could execute so comprehensive a retreat as the New Economic Policy in the confident expectation that he could retrace his steps. It is the grave flaw in Stalin's technique that he has built his dictatorship upon a pattern which excludes these possibilities. He has always to be victorious; he has always to be right; he has always to be successful. He has always to have men to blame whom he can convincingly blame. But that means that even his closest associates are never secure of their hold; and this means, in turn, that the loyalty upon which he has to rely is rarely, even in the central direction of affairs, the spontaneous loyalty of rational conviction. How little it is this kind of loyalty is evident to anyone who knows the Soviet system from within; or observes the growth of adulatory Byzantinism in the habits of the régime.

The future of the Soviet system is necessarily compromised by these developments. For they have threatened its success at home, as they have injured its prestige abroad. Abroad, it needed the authority which came from the conviction not only that it was the leader of the socialist forces of the world, but, also, that it could be counted upon to stand firmly against systems which, like that of Hitler, threaten at its root the power of the working-class to go forward. The German-Soviet Pact was, from this angle, a cynical manœuvre which, as the Communist International sought to provide it with a logical justification, became a shameless exhibition, on Stalin's part, of complete indifference to the fate of the working-class outside the Soviet Union; and the attack on Finland, like the absorption of the Baltic republics, was an example of strategic imperialism in the direct tradition of preventive wars. Both policies had a bad result on the internal aspect of the Soviet Union.

For their result was, necessarily, to prolong the power of a despotic system which no one had done more than Stalin and his colleagues to expose as the vital enemy of the workers. By prolonging that power, therefore, especially in the context of Stalin's inevitable knowledge that Hitler would abide by his agreement only so long as he felt it advisable, he risked the danger of exactly that isolation it should have been the central purpose of his strategy to avoid. It was above all his interest to keep the Soviet Union a factor in world affairs whose zeal for peace and whose hostility to aggression even his profoundest enemies could not successfully deny. That was his fundamental psychological safeguard in the evil atmosphere of power politics, which had been made so much more evil by the policy of Hitler. When he decided to compromise with Nazism, and to profit by the compromise in the Nazi manner, he could not fail gravely to impair the credit of the Russian Revolution even with its warmest friends.

The safety, in fact, of the purposes of 1917 now rests, in my judgment, less upon factors inside the Soviet Union than upon factors outside it. It depends, first, upon the rapid defeat of the Nazi government. For that defeat alone means a chance of reorganizing collective security against aggression, and, thereby, a breathing-space of pivotal importance to civilization. It is a breathing-space which gives the Soviet Union relief from the fear of external attack, and the chance that the nature of the economic problems post-war Europe will confront will hasten the evolution of the Western powers to a socialist synthesis. If that occurs, it will markedly advance the compulsion to internal democracy in the Soviet Union; for nothing else, within the time of which our generation need take account, can give its citizens that sense of security of which the return to freedom is the necessary outcome.

I doubt whether it will be a rapid return, unless some radical change occurs in the structure and habits of the Russian Communist party; for men who, like Stalin, have become accustomed to the habits of unfettered command do not easily recover from them save as the condition of survival. It is always, moreover, a hard thing to break the power of a bureaucracy many of whose members have attained positions of privilege by obsequious service to those habits. That is even more the case when the path of the dictator, as with Stalin, has been marked by the imposition of penalties so cruel upon those who have differed from him. There is the danger of revenge, the fear that a new terror may take the place of the old. Action and reaction are equal in the dynamics of politics not less than those of nature. It is part of the price that the Soviet Union will have to pay for the scale of its experiment, and the tempo at which, in its difficult environment, the experiment was made, that it will find the path from collectivist economics to political democracy so much more steep and difficult than its makers deemed possible. But that is the price they always must pay who do not measure the cost of means in their relentless pursuit even of the greatest end.

One final remark upon the Russian Revolution is worth making. There can be little doubt that the intensity of its dictatorship, its ruthlessness, even, makes less impact upon those over whom it is exercised than it would do among a people who, like ourselves, have a deep-rooted tradition of political democracy. After all, there had been nothing in Russian history to compare with that experience of self-government in trade unions, in Nonconformist Churches, in the co-operative societies, and in local politics, which made the working man in Britain increasingly anxious himself to shape his own destiny. The Soviet dictatorship, in Stalin's hands, carries on the Byzantine tradition of Czarism; there is a sense in which its results are more akin to those of Peter the Great than of a Western agent of emancipation. We cannot omit to recognize that, short of military defeat, those results are bound, in the long run, to be fatal to the dictator's power; the educational implications alone are, over a period, the guarantee of that. No one who knows the Soviet Union can doubt that its results stir up ways of behaviour which, when there is external security, will begin to question, will ask for a unity that grows from below instead of a unity that is imposed from above. How long those ways of behaviour will be in developing, I do not think anyone can tell; that the period of their emergence depends very largely on the international situation is, I think, a legitimate inference from our experience. Danger always holds together a nation that lives under strict coercive authority; and the danger that confronts the Russian Revolution has been beyond all question real. It has given Stalin psychological defences which a wiser policy in Britain and America would, over the last decade, have stricken from his hands. If their rulers, if, even more, their peoples, have learned one of the supreme lessons of this war, they can, I think, restore to the Russian Revolution that power to achieve the balance between individual liberty and social security which is the objective of all political effort. The first condition of that restoration is the defeat of Fascism; the second is the creative use of the victory. But to understand what these imply we must grasp the nature of the Fascist adventure. It is to that analysis that I now turn.

Chapter III

THE MEANING OF FASCISM

I

THE phenomena presented by the Fascist states preserve a certain regularity of rhythm of obvious importance to their understanding. In each case, their rulers have come to power either in a society that was defeated in the war of 1914 or in one that was dissatisfied in its expectations by the outcome of that conflict. Disappointed national ambition, that is to say, has in each case been an element in the rise of the Fascist party to power. In each case, further, the appeal of the Fascist party, in its predominant public expression, has been an appeal to the oppressed elements in the national community; the small shopkeeper, threatened by the progress of the co-operative store or the multiple shop, the unemployed, especially the unemployed ex-officer, the small manufacturer jeopardized by the growth of corporate organization, the *déclassé* intellectual, unable to find a career in one of the historic political organizations, the *petit bourgeois*, less able than at any previous time to become his own master, it is to these that, as it made its way to power, the Fascist party has sought to appeal.

But, in each case, also, the formal programme of the Fascist parties has been a façade to cover very different connections. A large part of their finance has been derived from affiliations made with big business; and a vital part of their leadership has been pledged, from an early stage, to hostility towards proletarian aspirations. There has been penetration of, or, at least, an understanding with, the governmental apparatus of the state; officers of its defence forces, the police, and even the magistracy and the civil service, have connived at considerable illegalities on the part of Fascists. Having attained power, they have invariably proceeded not only to throw overboard their announced programme. They have also, by a system of terror more or less proportionate to their fear of resistance, to destroy their opponents and to liquidate all organizations which might serve in the future as a contingent source of hostility. They have invariably established a monoparty state, of which the essence has been the identification of the party-structure with the apparatus of state-power. This has meant that all opposition to the party has become opposition to the state, with the result that, more or less rapidly, every aspect of the national life—cultural, political, economic, social—has become subordinated to the single need of the party's retention of power. This has, of course, implied at once the overthrow of all the constitutional habits which representative democracy had sought to establish since the French Revolution; and this, in its turn, has involved the denial that the individual is an end in himself, in whom, because he is so regarded, rights inhere. He has become, on the contrary, a means to an end.

That end is a constant increase in the power of the state, regarded as the authoritarian embodiment of the national purpose. But since the state is, for all essential purposes, the Fascist party, the subordination of the individual to the Fascist party is the inevitable accompaniment of its evolution. And this has set the perspective of both the internal and external policies of Fascism. Internally, it has been compelled to interventionism lest grievance accumulate and, thereby, threaten its power; compensation has to be offered to the multitude for the suppression of the institutions whereby, in a capitalist democracy, they sought to improve their standard of life. Externally, moreover, the very fact that Fascism was nourished by disappointed national ambition has meant its necessary concentration on an aggressive foreign policy. That has served several purposes. By the pursuit of "glory" abroad it has tended to draw attention away from grievance at home. The pursuit of "glory" has involved an increase in armaments proportionate to the ambitions such "glory" demanded, and that increase, accordingly, acts as a form of public works and so has the effect of decreasing unemployment; thereby it can be represented as proof of the triumph of the Fascist régime in the economic realm. But the pursuit of "glory" must have tangible achievements to its credit. It therefore becomes necessary for the Fascist power not only to threaten aggressive action, but also to move towards its achievement of "a place in the sun." For this purpose it selects an opponent who can either be compelled, through its weakness, to give way, or, if it resists, makes embarkation upon war seem at least a legitimate gamble. Since war, or the threat of it, is always a means of consolidating the psychological unity of a nation, at least to the point where it suffers defeat in the field, this has the effect at once of making resistance to the régime more difficult and, to the point where it is victorious, of enhancing its prestige. And the advance of the nation by conquests of this kind has the advantage of satisfying the national ambitions which have been defeated or disappointed in the past. There will be few of those who are not outright opponents of the system who will not be moved by its successful use of the technique of imperialist expansion.

The Marxist critics of Fascism have dismissed it as simply the expression of monopoly-capitalism in decay. They have pointed out, quite rightly, that it does not disturb the vital class-relations in any society it comes to dominate; individuals, or special groups like the Jews, apart, it is characteristic of its functioning that the rich remain rich and the poor remain poor. They have pointed out, also rightly, that in each Fascist state not only have the great monopolies strengthened their position, but that the promised protection to the "little man" has never, in fact, been forthcoming. They have shown, with abundant proof, that the destruction of institutions like the trade unions and the socialist parties leaves the workers largely helpless before the demands of their employers; a diminution in the standard of living has been a consistent accompaniment of Fascist evolution. They argue, therefore, that the essence of Fascism is that it represents the replacement of capitalist democracy by the naked dictatorship of the big monopolies. It is the refuge to which capitalism is driven when it is no longer able at once to preserve the privileges of its ruling class and to make concessions to the multitude.

There is a real truth in this analysis, though it is not, I think, rigorous enough in character to cover all the facts involved. No one can study the history of the way in which Mussolini and Hitler arrived at power without seeing that they were, in a fundamental way, the condottiere of big business. From that element in society each derived a large part of his financial support; each repaid that support by destroying for big business the essential mechanisms of working-class defence. But there are two other elements involved which are essential to the understanding of Fascism to which its Marxist opponents have given inadequate attention.

The first is the fact that both Mussolini and Hitler were able to build mass-movements. They were able to weld together in a powerful organization the disinherited, whether the unemployed soldier like Roehm, or the *déclassé* intellectual like Rosenberg, the dissatisfied youth and the *petit bourgeois* trader; and they made an obvious and important appeal to women. The secret of this ability appears to have a twofold basis. Partly, it was built upon a skilful exploitation of nationalist sentiment. It promised success and unity to peoples which had been rendered miserable by failure and disunity. It offered them expansion through action at a time when the régime against which Fascism was a protest seemed incapable of growth and of action. Organized, moreover, as an army, it offered the prospect of a career with the right to command to those who joined it; they felt they were marching somewhere. They were given something to do. In fulfilling their task, they became somebody. Even if they only attacked a helpless trade unionist in a dark side-street, or beat up an elderly Jew, they were defeating those whom they had been taught to regard as their enemies; and it was an easy step to make their enemies the cause of the humiliation the nation had suffered, and thus to represent their defeat as a victory for the nation. In the pathological condition of post-1918 Italy and Germany, there were large numbers anxious to work off a sense of frustration and able to find in violence the means of aggressive compensation for it. And since most of those whom they attacked were either, like trade unionists, bitterly disliked by business men, or like the German Jews, still regarded as an alien element in the national life, Fascist violence was almost benevolently regarded as a contribution to a future order in which trade unionism would be sterilized and the positions and property held by Jews would be open to men who could not compete with them on equal terms. And when all this is set in the context of economic depression, and a political atmosphere in which the fractionalism of parties prevented any clarity of direction in government, it is clear enough that there was vast explosive material waiting to be organized. Had government, in either Italy or Germany, acted firmly against either Hitler or Mussolini in their early days, there would have been little difficulty in destroying the movements they symbolized. But the forces opposed to them were never united enough to make this possible.

For the solid capitalist class distrusted the mood of the workers and was not unsympathetic to men who would, as they were privately assured, dissipate that mood by destroying the organization which made it possible. The workers were divided, above all by the divisions which sympathy for, and reaction against, the Communist International had created; they even came to hate one another more than they hated their common enemy. They faced an organized and well-drilled army which said one thing and one thing only to the mass of unpolitical citizens while they were engaged in endless and complicated doctrinal disputes of which that mass could make little or nothing. In a large degree, further, whatever promise the parties of the Left seemed to offer, was explicitly affirmed by Fascism also; and the latter, in its propaganda, was far more skilful in its psychological exploitation of the national tradition. The Left gave the impression of a detachment from its mainstream; for

Mussolini and Hitler the recovery of its power was an essential element in their programme. To a nation in the bitterness of disillusion, an exaggerated nationalism is almost a necessary luxury. While the Fascists dwelt upon the glories of its past, the Left demanded a clean break with a hundred memories that recollection had rendered sacred. There can be little doubt that the technique of Fascist propaganda was, in this regard, far more in accord with established expectation, more easily grasped, therefore, than that of their rivals. The insistence that their attainment of power would mean action likely to compensate for past defeat was, I think, an index to a perceptiveness which was always absent from the propaganda of the Left.

And of that Left one vital failure must be noted that is of the first importance. It was preaching a revolutionary doctrine without ever studying seriously the dynamics of power. That emerges clearly in the brief explosion of Italian revolutionary sentiment when the workers, in 1920, seized the factories. Either they had to move on from that seizure to an assault upon the state; or they had to accept a defeat which was bound to create profound hostility among every element of traditional order. They chose the first alternative, and this inevitably meant, first, that they informed their enemies that they were incapable of seizing power, that their resentment was a mood rather than a movement, and, second, that they would submit to strong government if it was imposed. It was that discovery which cemented the alliance between Mussolini and the governing class of Italy. Thenceforward, he had only to take power in an atmosphere carefully dramatized to convey the appearance that he was irresistible; and in the first two years in which he uneasily felt his way to absolutism, none of his opponents had the courage to challenge his assumption of authority. He acted while they were content to discuss.

If the German experience was more complicated, it nevertheless conveys the same lesson. It was not only that the Weimar régime was, from the outset, unpopular because it had to govern a Germany embittered by defeat. It was not only, also, that none of its many governments from 1918 sought to build either a civil service or a defence force upon whose loyalty it could genuinely count; the relation of Hitler to the Bavarian government after the putsch of 1923 is sufficient proof of that. It was not only, further, that the régime suffered from the tragedy of the inflation and the wholesale misery of the economic blizzard, and that it was, right down to the advent of Hitler, treated as an inferior state by France and Great

Britain. It never possessed, in the fifteen years of its history, a government with power enough to pursue either a strong or even a continuous policy. German communism dismayed it by playing at revolution and, thereby, terrifying its bourgeoisie without ever having the material power to subdue it. German socialists divided their time between fighting the Communists, on the one hand—an attitude for which Communist provocation has, indeed, a large responsibility—and in maintaining a tenacious legality of which their Fascist opponents took the fullest advantage. No one, to take a single, but crucial, instance, can study the tame surrender of the Social Democratic government of Prussia to von Papen in 1932 without realizing that the party, however well organized in a formal way, never understood the dynamics of power. From the moment of that abdication, there was no hope for the Weimar régime except in revolutionary action. The fact that the socialists, whose supreme interest was in its defence at all costs, refused to embark upon it meant, and could only mean, that they were acquiescing in their own destruction.

They desired to rule who were afraid to govern; that is, I suggest, the meaning of socialist experience in Italy and Germany before the advent of Mussolini and Hitler to power. They refused to be the state; and they encountered opponents who were determined to utilize to the limit the full implications of its supreme coercive power. And this leads me to the second aspect of Fascism in which, as I think, the Marxist analysis of its nature has been defective. While it is true, as I have said, that its rise to power has been associated with a partnership, revealed only after the event, between its leaders and the ruling elements in the capitalist democracy they destroyed, its use of power has made it more than a simple tool in the hands of monopoly-capitalism.

For it has been driven by its own inner logic to the destruction of capitalism in its historic liberal form. Granted the problems Fascism confronted, this was, I think, inevitable if, as an organized movement, its leaders, whether in Italy or in Germany, were to retain power. For they had to do two things. On the one hand, they had to grapple with the problem of unemployment; on the other, they had to renew the national tradition, to dissipate the deep sense of frustration that had been brought by the post-war years. They could not do the first according to the classic formulae of capitalism; Dr. Brüning's experience in Germany had made that clear. They could not, either, do it by inflation; the memories of the crisis after the French invasion of the Ruhr were still too vivid.

They therefore required a programme of public works which yet permitted the pursuit of a spirited foreign policy. The first would absorb the unemployed; the second would draw attention away from domestic grievance.

But a spirited foreign policy, if it is to have any prospect of success, must be built on rearmament; the statesman who makes large demands must have the material power with which to back his demands. A disarmed Germany, a weak Italy, could argue and plead and cajole; they could not insist. A policy of large-scale rearmament therefore presented obvious advantages. It acted as a programme of public works; and it enabled the Fascist leaders to pitch their demands ever higher as their strength in armament proceeded. It was obvious that the major European powers would do much, at least, to avoid war; concessions, thereby, could be obtained by threat which would restore the national prestige. Rearmament would absorb the unemployed; and this would not only appease the discontent the previous régime was unable to overcome, but would, also, to the degree of its achievement, enhance the reputation of Fascism among the workers, would even act, to some extent, as a compensation for their lost liberties. We must not forget—as the Fascist leaders have not forgotten—the magic appeal of the Soviet Union to the workers as the land from which unemployment has been abolished.

But a programme of this character could not, under a capitalist economy, be carried out on any considerable scale. It required the control of investment by the state; it required the control of imports by the state; it required the limitation of profit by the state to promote continually the extension of rearmament by investment in the manufacture of arms of surplus profits. More than this. As rearmament proceeded, there were the twin dangers that approximation to full employment necessarily brings—a rise in wages and therewith a rise in prices; and the related danger, also, of the movement of labour into the industries, and the firms within each industry, which paid best. It was therefore necessary for the government to limit the possibility of wage-increases; this involved, in order to prevent discontent, the fixation of prices, and this, in its turn, especially in the context of the devotion of profits to investment in armaments, to the rationing of consumption. Germany, by 1939, and in a less degree Italy, had abandoned every characteristic symptom of a liberal capitalist economy.

This development had further consequences. If it was facilitated by the abolition of the trade unions, which made any struggle for a higher standard of life impossible, its scope resulted in a rapid decline in mass-consumption. This in its turn did grave damage to the small shopkeeping class; they found themselves unable to maintain their position and were driven into the ranks of the wage-earners. From this angle, Fascism has undoubtedly strengthened the power of the large industrial units. But it has also weakened them because their authority, being subordinated to the requirements of the rearmament programme, is limited by the purposes of that programme, namely, the recovery of national prestige. But as the political system of Fascism is the dictatorship of the party, it follows that the definition of what national prestige requires is a matter for the party leaders. And since their object, like that of all *condottiere*, is simply to remain in power, that definition is made in terms of what they judge is most likely to keep them in power.

Granted this is, that they had (i) to deal with unemployment in a spectacular way, and (ii) that they had to restore the national prestige, they were compelled to rearmament and thence, inescapably, to a complete control of the productive system. In the light of the past, they had to avoid inflation. They had, therefore, to prevent, at the least, a rise in the standard of life at the same time time that they were increasing productivity. Aware that any continued depression of that standard over any long period was bound to result in discontent, they had to do two further things. They had to control profits, lest the workers contrast their own situation with that of their employers; and this was necessary, also, in order that the necessary capital for rearmament could be attained. But the limitation of profit was not enough. It might prevent the rise of anger and envy; it had a negatively beneficent effect psychologically. It did not, however, create hope; and a régime which seeks for permanence and stability must be able to create hope. The Fascist leaders, therefore, were bound to make rearmament the foundation of an imperialist policy of conquest. They had to be able to promise great future benefits in return for present sacrifice. Unless conquest was possible which presented the prospect of an exploitation from which the nation, whether Germany or Italy, would benefit, they could not satisfy either the workers, on the one hand, or the owning class on the other. The first would be impossible by reason of that proportion of production devoted to rearmament; the second because the removal of the limitation on profit would exacerbate working-class opinion. And they could not escape from the necessity of rearmament, because, if they did so, they would have to abandon that spirited foreign policy which enabled them to claim that they were renewing the national tradition; and they would have to find some substitute for rearmament as public works if immense unemployment was not to recur. Caught in that dilemma, both in Italy and in Germany, conquest became the inevitable end of their policy; and it was, of course, certain that, at some stage, conquest was bound to lead to war.

II

This is, of course, an excessive simplification of the complicated economic processes of which Fascism has disposed. What I am here concerned to emphasize is that the leaders of the Fascist parties have in each instance used the power of the state to make themselves the masters alike of the working classes and of the capitalist class in the interest of perpetuating their own authority. They have won some approval from the first by solving the problem of unemployment and by limiting profits; they have won the approval of the second by abolishing the organs of working-class advance and by making the industrial machine work at full pressure. They have won approval from all by making their respective nations feared by other nations; and this has been equated with a revival of national prestige. And that fear has led to the extension of the territories of each nation; with the prospect of continuous profit as the result of the extension. Profit offered the hope that, at some stage, there would be an increase in the standard of life; as that came, it would ensure security for the masses and stability for the régime.

The weakness of the scheme is apparent. It was dependent upon conquest without in order to maintain its conquests within. Its terror at home was matched by its threats abroad; and those threats impelled those whom it menaced to arm against their possible implications. I do not need here to summarize the history of international relations in the post-war period. The effort of the capitalist powers to "appease" Fascism is too well known to need detailed analysis. What is clear now from the history of that effort is that the purpose of "appeasement" could not possibly have been fulfilled. For the price that Fascism would have exacted would have left Great Britain and France with problems fatal to the maintenance of their own economic well-being; and there is no evidence that the surrender would have enabled the Fascist powers to accept a policy of peace. For that policy would have meant a threat to the authority of their leaders which would have been rapidly fatal to them. Peace would have meant that attention was withdrawn from foreign adventure to domestic grievance. It would have been necessary for them to confront the problem of the workers' standard of life, of the transformation of a war-economy to a peace-economy, and of the claims of the capitalist class for a return to less rigid controls. They were bound, therefore, as in the case of Germany with a rapidly increasing tempo, to make ever more demands, to convince their neighbours, that is, that a settled Europe was impossible while they remained in power. Once that conviction was clear, as it became clear after the seizure of Prague, the only question was the incident which would precipitate the catastrophe of war.

What, then, is the essence of Fascism? It is the outcome of capitalism in decay. It is the retort of the propertied interests to a democracy which seeks to transcend the relations of production implied in a capitalist society. But it is not merely the annihilation of democracy. It is also the use of nationalist feeling to justify a policy of foreign adventure in the hope, thereby, of redressing the grievances which are the index to capitalist decay. Wherever Fascism has been successful, it has been built upon a protest by the business interests against the increased demands of the workers. To make that protest effective, the business interests have, in effect, concluded an alliance with some outstanding *condottiere* and his mercenaries who have agreed to suppress the workers' power in exchange for the possession of the state. But as soon as the *condottiere* has seized the state, he has invariably discovered that he cannot merely restore the classic outlines of capitalism and leave it there. Not only has his own army expectations. Having identified himself with the state he has to use it to solve the problems through the existence of which he has been able to arrive at power. He has no real doctrine except his passionate desire to remain in authority. His test of good is the purely pragmatic test of success. And he finds invariably that success means using the state-power over the nation partly to coerce and partly to cajole it into acquiescence in his rule. That acquiescence is the sole purpose of, and the sole justification for, the methods that he uses. The only values he considers are those which seem likely to contribute to his success.

He is, in fact, and in the worst sense, Machiavelli's Prince in action. To continue in office, he must destroy the possibility that any constitutional procedure may throw him out of office; hence he must be a despot of unlimited authority and unlimited tenure. But unlimited despotism can only impose itself by fear; hence the rule of law must go, to be replaced by that of terror. But, in its turn, terror alone is not a method which permits of permanent power. The despot must therefore discover ways of evoking acquiescence in his authority. He can do something by propaganda; but the propaganda must be directed to satisfying the variety of interests which even a despot must placate. His principles of action, for this end, are essentially two in number. The first is the exploitation of national sentiment; he redresses real grievances, he discovers imaginary ones for which he can demand an accounting. But to do this, once more, he must be armed. To arm himself means at once to dominate the economy of the nation and to minimize the risk attendant upon the redress of grievances which imply a threat to other states; it also means that, by giving the defence forces of the state continuous occupation, and an enhanced position in the national life, he diminishes the danger that their power may grow beyond his control. The second principle is to have no fixed principle of social or economic organization, to establish or to relax controls not as a permanent feature of the landscape, but in terms of the changing necessities he encounters.

That this second principle has actuated both Mussolini and Hitler has been obvious from the policies they have followed. To the workers' complaint of a decline in the standard of life, they have been able to reply that they have limited profits and controlled the direction of investment, while, at the same time, their rearmament policy has involved full employment. To the employers complaint that enterprise is no longer free, they are able to respond first that, with the destruction of the workers' organizations, a docile labour force has been provided, and, second, that the new imperialism of economic penetration and conquest offers the prospect of future latifundia to be exploited by the class with the power to invest. The army of the *déclassés* upon whom they relied in their march to power are easily satisfied with more or less important political and industrial positions which, in each instance, have been the road for them to power and pomp and wealth they could not otherwise have obtained.

Much effort has been expended to discover a philosophy of Fascism. It is a waste of effort. Fascism is power built upon terror and organized and maintained by the fear of terror and the hopes to which conquest gives rise. It is the disciplining of society for a state of war in which martial law is permanent because the nation is forced to spend any brief period of peace in the preparation for war. It survives in peace by the intensity of the terror it imposes;

it survives in war just to the degree that it is successful in war. Its authority depends, in the period of peace, partly upon its power to prevent the organization of its opponents, and partly upon the expectations of benefit near at hand it is able to arouse. In time of war, its authority depends upon the continuous achievement of victories, and the recognition, by the nation, that the price of defeat is bound to be heavy.

There is no philosophy, in short, in Fascism in any of the forms in which we have known it. All the fustian of doctrine its exponents have presented us with reveal themselves, on examination, as propaganda expedients which have no meaning except their power to bolster up the particular régime. The doctrine of Nordic superiority works in Germany; the doctrine of the Latin genius works in Italy. Anti-semitism is the historic weapon of every ruler who needs an enemy to exploit and property to distribute; and it is always popular with the illiterate masses in a period of economic strain. The insistence on the "manifest destiny" of the nation, whether Germany or Italy, is, at bottom, simply the search for new sources of wealth to be exploited as a means of maintaining acquiescence in the régime. Conquest means posts, investments, a market to be politically controlled. The attack on the democratic principle necessarily follows from the need of the leader to justify his own exercise of absolute power. If a constitutive principle in Fascism exists at all, it is simply and solely the principle that power is the sole good and that values attach only to those expedients which sustain and enlarge it.

III

There is, in fact, nothing in the argument of Fascism which was not foreseen by Aristotle in his description of Hellenic tyranny; all that is new in its technique is the scale upon which it has been applied and the character of the weapons which modern science has placed at its disposal. This does not, of course, make any the less urgent the problems to which it gives rise. We have to understand why its seizure of power has been possible; we have to understand, also, by what methods it can be destroyed. For in any civilized community of nations the necessity for its destruction is axiomatic. A system which annihilates all values save that of power, and is prepared, without repining, to use war as the natural instrument of national policy, must either be destroyed or enslave mankind. There is no middle term between these alternatives.

In a sense, the Fascist conquest of Italy is not surprising. Parliamentary government had not been successful there; illiteracy was widespread; Italian ideas of expansion were wholly disproportionate to the actual achievement. The balance of power between different classes was nicely poised; quasi-feudal traditions were still deeply rooted in the agrarian regions. Italy was seeking to adopt the posture of a great power without the resources necessary to its maintenance. In the peculiar configuration of European politics, it possessed the strength, in 1915 as in 1939, of the blackmailer's position. Given the traditional habits of violence to which centuries of misgovernment and alien rule had accustomed it; granted further, the inability of its economy to satisfy any class within the premisses of capitalist democracy; granted, further, the absence of any profound tradition of representative government; the destruction of internal cohesion by the war and the frustration of its aftermath made it a likely enough victim for the *condottiere* of Mussolini's stamp. Italians recognized him without difficulty as the historic successor of Cesare Borgia. Parliamentary democracy, barely fifty years old, slipped back quite naturally into the position of a curious episode between periods of dictatorship.

But the Nazi conquest of Germany presents profounder problems. No nation of the modern time was more literate than the German; in educational standards, in perfection of industrial technique, in quality of scientific achievement it led, and for fifty years had led, the whole world. Its socialist movement was well organized; its trade unions seemed firmly based. In intellectual prestige it hardly yielded place to France; and the fuller the freedom its citizens enjoyed the greater appeared the range of that intellectual prestige. That a nation of this calibre should have submitted, practically without a blow, to Hitler and his legionaries is, on any showing, startling. That it should have acquiesced not merely in the exile of almost all those who had made the German name honoured abroad; that its scholars who remained should tamely have submitted to the imposition of a Byzantine adulation for men and methods most of the civilized world united to condemn would have been unbelievable if it had not occurred. That a system which had never, in times of free choice been able to obtain a majority of the electorate was able to insist upon the slavish support of practically the whole population is, on any showing, an overwhelming phenomenon. And it is not the least remarkable fact of all that acceptance of, even devotion to, the new rule and its gospel should characterize hundreds of thousands of Germans living among free peoples and devoid of the pressure and inhibitions to which Germans under the yoke of Hitler were subjected.

It is tempting, but it is also foolish, to find the explanation in the national character of the German people. They like, we are told, to be ruled; they instinctively accept the dominating hand; they are made for the habit of obedience. But explanations of this kind are too near to that which explains why clocks go by the principle of horologity to be satisfactory. They omit the long effort of the German working class to obtain its freedom. They take no account of the fact that Germans abroad do not retain the faculty of submissiveness as they move to a climate more favourable to free institutions and ideas. They forget the important principle so well expressed by Marx when he said that the ruling ideas of a nation are the ideas of its ruling class. The idea of innate and unchangeable characteristics in a people is an unscientific piece of unedifying mythology. To attribute the power of Hitler to innate dispositions in Germans which distinguish them from all other species of the human kind is not only completely irrational, but it is to prevent the consideration of other factors which reduce the problem to intelligible proportions.

As with Italy, much must be attributed to the late achievement of national unity, and a good deal to the fact that national unity was imposed, in the face of foreign opposition, in large part as the outcome of military success. For a century, Germany was a soul without a body; the achievement of "bodiliness" was secured only by the grim discipline of the sword. Something, too, is the outcome of the fact that Germany did not, like France and England, ever have a middle-class revolution. Like Japan her industrialization was the outcome of an alliance between business men, on the one hand, and the army, the aristocracy and the bureaucrats on the other—an alliance, moreover, in which the business men always remained the junior partners. For throughout the imperial period, the pivotal positions in the state always remained in the hands of the same class that held them in the eighteenth century. Germany, until the close of the war of 1914, was, in fact, an eighteenth-century state disposing of the power of modern technology; the greatest event in its history during the nineteenth and twentieth centuries was the revolution which did not happen.

In a sense, all German history contributes to the failure of 1848. Partly, it failed because the alliance between the middle class and the workers, which is the condition of a successful bourgeois revolution, did not occur. Partly, it failed because industrial conditions in pre-imperial Germany were not advanced enough to permit the consolidation of the anti-feudal forces into an unbreakable front. Partly, again, it failed because the particularism inherent in the political structure of Germany made impossible the unity of striking power in those who sought great changes which alone could have guaranteed success. Empire, unity, economic modernization, all these were imposed from above by the very forces against which a bourgeois revolution would have been expected. And when the new Germany was built in 1871, its opportunities of growth and power were set for it in a framework organized and controlled by those same forces. Middle-class Germany was given wealth, but always on the condition that essential authority remained in the hands of those who had governed it in the eighteenth century. They retained the power and prestige of the governing class. The purposes of the German bourgeoisie were always subject to their purposes. And the German bourgeoisie accepted their inferiority in return for an immense increase in material well-being.

The defeat of the empire in 1919 resulted in the alliance of the bourgeoisie and the workers to overthrow the prestige of the men responsible for the defeat; Versailles imposed a revenge for the failure of Frankfurt. But the Weimar Republic never completed the revolution it attempted. Partly, it came too late; within the framework of democracy, the day of the middle class was over in Germany at the very time that it assumed power. The makers of the Weimar Republic, moreover, could not complete the revolution they attempted for two reasons. To have done so, firstly, would have meant a civil war between the workers and the middle class; for that they were psychologically and doctrinally unprepared. They could not do it, secondly, because Great Britain and France were not prepared to allow its completion through fear of Bolshevist infection. They were prepared to see Germany a middle-class and constitutional republic on the lines, say, of France; they were not prepared to see it become a workers' republic. With the terrible weapon of the blockade in their hands, they assisted in the birth of a Germany which had no chance of survival.

For the new Germany had not merely the bitter inheritance of defeat. It had not merely to win the loyalty of its citizens while it endured the ignominy of the occupation and the seizure of the Ruhr. It saw vast sections of its middle class reduced to penury by the inflation. It encountered long years of mass-unemployment which it could not control within the framework of a capitalist democracy. Universal suffrage, under that system, was bound to mean that the citizens would use their votes to express above all their sense of frustration; the millions of votes that Hitler and the Communist Party secured were, above all, an index to the frustration of that sense. Nor is that all. The makers of the Weimar Republic, seeking hastily to improvise a political order which would satisfy their enemies, made the intelligible, but profound, mistake of entrusting its administration, in defence, in the personnel of the civil service and the law, to the men of the old régime who hated the new. The one thing that was certain of the main body of the officials during the period of the Weimar Republic was their disloyalty to it, and their nostalgia for the power and the glory of the old empire. Under the Republic, moreover, economic expansion was halted, and business men, big and little alike, ceased to have faith in a régime which presented them with none of the opportunities of the old. The disarmament imposed by the victors, and the loss of the colonies, meant the existence of a considerable class of people who had training without opportunity, to whom, therefore, the acceptance of the Weimar régime as permanent meant, once again, frustration. The combination of injured national pride with continuous economic misfortune laid the Republic continuously open to the assault of its enemies. It was hated by big business because it could not provide that expansion the empire had seen; it was hated by the officials, military and civil, who had dominated the state under the old empire; it was hated by the petit bourgeois who saw his economic security disappear in the inflation and the great depression; it was hated by millions of workers to whom the events of 1919 were no more than an unfulfilled promise they were anxious to bring to maturity.

Hitler is essentially the executioner brought to power to end these internal conflicts. To maintain power he had to do three things. He had to recover German prestige in the international realm. He had to restore the habit of obedience in the civil population. He had to provide careers for the thousands of frustrated careerists, without security and without principles, who knew only that they wanted power and material comfort and could not obtain them under the Weimar régime. He attained power because he promised all these things and was utterly indifferent to the fact that every social group in Germany placed a different interpretation upon his promise. Having himself no commitments to doctrine, being, as *Mein Kampf* made obvious, above everything an opportunist to whom rational principle was devoid of meaning, he achieved power simply in order to maintain power. He could not keep himself in power without terror; he therefore used terror. He needed it partly because, like every frustrated human being, the infliction of cruelty was a form of revenge for maladjustment to a normal world, and partly because the creation of impotence, above all of abject impotence, in his opponents was the easiest way of convincing himself that in fact he possessed power. He needed it, also, because, having no doctrine which he could translate into a way of life, there was no other method but that of terror by which he could impose himself.

And from this first step, all else has logically followed. Hitler came to destroy; he did not come to fulfil. There have been dictators in the past, like Napoleon, who were the residuary legatees of a revolution; they made war, they used terror, but they were the missionaries of an idea. Hitler had no idea to propagate except his hate of a civilization in which he failed; his genius was that he organized into the service of its destruction every element which had complaint to make of the social order it established. Having used those elements to become its master in Germany, there was nothing he could do with his power except to gain more power. First, therefore, he had to destroy all opposition within. That accomplished, he had to extend his power without for two reasons. First, by so doing, he could secure a factitious glory at home; this would prevent or, at least, postpone the rise of a new opposition. Secondly, the very nature of the régime was a threat to the settled arrangements of the outside world. He had to be powerful because, sooner or later, he would have to render account to it. To grow in power meant that he would become the apostle of militarism. That, again, temporarily strengthened his power. It provided work for the unemployed, and it satisfied the German tradition that the army was the primary element in the state. Since, moreover, he was dealing with a world which had grown into the hatred of war, he found that his first steps in the international adventure were unopposed. This served at once to feed his own ambitions, and to prove to his own subjects that the period of servitude to Versailles was over; by the methods of the bully Hitler reawakened in Germany a kind of parvenu national pride. And he harnessed to that pride all the skill in organization and power of work for which the German people is deservedly famous. He built the most massive war-machine in the history of the world. But, having built it, he became, inescapably, its prisoner.

For either he had to stop its operations; in which case he would have found himself confronted with the mass-unemployment grievance about which was a vital cause of his rise to power. Or, he had to use it, in which case, at some point, war was certain since, even if the smaller powers capitulated, like Austria, to his threats, it was certain that the great powers would refuse to accept his mastery of Europe. But if he stopped his operations, he had to have some principle upon which to organize the internal life of Germany; and it was grimly clear, both from his own utterances and those of his chief lieutenants, that he had no such principle to employ. He had, therefore, to continue the operations of his war-machine since peace would have been fatal to his retention of authority. It would have revealed the nakedness of his attitude, the fact that while he knew the things he hated, he did not know the things he loved. He had never been the exponent of a single positive idea. He had only fulminated against the authors of German misfortune and insisted that, given power, he could right the wrongs, internal and external, from which it suffered, and punish their authors. A series of complicated manœuvres and intrigues had given him power. But, beyond the destruction of his enemies, he had shown only that he did not know positively what to do with it when he had achieved it. Germany was militarily weak; he would make it militarily strong. Having accomplished that purpose, he had to hew his way to expansion without in the same way that he had hewn his way to authority within. And he could use expansion as the basis of an assurance to terrorized and half-starved Germans, slaving to satisfy the demands of his military machine, that once his expansion was complete, they would be rich for ever and might hope for a cessation from their toil.

He had therefore to take the gambler's throw of war. The real brilliance of Hitler's genius for destruction is most fully seen in the external forces he employed in his preparations for it. In these, there are three elements upon which emphasis must be laid. There is the concealment of the extent and nature of his schemes. There is the alliance, part open and part concealed, with movements similar to his own in other countries, the use not only of miniature Hitlers like Henlein and Franco, to undermine the strength of his opponents before ever the struggle commenced; and there is the degree to which in each nation likely to be involved in the struggle against him he used the fears within itself which revealed the depths to which the contradictions of capitalist democracy had moved.

His protestation that he wanted only peace profoundly affected pacifists to whom any appeasement was better than war. His insistence that the enemy was Bolshevism won him first the interest, and then the blindness, of large sections of the privileged classes in most of the democracies who feared that the waging of war might well be the prelude to a social revolution of which Bolshevism would be the residuary legatee. His attacks on "plutodemocracy" fell not ungratefully upon the ears of those unthinking socialists to whom any war waged by a "capitalist" government must necessarily be a "capitalist" war in which the workers could have no interest. He was able, in a word, seriously to divide the forces of his opponents long before it became necessary to fight them by preying ceaselessly upon all the fears which stood in the way of that unity of national outlook which modern war necessitates. By these means, he gained two immense advantages. In the first place, he had almost six years' priority in the preparation for a struggle in which the full use of industrial technology was a fundamental weapon; the size of his air force and the number of his tanks is the measure of how vital that advantage was. In the second place, he undermined the confidence of even the strongest of his enemies in their own cause at the point where the power to retain that confidence—as the example of France makes clear—was supremely important. He undermined, that is, the will of his enemies to resist before ever they entered the field. He had made the psychological preparations for victory before ever he had entered upon the campaign.

He had made the psychological and the material preparations for victory. Yet, in making them, he revealed, as in his domestic policy, precisely the defect that prevents him from finding that point, in all revolutions an essential point, where the processes of coercion can be transformed into processes of consent. He made the preparations for victory, but victory had no purpose save the material extension of his power. To win, he had not only to lay Europe waste by the ravages of war. To win, he had also to hold down by terror all the nations he brought under his dominion. But to hold them down by terror meant two fatal things. It meant, first, the continuance of militarism, the withdrawal, that is, of immense human forces from constructive service to society; and it meant, secondly, the transformation of vast masses into corps of economic slaves at the cost exacted by slave-labour to those who impose it not less than to those upon whom it is imposed. The Hitlerian technique, in a word, meant the reduction to impotence and poverty of millions who remembered freedom and material well-being. And there was no compensation for the slavery proposed for them except the comforting assurance that it was the necessary condition—disguised as the doctrine of Nordic racial superiority—of Hitler's supremacy over Europe.

I have discussed this development in terms of the Hitler movement; in large outline, it applies also to that of Mussolini as well. The construction of the Axis is, after all, nothing more than the alliance of two outlaw powers to use war as a means to a victory in which they may hope to divide the spoils. Less forcibly and less dramatically, the evolution and habits of Mussolini are the evolution and habits of Hitler—the difference is only that between the jackal and the tiger. Each stands for the failure which seeks to break the mould of social forms because he cannot attain success within it. Each attracts to himself all the gangster-elements in society. Each is able to use the contradictions of the society to arouse hopes which provide a road to power. Each, having attained it, does not know what to do with it except to maintain his possession of it; and each, as ruler of the state, transfers the gangster-methods by which he has attained legal power to the consolidation of his authority. The prospect of challenge is met by terror; the inability to solve the problems with which possession of the state presents each of them is met by embarking upon imperialist expansion. In each case, also, the necessities of that expansion involve two things. They involve, first, the complete suspension of the ordinary rules of international trade, with a consequential worsening of the prospects of world international recovery. They involve, secondly, a denial of the normal rules of international relations, and the consequential acceptance of the crudest methods of power-politics. And the tempo of that power-politics is enormously quickened because the very crudity of the methods employed naturally operates to heighten the strains and fears implicit in the international system.

IV

Civilization depends above all upon two things. It is dependent upon the power of reason to extend its empire over the minds and habits of men; and, as a function of that power, it is dependent upon our ability to replace arbitrary discretion in any man or group of men by settled legal principles within the ambit of which their conduct must be controlled. It is the fundamental indictment of Fascism, whether in its German or in its Italian form, that it is in its essence a denial of the validity of both of these. And, by denying them, it defines itself as the enemy of civilization.

It is the enemy of reason. It is its enemy because it rests upon the insistence that violence without principle is a justifiable method of obtaining power. It is prepared to coerce where it cannot convince. It regards any doctrine which dissents from its claim to power as invalid by reason of its dissent. Fascism therefore contradicts the fundamental affirmation of Western civilization in the last four hundred years. For its exponents, the strength of a principle is not the weight of the verified human experience that it embodies, but the massed physical power that it can organize on its side. The Nazi who said, "When I hear the word 'culture,' I reach for my gun," expressed in a single sentence the quintessence of the Fascist idea.

It is the enemy of the rule of law. That has been grimly evident in the experience of the Italian state since 1922 and the German state since 1933. Each has been built upon arbitrary aggression both within and without. Each has refused to submit its claims, whatever of substance they may have possessed, to any discussion but the sovereign will of which each disposed. The murder of Mateotti, planned, as we know, by Mussolini, and the night of June 30, 1934, are examples of that contempt for the rule of law in internal matters which has now become the settled routine of each dictator. Difference of opinion within the realm is identified with treason when the dictator is so minded; the penalty imposed for such difference is a matter of his discretion. And to prevent the rise of difference of opinion the barbaric apparatus of secret police and concentration camp are used on a scale which makes the cruelty (and the efficiency) of Czarist Russia sink into insignificance by comparison.

The rejection of any settled principles of law in the domestic sphere has been more than paralleled by the contempt for treaties and the settled rules of international intercourse in the realm of foreign relations. The dictators have never failed to break their pledged word when they were so minded. They have given the most solemn assurances which they have broken almost before the promise it was hoped they might imply could be discussed. They have rarely negotiated without the fact of mobilization in the immediate background of their diplomacy. They have openly glorified war, and insisted to their peoples that it was the natural way of settling international disputes. The education of the young has, both in Italy and Germany, been consciously adapted to serve their imperialist ambitions. They have set out to corrupt in wholesale fashion the well-springs of opinion in foreign countries. The grim pageant of their victims since 1933 is the measure at once of the insecurity they have caused and the unlimited ambitions in the service of which they have organized their resources. Assuming—it is a large assumption—that after their victory had been won, they could agree upon the division of the spoils, it is clear that they broadly contemplate a world in which at least Europe and Africa are reduced to the condition of immense *latifundia* to be exploited in the interest of their authority.

And let us ceaselessly remember that it will be an exploitation without meaning except as it serves that interest. What Mussolini called "the decaying corpse of liberty" is the index to their view of human nature. They have no respect for it; they deny its capacity for self-mastery. They believe that the masses are sheep to be used for whatever purposes they may determine. They deny the validity of any aspiration or belief which threatens their right to power. They insist upon a slavish obedience to their will which, at the best, makes hypocrites and sycophants, and, at the worst, turns the dignity of which man is capable into a fawning imitation of their own cruelty. The victory, indeed, of the Fascist idea is the victory of the brute in man over his capacity to rise above the level of animal instinct. It makes of his intelligence the slave of his ugliest passions.

Efforts have been made by learned men to find the roots of this outlook in the metaphysics of famous philosophers. One tells us that it comes from Kant; another blames its evil upon the fierce nationalism of Fichte; a third tells us that it is Hegel who introduced this servile worship of the state-power; yet another insists that the poison of Nietzsche's superman is, as it were, by inheritance in the veins of every German. Or we are bidden to note the influence of Sorel's confused mixture of Puritanism and Marx upon the mind of Mussolini; there, we are told, and in the voluminous speculations of Pareto, are the true sources of Italian Fascism. Others explore the philosophy of the German historians; it is Treitscke or Von Sybel, Mommsen with his Caesar-worship, or Droysen, who begat this dread temper.

I believe all such efforts to be wholly mistaken efforts. Fascism, in any of its forms, is at bottom a doctrineless nihilism; the attempt to provide it with a philosophic basis is the usual attempt of scholars to explain, or to provide a pedigree for, something altogether remote from serious influence upon its fortunes. It requires no elaborate metaphysic to discover why two ambitious men like Hitler and Mussolini, unable to find within the confines of an ordered society the nourishment for their ambition, should have sought the means to reshape its form rather than suffer frustration. It requires no metaphysic, either, to see how they could attract to their banners the thousands like-minded with themselves, men who rejected our settled ways of behaviour because, within their confines, they had no prospect of success or security. Their existence and their ambitions are as simple and as obvious as the existence and ambitions of Capone in Chicago or "Dutch Schultz" in New York. They are the amoral fringe of any social organization, the men who live by breaking the rules because they cannot hope to attain their ends if they observe the rules. They do not need a philosophy to justify their conduct to themselves. Their practice is the simple one of taking what they can if they can get it. They break the law in the hope that they may somehow evade or fight their way through its penalties. And if the society remains ordered enough to be able to impose its will upon them, in the end, they are broken by the law they defy.

The problem represented by Hitler and Mussolini is not the problem of what they believe—that belief is the underlying habit of all social outlaws—but of how they were able in each instance to make their belief the code of conduct imposed upon a nation's life. Here I may digress for a moment to point out that, in any profound sense, it is a mistake to regard such men as revolutionaries in the sense that Luther and Calvin, Cromwell and Washington, Marx and Lenin, were revolutionaries. Men such as these were driven by a purpose wider than the end of satisfying themselves. They were seeking to change the behaviour of men in terms of principles to which they attached the significance of universality, by the acceptance of which they deemed that the world might be shaped to a nobler pattern. They were unmoved by their own fate in relation to its realization. They were the servants, the priests, as it were, of the doctrine they professed, and not its masters. They were seeking to make new principles into law by which they themselves would be bound not less than their contemporaries; they were not seeking to elevate their own private ambitions to the status of universal principle. To class such men with Hitler and Mussolini is to identify the revolutionary with the outlaw. The distinction is a fundamental one if the nature of Fascism is to be understood.

No one would think of making elaborate metaphysical researches to discover a doctrinal basis for the habits of Capone or "Dutch Schultz". But if either were to have shot his way to the White House, we may be sure that learned men would have appeared to find philosophic origins for the habits they imposed upon the American people. This is what has happened with Mussolini and Hitler. The outlaw has become the state; the outlaw, as state, must provide a rationale for his behaviour, for without such a justification its naked violence is obvious; and men rarely are long reconciled to habits of naked violence. The central problem of Fascism, therefore, is not its philosophy, for the simple and sufficient reason that it has none. It represents the negation of philosophy, because it represents, supremely, the refusal to accept order and law, reason, therefore, in the universe it controls. That it can find men to seek the provision of a philosophy for it is not, indeed, surprising; the Nuremberg festival is proof enough that what William James called the "bitch goddess Success" will always find votaries at her altar; and if the votary's vocation be learning, he will vow its fruits to her service.

The central problem of Fascism is a very different one. It is the problem of what conditions in a society will enable the outlaw, like Mussolini or Hitler, to attempt the seizure of supreme coercive power, to make himself, in a word, the state. That is the issue the understanding of which alone makes possible our power to deal with the problem they confront. For it is clear that the vast majority of those who, in Germany, for example, assisted Hitler in his achievement of power did not expect the outcome that has occurred, or were confident that it would be a different outcome, or believed that, if he attained authority, he could be tamed to purposes other than his own. That confidence is clear, in Hitler's case, in men like Hugenberg and Thyssen, Rauschning, and even Hindenburg. They assisted in the imposition of a legend in which they never believed. They created a Frankenstein's monster which they did not imagine could grow out of their control. And what is true of these particular men is even more true of the groups who aided him—the Jews who thought that subscriptions to his funds would prove the insurance of personal protection, the business men who thought that the conditions of profitability would be resumed when the trade unions had been destroyed, the petit bourgeois shopkeeper who thought that he would be freed from the dangerous competition of the chain-store, the working-man who was heartened by the promise that the tyranny of interest would be destroyed, the soldier who yearned for the opportunity to wipe out the shame, as he thought it, of Versailles. All of them, not with unity of purpose, but for contradictory purposes, united to serve the outlaw's ambition. All of them were hypnotized into identifying his ambition with their own. All of them were deluded by the faith partly that, when he attained power, he would be their man, partly by the belief that what secret fears they nourished of his habits would be dissipated by his experience of responsibility. None of them realized that he had no purpose but power. None of them understood the depth of his contempt as an outlaw for the hopes they built upon the routine to which each of them hoped to confine him. None of them recognized that they were elevating the denial of the rational principles of social order into the constitutive principle of government.

Yet that is what was in truth done by the men who brought Hitler and Mussolini to power. The point I want to make is the vital one that such an achievement as theirs is only possible in any society at an epoch when men no longer have the great ends of life in common. It is, in fact, the expression of a society that is hastening to dissolution. It means that the power of fear is so much greater than the power of hope that the forces of order can no longer command assent. The procedures of the society are rejected because men can no longer agree upon the ends for which they shall be used. Respect for the law is dying because there is no longer a common faith in the purposes of the law. Each group in the society sees those interests threatened which it identifies with its ultimate good. Its sense of security has gone. Its familiar routine, the traditions and habits by which it lives, seem in jeopardy. It feels that it has lost its anchorage; it is on a voyage to a possible destination which it regards with suspicion and foreboding. It does not know what should be done; it feels wildly and deeply that something must be done. If the group is on the Right, it becomes convinced that the traditional state-wisdom has broken down and that only strong executive authority can save it; if it is of the Left, it has a similar conviction, but it demands a remaking of the state, a transvaluation of all values. Each group denies the premisses of its rivals; each comes to regard them as incompatible with the public peace. Or, rather, each regards a public peace which permits its rivals to function as a condition it is not worth while to preserve.

The society, in fact, is in a state of civil war; the power of the state to impose its routine has broken down. The authority of the outlaw has become formidable enough not merely to compete with that of the normal political groups; it is in a position to challenge that of the state itself. For it has, as the experience of both Hitler and Mussolini makes clear, so undermined the traditional authority, so allied itself, even, to the forces upon which that authority depends, that it seems almost natural to call in the outlaw to restore the classic relation between state and subject. And he is called in to achieve that restoration by men who believe that he will be the willing instrument of purposes that are in fact contradictory. Given power, he can only maintain it by a clean sweep of the rules. Given power, he can do nothing with it except impose himself. His first need is to be supreme; and the first condition of his supremacy is the satisfaction of the fellow-outlaws whom he controls, and upon whose support he is dependent. His second need is to destroy any possible source of dangerous opposition. Such a source will clearly be any group in the society the purposes of which do not coincide with his own. And since, in any profound way, the only group whose purposes are his are his own mercenaries, the outlaws whom he has shaped into an army, it is that group alone to which he can give his confidence.

The problem then becomes the problem of being able to recognize when a society has ceased to have the great ends of life in common; that, I have suggested, is the moment when the outlaw can seize the state. The answer, I think, is that a society reaches this point when its relations of production are in contradiction with its forces of production. That contradiction produces a situation, when the operations of the state are no longer able to satisfy so large a part of its citizens that their obedience to its orders is constantly in doubt. There are strikes, riots, demonstrations, a continuous disturbance of the peace, a sense of general malaise and frustration. Demands are made on all sides which appear outrageous to those upon whom they are made. We have known such periods before—the Reformation, the French Revolution, 1848. Each of them has been accompanied by war and revolution. Each of them resulted. in a new equilibrium between the relations of production and the forces of production. Each of them, by reason of that new equilibrium, was followed by a renovation of authority, a power sufficiently to satisfy established expectations that the habit of obedience to the implications of law could be reaffirmed. In each case, the new equilibrium coincided—a matter of vital importance—with an expansion of productive power. That expansion made it possible to admit of the conference of a new standard of life, a new sense of power and well-being upon those who were not only clamouring, but showed themselves prepared to fight for it. The state-power is now deemed to be devoted to purposes which command a general approval. The society feels again that its members generally have the great ends of life in common. Fear gives place to hope, the adoption of new values gives a new exhilaration to the social adventure.

In any long-term sense, I do not think this can occur when the outlaws capture the state. For having no philosophy, they have no road along which they can move to permanent relationships of peace. They have to make civil war permanent within in order to maintain their power; they have to make international war permanent without in order to prevent their defeat in that civil war. For, very rapidly, it is discovered by most of the groups through whose illusions they have come to power that they have not, in any real sense, restored law and order, since permanent terror is not its restoration. The necessity of terrorism means that they cannot discover the conditions of economic expansion. That, obviously enough, depends upon exactly that sense of security and confidence which terrorism, by its own immanent logic, is compelled to deny. Men are afraid, afraid of their rulers, afraid of their neighbours, afraid, even, of themselves and their thoughts. They never know what the morrow may bring forth. They dare not trust one another; they are not trusted from without; they know by grim experience that their outlaw-rulers have no bonds of loyalty to each other. Their governance has become that *bellum omnium contra omnes* in which the vital sense is lost that successfully to govern a people the rulers must not drive it before them but persuade it to follow in the path they tread.

There cannot be economic expansion where there is Fascism. Its internal direction of its own economic life means the wholesale misuse of national resources for rearmament. Its control of the whole process of production and foreign trade to that end means, necessarily, the organized blocking of the channels of international trade. Fascism has meant, in the pre-war period, the continuous lowering of the standard of life for its own people. With the outbreak of war, as its forces have moved forward, the inevitable trail of destruction and devastation have followed in its wake; and the shadow of wholesale famine stalks grimly behind it. For the peoples whom it conquers, the future holds no prospect but forced labour at low wages in service to the Fascist military effort. If it were ultimately to prevail, those peoples obviously must continue to serve that effort; for it would be necessary to maintain and munition great armies of occupation to hold down the populations deprived of freedom. Clearly, in such a situation, the conditions of economic expansion are also absent. For the effect of a low standard of life among the enslaved peoples will obviously be a general shrinkage of international trade. That will have its effect even upon the societies outside the ambit of Fascist control—on the United States, for instance, and on Japan. To safeguard themselves, they will be driven to take protective measures in defence of their home-markets—a step which will reduce still further the volume of commercial intercourse. Even if, in short, Fascism is able to organize the territories it conquers as *latifundia* for itself, the grim condition of that achievement is the prevention of the power to expand. The necessary consequence of Fascism, wherever it imposes itself, is an economics of increasing scarcity for the masses who become, through terror, the slaves of their rulers.

From this, I think, two conclusions are to be drawn. The first is the simple conclusion that to placate the outlaw is not a genuine renovation of the state-authority but a postponement of the effort to effect it. The gunman does not exact an obedience that builds a rule of law; he reduces society to a vast conspiracy in which no one is safe. For even the outlaw depends upon his power to cajole and coerce the fellow-outlaws upon whom he immediately depends; his tyranny depends upon his power to shoot first. He lives only by being successful; the moment failure dogs his footsteps, his power to terrorize is in jeopardy. That is why no dictator has ever been able to afford a serious defeat. That is why, also, the moment he is uncertain of his direction, what are remembered are his crimes and not his achievements. That is why, again, he cannot determine the succession to himself. Because his power has no purpose except the satisfaction of his ambition, it can only endure by a permanent ability to triumph over competing ambitions. And because it is not based on any philosophy save that of terror, it is certain to release those competing ambitions the moment it is doubtful where and when to strike.

The second conclusion, though more complicated, is, I think, none the less certain. It is that Fascism is a contradiction of the objective movement of history. It is, as it were, a moment of arrest in its course; it is not an assistance to its fulfilment. Were it the latter, it would increase, as each new equilibrium between the relations and the forces of production has increased, the standard of living and man's power over nature. As I have sought to show, Fascism cannot do this by the very nature of its end. For it emphasizes in behaviour all the elements adverse to productive capacity. It disturbs peace; it is inimical to law; it destroys confidence; it is hostile to security. It is, indeed, itself the epitome of destruction. Since it comes as the denial of all values, it cannot harness the effort of men to any continuous purpose. Since it is the enemy of reason, every discovery save those which increase the forces of destruction is its enemy too. It cannot permit to men the luxury of thought, since consent and freedom are the necessary mental climate in which thought alone can be possible. Its whole atmosphere is that of terror; its chief votaries even are permanent conspirators watching at every turn for the felon's blow that may ruin them. It cannot build a society in which the principles of organization will seem to the masses to be just, for, in the long run, a régime is only recognized as just where established expectations are fulfilled, and the condition of that fulfilment is the presence of precisely that security which Fascism denies.

I believe, therefore, that Fascism, in both its German and its Italian forms, is a passing, and not a permanent, phenomenon in history. It could win purpose only by developing a philosophy; but, by so doing, it would cease to be Fascism. The reasons for expecting its ultimate defeat are powerful ones. Psychologically, men cannot live continuously in the strain and at the tempo that totalitarian systems require. Fascism throws them too grimly out of the private routine in which most of them wish to pass their existence. Its need to occupy them with continuous sound and fury is necessary to itself; it prevents them from the chance of that thought against which it must always be on guard. But it must be able, if they are to accept the strain it imposes, to make them believe in its capacity to assure peace; and, in the long run, the only way to create that belief is actually to assure peace. We know only too well from past historic experience that no government can impose either permanent war or permanent terror, even when either is built upon an idea; the histories of Napoleon and of Robespierre are the proof of that. Any system of coercion must, after a period, transform itself into a system of consent if it is to survive.

But every system of consent in modern history has required a faith as its basis that men can accept; and the roots of that faith are its ability, as a going economic concern, to satisfy the wants it encounters. This, again by its own inherent nature, Fascism is unable to do. It is not, indeed, interested in doing so; for a people that was satisfied would not submit to a government of outlaws. And anyone who examines the conditions of its rise to power will, I think, be convinced that this is the case. It divided the nations upon which it imposed itself less by the offer of a positive programme than by its capacity to set one hate against another among groups of men either afraid of the future or devoid of hope about its outcome. It persuaded those of its supporters who were not directly of its armies that it was not what they suspected it of being. It commanded, no doubt, even after it had come to power, a certain respect for its audacity and a certain admiration for its successes.

But it is, I suggest, notable that those who announced this respect or admiration, whether native citizens or visiting foreigners, were always careful, where it was safe, to dissociate themselves from the inner essence of the Fascist régime. They disliked the persecution of the Jews; they turned their faces away from the concentration camps; they sought to persuade themselves that the instant demand would in fact be the last. They were looking, in a word, for the dawn of normality; they knew that their lives were not worth living under conditions which denied all meaning to the most elementary principles of civilized living. The subjects of a Fascist state, no doubt, could not break its hold so long as it was continuously successful and so long as a common fear united their outlaw leaders in the common conspiracy of power. But if there was a halt to success? If conditions developed in which Balbo out-generalled Mussolini in the struggle for power, or Goering doubted the need to play second fiddle to Hitler? The Fascist leaders stood always poised on the steepest abyss, with death as the penalty for taking one mistaken step. Matteotti lost in 1924; but there will be new Matteottis once Mussolini makes a wrong move. Hitler defeated Roehm on the bloody night of June 30th; but there will be new Roehms once the leader is suspected of faltering.

They came to power in Rome and Berlin because the conditions of social unity had been lost; and they had been lost because national and economic failure combined to make men more aware of their differences than of their identities. They held power in a Europe that could, in their earlier phases at least, have broken them but was unwilling to do so because the price of their destruction was war. They were not believed to be outlaws by men who deliberately refrained from their examination of their habits for two reasons. First, they retained a confidence that those habits might be tamed; that is the history of the policy called "appeasement." Second, in each appeasing state the interests predominantly destroyed by Fascism were interests the implications of which troubled the appeasers in their own communities. And if they sought the overthrow of Fascism, what would come in its place? They regarded communism as its residuary legatee; and most of them, the professional representatives of privilege, regarded that alternative as even more deadly than the outlaws. For communism, they knew, was in very truth a philosophy, and for over twenty years they had striven vainly to build a Chinese wall about it. Their hope was either that Fascism and communism—to them twin outlaws—would destroy one another; or that they could throw enough to it to persuade it to responsibility. When it became evident that they could do neither, Fascism had become so strong that they were themselves in jeopardy. For having no doctrine but power, being compelled to move in an ever faster tempo, the Fascist leaders, in order to maintain themselves, were bound to look for spoils proportionate to the difficulties of their problems. Those spoils were available only in the empires of those nations which, at the outset, would have been able to overthrow the outlaws. They saw too late that they were the inevitable victims of the outlaws' ambitions.

The reason for that lateness of insight is clear enough. Those who described the nature of Fascism to them were the very men who, in their own communities, were seeking to deprive the "appeasers" of political power. And the object of that deprivation was, avowedly, a re-definition of class-relations in their communities. But, to the "appeasers" a re-definition of class-relations was as great an evil as any they could perceive. It meant that they would have to forgo time-honoured privileges. It meant the extension of the idea of democracy beyond that purely political sphere in which they had so far been able mainly to confine its operations. It made that marriage between the idea of liberty and the idea of equality against which they had always taken profound objection. Their difficulty was that, though many of them disliked, and even despised, the methods of Fascism, they were, on the whole, not discontented with its disciplining of the workers by the destruction of their defence-mechanisms such as the trade unions. In the blinding light of war, it is interesting to look back upon the eulogies lavished by eminent men on the Fascist handling of labour. Statesmen of distinction wrote as though the absence of industrial unrest in Italy, for instance, meant that Mussolini had solved the labour problem there.[1] The connection of that absence with the general need of the outlaws to suppress all possible questioning of their power was not perceived until the advance of Fascist power threatened the imperial interests those statesmen were concerned to safeguard. Then, of course, it was too late, for the stage was already set for conflict.

Fascism, in fact, has revealed, in its evolution, that as capitalist democracy loses its power to expand, its business men, and those whose interest is affiliated to them, will reject the claims of democracy as soon as these are seriously put forward. They reject them for the reason that Tocqueville predicted over a century ago. "The people," he wrote,[2] "had first endeavoured to help itself by changing every

[1] Cf. Lord Lloyd, *The British Case* (1939).

[2] *Recollections*, p. 99

political institution, but after each change it found that its lot was in no way improved, or was only improving with a slowness quite incompatible with the eagerness of its desire. Inevitably, it must sooner or later discover that what held it fixed in its position was not the constitution of the government, but the unalterable laws that constitute society itself; and it was natural that it should be brought to ask itself if it had not both the power and the right to alter those laws, as it had altered all the rest?" Tocqueville saw that the system of private property was what he termed the "principal obstacle to equality among men," and that it was the logic of universal suffrage in a capitalist democracy that the masses should seek to use their political power for the socialization of the means of production. Confronted by this logic, the business men turned to the outlaws for relief from the pressure of democracy. The outlaws were prepared for the alliance. It was an offer of power; what use of it, they themselves would determine.

For it is pretty certain that the business interests which made their secret alliance with Fascism were hardly less deceived by the outlaws than those disappointed and *déclassé* sections of the masses which believed that they caught the echo of their own experience and hopes in its slogans. They assumed that they would at least be partners; they found that they were subordinates who could only control the outlaws by defeating the very purpose for which they were brought to power. They therefore accepted their position; but they found, in its acceptance, that they were then at the mercy of their new masters. For, naturally enough, just because they were outlaws, their new masters had no more respect for individual owners of property than their socialist opponents had for the capitalist system. More: they might share the privileges of property with its owners. But they had also to keep the masses quiet in order to protect themselves in their new rôle of the state. That involved them, as I have shown, in a massive policy of rearmament, on the one hand to purchase the support of the army by offering it new prospects of glory, and, on the other, to deal with that large-scale unemployment resentment about which had provided them with so large a part of their opportunity. The business interests, in this situation, had either to revolt or to follow the new outlaws wherever they might lead. The first choice was a hopeless adventure, since they were simply leaders without an army; the fate of Hugenberg and Thyssen showed how easily their opposition could be dealt with. They therefore took the inevitable course of following their outlaw leaders on that path which led inevitably to war. And at its end, the vista they confronted was a victory in which there would be a new Europe, indeed, but one racked by famine and devastation, and the ultimate certainty of revolt among the conquered, conditions, in fact, incompatible with the economic recovery they sought; or they confronted the danger of defeat in which their utter destruction was inevitable. For the one thing that is certain is the fact that the defeat of the outlaws will bring down in ruin the interests which have acquiesced in their reckless gamble.

They who sought a peace found only the certainty of war; that is the real lesson of the triple alliance between privilege, the army, and the outlaws, by which it was sought to avoid the implications of democracy. It was an inevitable outcome. The psychological foundations of an ordered society are rooted in the belief of the masses that they enjoy social justice. When they lack that belief, their rulers must either make concessions to them or make war upon them. Their rulers chose the latter course. But war means tyranny, and that is psychologically acceptable only in the drama of foreign war. The decision to place Mussolini and Hitler in power may have seemed, when it was made, the disciplining of the masses to the purposes of capitalism; it was, in fact, the execution of bourgeois society. For it placed it in a state of siege; thereby it revealed the depths of corruption inherent in any order built, like bourgeois society, centrally upon the acquisitive principle. It ended the possibility of security; it made terror king. It therefore abolished at a stroke the relevance to action of all the acquired wisdom and ethic of the bourgeoisie. They were helpless before men with no values at all, as they had been unimaginative with those who doubted the validity of their values. Unable to confront the desirability of sacrifice, they organized the assassination of their opponents without the insight to see that they were, at the same time, organizing their own destruction. For the men to whom they entrusted their fortunes had no interest in their fate save as it served their own greed for power. Unwilling to experiment with social justice, the vested interests of Germany and Italy became the bondsmen of the enemies of civilization.

V

There are two minor points upon which it is worth while to dwell. There is a special interest in the means by which Fascist leadership in Germany and Italy, especially in the former country, has sought to obtain its psychological hold upon the masses whom it controls. It is an interesting combination of habits variously derived. Part of it is built upon the religious impulse—worship of and utter surrender to, the leader is made into a cult comparable in its outward expression of intensity only to the fanaticism of the historic religions. Hitler, for instance, is the especially chosen of God; he is infallible; he is omniscient; he is the father of his people. He is not bound by the laws of men; special insights are communicated to him. He is surrounded by his inner circle of followers, whose power is a function of his own magic. He may be as brutal as Goering, as snakelike as Himmler, as treacherous as Goebbels, as pornographic as Streicher; whatever the defects in him that the ordinary man may be tempted to recognize, are compensated for by his recognition from, and devotion to, the leader. He becomes a semi-sacred person, not to be judged by ordinary standards. He is half-ruler, half-priest, deified in his own lifetime, spoken of in terms of an adoring adulation it is sacrilege to doubt.

It is not, I think, blasphemous to suggest that it has been the deliberate effort of the Nazi party to make of Hitler in a real sense a god to the people; with, of course, the inference that all officials of the party have a special charismatic character since they are set apart from ordinary men by delegation from the Godhead. The officials, as the peculiar dialect of their speeches makes clear, have all at least the capacity to express themselves as missionaries of a faith the power of which is beyond human ken. And because it is such a power, because its origin is wrapped in a divine mystery, it is not subject to the scrutiny of ordinary rational processes, nor would it be fitting for it to be controlled by ordinary democratic procedure. The emphasis has the advantage that nothing needs be explained. To do right is to obey; to do wrong is to doubt the wisdom of the leader or of his delegate. And because the sanction of obedience is the leader's mystical character, the punishment for disobedience need not be rational either; hence, for example, the acceptance of so tremendous a penalty as the purge of Roehm and his colleagues.

But alongside this attempt to impose an almost ecstasy of religious devotion, there is another not less interesting side. The leader must be immensely above his followers, but he must be also one with them and of them; distance must not interfere with the sense of intimate communion. So that the leader, who is godlike, is also of common clay. He is the little man who failed in the "plutodemocracy" he came to supplant, so that all the little men who failed under that social order may recognize themselves in him. His doubtful war record develops epic proportions, so that he almost becomes, as it were, the unknown soldier; and every man who took part in the last war, or takes part in this, knows that the leader feels and shares his dangers. He that was nothing has become everything by devotion to the glory of his country; and the inference the common man is asked to draw is that if only he will emulate that devotion, immense opportunity knocks at his door.

There can be little doubt that this contributes, especially in the atmosphere of war, an immense *élan* and exhilaration to the régime. Men who are not set in their ways can feel that membership of an *élite* is continuously open to them; if not everyone has the marshal's baton in his knapsack, school teachers can become cabinet ministers, a gymnastic instructor can become a district leader, a former locksmith is the gauleiter of Norway. Party organization immensely stimulates the hope of dramatic opportunity which knows no bounds to its power; there were seven hundred thousand political leaders in Germany just before the conquest of Austria, each hoping to climb upwards. Something of the log cabin legend of the American presidency is woven, in a far more intense degree, into the system; and when it is remembered that these opportunities knock, above all, at the door of the young, they are bound to exert an immense attraction. In 1935, over thirty-five per cent of the Nazi party was under thirty years of age; almost twice the percentage of that age-group in the Social Democratic party in 1931.[1] And, in large part technical or administrative qualifications are not exacted for the post of leader. Twenty per cent of them were chosen because they took part in the party struggles before its arrival at power; they were mostly recruited from those who could not find secure occupation under the Weimar régime. For many of the rest, the supreme test of fitness is the proof of capacity for a blind obedience to orders; the reflective type who argues, who has a point of view of his own, is suspect. The object, indeed, of the party's training schools is to breed a type of cynical fanatic, to whom morality consists solely in the power to be loyal to the leader; a type comparable in character to the gangster's bodyguard in New York or Chicago.

That is the central fact we must continually bear in mind: the outlaws' machine of domination is modelled in the image of their own amorality. It gives power devoid of principle to thousands who have had no experience of responsibility. It legitimates for them, in

[1] On the composition of the Nazi party, see an admirable article by Hans Gerth, in the *American Journal of Sociology*, vol. 45, p. 517, to which I am much indebted.

their own eyes, the use of terror and violence as methods of controlling the lives of private citizens. The absence of any principle in the operations of power confers upon those to whom it is entrusted a sense of boundless horizons within their reach. It satisfies vanity, which is rationalized by every sort of pressure and personal interest into the performance of duty. It frees them from dependence upon the historic values, partly by its skill in associating these with past failures of the German people, and partly by the proof it can offer that those values do not pay. Men become accustomed to the medium in which they work; there are thousands of younger members in the Nazi movement to whom the ways of rational persuasion as a method of government are completely unknown. They have been taught by experience that they are entitled to what they can get; the only certificate of legitimate action they know is that it should be successful action. They have been schooled to regard violence as virility; they therefore assume that doubt and argument are the signs of weakness. They learn from the world into which they have been absorbed that the world is theirs for the taking, and that the only limit to their right is the might they can deploy. The more fully they give themselves to this creed, the more hope they have of fulfilling their ambition. And since they live in a constant stream of indoctrination which insists that criticism of the creed is enmity to the state; since they know that those who venture this criticism are the men under whom Germany was weak and defeated, since, too, they see that, under its present rulers, it has scored staggering military and diplomatic successes, it is not really surprising that they should accept the indoctrination to which they are subjected.

And to all this must be added the immense and elaborate ritual to which the general population is subject—the endless meetings, parades, the vast armies of workers under disciplined control, whose effort is subordinated to the outlaws' purpose. All of it is calculated, let us add not seldom brilliantly calculated, to break down the resistance of the common man to its appeal. Most of us, anyhow, are conformists; it takes a courage it is difficult to exaggerate to step outside the ranks of an army with flags flying and victories to report. It takes even more courage when the penalty for stepping outside is death. The legend of the outlaws is bound to be successful until it becomes plain that there are those who will fight to the death for its exposure. And that fight must be organized if it is to have its chance. The lone voice which makes its protest, above all if it comes from abroad, has no chance of being heard as long as it is drowned in the clamour of applause the outlaws organize upon their own behalf. Only the extraordinary man will listen to catch the accent of protest in such an atmosphere unless it forces itself upon his attention. And it cannot so force itself unless it has the strength at its disposal to challenge the power of the outlaws to impose their authority. Only, that is, as they are broken as a government, is there the prospect that their power will fade.

All this means, I think, that the breakdown of Fascism depends upon one of two factors. There must be its external defeat; or there must be that internal confusion produced by conspiracy which is staged at that focal point when fatigue and insecurity have provoked widespread disillusion. But the second of these possibilities is itself the consequence of defeat, since a successful challenge to the authority of a state can only be made when the failure of its leaders is evident to a large number of their subjects. For the essence of Fascist practice is to break the will of those who seek to resist it; and that will can only recover its resolution to go on opposing when it discovers the prospect of success. Otherwise, it sinks into that apathy of despair which is the very condition the outlaws seek to promote; a people in despair obeys the orders it receives. Resistance comes with anger, and anger is provoked by the recognition which, with a myth, only defeat can confer, that the legend men have been accepting is proven to be false.

Here, clearly enough, all the evidence points to the necessity of external defeat. It does so for two reasons. In the first place, the fact that Mussolini has been in power for over twenty and Hitler for over ten years, makes it obvious that no sort of Blanquist conspiracy can be effective against either. Granted the technical means of control at their disposal, it is an obvious condition of their internal overthrow that they should not be able to rely upon the obedience of the army. But it is also obvious that each of them has, so far, been able to retain that allegiance by making the army career one of the supreme sources of distinction in the state; the army would risk that distinction by turning upon the outlaws. And without its support, any other conspiracy has not only but little chance of success, but runs the risk even of strengthening the régime by failure, since failure only deepens the despair of those who look for conspiracy, and the apathy of the general population. A conspiracy which fails intensifies the power of the Nazi myth by proving that it has the continued power to triumph over its enemies.

To succeed, this is to say, a conspiracy against Fascism, whether in its Italian or its German form, must be more than a conspiracy;

it must be a movement. It must be able to throw into disrepute and doubt the whole mythology and apparatus of Fascism. To do so, it must be able to demonstrate its weakness, to arouse the conviction among, not only those who have the courage actively to oppose it, but, even those who passively acquiesce in the imposition upon themselves of its power, that its authority is in process of being undermined. My own view is clear that while the Fascist powers were at peace, this could only have been done by making it definitively clear that they could not have their way by aggression. It would have been necessary, that is, to reverse the fatal policy of "appeasement" that was followed up to Munich, and even beyond; when it was reversed, after March 1939, it was already too late, partly because Fascism had then organized the material resources that it believed to be proportionate to the gamble for which it was prepared, and partly because its record of successes up to that time had organized also, both at home and even abroad, the psychological foundations necessary for the adventure. The main bulk at least of the German people accepted the idea of Hitler's invincibility; and in the countries with which war was by then rapidly becoming inevitable important sections of opinion were ready to believe that his strength made any reasonable sort of peace better than war. Their defeatism, as the experience of France was to show, was profound, and it was built upon the failure to recognize that waging war upon Fascism meant mobilizing against it the spiritual forces of democracy. But that mobilization, in its turn, implied a need to recognize that privilege must show itself capable of great sacrifices in the material sphere. Too many of the privileged were doubtful of this need. They wanted victory; but they did not understand the price they must pay for it. And some of them, at least, as, again, the experience of France made clear, were not prepared for victory on those terms.

If this analysis be correct, it follows that the defeat of Fascism is necessarily consequent upon its military defeat. That alone can break the legend of its invincibility. That alone can put its immense mythology in the perspective which exhibits its real nature. I do not mean by military defeat simply victory in the field, though I think this is of vital importance. I mean by it the ability to produce by the depth of the resistance Fascism encounters first the doubt whether the promises of its leaders can be fulfilled, and, following upon that, the increasing realization that because those promises are unfulfilled, its defeat is a prospect seriously to be weighed. That, as I think, is the only situation which can at once break the submission of the masses to the outlaws, and, on the other, induce within the ranks of the outlaws themselves that distrust and disloyalty which they always feel to one another, but which, while they are successful, they are able to overcome. Just as Capone and "Dutch Schultz" can always impose themselves upon their mercenaries so long as they can evade or defeat the law, just, also, so soon as the law asserts itself, their hold upon their followers vanishes, so, also, with Hitler and Mussolini. The machine-gun compels so long as there are not more massive machine-guns in action against it; trickery and deception succeed as long as it is not willed that they shall cease to succeed. Persuade the peoples of Italy and Germany that, under Mussolini, they have no prospect of the full victory they promise, even more, that they are likely to bring upon their people the certainty of defeat, and there is then loosed in those countries those movements of opposition they have coerced by terrorism into passivity. The law is vindicated, internationally not less than nationally, by the certainty that it will not permit itself to be violated. And at the stage of Fascist evolution we have now reached, this means the military defeat of those who control its development. The conflict that Fascism has been driven by its essential nature to stage permits of no alternative. It must conquer or be defeated. Civilization can no more remain part free part gangsterized than the United States could have remained half slave, half free. There are ways of life the fulfilment of which admits of no compromise with its opposite; Fascism is one of them. It is the rising of the underworld against the habits of an ordered cosmos. Its significance lies, above all, in its determination to destroy the values which, however inadequately, that ordered cosmos is seeking to realize in the individual lives of its citizens.

VI

Fascism, I have said, is the rising of the underworld. That it should have the capacity to rise is already important evidence that a whole epoch in human history is drawing to its close. For the very fact that it would not merely rise but impose its authority on so large a part of European civilization is itself the proof of a fatal weakness in its structural foundations. It is the proof that the rulers who invoked the aid of the outlaws cared more for their privileges than for the values the social system was seeking to realize; or, perhaps better, that they made the cardinal error of identifying their privileges with the preservation of those values. It is the proof that a social system which in the last analysis bound man to man by the purely material relation of the cash-nexus was inadequate to the ends that it had in view.

For, obviously, to have reached this pass, it must have been torn by a central contradiction. The civilization which arose from the breakdown of the medieval world has lasted roughly for four hundred years. What the war with Fascism reveals is how fragile were the foundations of its spiritual unity. And these were fragile for the simple reason that the professed purposes of European civilization were always in large part denied by its actual achievement. Its validity, as a going concern, depended upon its power to satisfy, and constantly to elevate, the common man. But it was prepared to do this only on the condition that his elevation left unhampered the privileges of its ruling class. It made concessions to the common man; it never sought effectively to place him in power. On the contrary, its whole predominant ethos is set in terms of the fear of its rulers of what might happen to themselves if he were called to power in society. He remained poor, in considerable degree uneducated, in large part prohibited from that organization which would enable him to make his wants effective. In periods of well-being, his rulers gave him concessions; in a wholesale way, they never gave him justice. In periods of economic expansion, they were able to contemplate the edifice they had built with some confidence in its power to endure. But in periods of economic contraction their policy was built always upon their fear and not upon their hopes.

They were prepared to accept democracy so long as they were not alarmed by its demands. But they were suspicious of its claims the very moment they were thrown into that alarm. When it came to the point where they had to choose between their privileges and democracy, it was their privileges they sought to preserve. And they called in the outlaws to preserve them exactly as a great American business corporation calls in its army of guards and thugs and agents-provocateurs[1] to prevent the growth of trade unionism among their workers. They had themselves used their political power to shape the law to their own purpose; they thought it unreasonable that the masses should do likewise. But what they meant by "unreasonableness" was the affirmation of a way of life which denied their permanent title to power. When they feared that their title was in jeopardy they preferred the risk of alliance with the outlaws to the possibilities involved in an alliance with the people.

[1] See Leo Huberman, *The Labour Spy Racket* (1937)—a sober summary of testimony before a committee of the American Senate.

What, perhaps, is most astonishing in that choice is that they should never have had any measure of the risks they were taking. The outlaws, no doubt, had a contempt for the people; they were, for the outlaws, the drab routineers disciplined to the acceptance of their failure in life. But it was of the essence of the outlaw's standpoint that they should reject altogether the scheme of values upon the maintenance of which the privileged depended. It was precisely that scheme which made them outlaws; it was precisely that scheme the boundaries of which they could not, without support, hope to transcend. So long as they were outside the law there were rules by which they were confined. But the moment they became the state-power, the outlaws made the rules. And since their lives were, above all, a denial of all values, the only purpose for which they could make their rules was to secure themselves in possession of authority. To do so, they had necessarily to convert society into a state of siege. That was the only way of life to which they were accustomed. There was no other atmosphere in which they could maintain their power. And that conversion meant civil war within, and foreign war without. It meant, in fact, exactly the conditions which are fatal to any privileged class. For a state of siege means martial law, which is no law at all; and since privilege is the child of law, the government of the outlaws meant the inevitable subordination of the privileged class to an anarchy in which their privilege would rapidly cease to have any rational meaning.

If this interpretation be correct, the only way to fight Fascism is with a faith that has the power to go beyond the terror it imposes upon those whom it defeats. Obviously enough, that faith must have deeper roots than those which capitalist democracy was able to strike; for Fascism came to power at the breakdown of capitalist democracy. And it did so, I suggest, for the vital reason that, in the last analysis, in capitalist democracy the principles imposed were always more capitalist than democratic; the dynamic of capitalism was always in contradiction with the dynamic of democracy. Capitalist democracy, so to say, was always democracy on conditions approved by the capitalists. It was admitted its place always upon the condition that it did not strain their allegiance to democratic principles. And that allegiance was obviously strained the moment that democracy seemed gravely to jeopardize the privileges which the owners of property had accumulated. The law it was sought to transform was their law; the rights it was proposed to abolish were their rights; the values called into question were their values. All these things had become for them habits so deeply entrenched that they identified them with civilization itself. That there was another law, other conceptions of rights, other schemes of value, was, for them, unthinkable. Driven into panic by the challenge, they preferred to fight rather than to discuss. They believed that they could fight upon their own terms and for their own ends; they did not recognize, in their panic, that conflict always breeds the conditions of revolution.

They saw democracy destroyed over wide areas; like the dwellers in Dante's hell their punishment was the fulfilment of their own desires. But that fulfilment was, at the same time, their subordination to new masters against whose habits they had passed their lives in building safeguards. To escape from fear they entered a prison; and they then discovered that to be free from the new chains they must, somehow, build a partnership with those masses the fear of which had driven them to prison. Yet to build that partnership demanded exactly the abdication they had, when they called in the outlaws, refused to make. They had to appeal to the men they had denounced. They had to defend the principles they had denied. They had to admit the values insistence upon which by the masses had thrown them into panic and fury. To enchain the masses, they had set the world on fire. Now they were to discover that only by liberating the masses could they hope to extinguish the flames.

Chapter IV

THE DEMOCRACIES AT BAY

I

None of the great democracies presented a satisfactory spectacle in the inter-war years. They were challenged both by ideas and men directly hostile to their constitutive principle. Not only did they shrink from meeting the challenge; it almost seemed as if many of their leaders were half-convinced by the defiance of their enemies. For not only was there, as in Germany and Italy, an almost bloodless surrender to men who openly avowed their intention to conquer power and maintain it for anti-democratic purposes. Here, however, democratic leaders might well reply that in neither society was the tradition strong that was destroyed, and that in both it had sought expression in highly unfavourable circumstances. What was more serious was the constant tendency of leading democratic statesmen to do two things. On the one hand, they urged on the masses the need to recognize limits beyond which the democratic principle must not seek to go; on the other, they were open in their avowals of admiration for the achievements—which they can hardly have submitted to a critical examination—of the Fascist leaders. An incredible anthology could be compiled of the almost fawning enthusiasm heaped by British Conservative statesmen on Mussolini and his system.

It is obvious, on the record, that scepticism of democracy had penetrated deeply into the democracies themselves in the period before the outbreak of war. The literature begins to reveal, in the new world as well as in the old, a movement away from the optimistic confidence of the Victorian sunset back to the fears and hesitations of the period between the fall of Napoleon, and the end of the revolutionary movement in 1848. That movement is shown in many ways. It is revealed in a new emphasis on the ignorance the masses, an insistence on their incapacity for the task of self-government; the growth and popularity of arguments which sought to show that politics is the function of an élite are almost as notable as the inability of those who employed them to agree upon criteria by which the élite may be defined. It is exhibited in the sorrowful conclusion of men like Elie Halévy that the socialist tendencies of democracy are incompatible with freedom. Socialism, he thought, means the necessity of planning, and the essence of planning is the acceptance of an authoritarian principle fatal to personal liberty. It is revealed, perhaps, even more starkly in the argument of Lord Eustace Percy that politics is a matter necessarily for the few, and that the many must find their fulfilment in the satisfaction of the religious impulse. The popularity of books like those of Pareto and Spengler, the revival of an anti-rationalist philosophy of history in Toynbee, are symptoms of the same temper. So, too, has been the influence of the psychoanalysts, and of those enthusiasts for mental tests who have regarded their results as a proof that science and democracy are antithetic terms.

Scepticism of democracy has two aspects which must be sharply separated from each other. On the right, its main motive was fear; on the left, its chief source was disappointment. On the right, the suspicion was deep that the procedures of democracy led inevitably to a re-examination of the economic bases of society, and it was uneasily recognized that this might reveal the ultimate incompatibility of democracy and capitalism. Democratic procedures might thus involve an assault upon privileges which had behind them the power and the prestige of long tradition; and most of those who attacked democracy from the right were, in fact, rationalizing a desire born of interest to preserve those privileges from invasion.

On the left, the attack was the outcome of that sense, foreseen almost a century ago by Tocqueville, in the warning to his contemporaries that I have already quoted. Deeply influenced by events in Russia, the left was tempted to believe two things: first, that its opponents would not respect the procedures of democracy as soon as these seemed to compromise their privileges, and, second, that the methods of the Soviet government were a new expression of the democratic principle, superior in its efficacy to that of capitalist democracy which was limited by its obvious subordination to "bourgeois" necessity. Their necessity enabled them, without undue difficulty, to rationalize their enthusiasm for the Russian change in the relations of production, clearly achieved by the method of revolutionary dictatorship, into an insistence that, seen in its proper perspective, the Russian dictatorship was, in fact, democracy.

The period of the inter-war years had, in its conflicting ideologies, a remarkable resemblance to the sixty years after the outbreak of the French Revolution. Just as attraction to, or repulsion from, the first set of men's attitudes to its principles, so, in our own day, attraction to, or repulsion from, the Russian Revolution was the main factor, sometimes only half-consciously, which conditioned men's attitudes. An abstract liberalism in both periods was tested by an event which brought the fact that it was abstract up against the hard dynamic of reality; and men discovered that philosophies which seek to change the world divide men much more profoundly than those which seek merely to interpret it. All the characteristics of the earlier period are present in the later. Dawning enthusiasms become bitter disappointments; eager hopes become massive disillusions. Observers see what they want to see; what seems to one immense achievement seems to another an assault upon the very foundations of civilized living. Bewilderment, anger, contempt, fear, these are the emotions aroused on the right by the spectacle of Russia in travail; and they enable the exponents of Conservative philosophy to view the emergence of an anti-democratic philosophy with tolerance, and even enthusiasm. But the wider the hold that anti-democratic philosophy secures, the more, not unnaturally, it provokes the left to assume that the faith of the right in democratic procedures will break down at once when its interests are in jeopardy. The general result is that both sides begin to arm themselves for a collision they do not believe they can escape; with the result that, as they arm, their faith in the procedure of democracy suffers a further decline. For men arm to do battle, not to reason with one another; and the power to maintain faith in democracy depends upon the ability to preserve faith in the procedures of reason.

Another feature of the life of the democracies contributed to the same result. The war of 1914–18 ended with an apparently overwhelming democratic triumph. But its dramatic intensity had aroused vast expectations among the masses; and these were only in a small degree fulfilled. Great economic insecurity; grave numbers of unemployed; the increasing revelation of the abyss which separated the possession of political, from the control of economic, power; the seemingly unbridgeable gap between the depth of the frustration felt by the masses and the inadequacy of the remedies proposed by the political parties which sought to assuage it; the unwillingness of any government to attempt any fundamental experiments; these are, I think, the outstanding political characteristics of democracy in action in these years. It is no doubt true that, compared with the period before 1914, the scale of social legislation was impressive; the point of importance is that it seemed far more impressive to those who bestowed it than it did to those upon whom it was bestowed.

The right to work for reasonable hours at a reasonable wage had become, by 1919, a fixed article of faith in democratic communities; and the masses were tending increasingly to judge the validity of political and economic systems by their power to realize that article of faith. They were not interested in the technical debate between economists upon the issue of whether state-intervention did, or did not, either in the long run or in the short run, interfere with the prospect of full employment. They were impressed by the fact that, whether state-intervention was on a large scale, as in Great Britiain, or on a small scale, as in the America of Mr. Hoover, the masses were denied the fulfilment of the right to work. They learned that, when state-assistance developed on any considerable scale, its recipients were the objects of hate and anger to those who were taxed to make it possible. They watched the deliberate organization, under state-patronage, of restrictions upon production at a time when the main experience they knew was poverty.

In Britain and France, they returned governments of the left to office in the hope that the attack on poverty might assume a new vigour. They found that it not only deepened, in each case, the crisis from which they suffered, but also sharpened the suspicion of democracy among the rich. If, in angry despair, they resorted to the strike as a method of remedying their grievance, they were informed, with equal anger, that they were seeking to coerce the community. Since they felt themselves no inconsiderable part of it, it is not surprising that they were bewildered by the accusation, nor that they deeply resented the decision of the government to identity the state-power with the employers' case, in the name of a law and order the masses had never conceived themselves as threatening. No democracy can be in a healthy condition in which the premisses of action have become so different between different classes in the community; for it is of the essence of democracy that the central premisses of action must be held in common by all classes which count. Not openly, but in a veiled way, that was gradually ceasing to be the case in all the major democracies in the inter-war years.

The reason for this development is set out in the quotation from Tocqueville to which I have already referred. It is not enough to answer that the masses were better off in the democracies than in any previous period; nor is it sufficient to say that at no time in the past was the state-power so widely exerted to mitigate the consequences of poverty. For what is more important than either are the facts, first, that the improvement in the condition of the masses was at no point equal to their expectation of improvement; and, second, that as they began to be influenced by the new level of education produced in the last forty years, they began to perceive more sharply the meaning and significance of the contrasts between rich and poor. It is not an exaggeration to say that, by the outbreak of war, the power of classes in the major democracies to understand one another was less than it had been for a century.

This was, I think, because, in this period, two major developments had occurred. The first was the growing inability of the capitalist system to exploit the forces of production; everywhere restrictionism was necessary in order to maintain the principle of profit-making. The second, growing out of the first, was the shrinkage of opportunity. That shrinkage was, perhaps, more dramatic in a society like Great Britain, where the idea of social equality followed with precarious slowness on the acceptance of political equality than it was in the United States and France which had both, by the middle of the nineteenth century, made the one aspect of equality coincident with the other. Only in Britain was there one system of education for the rich and another for the poor; only in Britain was it true to say that the professions, the chief posts in the civil service, the established Church, the commissioned ranks of the Army, Navy and Air Force, in overwhelming degree were recruited from the middle and upper classes; only in Britain, again, was it true to say that it was exceptional, even after the war of 1914, for the son of a working man to become a cabinet minister. The forms of political democracy had, in Britain, only very partially expressed themselves in terms of social democracy by 1940.

But it is notable that the tendency to insist upon the stabilization of political democracy at the point where it does not threaten economic foundations was growing before the war in both France and the United States. The growth of this temper in France was revealed in all its naked strength by the collapse of 1940; the men who made the Vichy government preferred subordination to Hitler to experiment with the dynamic of democracy. But it was revealed before the collapse in a number of important ways. The France of the *universitaires*, for example, which, before the Third Republic, had produced teachers with the democratic enthusiasm of Michelet and Mignet, after 1870 produced teachers whose main emphasis, as with Faguet and Brunetière, was either sceptical of it, or frankly hostile to its claims. French finance, after 1919, may have been anti-German; but it showed with insistence on each occasion that a government of the left came to power that it was less anti-German than it was anti-democratic. It assisted in the organization of a series of Fascist movements which narrowly failed to overthrow the Republic from within in 1934. All the testimony we have about the breakdown of 1940 is clearly to the effect that it was the leaders who failed the nation, not the nation which failed its leaders. And it is significant that the men who sought to organize France for collaboration with Hitler deemed it their duty to attack both the doctrinal and the institutional expression of 1789—the principles and methods, that is, which had overthrown feudal France, and begun the function of its democratization. Hierarchy, discipline, faith, these were the new watchwords. A mystical escape from reason and its consequences was presented as a purification through suffering. What it meant in fact was that the pretensions of the masses to a full share in the exercise of power was checked by destroying the organs through which they might fulfil their claims.

The American experience is more complex, though its drift has been in much the same direction. It is, of course, of decisive significance that, within the framework of the system, the economic absorptive capacity of the United States ended in 1919; thenceforward the massive controls it became necessary, above all through pressure from the working-classes, to impose showed that the margin of opportunity had been reached. It has been shown, moreover, that the sources of business leadership in the last generation have become increasingly narrow. The growth of a private-school system for the children of the rich, on something like the British model, was rapid in the first third of the present century. There began, moreover, to emerge in the United States—though its evolution was arrested by the Great Depression—a leisured class with many of the habits, and much of the outlook, of the functionless aristocracy of Britain and France, above all with the same deep concern lest its economic privileges be invaded. It is probable, moreover, that no business men exercised an autocracy more extensive or more profound than those of the United Staes. Men like Mr. Ford, the steel magnates of Pittsburgh, the coal barons of Kentucky and Pennsylvania, disposed of industrial empires with an authority which often challenged, and sometimes even mastered, the power of state and federal governments. No one can read the literature of the United States in the nineteen-twenties and thirties without the sense that the frontiers of political democracy were threatened as profoundly as at any time in American history. It is particularly notable that, until 1932, the legislation which characterized the emergence of the positive state in Europe, had hardly even begun to secure acceptance in the United States.

No doubt the explanation of this is psychological as well as economic. The hard-bitten individualism of the frontier, its optimism, and its self-reliance, persisted in the United States long after the pioneering conditions of the frontier had ceased to exist. But nothing reveals more fully the dangers to which American democracy is exposed than the history, between 1932 and 1940, of the Roosevelt administration. Most of its measures were of the type that we associate with the Liberal government of 1906–14 in Britain—social insurance, the public provision of relief for the unemployed, government housing scheme, federal control of public utilities, a few important experiments, like that in the Tennessee Valley, in public ownership, an insistence upon the right of trade unions to bargain collectively on behalf of their members. That the "New Deal" had public opinion on its side was impressively demonstrated in the two re-elections of Mr. Roosevelt to the Presidency—a choice which broke the deeply-felt precedents of a century and a half.

The "New Deal" had public opinion on its side. Yet it may be doubted whether any American President has encountered a hate so organized or so virulent as that which Mr. Roosevelt incurred for his programme. It was dictatorship; it was Communism; it was un-American. The attack upon him was almost wholly confined to the rich. The antagonism his measures aroused divided families and severed ancient friendships. That they were measures rendered in their large outline inevitable by the massive character of the problems he faced; that most of them were reforms long overdue; more, that his opponents, when they challenged his re-election in 1936 and 1940, offered a programme for acceptance the general principles of which were indistinguishable from his own; all this did nothing to diminish the hatred of privilege for his record. And it is significant that many of those who expressed their opposition did not hesitate to build connections with the darker forces in American politics, men like the late Senator Huey Long, like Father Coughlin, and like Dr. Townsend. It is, too, notable that the era showed a decisive growth in anti-semitism in the United States, always itself a primary index to the decline of democratic power in a society.

The experience of the Roosevelt administration is the more startling to anyone who is aware of the character of the epoch which preceded it and the impressive proof marshalled by its various investigations of the anti-social habits of those business men to whose power it sought to set limits. It becomes more startling still when it is remembered that, in the first months of his Presidency, Mr. Roosevelt was recognized even by the most bitter of his opponents to have steered the United States successfully through a crisis graver than any it had encountered since the Civil War. What, I think, was revealed in the first nine years of the "New Deal" was the emphatic conviction of American business men that democracy meant *laissez-faire*, and that as soon as democracy denied the validity of *laissez-faire*, they became sceptical of the validity of democracy. Violent behaviour is more characteristic of American social relationships than it has been of those of Britain or of France. Yet I doubt, even when allowance is made for this difference, whether public opinion in France or Britain would have suffered the extra-legal interferences with civil freedom that were deliberately organized by business men in the United States. It is necessary to read in all its details a document like the report of the La Follette Committee of the Senate on civil liberties to attain a just view of the proportions of that interference. Corruption, espionage, blackmail, hooliganism, the deliberate misuse of even the highest state courts, and the lower Federal Tribunals, these are only the bare categories into which the habits of the business leaders of America fall. There were few great industrial corporations which did not have their private armies, with machine-guns and tear-gas, to prevent the invasion of their plants by trade unionism. There were, moreover, areas in the United States, Louisiana under Senator Long, Jersey City under Mayor Hague, the Imperial Valley in California, to take instances only, in which the American Bill of Rights had no authority against the determination of busines men to eke out the last ounce of privilege from their undisputed possession of economic power. It is not, I think, an excessive judgment to say that, by 1940, beneath the formal acceptance of democratic principles, the Fascist idea had penetrated deeply into the minds of American business men.

This is not, of course, a new situation in American history. It is merely the modern form of a conflict which goes back to the struggle between Federalists and Republicans, a struggle in which John Marshall's mastery of the Supreme Court gave the victory to the former group, even though, as under Jefferson and Jackson, they were defeated on the electoral field. The trend of the future was then clearly foreseen in the remarkable diagnosis of John Taylor of Carolina. It was, he saw, the fate of the masses to have been exploited by their rulers under all previous economic systems. Under the aegis of Hamilton, the exploitation had merely changed its form. Under the slogan of "public faith, national integrity and sacred credit," he had provided it with the institutions whereby wealth could be stolen from the labour which was its true source. Business men had no political principles; they would adapt themselves to any form of government which gave them security for profit-making. But they would adapt themselves to no other form, and there was no way to the preservation of American democracy save in the destruction of special privilege.

No doubt the background of John Taylor's thought is set in the special circumstances of his time. But he saw with incisive clarity that, whatever the political forms of a society, it is in all essentials true that effective authority rests with the holders of economic power. He realized that the inner principle of the system upon which their special privilege depends gives its character to all the ideas and institutions by which the life of a society is shaped; the state-power is thus geared to the protection of their privilege, and its authority is invoked against all who may seek to invade it. Writing at the beginning of the nineteenth century, at the flood-tide of the Jeffersonian triumph, he not unnaturally saw the safety of democracy in the preservation of that relatively simple agrarian society which was beginning to be obsolete even while he wrote, But the central idea of which he had firm hold is the clue to the main character of American history. It explains, as no other idea can explain, the struggle for power between classes in the United States; above all, it explains why those who possess special privilege have never been willing to admit the full logic of the democratic idea even in a society which seemed, by the extent of its natural resources, historically destined to realize it.

Taylor had to contend with an opposition which assumed two forms. Men of the stamp of John Adams repudiated democracy because they assumed that it merely provided an amphitheatre in which the struggle between rich and poor, which, for Adams, was the struggle between the able and the inefficient, was so bitter that tyranny was its natural outcome. Men of the school of Alexander Hamilton simply assumed the inevitability of exploitation and insisted that the exploiters were entitled to the state-power because the alternative was anarchy. Both Adams and Hamilton inferred from the contemporary situation that barriers must be erected against the claim of democracy to an equal interest in the results of the social process.

It is well known that both men were pessimistic about the future of America, and convinced of the fragility of its institutions. What, of course, they underestimated was two things. They could not foresee how vast were its natural resources, how long, therefore, they would permit the continuance, side by side, of exploitation made acceptable by concession; and they could not estimate the degree to which the ideology of the exploiters would, through the growth of the productive forces in America, almost convince the exploited that the interests of wealth and commonwealth were identical. Again and again in American history, crisis seems to provoke the masses to the use of their democratic power against their masters; that is the meaning of the Jacksonian revolt, of Bryanism, and of the New Deal. But, until our own time, America presented the striking spectacle of a society always capable of recovering from its crises, of offering, at their close, new hope, by way of improved conditions to the masses. Democratic institutions were safe in America, in the first century and a half of the republic essentially for two reasons. First, the fluidity of its social relationships made the fact of opportunity more widespread than elsewhere, its dramatic expression more appealing; and, second, if what Theodore Roosevelt called the "malefactors of great wealth" were, on occasion, bitterly assailed, the system on which they depended for their privilege did not seem to them in jeopardy. In the main relation between master and servant, the state-power gave their conception of its character the ample protection of the law; while in the recognition of the place of prescription in their title to property the main ethos of the American idea could scarcely, until very recent days, have been deemed inadequate by John Marshall himself. No modern society since the England of Cobden has, until our own day, more fully exemplified the famous aphorism of Marx that the ruling ideas of an age are the ideas of its ruling class.

That is, I think, most remarkably shown in the absence of any serious socialist movement in the United States. There have been scattered experiments in communist living; there has been a persistent efflorescence of minor groupings one of which, in 1920, secured over a million votes in the Presidential election; and there have been contributions of notable quality to socialist literature. But it is, I think, true to say that socialism as an organized body of doctrine has made little impact, as yet, on the American mind, and has shown none of the power it has developed in Europe directly to influence the trade union movement. On the contrary, it would rather be true to say that, with personal exceptions, predominant trade union opinion in America has hardly begun to develop a socialist philosophy distinct in character from that of business men. Naturally enough, the trade unions have sought for higher wages and for shorter hours; but these are the effective limits within which their doctrinal outlook has moved. A successful trade union leader in the United States has far more of the habit and outlook of a prosperous business executive there than he has of the outlook of a trade union leader in Europe.

That is not because an American proletariat is lacking; the "poor whites" of the South, the pecan workers of San Antonio, the vast bulk of the Negro population have all the characteristics of a proletariat. The absence of a socialist movement of serious proportions is due to a complex of causes. Partly, it is the outcome of the intense social mobility of America; that has meant the absence of anything like the deep caste cleavages which are known over most of Europe. Partly, again, it is due to the fact that so large a proportion of Americans are emigrants, or their descendants, from Europe who have found in the New World relief from the trammels and handicaps of the old. Partly, further, it is due to the fact that the horizons of opportunity are still, in the United States, wider than anywhere in Europe except the Soviet Union. The result of these forces is that, despite the grim statistical facts, few Americans expect that their incidence applies to themselves. The expectation is still that of Woodrow Wilson's "New Freedon"; "do you not want," he asked, "to see your son the head of some small, it may be, but flourishing, business?" Few, in fact, are chosen for that position; but the vast majority feel "called" to it. The result is that the atmosphere perpetuates an intense individualism of outlook long after its possibilities of fulfilment have passed away. And the culture-lag of that individualism still opposes a formidable barrier to the alliance between socialism and the workers which is endemic in Europe. Socialism seems "un-American"; it is the denial of the legend to which every schoolboy is disciplined; it is the expression of conditions that have no relevance in the world where the gospel of self-help is still accepted as the proper philosophy of the average man.

In fact, the character of the Roosevelt epoch has shown beyond all doubt that the inherent contradiction between capitalism and democracy which has produced so decisive a crisis in Europe, is in full operation in the United States, if with retarded influence. All the problems by which Europe is afflicted are present there, even if their incidence and emphasis are different. They are present because a political democracy requires, if it is to be secure, an economics of expansion; in the United States, as elsewhere, an economics of expansion is no longer open to capitalism. The stage has therefore been reached in American evolution that has been reached in Europe where the masses seek to use their political power in order to improve their condition. They find, as they have always found, that they can only do so as they are able to secure fundamental changes in the property-relation. But so soon as they seek to secure these changes, they discover that the procedures of democracy are questioned. For they cannot, as John Taylor saw, touch the property-relation in any fundamental way without calling privilege into hazard. To privilege there is attached a power of prescriptive tradition which has about it almost the sanction of a religious faith. For privilege has stabilized a way of life for its votaries upon which they have erected a body of values round which their whole lives are built. Its surrender is as impossible for them as it was for their predecessors under earlier régimes. They are asked, as they feel, to acquiesce in a revolution which not only endangers their own interests, but that of the whole society. For at the basis of their thinking is the inescapable conviction that their interests and the good of the society are identical.

It is this outlook, I suggest, which explains two features of the American scene which are otherwise bewildering to the outsider. It explains, in the first place, why measures so modest as those of the Roosevelt administration should have not only aroused an indignation so profound, but should also, broadly speaking, have divided American opinion fairly precisely in terms of income. On the side of the Presidential experiment have been, generally, the trade unions, the unemployed, the small farmer, probably the bulk of independent professional men, and, significantly, the overwhelming majority of the intellectuals. Opposed to him have been the leaders of finance and business, the rentier class, the executives of business management, and the corporation lawyers. It explains, in the second place, why the advance of Fascism aroused profound indignation in the first group and, as a rule, an interest that was occasionally enthusiastic in the second. It is, of course, true that the enthusiasm was greater in the period of Mussolini's dominance than it was when Hitler took the centre of the stage; and there was general repugnance for his religious and racial persecution. But the feeling in the second group was widespread that Fascism was the natural response of property to the Communist threat; it was a good thing to have strong men in a position to keep the masses in order. Not a few thought, especially in the Roosevelt epoch, that American labour "needed a Hitler." What was surprising was the small number of those among business leaders in America who thought that the most effective answer to Communism might possibly be social and economic reform.

My argument is thus the simple one that the inter-war conditions, all over the Western world, challenged the democracies to extend their frontiers into the economic and social fields. Their ruling classes were unwilling to do so because they saw in that expansion a threat to the privileges to which they believed themselves entitled. If they had to choose between democracy and those privileges, at the best, their mood was one of uncertainty; at the worst they did not even attempt to conceal their preference for privilege. And this attitude must be related to the contrast in the reception given by these ruling classes to Communism on the one hand, and to Fascism, on the other. For the first they had a fear and a hatred which revealed their sense of their own insecurity. They welcomed every sign, however unplausible, which might be taken as evidence or failure in the Soviet Union. Fascism, in general, aroused no such emotions in them; on the contrary, it seemed to a large part of them a healthy form of mass-discipline. The intensity of their efforts to find accommodation with its leaders in the international field stands out startlingly in comparison with their wholesale intervention in the Soviet Union. Taking the total spectacle of the inter-war years it is difficult not to conclude that only economic revival would have sustained the faith of the ruling classes in the validity of the democratic idea.

II

The war brought a renovation of what may be termed the rhetoric of the democratic idea; it has not yet assured it of the capacity for survival. It renovated its rhetoric for the simple reason that, whatever the world a Fascist victory might shape, its outlines were a challenge to the privilege of those who ruled the democracies. In a broad sense, the solution of the issues proposed by the Fascist leaders was to transfer to their own peoples those sources of wealth through the control of which the rulers of the democracies had been able to maintain their delicate relationship with capitalism. Deprived of these, they confronted a bleak future in which their prospects depended upon what charity they might be offered by their conquerors. They would lose their economic independence; it was plain from the fate of the Jews, of Austria, and of Czechoslovakia that the Fascists had no respect either for traditional status or the claims of property. They would lose, also, their national independence and, with it, their separate culture and way of life; for the Fascist leaders understood nothing so fully as the fact that national independence was, by its inherent implications, a continuous threat to their victory.

Up to the fall of France, it is, I think, fair to suggest that a grasp of what Fascism implied was more widespread and more profound among the masses in the democracies than it was among their leaders. In a formal way, these paid to democracy the tribute of eulogy the situation required; they were bound to exalt the system which was making the war. They needed the assistance of the masses not only for the fighting services, but, almost more, for the arms upon which the fighting services depended. They were compelled, therefore, to emphasize their acceptance of the democratic idea. But it is also obvious that in this first year of the conflict there was no clear notion in their minds of the gulf between Fascism and democracy, no willingness to evoke the dynamic of democracy as a fighting faith to set over against the *élan* of their enemies' assault. That is, I think, clear from three things. It is evident from their inability to surrender their belief that, somehow, a compromise peace could be arranged. It is implicit in their desire to distinguish between Fascism in its German, and Fascism in its Italian, form. It is inherent in the way in which they waged the war. There was no search for the offensive; the initiative was left to their opponents. There was no attempt to evoke the mass-enthusiasm of the democracies; that was seen in Mr. Chamberlain's treatment of the trade unions and in his approach to the crucial problem of India. The policy of "appeasement" still lingered in the inner framework of the methods to which they clung—appeasement of Spain, appeasement of Italy, appeasement of Japan. It is not unjust to emphasize that, until Dunkirk, the democracies were, indeed, waging a war but had not yet, so far as their leaders were concerned, made up their minds about the character of the war that they were fighting.

They were agreed, of course, that Hitler was an evil man who must be defeated. But, however eagerly they might wish for his defeat, they did not desire to upset the social and economic equilibrium which the war had disturbed. They were terrified that Bolshevism might be the residuary legatee of their exhaustion; and they still saw in the system of which Hitler was the embodiment only an evil exaggeration of a discipline for the acceptance of which many of them were prepared. That, I suggest, is plain from the statement of the British case made by Lord Lloyd in 1939, and commended by Lord Halifax, then Foreign Secretary, in a preface in which he appeared to have no difficulty in accepting Lord Lloyd's argument.

"The Italian genius," wrote Lord Lloyd, "has developed in the characteristic Fascist institutions a highly authoritarian régime which, however, threatens neither religious nor economic freedom, nor the security of other European nations. . . . The Italian system is founded on two rocks: first, the separation of Church and State, and the supremacy of the Church in matters not only of faith but of morals: second, the rights of labour."[1] This, it must be remembered, was written after seventeen years' experience of Mussolini, which included the attack on Corfu, intervention in Spain, the extinction of Albanian independence, the Abyssinian adventure, and the introduction of anti-Jewish laws. It takes no account of the forcible destruction of the Italian socialist and trade union movements; it pays no regard to the outlook of the man who declared that "war is to man what maternity is to woman. . . . I do not believe in perpetual peace . . . I consider it depresses and negatives the fundamental virtues of man which only in bloody effort reveal themselves in the full light of the sun." Its easy assurance that the Fascist state in Italy is built upon the "rights of labour" should be set in the background of the notorious remark of a prominent Fascist official, Olivetti. "It is an illusion," he wrote, "to presume that class war has been finally abolished. It has been abolished . . . for the workers. On the other side, class war is being continued."

How deep, indeed, was the half-conscious acceptance of Fascist ideology among the democratic leaders the fall of France decisively demonstrated. For the ruling class of France took their defeat to be a judgment upon the democratic principles of the French Revolution; they abandoned the struggle, and set themselves the task of saving from the wreckage whatever their conquerors would permit them to retain. The rapidity with which men like Laval and Darlan accepted the ideology of Fascism was only equalled by their inability to persuade the French masses to co-operate in their dishonour. Defeat offered the ruling class of France the choice between property for the few and surrender, on the one hand, and democracy for the many with continued resistance, on the other. It is an index to the democratic malaise that they did not hesitate to choose property and surrender.

Yet their choice, on a considered view, was the real turning-point of the war. For the depth of the ignominy it involved awakened the dormant nationalism of the British ruling class and brought its aid to the support of the democracy. The French defeat revealed that the Fascist conquerors proposed not only the national enslavement

[1] *The British Case*, with a preface by Viscount Halifax. London (1939).

of their victims but also their economic ruin. What we know of the armistice terms they imposed on France have made it sufficiently evident that the Treaty of Versailles was a profoundly generous instrument by comparison. The humiliation it foreshadowed for Great Britain swept on one side the doubts and hesitations of the Baldwin-Chamberlain epoch. It became clear even to the most blind that the very existence of Great Britain as an independent nation was at stake. That revelation made the necessity of national unity more starkly clear than at any period of British history. It did more than a decade of discussion, more, even, than the pitiful narratives of a hundred thousand refugees, to make even the most Conservative of Englishmen understand that no price could be too great for victory. In the summer and autumn of 1940 there was something that it is difficult not to describe as a regeneration of British democracy. The character of the struggle was defined in terms which made the identities between citizens a hundred times more vital than the differences which divided them. They learned, in the lightning-flash of overwhelming danger that their choice was between victory and death.

It is important, moreover, that the impact of this revelation was not confined to Britain merely. It swept a large part of the world. It altered the outlook of Greece; it secured something like a popular revolt in Jugo-Slavia against acquiescence in surrender. In the United States it evoked the unprecedented result of electing Mr. Roosevelt for a third Presidential term, above all because he had come to embody for the masses the idea of resolute challenge to the dictators' claims. Within a year of the fall of France, it was, I think, universally understood wherever men could even whisper their faith in freedom that its maintenance was bound up with the victory of democracy. The strength, indeed, of the Fascist powers was still too great for any sudden reversal of the tide of their conquests. It was understood, increasingly, that the road to victory would be long and hard. More, it was increasingly realized that the road to victory would involve social and economic changes so profound that there would be no possibility of a return to the pre-war equilibrium. What the new equilibrium would be few could venture to prophesy and none could, in any fullness, diagnose. Yet that uncertainty had ceased to matter. What counted was victory, for victory had been revealed as the price of national survival. And a ruling-class which, all over the world, was suspicious of, and hesitant about democracy, was driven to renew its homage to the democratic idea by reason of its sudden grasp of the implications of defeat. Dying democracy in

France paid its last tribute to freedom when its surrender revealed the full cost of slavery.

III

It is, however, important to be quite clear what is implied in this new homage to democracy which transformed the international scene after the French surrender. What was aroused in the ruling class of Britain was not a sense that the relationship between capitalism and democracy was obsolete. What was aroused was, partly, the deepest impulses of national sentiment, and, partly, the anger which comes to men who have been betrayed by concepts they thought they understood. This took the form of a renewed dedication to democracy because that was the political form of state through which the British national idea was expressed. Democracy received a new support because it was the idea under which the maximum opposition to the Fascist danger could be organized. Everyone was sure, alike by instinct and by reason, that the defeat of Hitlerism was vital. No one was certain for what Hitlerism was to be beaten. No definite purposes beyond his overthrow were evolved under the stress of danger.

That must be emphasized because it is the clue to the unresolved contradiction in the democratic case which is obscured, for the time being, by the pressure of events. All classes in the British nation are resolved to win. All free men and women, everywhere, know fully that a British victory is the condition for the liberation of those nations Hitler has reduced to slavery. But the question of the ends to which victory is to be devoted is not a question upon which there is evident any clear reply. Mr. Churchill's aim is victory; beyond that he has refused to speculate. Mr. Eden and Lord Halifax are clear that there must be greater freedom of trade, greater economic security for the individual, and political and religious freedom; for Lord Halifax the war is a crusade for a somewhat nebulous body of doctrine which he calls "Christian principles." President Roosevelt has set out a noble body of the ends a democracy must secure for its citizens, and has insisted that their realization is possible within our own generation. The British Labour Party has insisted that only the socialist transformation of Great Britain can lay the foundations of a democracy safeguarded against injustice within and war without. The British Liberal Party has reaffirmed its faith in the principles of private enterprise. Until June 22, 1941, the Communist parties of every country, though insistent on the necessity for the ultimate defeat of Fascism, denied with passion the democratic claims as these were embodied in the British and American governments; and they pursued a policy of revolutionary defeatism which, had it been successful, would have ensured the victory of Hitler. The Independent Labour Party in Britain, and the American Socialist Party, both held aloof from the war, partly in terms of a deeply-felt pacifist tradition, and partly out of a refusal to believe that a war waged between competing capitalist states could have meaning for those to whom a socialist solution was alone significant.

The democracies were aware that their survival depended upon victory; but they had not begun, in any serious way, to bend their minds to the problem of what they were to do with their victory if they won it. There were presented for the consumption of their citizens a mass of competing Utopias each of which presented the alluring prospect of permanent peace. One group of thinkers saw in Anglo-American union the solution for all our ills; though none of its advocates could explain how India could be democratically related to the new partnership, nor how such a marriage of capitalist democracies would solve the central problem of making the relations of production proportionate to the forces of production. Another group preached with ardour the ideal of a federated Europe, though there was little agreement between them either upon the constituent nations in the federation or the manner in which power should be divided between the centre and the circumference. Still another group demanded the revival of the League of Nations, sometimes with powers beyond those of the Covenant of 1919, sometimes with less than such powers. Others saw the future in terms of a system of continental federations linked, perhaps, together for some common purposes in a confederative superstructure. To the schemes of re-organization there was no limit save the imaginative discretion of the particular inventor.

The vital thing for the serious observer is to keep his mind firmly fixed upon three facts. The first is that though the Churchill government has been responsible for a number of admirable, and even important, social reforms, nothing in its record, so far, has made any effective change in the parallelogram of social and economic forces in Britain. If victory came to-morrow, the problems of capitalist democracy there would be as real, though more intense, than they were in September, 1939. The second fact of importance is that, all over the world, the war has been responsible for changes, not least psychological changes, which are revolutionary in their profundity. The wholesale abandonment of *laissez-faire* was the first consequence of the need to plan production. The prescriptive rights of property, both internal and external, have suffered invasions on a scale which have deprived them of their traditional authority. It has been shown that state-planning can not only abolish unemployment, but is capable, even in war-conditions, of preserving the health of the population at a higher level than the free economy of capitalist democracy in peace-time, There have been no significant changes in the relations of production; but the changes in the unit of production, in the power of the state over financial institutions, price-control, consumption, and the objects of manufacture, have been of a momentous order. The risks, moreover, of bombardment from the air have created new habits in the population of which we are only beginning to know the import. And this new factor in our lives has revealed defects in the traditional structure of local government which makes certain massive adaptations in area and function in the future. The cost of the war, moreover, has compelled the ascent of taxation to heights which even in the last war would have been regarded as impossible. Since, too, not the least essential front of the war is in the factories, the place of the trade unions in the state has become ever more significant; it is not, I think an exaggeration to say that a regulation like the British Essential Work Order of 1941 owed its acceptance, in part to the fact that it was sponsored by Mr. Ernest Bevin, the trade union member of the War Cabinet, and, in part, to its acceptance by the trade unions as a necessary element in victory. Less obvious, but none the less real, were the powers of the government to take over farms or factories the operation of which did not conform to standards it was empowered to impose.

All of this has effected a breach in familiar habits of revolutionary proportions. In the first two years of war, but especially in its second year, the tempo of life, the response to its established expectations has become utterly different for the overwhelming majority of the population. These, in their turn, have induced an experimental, temper, a familiarity with the need of sudden adaptation, upon which too much emphasis can hardly be laid. There is everywhere a sense of the opening of new vistas, the acceptance of the need for the experimental temper, which, in its contemporary intensity, mankind has hardly, I think, known since the age of the Reformation and the Renaissance. It is not a mood confined to any class within the democracies; it goes too deep for that. It may be welcome or unwelcome. What is important is the fact that, as a mood, it has become an integral part of our habits. The sense is abroad that humanity is on the march, even if there is profound uncertainty about the direction of the voyage.

To these two factors must be linked the third, the alliance, since June 22, 1941, of the Soviet Union on the side of the democracies, That is a portent of which the psychological implications are not less urgent than the material. I have already pointed out how much of the texture of our thinking in the inter-war years has been set by the gigantic fact of the Russian Revolution. Its active alignment against the Fascist powers has repercussions to which it is difficult to set limits. It domesticates amongst us a body of ideas to which every government in the future will have to accommodate itself. The first and, I think, the most immediately important is that it is within the competence of state-power to abolish unemployment; at a stroke, this sets the problem of economic security in a new perspective. The second, and in the long run the most significant, is the idea that the state-ownership of the means of production enables planned production for community consumption to be attempted; this, once more, supplies a new horizon to the future place of the profit-making motive in society. The third idea, which will be grasped more slowly, but of which the results are bound to be far-reaching, is the public endowment and collective organization of scientific research for social benefit; the man of science will slowly, no doubt, but inescapably, come to have that place in society which, in the public imagination, the successful pioneer in business enterprise possessed, especially in the United States, in the period of capitalist expansion. The fourth idea is the attachment of social esteem to achievements in fields hitherto regarded as negligible in bourgeois civilization. The exceptional worker in field or factory will have a status comparable to that of the exceptional executive; he will be rescued from the insignificant anonymity which, hitherto, has been his lot; and this will, in the long run, give a new dignity to manual labour, a realization, if in a different form of William Morris's dream. And I must emphasize, finally, the overwhelming importance which attaches to the fact that the Red Army is, in structure, a democratic army, and, in social ideas as well as in technical demand, in the vanguard of Soviet progressivism. The contrast here with the traditional structure and ideas of the armies of the capitalist democracies can hardly be exaggerated. And it should be added that, in the degree of the Russian contribution to the defeat of Hitlerism, so will these factors operate to influence the mind of the masses all over the world.

It is in this background that the contradiction in the democratic purpose, to which I have referred, must be set. Its status with the ruling classes aligned against Hitlerism depends upon its association with the national idea. They are not, as Mr. Churchill has made evident, thinking of victory in terms of a new social order; they think of victory in terms of the maintenance of what he himself has termed "traditional" Britain, revised, to use his phrase once more, by "a few practical measures of reconstruction." But to the masses, as distinct from their rulers, victory means the extension of the frontiers of democracy from those political boundaries at which they now so largely halt to the social and economic fields. I do not mean by this that the masses have in their minds the application of a concrete body of socialist measures, or even that they have considered with any care the dynamics of social change. I mean only that, given victory, there are certain objectives upon which they are determined, and that they will use their political power to secure them. They will not endure, after victory, the persistence of mass-unemployment; they have seen that it can be prevented by the planned use of the state-power. They will not accept the re-emergence of distressed areas, Jarrow, Durham, South Wales, as we knew them in the inter-war years; they have seen that these arise from the unplanned use of social resources which need not be sacrificed to the ruthless exactions of private ownership. They will not submit, at least peacefully, to any rebuilding of Britain which enables the ground landlord and the speculative builder to profiteer out of the sufferings of Coventry and Plymouth, East London and the Merseyside.

Our central problem is whether the fight of the democracies against Hitlerism is, as I think Mr Churchill conceives it, a fight for the survival of a national tradition the main historic contours of which he proposes to preserve; or whether there is room in that tradition for the acceptance by consent of the three basic principles, with all their immense consequences, that I have just enumerated. It is not enough to say that all parties in the democracies are committed to "justice between classes," or to "social security" or what not. Agreement can always be reached on ends, if they are defined comprehensively enough; it is upon the different content different classes give to those ends, and the conflict over the methods by which they may be reached that men kill one another. The Polish government in Britain is committed to the establishment of a democratic Poland after the war; but no small part of its membership belongs to parties which, while they shared power, exploited the workers and peasants of Poland and still issue, if indirectly, virulent anti-semitic propaganda. Most of the promises which members of the Churchill government are making to-day were made, with much the same kind of class-support, after the last war; that was also a war "to make the world safe for democracy," and the workers, at any rate, ceaselessly emphasize that, as soon as victory was won, the promises were conveniently forgotten. It is not cynical, but common sense, to insist that the same dangers confront us as in 1919, and that their consequences will be far more serious in our generation than they were in the last.

We have, this is to say, to confront the fact that the victory of political democracy over the external danger which threatens it is a stage in, and not the end of, a process. It is a necessary stage; without it, quite certainly, there would be no need even to consider the future of democratic institutions. But the overthrow of Hitlerism still leaves in all their formidable complexity the problems out of which Hitlerism emerged. It still leaves untouched the frame of mind in the ruling class of every democracy which was prepared to consider accommodation with Hitlerism, because it was unprepared for accommodation with the economic and social implications of democracy. Victory is in itself an opportunity, and not a fulfilment. It gives democracy another chance; it is not in itself an assurance that the chance will be taken.

It is, I say, common sense to be aware that this is the reality; we shall confront it honestly and resolutely only in the degree that we are aware of it. There is plenty of evidence to suggest that, when our dangers are overcome, we shall begin to remember less our identities than our differences. There are plenty of people anxious to put a ceiling to wages who protest with indignation that our taxes destroy the manufacturer's incentive. "We are told," said Mr. Churchill himself,[1] "how badly labour is behaving, and then a lot of people who never did a day's hard work in their lives are out after them." "The critics of the workers," said Mr. Lawson in the same debate, "seldom pay any attention to a considerable section of society which never does any work at all, which has sufficient wealth to get as much food as it likes, which can roll in its motor cars to certain places and pay for what it gets, and very often get what is denied to other people. We do not hear much about that class. Neither do we hear that in the past year the mass of the workers have, in the main, almost exhausted themselves in order to contribute to the nation's need." "If," Mr. Bevin told the House, "somebody gets £1,000, £2,000, or £3,000, it is purely a conception, but if a

[1] Hansard, vol. 373, No. 91. July 29, 1941. Col. 1300.

workman gets over £5, somebody thinks the world is coming to an end."

"We declare," said Mr. Bevin, "that we will carry on to the bitter end to remove the Nazi régime and its spirit of domination and aggression; we will weave into the fabric of society the spirit of freedom and equality for all."[1] I do not doubt that in those words Mr. Bevin summarized the aspirations of the workers all over the world. But aspirations can only be fulfilled where the conditions directly lead to their realization. It is of no use to aspire in their absence. The present economic system requires a permanent reserve of unemployment; it requires to produce so that a profit may be earned for the owners of the instruments of production; it is inherently indifferent to social considerations whether in relation to its principles of production or its principles of distribution; it accumulates and invests in terms overwhelmingly of morally neutral supply and demand. It has shaped most of our institutions and our habits of thought to its inner and immanent necessities. It knows no test of survival save the power to make profit. It has accepted no social reforms save those that were forced upon it. The freedom for which it has invariably been concerned has been that of profit-making; the operation of the equality upon which it has insisted has invariably been limited to the owners of property. The history of democracy, as Tocqueville and Marx both saw from their very different angles of vision, has thus far been overwhelmingly conditioned to the service of the profit-making motive.

It is, of course, true that the last three-quarters of a century have seen the negative state transformed into the positive state; many of its functions are deliberately conceived to mitigate the consequences inherent in the principle of capitalism. But, upon this, there are two observations to be made. Historically, the owners of property have fought every concession they were ultimately driven to make until it could only be denied at the cost of violence; historically, also, it has made every concession without decisively touching its hold upon the central citadel of its power. The struggle for national education, the establishment of a system of factory inspection, the achievement of Plimsoll's safety line in ships, the effort to prevent sweating in industry, the establishment of a standard of unemployment benefit which makes possible reasonable living conditions, the recognition of the right of the workers to use their collective strength in industrial bargaining, all these are merely illustrations of the two observations I have made. Capitalism in its pursuit of profit has been, again

[1] Hansard, vol. 373, No. 91. July 29, 1941. Col. 1334.

as a simple matter of history, without conscience and without pity. The record of imperialism in Africa, reaffirmed in the war by the report on the copper mines of Rhodesia, the slums .of our great cities, the denial, on profit-making grounds, of elementary amenities like lightning and water-supply to the great majority of the rural population, the fate of Jarrow in the inter-war years,[1] the fact that in our civilization, the second richest in the world thirty per cent of the population suffer from defective nutrition, these, and things like these, are the framework within which the aspirations Mr. Bevin has noted have to be met.

Nor is this all. The defeat of Hitlerism removes a grave threat to our security. It assures the ruling class that their privileges are free from the danger of external aggression. But it leaves our social and economic structure in a jeopardy the more profound because the chief motive to national unity willl no longer be operative. There are the vast problems of the change-over from a war-economy to a peace-economy. There are the concurrent problems of demobilization with their implication of massive, and dangerous, psychological frustration. There is the need to reorganize the export trade, much of it with peoples likely to be long impoverished by the results of the war. There is the loss of our American investments, and our transformation into a debtor to the United States. There is the problem of transforming a European continent racked by hate and suffering to something approaching an ordered and stable life. There is the repercussion of the natural desire of men and women so long subject to the intense strain of total war to recover, if only for a brief hour, the wonted routine of that privilege to which they clung so passionately in the inter-war years. It is the habit of property to be timid and distrustful. Its power of ideological innovation has, historically been always well behind the needs that it confronts. In the inter-war years, with issues before it of much smaller magnitude, it shrank from the hazard of bold experiment. Not only did it distrust democracy; where it had the power, and could organize the opportunity, it co-operated in the overthrow of democracy. Can we, before such evidence, conclude that the ruling class will assist in, perhaps preside over, operations which are intended to terminate their privilege?

For, once again, I must emphasize that the character of our epoch will not be understood unless we think of it in terms of an age like that of the Reformation. It is an epoch when the principles of the dominant economy can no longer fully exploit the forces of

[1] Cf. Miss Wilkinson's amply documented record, *Murder of a Town* (1938).

production that are at their disposal. Its capacity to expand is exhausted; its contradictions have become the master of its purpose. That is why the values it was able to impose in its hey-day no longer command a general confidence. For their imposition is no longer associated with the fact of economic success. Within the legal framework of capitalist economy the achievement of profit is only possible at the expense of the well-being of the masses. And the fact that the masses have the franchise, the fact, further, of their organization into strong trade unions for the protection and enlargement of their standard of life, means the certainty they will use their political and economic power to secure fundamental adjustments in that legal framework.

It is inevitable that this should occur. When it is felt that the legal framework of a social order inhibits men's power to realize the full potentialities of production an age of revolution is always at hand. And nothing exhibits its revolutionary character more profoundly than the moral crisis through which it passes. The sense that the classic values are in decay, the yearning for a new faith, the presence of innumerable little groups which stand aside from the central movement of social forces, and proclaim that the truth is in them, the breakdown, in a word, of the contemporary culture which some given system of economic relationships supports, all these have been, in the past, as they are with ourselves, the index to the decisive breakdown of a way of life. Just as the replacement of feudalism by capitalism exhibited these phenomena; just as, also, the replacement of the way of life of feudalism meant war and revolution, so it is with the end of capitalist society. That society expressed itself in the political form of democracy because those who profited by the transformation it achieved were in need of the support of the masses to overcome the opposition they encountered. But the democracy they established after their victory halted at the frontiers of privilege. It was incomplete because it assumed that right was a function of ownership, and where there was no ownership there was, instead of right, concession. The spectacle of capitalist democracy was, in fact, always a curious one since the immanent principle of each part of the alliance was in contradiction with that of the other part. But it was accepted because the range of the concessions the owners of property could make was wide enough to satisfy the masses who clamoured for them almost until our own day.

It was accepted, further, because, above all after the French Revolution, it was supported by the prestige and power of the national idea over all but a very small number of persons in democratic communities. It is, I think, broadly true to say that it has been exceptional for men to feel, as Lenin felt, that economic injustice is worse than alien rule. Nationalism has therefore been able to unify men in the face of a common danger; and where the enemy has had the character of Hitlerism its power to unify has been wholly intelligible. The fact remains that, when the common danger is withdrawn, the economic issue between classes which the contraction of capitalism involves becomes once more urgent. The problems then before democracy assume the form of an inescapable dilemma. Either capitalism must be able to resume its power to expand, and thus maintain its compatibility with democratic forms by resuming, also, its power to make concessions, or it must separate from its democratic context. In the latter event, it either ceases to be democratic, which, almost certainly, means a rapid drift to some form of Fascism, or it is itself transformed by the acceptance of a new constitutive principle in economic organization.

So stated, of course, I unduly simplify; the facts are more complex than we can summarize in our categories of thought. I am concerned to emphasize that the economic rulers of our society have moulded the state to purposes which sought, above all, the protection of the privileges inherent in their ownership; and that they could maintain their possession of the state as a democracy only so long as they were able to satisfy the masses. I am arguing that their ability to achieve this satisfaction has broken down, and that the profound moral crisis in which we are involved is the proof of its breakdown. It follows that the resolution of this moral crisis is only possible by restoring to the state the power to enforce its traditional discipline; and this power is a direct function of the economic success of the property-system which the state supports. In the absence of this success, there are no common ends in which members of the community feel that they sufficiently share to accept without conflict what they conceive to be its injustice and its irrationality.

Here, of course, we encounter the great difficulty inherent in any society marked by inequalities as great as those between different classes in Britain or the United States. The inequalities which seem patently indefensible to one class seem coincident with national well-being to another. The Marquess of Salisbury cannot conceive of a House of Lords the main purpose of which is not to frustrate the coming of socialism in Britain; the Labour Party cannot conceive of a House of Lords justified in frustrating the will of a government which has behind it a socialist majority in the electorate. American trade unions see in the Wagner Act something like the Magna

Carta of their freedom; American employers, in general, regard it as a wanton interference with the rights of business men to determine whom, and upon what terms, they shall employ. And behind these antithetic judgments there lie, often enough, long years of habit and prescription which make those who pronounce them deaf to the premisses upon which their opponents proceed. Periods of economic expansion give the leeway for accommodation because they give the time for adjustment. Periods of economic contraction make accommodation far more difficult for the very simple reason that they tend to annihilate the category of time. They force men either to yield what they have been taught by long experience to regard as fundamental or they compel them to fight. That is the situation in which we find ourselves. It is merely postponed, it is not met, by the fact that, until Hitler is defeated, there is an overriding objective.

The problem that the democracies confront in this regard could hardly be symbolized better than in the attitude of Mr. Churchill, in Britain, to reconstruction. The depth of Hitler's threat to British independence meant that he had to form a government of all parties when he assumed office as Prime Minister; for without the direct participation of the Labour Party he would not have been able to mobilize the full support of the working-class behind it. But, throughout his period of office, Mr. Churchill has been, quite obviously, in a serious dilemma. Upon the issue of the need for victory there was behind him a nation than which, in all history, none has been more united. There was even considerable unity upon the nominal ends for which victory must be achieved. It was regarded on all hands as imperative that a defeated Germany must never again be able to use aggression as an instrument of national policy. It was universally accepted that there must be greater economic security for the masses after the war. It was agreed that methods must be accepted which raised the standard of life for all peoples; a common prosperity, it was widely recognized, was the foundation of international peace, even that Germany and Italy must be participants in that prosperity.

In the declaration of these aims, Mr. Churchill confronted no difficulty. On the methods by which they were to be secured he could make no pronouncement because there was no real agreement about them. On the one hand his leadership of the Conservative Party compelled him to insist that he stood for "traditional" Britain, with "a few practical measures of reconstruction." On the other hand, his Labour colleagues confronted a constituency pledged to the radical transformation of "traditional" Britain, and uneasily aware that it would be profoundly dissatisfied with any reconstruction which did not at least begin the reorganization of capitalist foundations. Mr. Churchill understood that European recovery, when peace comes, was dependent upon the leadership of a Britain able to maintain the great ends of life in common, at peace, therefore, within itself, and thus able to devote its main energies to the task of reconstruction. He expressed the hope that the Coalition Government over which he presided would last for some such period as three years after the Armistice that it might preside over European stabilization and recovery.

Clearly enough, the continuance of the Coalition Government would depend upon the character of the terms Mr. Churchill could offer to the Labour Party. Publicly, at any rate, he would not announce those terms; and, publicly, also, the Labour Party could not ask for them lest their revelation showed the distance between the conceptions by which the partners in the Coalition were moved, the certainty that, once the overriding danger of Hitlerism had been overthrown, it could not in fact be bridged. More than this. The problems of an alliance between parties wedded, like Mr. Churchill's, to the maintenance of capitalism, and one which, like the Labour Party, has formally, at least, accepted the necessity for a socialist transformation of Britain was apparent in the character of the domestic measures for which the National Government has been responsible in the first two years or so of its life. Conservatism has been satisfied by the fact that no essential change has been made in the ownership or control of the economic system; the central citadel of capitalism in Britain remains untouched by the necessities of organization for war. Labour has been placated by a series of social reforms, the virtual abolition of the household means test, the increase of old age pensions and workmen's compensation payments, the advance of agricultural wages, and so on, all of which put plasters on old economic sores without raising the more delicate question of preventing the occurrence of the wounds. Each aspect of the compromise is a necessary process, because neither party to it dare risk the danger of raising, in any fundamental way, those questions which might strain that national unity the necessity of which danger imposes. The Labour Party has ceaselessly to remember that the owning class in France preferred defeat and collaboration with Hitler to the abandonment of their privileges; the Conservatives dare not forget that, without the support of Labour, they cannot win a victory without which their privileges have no future.

I am aware that immense impersonal forces are at work in Britain which, whatever men may will, are certain, with peace, to bring profound changes in social and economic organization in their wake. The evacuation, the consolidation of industry, the new levels of taxation, the implications of the "Essential Work" order, the new techniques of production, the vast expansion in the potential sources of productivity, the changed face of Britain which bombardment from the air has effected, all these are big with revolutionary incidence. I am aware, too, that there is a great hunger everywhere for a new faith in which men can continue the unity of the war-years, and a willingness to see experiment for the discovery of that faith.

But there are three great difficulties which we would be foolish to underestimate. The first is the difficulty that men always feel when they are asked to surrender settled habits to the possibilities of the unknown. More people are in favour of great changes in general than will support any specific change in particular; and where the group deems itself adversely affected by some concrete proposal for specific change all its ingenuity is exerted to secure, usually successfully, its postponement until "after the war." Postponement is the vice of coalitions. There is postponement of any real decision over the future of the banks, over the future of the land, over the future of railways and mines. There is postponement of the need to confront the issue of Indian self-government, the grim poverty of the colonial populations, the problem of whether democracy can survive when the mass of its members cease to be educated just at the point where knowledge begins to exercise its fascination. A nation can afford the luxury of compromise when it has decided upon the goal at which it aims. It cannot afford that luxury when it is fearful of choosing the goal.

The second great difficulty is the widespread tendency, clearly related to the first, of thinking of reconstruction as something to be planned after the war instead of conceiving it as a process the nature of which is in fact determined by the social and economic methods by which the war is waged. For it is surely clear that if the goal cannot be defined when men are ready for great experiment, when the sense of danger has made them understand their intense dependence upon one another, it will be far more difficult to define it, at least in terms which command wide assent, when victory has made the need for sacrifice and accommodation seem so much less urgent. Every privilege, every injustice, every inefficiency, that go unchecked in wartime are given new vigour with which to protect themselves when peace comes. Vested interests which, in war, have staved off full subordination to the national effort are not likely, when its profound compulsions are withdrawn, to prove more amenable to adjustment. The evidence is already profound that, in this realm, immense opportunities have been missed. There is not, I think, any doubt that when, as France was falling, the Churchill government took absolute powers over the persons and property of its citizens, the nation was in a mood that would have permitted, even rejoiced in, large-scale experiments which, by defining the contours of reconstruction, would have shaped the necessary basis for its pattern in peace. But, in fact, while the power over persons has been exercised drastically, little use has been made of the power over property. A few farmers have been displaced for the inefficient use of their land; a few business firms have been reorganized on similar grounds. But, in the main, the disposition of economic forces will remain the same at the end of the war as it was at the beginning; with the important difference only that the concentration of industry, in the interest of the most efficient use of manpower, will give the large units of production a position of pivotal advantage over the small man. Since large-scale state-intervention is inevitable at the end of the war, this means, in the absence of safeguards, a direct and massive strengthening of the general drift towards monopoly capitalism.

The third great difficulty to which I must draw attention is, naturally enough, more obvious in Britain than it is in America. In an epoch such as our own, nothing is so essential to the maintenance of democracy as great leadership, and, in an ultimate sense, great leadership means the power to make the possible inevitable. Democracy has not merely, if it is to survive, to win the war; it has got, as I have sought to show, to decide while it is organizing victory, what it is to win the war for. But the organization of the war-effort is itself so immense and absorbing a task that the main energies of our leaders is devoted to its problems. The war receives their attention; the future receives the rhetoric of their perorations. When the battle sways over half the world, the ability to separate themselves from its immediacies is the rarest of qualities. The tasks of the day press so insistently upon their attention that it seems extravagant to give their time to what they think of as the problems of tomorrow. What, so far, they have either failed to see, or failed to act upon, is the fact that the problems of to-morrow are already the problems of to-day; for the decisions they take to-day set the frame in which the problems of to-morrow are shaped. No British statesman, for example, has given this nation any guide comparable in character with the chart provided for the American people by President Roosevelt in his message to Congress of January 6, 1941. It is true that no statesman of any nation has surpassed Mr. Churchill in his power to steel the endurance of our people to whatever dangers it may have to meet. But beyond his emphasis on the need to endure for victory Mr. Churchill has not gone. He has not asked the nation to accept the ends he conceives that endurance should serve. It is with the maintenance of past glories rather than with the organization of future promise that he had been overwhelmingly concerned.

I have said that the problems of to-morrow are already the problems of to-day; and there is one aspect of the failure to act upon this view which deserves a special annotation. This war is a war for the soul of the peoples of the world. We have the task not only of breaking Hitlerism but also of enabling those whom he has conquered to recover their self-respect by participating in his overthrow. We seek, that is, to provoke such a resistance to his authority as will assume, when the shadows of his defeat begin to lengthen, the proportions of a revolution. But this resistance and this revolution we seek to provoke to reaffirm the faith of the peoples in the democratic principle. It is hard to see how this can be achieved save as we demonstrate the power of democracy to master those economic problems, poverty, insecurity, the life of endless toil, ignorance, which were the environment out of which Hitlerism was born. We know that Hitlerism is evil, ugly, ruthless; we have got to reckon with the fact not only that it is an idea which has imposed itself, but an idea against which its victims are impotent save as we give them the hope of a future in which they find the present courage to resist. What we have to prevent is that they should fall into that numb acceptance of their servitude which is the predominant mood of the German and Italian peoples.

And what we have to remember is that every evil which defaces our national life, every injustice which can be exploited in our system, every problem we fail to tackle, is a weapon in the hands of Hitlerism. We summon the conquered peoples to revolt; but there is the danger that our summons to them may seem a call to exchange one master for another. They hear ceaselessly from the exponents of Nazism of the limitations of our democracy; we have to make it plain to them how we are transcending those limitations. But the way to make it plain is to embark now upon the task of transcendence. The defect of all our political warfare is that it consists of eloquent, but vague, pledges about the future, instead of the narrative of concrete achievements in the present. It is not an effective answer to the Nazi idea to promise the preservation of "traditional" Britain, even with a few, but unspecified, "practical measures of reconstruction." We evoke the resistance that becomes revolution, we maintain the self-respect that becomes democracy, by example and not by precept, by great measures and not by great perorations.

I have already emphasized the resemblance of the mental climate of our time to the age of the Reformation, and that resemblance provides an example upon which it is worth while to dwell. One of the striking features of that age is the courage and endurance of men who braved torture and death for their beliefs. The secret of their courage was their faith in a certain salvation. Our problem consists in providing a similar faith for our own generation. So far, it is obvious, we have not provided it. Nor will it come, as some speculate, from a miraculous recovery of faith in the supernatural. The conditions which made Catholic and Protestant alike faithful, under all hazards, to their ideal have largely disappeared; for our day, the promises which matter are not the rewards of an after-life, but the rewards attainable in this world. There is, for the masses, no promise of such rewards, save with the possible exception of the Soviet Union, and until that promise becomes real and tangible, the faith we require is not likely to be forthcoming. Of the impact that faith can have, of the *élan* it contributes to effort, I have already spoken when, in an earlier chapter, I compared the psychological habits of the Puritan with those of the Bolshevik. It is, of course, an attitude which has its dangers, not less than its merits; but it is the fundamental temper in which great achievement is possible.

My point is that in the present condition of democracy, both in Britain and in America, that faith is not available to the masses. There is, no doubt at all, courage in abundance, resolution, a power to hold that has not been surpassed in any previous age. But the circumstances in which these qualities operate are negative and not positive circumstances. No one can have any deep or frequent contact with the masses in this country without the conviction that this is the case. The deep determination for victory is accompanied by an anxiety about the shape of things to come not less deep. There is vivid remembrance of the promise and hopes of 1914–18 and their frustration in the inter-war years. There is a passionate yearning for economic security, a ceaseless demand that statesmen offer proof that it can be made real. Talk of "a new world after the war" is received with scepticism and not with conviction. There is a restless fear that none of the political parties will prove equal to the tasks before them. Even those most convinced that, under Mr. Churchill's leadership, the nation can win this war proffer no certitude that it will win the peace. It is a nation brooding over its issues, watchful as never before, of its leaders, eager for assurances that it does not yet feel it has received. It is keenly alive to the nature of the problems it will face; it is grimly dubious whether its leaders have the imaginative audacity to face them.

But of two things it is, I am confident, sure. From its awareness of what it has endured, it has recovered that self-respect which it visibly lost in the "appeasement" period. And because it has recovered its self-respect, it is in a fighting mood about its freedom. It sets that freedom, as never before, in the context of equality; it will enforce attention to that context. The common people will fail in nothing that victory calls for; but anyone who has seen and talked with them, at night in the air-raid shelters, in the hours when darkness approaches when the long trek commences to some hoped-for safety in the countryside, or at the benches in the factories when they discuss with freedom the habits of their masters, anyone who has seen and talked with them can be quite certain that the freedom for which they are told they are fighting is a freedom for which they propose to fight. Soldier and sailor, airman and the seamen of the merchant navy, docker and engineer, shipbuilder and miner, they know that they have saved Britain; in a half-articulate way, they suspect that they have saved civilization. They will demand their price. They are not going back to a Britain of mass-unemployment, of distressed areas, of a Coventry and a Plymouth, a London and a Merseyside, to be rebuilt for the profit of the ground landlord and the speculative contractor. They will fight for their right to be safeguarded against these things against any force that privilege may deploy against them. I do not think they are certain that they will win. I am confident only that they will not be deprived of security and hope without conflict. If, they say, this is a people's war, then it must issue in a people's peace.

That is the problem they pose to their rulers; that, also, is the problem about which their rulers have to make up their minds. I do not think there is ground for saying that their rulers will satisfy their aspirations. It is, no doubt, true that, on their own premisses, their rulers will make a genuine, even generous, effort to satisfy them. The issue is whether the premisses of their rulers are near enough to the premisses of the masses to make possible a revolution by consent. It is an issue vaguely felt as the fundamental issue all over the world. It is, indeed, seen fundamentally, the issue about which this war is being fought, for the real purpose of Hitler is to transform the world into a vast *latifundium* operated for the benefit of the German people in exchange for his retention of autocractic power. It was the issue, also, about which cohered the main differences between President Roosevelt and the business men of America. Quite simply, it is the issue of whether, in the terms Matthew Arnold liked to use, the privileged class in a democracy will, without compulsion, choose equality and flee greed. Were it to make that choice the relations of production would become, once again, proportionate to the forces of production; democracy could transform capitalism and so surmount the contradictions which at present threaten its destruction. Were it to make that choice, a democracy at bay would have made its supreme hour of danger its supreme hour of opportunity as well. The choice, on any serious analysis, is a very clear choice. A revolution by consent permits the affirmation of democratic principles over a wider area and with greater strength. A revolution by violence, even if it be successful, is bound to suspend the procedures of democracy. Even if it be successful, we know from 1789 and 1917 that it ushers in an iron age. If it fail, it takes men, as Hitler seeks to take them, into an ugly jungle in which the dignity of man is sacrificed to the crude lust for power.

This, I say, is what we are deciding. It is important to remember that the time for our decision is short. The possibility of revolution by consent will last only as long as the drama of war makes the common interest more compelling than any private interest; it will not survive the natural urge that peace will bring to recover our wonted routines. With peace, men will stake out their claims with a fierceness made more sharp by expectation, on the one hand, and prescription on the other. Their differences will be the more incapable of compromise because the sense of frustration will be so much the more deep. The time for our decision is short. The prospects which hang on that decision quite literally determine the character of civilization in the next epoch. Rarely has there been an age in which so many have given so much that freedom may have a new birth. What response their generosity will evoke we do not yet know. We may at least dare still to hope because the die is not yet cast.

Chapter V

THE INTERNAL CONDITIONS OF DEMOCRACY

I

THE confusion of a revolutionary epoch makes all simplicity in political speculation a dangerous luxury. It is easy to define ends; it is far more difficult to agree upon the means of their realization. It is easy to say that this is a war for democracy and freedom; it is far more difficult to translate democracy and freedom into the individual lives of men and women. It is easy to say that we fight against the totalitarian idea; it is less easy to admit that to fight against it successfully means running grave risks of becoming like our enemy. When nations are fighting for their lives, ethical precision is not one of their primary considerations. We insist that the world cannot endure half-slave, half-free; but we can convince ourselves of the need to "appease" General Franco who has turned Spain into one gigantic prison. We placate the authoritarian Salazar in Portugal. We denounce the ugly anti-Semitism of Hitler; but we patronize a provisional Polish government which uses the funds we place at its disposal for the indirect propagation of an anti-semitism hardly less vicious. We speak in high terms of the right of a people to govern itself; but we keep twelve thousand Indians in jail because they take that right to heart. We denounce the racial arrogance of Nazi Germany; but we confine the major positions in the colonial civil service to "persons of European descent."

To find our way through the complicated maze of contradictions in which we are involved makes it impossible to accept any simple formula as the certain way to peace and the plenty that might be built upon peace. Too much of the future is a sealed book we cannot open. Too many of the interests, national, economic, racial, for which we have to find a common level of well-being, exist at different levels of power and of development to make the road to our ends direct and obvious. Too many legacies of hate will be left by this war for the necessary collaboration to be easy. All we can do, in any assessment of the possibilities before us, is to follow the few gleams in the dark which seem to beckon us forward, to remember, above all, that it is hopeless to attempt even any conscious control of our fate unless we bring experimentalism and audacity to the ends we seek. The one quality which will assure our failure is lack of courage.

Yet, vast though our ignorance is, certain things in our situation are clear. The two world wars mark the close of the epoch which began with the Reformation. They bring us, whatever we may wish, to the certainty of a planned society. Either, as it develops, we find ways of redefining a common system of accepted values, and a common procedure to give them currency, or we can be certain that divergencies between state-interests in this interdependent world will lead inescapably to a new outbreak of war. But this means that our movement into a planned society involves agreement upon the purposes of planning. There is not an atom of reason to suppose that a planned society as such means an increase of well-being for ordinary people unless the plan is deliberately geared to that end. Compared, indeed, with Britain and America the experience of planned societies we have so far had has meant a diminution and not an increase of well-being. They have been built around the acceptance of three general principles the ugliness of which is manifest. They have relied upon a massive secret police to control the public expression of any private experience critical of the planners. They have prevented the free choice by the masses of those who control the state-power. To maintain the planners in control of its authority they have been driven, by a dreadful logic, to identify all serious opposition with treason. Hence Mussolini's murder of Matteotti, Hitler's purge of June 30, 1934, and the grim series of treason-trials in the Soviet Union.

A planned society may easily be built by the sacrifice of individual freedom to that collective state-power operated by the rulers of the society. To fight totalitarianism, we are ourselves compelled to plan; and, thereby, we run the danger that, in defeating it, we reproduce its habits in our own lives. For we know that the price of its defeat is that we cannot preserve the traditional civilization of the past. The war has meant an economic revolution the whole impetus of which is towards the development of giant industry at the expense of the small producer; there will be no going back upon that development. It has meant a degree of state-intervention which has altered the whole pattern of social and governmental habits. If we are to plan our civilization for democracy and freedom thereby, *a priori* we rule out a return to the basic pattern of the inter-war years. For implicit in that pattern were the strains and stresses which made Hitler and Mussolini possible, which brought Britain and the United States to the verge of economic disaster in the great depression. The inter-war years have made it clear that democracy cannot survive in the presence of things like mass-unemployment and distressed areas. The citizen looks to the state-power to redress their consequences; and if those who build its authority fail him, then he will listen to any voice which pledges its use for his aid. The pledge may be given, as Hitler and Mussolini gave it, with no serious thought of its redemption. But, given honestly or dishonestly, the pledge will be exacted; its exaction means interventionism; and interventionism means planning. At some point our historic situation marks its inevitability. What we seek to plan for are democracy and freedom; for planning that does not aim at these must make war that it may offer by conquest the fruits it cannot gather by peaceful advance. What, then, do we mean when we say that we seek to plan for democracy and freedom?

A democratic society is as much a matter of the spiritual inter-relations of its members as of the forms through which it is ruled. It requires that the effective responsibility of rulers to citizens shall be capable of continuous enforcement without resort to violence. It requires the choice of those rulers by citizens against whom there is no discrimination on grounds of religion or race or sex, colour or wealth. This is its procedural foundation: a system of universal suffrage which enables the peaceful and periodic choice of the rulers to be made.

But let us be clear that this procedure cannot be separated from certain conditions which alone give meaning to the idea of responsibility. A democratic society lives by maintaining a rule of law to which no citizen is superior. It depends, therefore, upon its capacity continuously to maintain respect for the laws it seeks through its government to enforce. In the long run, respect for laws is born of their outcome from consent and not from coercion; a society in which the secret police and the concentration camp are the main instruments of obedience will not for long retain a unity of purpose within its membership. And the habit of respect for law is, again in the long run, born of the citizen's sense that the society as a going concern affords him and his like the capacity to satisfy the expectations he deems legitimate and that this capacity is maintained by the law for which his respect is sought. If that sense is absent over a period from any considerable or powerful minority, democratic methods are certain to break down.

That is why, as I have sought to show in the first chapter of this book, democracy depends upon the power of reason over men's minds, why, also, fear and insecurity are fatal to that power. That is why, further, a democratic system is only likely to endure so long as men feel that they have the great ends of life in common, that the values they seek to realize are the same values. They are likely to feel this whenever they share in an expanding welfare under institutions rendered dear by traditional prescription, or whenever, as with ourselves to-day, their differences are forgotten in a great common danger they can unite to repel with all their energy. My argument therefore depends upon the premiss that, with the defeat of Hitler, democracy will be in jeopardy everywhere unless it expresses an economic system capable of offering the world expanding welfare. I have argued that this welfare cannot any longer be attained within the framework of the productive relations capitalism imposes. We have, therefore, to transcend those relations if we wish to maintain democracy.

To plan, of course, is essentially to disturb existing economic relations, and the difficulty, even the danger, of such disturbance needs no emphasis. Revolution in Russia, counter-revolution in Italy and Germany, these have been the price of the disturbance in our own generation. Even under the grave compulsion of total war, our rulers have sought so to plan that no powerful interest was disaffected by the disturbance that it suffered; how great an influence the example of those Frenchmen who preferred surrender to disturbance has wrought in the British government, both consciously and unconsciously, we shall never know. The United States is less habituated than ourselves to a gracious screening of its governmental relations from the public view. There, at least, we already know in ample measure that the President has had gravely to limit the possibilities of planned production, in almost every phase of the American rearmament programme, by the fear that under disturbance of existing economic relations it would jeopardize the co-operation he needs from big business; and the entry of some, at least, of its leaders into the Office of Productive Management was set at least as much by their resolve to set the limits of disturbance as by their desire to speed production. Ideally, we should have planned the maximum use of our resources for victory without regard to the effect of planning upon vested interests. Actually, we have known that such planning would have broken against psychological resistances it would have been powerless to overcome.

I do not for one moment say that those resistances have been unpatriotic. They are the outcome of a system the mental climate of which made a different way of thought impossible. They are part of the price we pay for an unequal society in which production is geared to the profit-making motive. A system of habits behind which there is the drive of some three hundred years of successful enterprise does not, even in an emergency, abandon its premisses in a sudden flash of inspiration, as a man suddenly catches a vision of new truth in the realm of religious faith. Habit dies hard, and it is not easily amenable to a reason which does not start from its own premisses. We can see that if we compare the relative ease with which the poor adapted themselves to the billeting necessitated by evacuation with the difficulties of adjustment encountered by the rich. With the poor, narrowness of accommodation and the sharing of burdens were, with a lack of privacy, part of the normal background of experience; the reception of evacuees was a quantitative change only in their lives. But for the rich is was an invasion of habits by people whose *mores* were set in a different perspective from their own; and the effort acceptance of it, even as a temporary measure, required of them was only less great than the ingenuities they displayed in finding ways of evading their responsibilities.

The central problem of the war for British democracy has been the full mobilization of its resources and the adequate adaptation of its habits to a purpose the fulfilment of which meant massive changes in the assumptions of the pre-war way of life. Predominantly this had to be done by consent; to do it by coercion would have destroyed that unity of the national will upon which victory depended. That has meant that much of the planning we have embarked upon has been an inadequate compromise. It has meant, also, that the degree to which we could go beyond the limits compromise involved has been dependent upon the degree to which men and women have felt the gravity of the danger. Clearly, for example, the grim weeks after Dunkirk evoked a greater effort and offered greater possibilities of innovation than the weeks, in the summer of 1941, when the concentration of the whole German effort against the Soviet Union seemed to remove the instancy of attack. The ease with which citizens returned, in this later period, to many of their normal habits measured something of the difficulties a planned society will face when the absence of the dramatic compulsion of war involves the interference with economic relationships without the psychological background which persuades men that it is necessary and justified.

If we are to plan for a society capable of expanding welfare then it is clear that we must dig long fingers into the foundations of property. Unless we change, with a reorganized productive relation, the motives of our society, that capacity will confront vested interests which will strike it into impotence. For this capacity is not a function of an abstract goodwill functioning in a vacuum; it is a function of a concrete goodwill which has the possibility of fulfilment within the framework of the society in which it operates. For we must remember that planning, as such, is a neutral exercise; whether it be democratic or undemocratic depends upon the purpose by which it is informed. Planning in Italy and Germany has been harnessed to the service of the privileged few; planning in the Soviet Union has been harnessed to the service of the masses. With ourselves, the purpose of such planning as we have attempted has been victory in the field; the end that victory is to serve has not, save in a purely conceptual way, entered into the calculations of statesmen. The whole effort has been a vast improvisation the parties to which have, by almost a conspiracy of silence, agreed not to raise questions of principle which might create difficulties for the constituency to which each appeals. By common consent, the waging of total war is revolutionary in its incidence; but, by a consent among political leaders almost as universal, the purpose of the revolution is a matter postponed from consideration until victory is won.

It is central to the argument I am making in this book that we cannot postpone the issue of the purpose of a planned society without jeopardizing the existence of democracy when the war is over. The reason for this is simple. The atmosphere of war permits, and even compels, innovations and experiments that are not possible when peace returns. The invasion of our wonted routine of life accustoms us to what William James called the vital habit of breaking habits. We adjust ourselves to the claims of a new world. We make responses to demands to which we were previously deaf. We find ourselves stimulated to exertions, even sacrifices, we did not know we had it in us to make. Common danger builds a basis for a new fellowship the future of which is dependent wholly upon whether the foundations are temporary or permanent. If they are temporary, then the end of the war sees the resumption of all our previous differences exacerbated tenfold by the grave problems it will have left. If they are permanent, then there is at least the possibility that we can find our way peacefully to the end we seek. What, above all, we require is time to discover how, in the new world we shall have entered with the cessation of hostilities, we can maintain the great ends of life in common. The menace of external danger will have gone, with it the major impulse to adaptation and sacrifice. Unless, at that stage, the foundations of a world have been laid in which men can discover the right to hope they will think too differently to settle their disagreements in terms of peace. The margin between their assumptions will be too wide to be bridged by discussion, by the give and take of rational compromise. If that becomes the position, it is obvious that the preservation of democracy will no longer be possible.

II

It is only necessary to think of the scale our post-war problems are certain to assume to recognize that this is neither a distorted nor an exaggerated picture. The transformation of our economy from a war to a peace basis; the demobilization of the armed forces; the rebuilding of the vast areas that have been bombed; the return of the innumerable evacuees in some ordered and coherent plan; the establishment of those priorities in material reconstruction which the nature of the rebuilding will call for, the agreement about the future place of agriculture in our national economy; the terms of maintenance for the unemployed in the period in which they await economic reabsorption; the resumption, and the level of resumption, of services like education; merely to enumerate items in the range of our problems is to give an index to their scale but not to their intensity. And we have to face those problems with the knowledge that, during the war, we have purchased our national unity by accepting, as common ground between all classes, those four freedoms of which President Roosevelt has spoken so eloquently. They mean that, on the economic plane, we are committed to three principles. We have to prevent the re-emergence of mass-unemployment. We have to prevent the re-emergence of distressed areas. We have to prevent the rebuilding of Britain from becoming an opportunity to profiteer by the ground landlord and the speculative builder.

What we have demonstrated in the war-years is that an overmastering social purpose can, in terms of planning, prevent these things. Within limits, no doubt, we have subordinated the profit-making motive to the victory of that purpose. By common agreement, that subordination was necessary if victory was to be won; the only real debate, since 1939, was whether the degree of subordination effected was adequate to the end in view. Planning for victory in war has created inescapable expectations in the masses of the possibilities of planning for increased material welfare when peace comes. But it is important to realize that, so far, every conscious step we have taken is temporary in character. If the war were to end to-morrow, no permanent change would have been effected in the relations of production; and we should have lost the decisive urge to innovation. Exactly as after 1918 the pressure on ancient habits and traditions would suddenly be withdrawn. The old motives would imperceptibly resume their sway; and the power of reason to prevail would be limited by the necessity of its operation within the limits provided by those motives. On experience, that means a post-war boom of a temporary character; and then a grim period in which we settle down to the recurrence of boom and slump which leads to political crises no longer compatible with democratic institutions.

I am not arguing for a moment that anyone, whatever his political complexion, desires a return after the war to the conditions of the inter-war years. No one wants mass-unemployment; no one wants distressed areas; no one wants to see profiteering out of the rebuilding of Britain. But unless we make fundamental changes now in the fundamental character of our economic system all these things will inevitably occur whatever may be our desires; for, in the absence of planned control, all these things are inherent in the economic system. We can begin those changes now because the atmosphere is prepared for their reception. It is highly doubtful whether we can make them by consent when that atmosphere is absent. It is the more doubtful because the effort the war requires will induce in many, above all in those who have agreed to the suspension of privilege, a fatigue, a hunger for the ancient ways, which it will be difficult to resist. Each class in the community will remember its own sacrifices; it will find it difficult to retain proportionate remembrance of the sacrifice of other classes. Our attitude to the soldier and sailor and airman who are, to-day, winning the war for us, is going to be very different from our attitude to them as unemployed men, supported by the community, and making no return to its productive effort. We must not forget that in all of us will be the knowledge that poverty and insecurity are our failures; and our sense of guilt will transform itself into hate of those who suffer from our guilt. The victims of the system will, in their turn, have a sense of anger and indignation deepened by the knowledge that this will be the second time in a generation we have chosen an economics of scarcity instead of an economics of abundance. We shall have the same tragic spectacle as after 1919 of demand for economies in national expenditure that the level of taxation may be reduced; there will be, as in the period symbolized by the axe of Sir Eric Geddes, the sacrifice of the amenities of the many to the maintenance of the luxuries of the few. That way, assuredly, lies disaster.

But that way, assuredly, we shall take unless, with conscious purpose, we set out now upon another way. Either we build now to make possible the movement from an economics of scarcity to an economics of abundance, or, with, no doubt, special features which our own historical traditions will provide, we shall move irresistibly towards a fascism of our own making. Indeed, we have to recognize that, without the organization of fundamental change now, the changes which the war has compelled will set our feet irresistibly in that direction. For a planned economy which has concentrated the ownership of the means of production in fewer hands than ever before is bound to gear the purposes of the state-power to their purposes. Historically, the character of an owning class is the determining factor in those purposes; the masses can only either vote to change the seat of economic power or vote to maintain it. But, historically also, the acceptance of a change by vote is one of the rarest phenomena of history. It is achieved only when the class in possession of the state feels confident that it will be defeated. On the evidence, it appears that Solon was able to secure an acceptance of this kind; and there is a sense, perhaps, in which the passage of the Reform Act of 1832 was the peaceful registration of a transfer of political power to the class whose economic authority was already predominant—a transfer, it must be added, directly related to the results of twenty years of violent conflict in the seventeenth century. The movement of things in our own epoch seems to me to make it highly unlikely that the precedent—if it be a precedent—of 1832 will be repeated. For, in the first place, economic power is not predominantly in the hands of those who press for a re-definition of the state-purpose; and, in the second place, the impulse to a peaceful settlement will be far less compelling then than it is to-day. The owning-class, in choosing peace, may be asked to surrender privilege, but they are bound to remember that they can retain privilege at the expense of democracy. They can easily recover all the arguments of the pre-war years by which so many of them almost convinced themselves in the disturbed atmosphere by which they were irritated that there was a good deal to be said for Hitler and Mussolini. They know now, of course, that both are evil men. Would they feel the same sense of evil about a British Fascist leader if, after victory and some months or years of profound internal strife, he would assure them of safety for their privileges?

It is, of course, easy to say that this is not the British way. Centuries of political experience have given us a genius for compromise. We stumble into solutions because we have, as perhaps no other people but the American, the political instinct. The democratic principle is too deeply rooted in our experience for its surrender to be possible. I think there is a core of truth in all these affirmations. But what has given them that core of truth is, I suspect, a special set of historical circumstances the impact of which no longer carries with it the old validity. I think all those affirmations were reasonable when three conditions obtained. They were reasonable when our economic supremacy was so outstanding that the power of privilege to go on making concessions without injury to its essential authority was a continuous power; that is no longer the case. The economic leadership of the next generation belongs to the United States, and we shall find it difficult enough, on any basis, to maintain our ground. They were reasonable, secondly, when our insularity was a vital protection to us in any conflict in which we were involved; it meant that we did not need a standing army based upon conscription—the absence of which was the real basis of the middle-class triumph in Britain—and that by reliance on that naval supremacy bought with our economic predominance, we were a vital factor on land in any European war. The course of events since 1939 has profoundly and permanently altered our situation in this regard. These affirmations were reasonable, thirdly, when the postulates of our economic system implied expanding welfare. This, as I have argued, is no longer true of ourselves or of any society built upon those postulates. We are losing, if we have not already lost, the elbow-room which permitted to us, as it permitted to no other major European power, the maintenance of democracy upon a capitalist basis. And to these peculiar characteristics there may well be added that the imperialist basis of our compromise is quite certain to lose, above all in India, in the post-war years the impressive material contribution it made to the maintenance of social peace.

We have passed, in short, the stage when we can rely upon some mysterious virtue in our national character to pull us through our difficulties unless we provide that national character with adequate opportunity to display once more its mysterious virtue. If we maintain capitalism as the basis of our economy, then we must operate our system within the categories of the logic it entails. We must maintain, that is, an acquisitive society dominated by supply and demand in terms of profit-making; the purposes of the state-power must be harnessed to the need of those who own the instruments of production to make profit. On these terms, both the commodities we produce and the principles of distribution must be set by the social habits a capitalist system enforces. We can amend its results to conformity with the habits of democracy precisely so far as we do not thereby injure the central requirement of capitalism that it is worth while for capitalists to go on producing in terms of their ability to make profit. But if, as I am urging, that amendment has been raised to a level where this ability no longer exists, it follows that we must either abandon capitalism or abandon democracy. We cannot make the best of two worlds whose basic principles are in contradiction with one another.

This it is, I add, which makes nonsense of Mr. Churchill's insistence that he is not interested in a new economic order; that he seeks to maintain "traditional England" subject only to a few practical measures of reconstruction. That possibility is not open to him for two reasons: first, "traditional England," in his sense, has already been made obsolete by the changes the war has involved; and, second, anyone who seeks to maintain it seeks to perpetuate a system from the implications of which at least a third of the electorate vigorously dissented. The conditions which built "traditional England" no longer exist. The question that men in Mr. Churchill's position have to answer is, what is to be the basis of the new England? As I have sought to show, the character of the new problems it is already obvious that new England will confront make it fantastic to suggest that a "few practical measures of reconstruction" can cope with them. By the inherent nature of our position the need is now inescapable to remake the foundations of our society; and the vital decision we have to take turns on the purpose which is to inform those foundations.

If we are agreed that the purpose is to maintain democracy in Britain as a going concern, then the issue it raises is twofold. First, it is the issue of renewing the power to expand welfare; second it is the choice of the appropriate moment at which to begin that renewal. The renewal of the power to expand welfare is, as I have argued, dependent upon an alteration in the basic productive relations of society. We have reached a point in the evolution of capitalism where the vested interests it protects makes it impossible for its habits any longer to exploit with adequacy the implications of our potential productive capacity. This impossibility is revealed by four basic weaknesses in the functioning of our system. Capitalism, first, involves a progressively increasing number of employed, and a lower relative wage for those whom it does employ. Capitalism, secondly, progressively raises prices without a corresponding increase in wages; the result is its inability to solve the problem of distribution. Capitalism, in the third place, distributes an excessive proportion of social income to the rich; with the result that wealth, and, therefore, economic power, is increasingly centralized in a few hands. Capitalism, finally, ceases to be capable of that continuous expansion which enables it to make continuous concessions of welfare to the many. In the face of these basic weaknesses, the relations of a capitalist society are in contradiction with its forces of production in precisely the same way as the legal relations of feudalism were in contradiction with the productive forces of the sixteenth century. Either we resolve that contradiction, or we face the same attempt at its forcible adjustment as characterized the three centuries before 1789.

I have discussed this issue with special reference to the situation in Great Britain; it is important to realize that the same tendencies are at work, if with retarded effect, in the United States.[1] The great depression, and the New Deal which was its direct consequence, warn us that the history of American capitalism has reached, with the disappearance of the frontier, much the same situation as we ourselves confront. That is why the policy of President Roosevelt has resulted in reform appearing to American capitalists as the antithesis of recovery; that is why, also, there has appeared on the American horizon that profound suspicion of majority rule which always marks the end of that leeway which, in the past, has enabled capitalism to respond to the insistent demands of democracy. It is significant that, all over the world, a public works programme initiated by the state is essential to the maintenance of democracy. In Fascist states, that programme assumes the character of a drive to military conquest; it is hoped to discover a new equilibrium from the loot of empires. But democratic states are endangered by the Fascist threat; and they are relentlessly compelled to a competition in the realm of armaments of which the consequence is the fear and insecurity which lead to war. We reach the fantastic position, in a capitalist régime, that war is necessary to obtain that full employment internally which makes possible domestic peace.

[1] The American position is admirably set out by Lewis Corey, *The Decline of American Capitalism* (1934), and J. M. Blair, *Seeds of Destruction* (1938).

Obviously, this is no permanent solution. Obviously, at some stage, we have to discover the conditions, economic and psychological, which make possible the peaceful resumption of expanding welfare. At the moment, it is upon the second of these issues that I wish to lay emphasis. It seems to me clear that the moment to embark upon innovation is that at which the minds of men are attuned to the idea of change. If we let that moment pass, we lose the chance of making the adjustments which are called for in a mental climate prepared for their acceptance. And the moment does not return. We cannot go on exhorting to sacrifice without the definition in time of a specific objective for which the sacrifice is made. The mood of those epic weeks after Dunkirk cannot be crystallized in perpetuity. It may be renewed at intervals, in circumstances of equal drama; it is a mood which, by the sheer physical demands it makes, is temporary and not permanent in character.

I am, therefore, arguing that the changes which we require we can make by consent in a period in which, as now, conditions make men remember their identities and not their differences. It is, at the very best, at least highly doubtful whether such a chance will again be available to us. An epoch like this, in which agreement is the very condition of survival, creates opportunities which do not recur when the danger of defeat is past. In such an epoch men can transcend the limitations which their economic position imposes on their thought. The drive to accommodation is too vital to be overlooked. No one suggests that party differences can be subordinated to national necessity after the defeat of Hitler. And if national necessity, as I am suggesting, requires a re-definition of class-relations in order that the expansion of welfare may be available to us, the moment for re-definition is when men can take experimentation in their stride. To wait until the perspective of urgency has disappeared, is to lose the favourable moment when the possibilities of history can be made into its inevitabilities. Such moments do not recur.

This may be put in another way. There is no democratic statesman to-day in any party who does not seek to maintain the morale of those who are fighting Hitlerism by the promise of a world organized for international peace and economic welfare and security. That promise was incapable of fulfilment in the inter-war years because the world was not organized upon the postulates necessary to that fulfilment. The urgencies of the war have thrown all vested interests into the melting-pot. I do not say that there is no sacrifice for which men are not prepared in order to win; I do say that in order to win they are ready for far greater innovations than they will be prepared to accept when they have won. Not to embark upon those innovations now, not, this is, to prepare the necessary postulates which make our democratic society safe, is to leave in being all the conditions which led to the war of 1939. Those conditions will lead to the same frustration of our will to peace and welfare unless we transcend them now. They may even lead to a more rapid frustration because the margin between promise and fulfilment will seem far more disastrous after a second failure than after a first. We cannot invite men to die a second time for democracy and freedom unless we take the steps that give these a firm foundation upon which they have the right to hope.

I am not for one moment denying that, even in war, it is difficult to lay that foundation; I am arguing only that, if it is difficult in war, it is ten times more difficult in peace. I am arguing that the incentive to agreement now has a claim upon men far more compelling than it can possibly have in the future. Men who share in the common effort to repulse great danger know the creative implications of magnanimity. There is bred in that experience a power of reciprocal understanding rarely available at other times. The middle ground is sought for; the logic of extremes is less attractive; the compulsion of the past lies less heavily upon us; we are less grimly the prisoners of our traditions. Danger breeds in men that exhilaration of mind which takes innovation in its stride. It offers a temporary spaciousness receptive, as no other situation is receptive, to experiment. But it is not a lasting mood. The human mind can dwell only rarely upon the heights. The history of every revolution is the history of the rise to a new equilibrium which the fatigue of great events threatens always to destroy. It was so in seventeenth-century England; it was so in 1789; it was so in the Soviet Union after 1917. Innovating government requires the extraordinary period if it is to meet the mood ready to accept innovation. Only urgency can persuade prescription to the abatement of its claims.

This, then, is the appropriate moment to organize the basis upon which we have at least the chance of maintaining the conditions of a democratic society. There will be no moment more appropriate than now. At a time when the state-power enjoys its midsummer of high credit, and political parties search for the formulae of unity, those who oppose experiment seem to sacrifice to private advantage the claims of public necessity. After Dunkirk, no trade union would have been heard with patience which put its special privileges before the needs of the nation; after Dunkirk, also, a refusal of the banks to acquiesce in the orders of the Chancellor of the Exchequer would have been swept on one side in universal indignation. The potentialities of that mood remain for evocation by great leadership. They are not a permanent thing. We have seen in the summer of 1942 how easily a temper of high resolution slips back into a hesitant complacency. If that can be the case when any realistic analysis tells us how far we are from even a Pisgah sight of victory, how much more true is it bound to be when the victory is certain. Our choice is an inescapable one. Either we build now into the foundations of our society the necessary postulates of democracy and freedom or we shall watch the swift eclipse of the chance to build them. History gives us our opportunity; it reveals the conditions under which it can be employed. But only our own wisdom can take advantage of it.

III

If we desire a revolution by consent, then the appropriate moment for action is now. The purpose of the revolution is plain. It is to reopen the prospect of expanding welfare; thereby, it is to make possible the maintenance in our civilization of those democratic processes the implicit values in which we set over against the new order our enemies seek to impose. We accept those values upon the premisses first, that men and women are ends in themselves, and not means to someone else's end, and, second, that the more profound the fulfilment of individual personality, the richer is the society in which it plays its part.

It needs no argument to prove that it is these implicit values, upon which the power of orderly government by consent depended, which are breaking down in our generation; and it is to that erosion that we may attribute the disillusion, the pessimism, and the anti-rationalism of our time. They are wholly right, I believe, who urge that without a renovation of faith there can be no restoration of confidence in the values we seek to establish. They are wholly right, also, in their insistence that, in a fundamental sense, those values are principles of social life which were first given a universal status with the acceptance of the Christian religion; though it is, of course, important to remember that they were not specifically Christian in their origins, and that they owe much of their power to both men and movements with which the predominant Christian Churches of every age have been at war.

But I do not think a renovation of faith means that we must

restore the authority of the Churches in our civilization. This view is based upon the belief that the historic claim of the Churches is true and that their renovation is possible. All the evidence we have points strongly against that belief. It suggests a power to renew faith in dogmas which have long ceased to have any precise meaning for the overwhelming mass of men. They have not, as dogmas, been able to withstand the impact of four centuries of historical criticism; and the Churches which have professed them have lost their hold because, in the end, they have always adapted their requirements to worldly considerations rather than sought to transform a society so large a part of whose habits and institutions were in plain contradiction with the behaviour the Churches were, by the commission they claimed, supposed to exact. That is why every movement for Church reform has always been a plea for the recovery of primitive simplicity. and why every Church, as it has passed from protest to power, has compromised with the reality it was born to deny.

To renew the authority of the Churches in modern life would require a reabsorption of the state into the Churches, the surrender of territories which they were unable to cultivate with success. Such a reversal of the historic process is not open to us. The secularization of society is a final achievement in the evolution of mankind. It will extend, and not diminish, its power. The faith we have to build is a faith in the values of this world, not in the values of another. The claim we have to establish is that of man upon the brother that he sees, not the claim of the unseen God upon man. It is, no doubt, a problem of gigantic proportions; it means the moralization of an increasingly anthropocentric universe. But it is at least certain that if we cannot establish the claim, we cannot hope to give a rational social ethic an effective place in our society.

The problem with which we are confronted is that which was so incisively seen by Rousseau in that famous chapter on civil religion which, so far from being an afterthought in his work, is the very core and essence of the *Social Contract*. He realized that no pagan religion provided the values which bound men together unbreakably in a common faith; he saw that the weakness of Christianity, on its civic side, at least, was that, in its Protestant forms, its emphasis on individual salvation emptied its expression of that power to control the public behaviour of men which is vital to the needs of the Commonwealth; while, in its Catholic form, it precipitated endless conflicts over jurisdiction which made power, and not virtue, the main end of religious organization. His own remedy, a civic religion of "a few simple dogmas," is unlikely to make the appeal he believed; partly because the dogmas have, in fact, none of the simplicity he attached to them, and partly because they involve the operation of a coercive apparatus for their imposition which would be fatal to the free play of the mind.

I think, nevertheless, that Rousseau in this chapter put his hand on a vital element in our problem. A civilization built upon the mere growth of material power will break down, as ours is breaking down, unless it can convince its members that the order it imposes is just. It was, broadly speaking, able so to convince them when the mass of mankind believed that there was a reward in another world for the misery of this life; that belief bred a patience and a humility which were, for long centuries, the cement of the social order. It was a cement which continually crumbled; few generations but displayed, even in its presence, the fragility of ordered government. The true basis of ordered government is, no doubt, as complex and as irrational, as the mind of man himself. But it is not, I think, beyond the facts to claim that the true basis has always been the ability of a social system to provide its members with the right to hope that they will be able to better their condition. So long as they have this hope, they accept the obligation to work and to obey; law and order are rooted in consent. But once, for any large and determined minority, this hope is gone, they become convinced that the foundations upon which law and order depend are irrational and unjust. Power is then, for them, stripped of its moral claims. A struggle develops which makes the rules embodying the ethical code of the society appear inadequate as sanctions of conduct.

The period before 1914 had witnessed the slow erosion of the religious sanction by which the claims of authority had been partly maintained. But the significance of its disappearance had been obscured by the immense material progress in the same era. In Western civilization, the fruits of that progress had been widely, though unequally, shared by all classes and by most nations; least in the East of Europe, most in Great Britain and the United States. But the progress had slowed down by the nineties of the last century, especially after the exhaustion of the American frontier; and the armed truce before 1914, the first world-war, and the revelation, in the inter-war years, that the economic system could not, by its inherent nature, maintain the rate of advance characteristic of its early phase, deprived literally millions of that hope of bettering their position which enables them to accept without undue scrutiny the justice of social arrangements. Hence the almost universal phenomenon of the decline of the birth-rate, a decline, it is significant, that no religious organization could seriously arrest. Hence, also, the growth of prohibitions upon freedom of migration which were the more grave and the more poignant because they imposed upon the poorest elements in civilization a suffering which led, inevitably, to things like racial persecution and intensified nationalism. Mass-unemployment, the growth of an insecurity which affected millions, the absence of that secret consolation which, in an earlier day, had given hope amid suffering to many of the disinherited, were bound to evoke the disillusion which is the main characteristic of our time. In the timid and the comfortable, it bred a fear at the claim that the foundations should be scrutinized, in the bold a determination to attempt their reorganization. And all this was exacerbated by the uneasy sense that we were on the threshold of an epoch in which the renewal of hope was possible if we could only break the psychological barriers which stood in the path of our access to it.

The challenge to our system of values is, if this argument be correct, the outcome of our failure to maintain the right to hope; and that failure, in its turn, is born of the fact that our relations of production do not enable us to exploit with sufficient adequacy the forces of production at our disposal. Spiritual values always go into the melting-pot at times like these; and the sense of frustration these times evoke make men into saints or devils. For they suspend that capacity to reason which gives men courage because they have the assurance that they can plan with confidence for the morrow. Nothing shows this more clearly, in the four centuries from the Reformation to the French Revolution, than the massive efflorescence of sects at each age of crisis; their particular vision and emphasis is the sign of the breakdown of accepted values. They have lost hope in these values; they seek, as best they may, for new sources from which to gather it. Baptist, Ranter, Seeker, Friend, Muggletonian, in the Cromwellian age, all express the search for a basis upon which to come to terms with a world whose order they either defy or ignore. All of them either perish or find a plane of relevance to the material forces of civilization in which they discover peace. We can trace in men, like George Fox or John Bunyan, the roots of an esoteric satisfaction with life born of the acute sense of disharmony with the normal environment, and lighting a flame in others the light of which persists while the disharmony and the original inspiration endure. And as the society recovers an equilibrium in which the right to hope is renewed the sects sink back, like the Baptists and the Quakers in the eighteenth century, into a conventionalism of conduct which means that, for them, the disharmony has been resolved.

The changed relation of religious belief in our own day is coincident with a situation in which the sphere of the state is increasingly coterminous with the sphere of society. Protest against a felt disharmony, therefore, rarely expresses itself in the form of religious sectarianism; a development like the Group movement, for example, is hardly comparable, above all because of its frank acceptance of worldly-values, and its social quietism, with the Commonwealth revival of the sects. The true analogy is in the field of political parties. There we have the evolution of prophets and doctrines which seek by their utterance to organize, like Fox or Bunyan, a change in the way of men's lives. The sect may, like Lenin or Hitler or Mussolini, develop in circumstances which give it control of the state-power; whatever its fate, what is of interest in its outlook is the compulsion it cannot evade to formulate a doctrine into which every aspect of conduct can be fitted. It develops its casuistry and its heretics; it has its ritual and its dogmas. The secularization of social life has meant the increasing assumption by the state of the character of a church. And that, in its turn, has meant that any decrease in the ability of the major political parties in a state to satisfy the wants of its members has led either to the multiplication of parties—the familiar phenomenon of sectarianism—or the need for a dictatorship to secure such a routine of behaviour as will maintain the society as a going concern.

This is the alternative before the democracies in our own day. They have to discover a plane of unity between their citizens or give way before a form of government which gives the great mass the right to hope. That plane of unity they can find only as they are able to resume the condition of increasing material welfare. Without that resumption, the right of their rulers to command, their ability to secure a willing obedience, is doubted and thwarted at every turn. When that right and that ability are in jeopardy over any considerable period of time—as in Germany under the Weimar Republic—dictatorship is accepted because it offers relief from the torture of uncertainty; and this torture is the greater in a capitalist society the main motive to production in which is profit based on the security of future expectation. We have, therefore, the problem that unless democracy can create relations of production which enable it to resume the condition of increasing material welfare, it has no power to establish a system of values which has validity for its citizens.

It is, I think, in this context important to note that, in the inter-war years, increasing material welfare has been characteristic of only two societies in Western civilization, and in two societies only has there been a period of optimism. There was increasing material welfare in the United States in what is broadly termed the Coolidge epoch; it was, indeed, a brief Indian summer of material progress which ended calamitously with the great Depression of 1929. It is clear that it left no profound psychological results except that it made the disillusion after the collapse more bitter for the masses by reason of the unbased hopes it had created. The other society is the Soviet Union. There, as most detached observers have agreed, something as genuinely new in civilization was coming to the birth as in the sixteenth century, or after 1789; its coming was marked, despite everything, by a spaciousness in experiment, an ardour of hope, a confidence about the future, which have stood the test not only of a quarter of a century's heavy sacrifice, but, even more, of the ability to maintain unity before the danger of war, and in the actual crisis of war itself. The contrast between the Russian defence of its achievements and that of France is remarkable; but not less remarkable is the relation between the Russian masses and their dictator, on the one hand, and the German masses and their dictator, on the other.

I have already sought to interpret the meaning of the Russian Revolution. Here, it is sufficient to emphasize that it was capable, when challenged, of alliance with the democracies and of evoking the confidence that, with the emergence of international security, its dictatorial character was a passing phase in its evolution. It was able, moreover, to speak in accents both to its own people and to the masses beyond its own territory, to which there was a response as spontaneous as it was heroic. It is significant that the German dictatorship, for survival merely, was compelled to seek the subjugation of the world. To attempt this subjugation, it was driven to an anti-rationalism of outlook which meant its deliberate and decisive rejection of the principles and habits of conduct which, until its advent, seemed the settled tradition of Western civilization. It lived by terror; to all but its own people it offered no prospect but of permanent slavery; even to its own people it dared not offer the prospect of internal freedom. That was because it was built upon the denial of the inherent dignity of human personality, the principle upon which the spiritual progress of Western civilization has depended. It is significant that the Russian Revolution has been built upon the acceptance of this principle. It is significant, also, that wherever a nation has come to terms with Hitlerite

Germany the denial of this principle has become, however unwillingly, a central part of its policy.

The reason, I suggest, for this contrast is, in essence, that Hitlerism is the apotheosis of the counter-revolution. Its purpose is to preserve a system of productive relations now inconsistent with increasing material welfare; it is therefore compelled to find means of satisfying its people by the loot it can extract from other peoples. It has therefore to adjust the values of society to that outlook; that is the penalty any system must pay which refuses to transcend its inherent contradictions. But it is important to emphasize that it is a penalty we ourselves must pay unless we embark upon the task Germany has, under Hitler, refused to attempt. The values of a civilization are always set by the proportion between its productive forces and its productive relations. Decay sets in when the barriers of interest prevent the maintenance of that proportion. Decay means the death of hope; and, where hope dies, the power of man to fulfil himself dies also. He ceases to feel that he is himself an end; he becomes an instrument, in the end a blind instrument, of purposes by which he is frustrated because he is not permitted to examine them. Since progress is a function of free examination what I have called the Hitlerite counter-revolution is, directly and, indeed, by self-avowal, the enemy of progress.

This view is not inconsistent with the immense power that Germany is to-day enabled to deploy in the field; that merely registers the fact that its rulers dispose of the accumulated stock of common scientific achievement. The problem before Germany is not of its level of knowledge and power of organization to-day, but of what that level and power would be after a generation of Hitlerism. We have some sense of their prospects if we compare the Spain of modern times, whether in terms of material welfare or of intellectual achievement, with Britain, or France, or pre-war Germany. There, after a great epoch in the sixteenth century, the obsolescence of its productive relations meant a material poverty incompatible with intellectual or spiritual advance; unless, indeed, we equate spiritual advance with the ceaseless repetition of historic formulae which had ceased to have intelligible content for the overwhelming majority of those who uttered them. It is hardly accident that every great name in Spanish history since the French Revolution is that of an opponent of the traditional régime. Were Hitler to be victorious, the same result would be true of German history within a generation. No more than in the Roman empire, can we make a desert of the mind and call it peace.

It therefore follows that to maintain the values of our civilization as living principles of belief and action we have to create the environment in which it is recognized by those with the power to decide that it is socially beneficent for them to function. That does not mean an attempt to unsecularize modern society; that has not been open to us since the scientific revolution of the seventeenth century. And it means more than the overthrow of Hitlerism, though that overthrow is a vital incident in the process such recognition requires. Put simply, the revival of faith in values among men means the creation of the conditions of expanding welfare. It means releasing the productive forces of society from the shackles by which they are now impeded. It means the deliberate adoption of an economics of abundance instead of an economics of restriction. The disease of the world is not merely the poverty of the world; far more, it is the frustration that poverty imposes upon millions who feel that it is unjust because it is unnecessary, to whom the irrationality of our present order so often betrays, as the masses in Italy and Germany were betrayed, into disrespect for reason itself. We have reached one of those periods in social evolution when the traditions of the past are in conflict with the rights of the future. So that even if we assume a military victory over Hitlerism, there still remains the deeper issue of a victory over ourselves. The gravest danger we face is that we shall assume the easier triumph to be the vital battle. In truth, it is already the deeper issue which should be our concern.

For that issue has not been born with the crisis that Hitlerism symbolizes; it has been slowly forcing its way to decision ever since the breakdown of feudal civilization. Something of its claims we can see as early as the sixteenth centruy in the *Utopia* of More, the Peasants' Revolt in Germany, the sermons of Latimer, the angry protests of Crowley and of Lever. The issue is whether, as Tocqueville put it, we are willing to effect the popularization of liberty. By the French Revolution we had given it concrete meaning for those who owned the instruments of production and to such of their dependents as it paid those owners to keep on their side; to the masses we offered a minor share in the vast horizon of expanding welfare opened by the release of those productive forces which the collapse of feudalism permitted. We offered them, too, a consolation, not seldom noble in expression and often more spiritually real, of faith in another world where eternal salvation would redress the sufferings of this earthly life; no one can read the *Diary* of George Fox or Bunyan's *Grace Abounding* without the perception that their confidence in those "trumpets that would sound for them on the other side" gave them an inner wealth of happiness attained by but few of those whose centre of gravity is in this world.

But the right, even the custom, of regarding this world as but a temporary vale of tears is a consolation which decreasingly carries conviction; and none of those who seek its revival can do more than proclaim the renaissance that would follow this revival without being able to give us the formulae upon which it depends. Whether the value of a revolutionary Christianity is preached, whether we are urged to take refuge in the ecstasies of a private mysticism—itself the expression of an individual escape from the responsibilities of social life—the fact remains that no values, Christian or other, can secure serious acceptance in a secularized society like ours without either being accepted by the state or capturing it. Either achievement means the renewal of hope among the masses; and the renewal of hope is dependent upon the popularization of liberty.

That has been seen time and again since liberty was set, with the sixteenth century, in the context of individual ownership. We can see it in the passionate debates of the Army Council under Cromwell, in the angry assertiveness of John Lilburne, in the noble, if premature, insights of Gerard Winstanley. It is expressed again in the French Revolution by the *Enragés*, and by those who, with Babeuf, made the last despairing effort to recapture the fraternity for which men hoped in the great days of 1789 when those "petty lawyers and stewards of manors" whom Burke regarded with such contempt, legislated a new world into being. We catch again the same accent in the spacious dreams of 1848 and, above all, in that supreme optimism which enabled Marx and Engels, in a hundred pages, to trace the whole pattern, past and future, of human evolution. It is present, again, in that sudden sense of emancipation felt by the whole world when the Russian people struck off the chains of Czarist despotism. There was a hint of it in the enthusiasm which created the League of Nations in 1919; we must never forget what was symbolized in the triumphant reception of Woodrow Wilson by the masses of Europe. I think it is true to say that when, after Dunkirk, the British people held, when, once more, in June, 1941, the Russian people withstood the assault of Hitlerism, the idea that freedom might assume a wider context began to take a new hold upon the minds of men.

IV

To grasp the meaning of that wider context we must note what has been denied in the society to which it seeks admission. The great cultural heritage of our society has been the possession of the few; even the bare literacy it demands for its understanding has been withheld from them. And that denial, we must note, has been in no small degree a conscious one; to withhold popular access to knowledge has always been one of the main instruments of unjust power. We can see in the development of educational opportunity in the United States and in the Soviet Union how largely the conquest of illiteracy is a matter of deliberate will; and we are entitled to conclude that where, to-day, that development is not organized it is because those who refuse to attempt it have vested interests enlightenment would weaken.

Only less significant are the material inequalities we permit, the difference in the health, the housing, the nutrition, the power to travel, of the rich and the poor. A society is intelligible enough which makes some differentiation in reward in terms of the social functions its members perform; in any ethical terms, it is difficult to regard a society as rational in which the response to want is proportionate to skill in the exploitation of an acquisitive impulse unrelated to social need. The adulation which is heaped upon wealth, the incredible elements which go to the making of social prestige, the transformation of charity into an organized profession, the relation of what Veblen called "conspicuous waste," to esteem, the fact that a "great Churchman" means, not a great Christian, but an important ecclesiastic, the persistence of the belief that the manual vocations are, in some mysterious way, less dignified than the clerical, all these indicate, in their different ways, a society which is sick at its foundations. And, in essence, its sickness is the outcome of the knowledge that it can no longer impose its values without challenge. Its wealth may continue to breed arrogance; the vital fact, of which it has to take increasing account, is that the association of its values with insecurity begets not servility but revolt in the masses. It is called to that supreme accounting which all civilizations face when the masses appear as the plaintiff at the bar of history.

At the moment of such an accounting the only way out for privilege is either to fight or to come to terms. If it chooses conflict, the experience, so magistrally different yet so decisive, of Russia and of Germany, makes it evident that, whatever the result of the conflict, it annihilates for a long period to come the prospect of democracy and freedom. If it comes to terms, it has the chance to find time for adjustment, the opportunity, that is, to experiment with the conditions which make possible the resumption of expanding welfare. Those conditions may be summarized by saying that they require us to put the idea of freedom in the context of equality. Instead of thinking of them, as in the past we have done, as antithetic terms, we have to discover how their implications may interpenetrate one another. For it is the characteristic of those who are free in an epoch of economic contraction that their freedom should appear the price of other men's misfortune. In some degree, indeed, it is the price; for it is the pitiful condition of the rich, in an age like our own, that even their generosity cannot ease, in any radical way, the frustrations from which men suffer. The scale of the issue before us means that we must dig into the foundations; it is the vast impersonal forces of history that we have to reshape.

This means the recognition, in the domestic sphere, that there are certain sources of power too vital to trust to private hands. It means the understanding that there are certain standards of living the maintenance of which is a charge the society must meet before the validity of difference in the return to effort can be admitted as rationally valid. It means that the frustrations to personal advance are banished which result from creed or wealth, race or colour. It means a society the members of which never live so differently that they are compelled to think differently too. The insight Plato had when, in the *Laws*, he insisted upon an upper limit to wealth appears the more wise the fuller the thought we give to its historical implications. For any society in which the few are so wealthy and the many so poor that their minds are driven to perpetual consideration of their wealth and poverty is, in fact, a society at war, whether the fight be open or concealed. It is a society, once its power to expand is arrested, which cannot think in terms of a common interest because whatever is taken from one class is given thereby to another. It cannot be a free society because its internal strains deprive it of security; it is therefore fearful and deprived of the climate in which the power to reason is assured. Every experiment it is urged to make is hampered by the conviction that it marks the beginning of a process of which disaster is the inevitable end. Needing great changes, even, on occasion, aware of the great changes it needs, it stands drifting helplessly before their necessity. It is in the presence of a challenge it does not have the courage to meet. Historically, a society which evades this kind of challenge is predestined to decay. For men go forward only when they are prepared to pay the price of progress.

It is necessary to be clear about the meaning of that equality in whose context I am arguing that liberty must be set. Equality does not mean identity; there is no more reason to ask for the same treatment of different people than to ask for the same clothes for men of different stature or the same food for men of different tastes. But it does mean that there is an equal right to the satisfaction of equal needs, and that no special privilege in any one citizen shall abridge the right of another to that satisfaction. It means the admission of a plane of general satisfactions in social organization where the minimum satisfaction of equal needs is at a level which permits the increasing fulfilment of personality. It argues that where unequal rights are bestowed their consequence tends always to sacrifice those who do not share in their bestowal to those who do share in them, whatever be the ground upon which the inequality is maintained. It sees in this inequality the source which has restricted freedom in the past to those whose special claim has been admitted; and it denies, therefore, that any principle or institution can be valid which is the basis of this special claim. Since, in our epoch, the main source of such special claims lies in the private ownership and control of the instruments of production, to set liberty in the context of equality means the social ownership and control of those instruments.

For whatever in a society destroys the unity of interest between citizens in the results of the process of government is bound in the long run to produce hatred and tyranny, is bound, that is, to destroy democracy and freedom. Our experience has made it clear that the present relations of production have this result. They prevent our power to plan for plenty because they assume that the satisfaction of the acquisitive impulse in individuals will result in a well-ordered society. We have learned that this is not the case. We have learned that, on the contrary, the creation of these private economic empires in any realm where the commodity to be produced is essential to public well-being frustrates the purpose of the commonwealth. Whether it be banking or transport, coal or oil, land or electric power, private ownership means vested interest, and vested interest means that the needs of the community are in pawn to the wants of the few.

"Mankind," said John Taylor, "may be governed by money or by arms." We prevented the anarchy which resulted from the power of the feudal lord to hold men to ransom by his ownership and control of private armies. We have to prevent the anarchy which results from the power of the banker or the coalowner, the oil magnate or the steel baron, to hold men to ransom by his ownership and control of economic power. For so long as each of these has an interest in its functioning which is separate from that of the community, it is bound to subdue the authority of the state to its purpose; in a fundamental sense, indeed, economic power determines the real complexion of the state. For the likeness between the economic oligarchy of our own day and the feudal aristocracy of an earlier period is unmistakable. The ownership of the instruments of production is the basis of power in the one, land is its basis in the other. And in each case the character of the social legislation which distinguishes the system is that it is subordinated to the privileges of the ruling class. Law must operate within boundaries that are satisfactory to those interests. They are, historically, overpassed only when some great convulsion reveals the antagonism between the privilege of the ruling class and the well-being of the many. For, in essence, private ownership means that distribution is governed neither by need nor by effort, but by the compulsive artifice of law. At some point, the contradiction between the artifice and potential production becomes obvious to those whom it has excluded from benefit, and they move to its re-definition.

That contradiction, I suggest, has become clear to this generation. Having seen that war secures full employment, that it suspends some part, at any rate, of the authority of the profit-making motive; that it compels the government to organize the scientific talent at its disposal; that it limits the right of wealth to command persons; that it secures the acceptance of taxation upon a hitherto unimagined scale; that it destroys the classic legend that a country is ruined which fails to balance its budget; that, to put it briefly, what I have called those compulsive artifices of law which capitalism has historically exacted must, in considerable degree, be suspended; having seen this, not once, but twice, in twenty-five years, it is at least reasonable to suppose that the masses still expect the application of some part of the lessons of war to the economy of peace. The alternative is an economic misery so wide and so profound that its implication is quite obviously social disaster. Either we deliberately reconstruct our foundations, or we drift rapidly to one of those crises where, because men no longer have the great ends of life in common, there is no alternative but to fight our way to a new scheme of relationships.

For consider the indictment the ordinary worker can draw up against the ruling class of this country. It emerged from the victory of 1918 with an authority and a prestige that no other class has commanded in history. It refused to allow any vital change to be made in the economic system. It sabotaged, in the League of Nations, the one hopeful experiment of the post-war years. With massive evidence at its disposal of the evils of economic nationalism, it embarked on Protection and a closed imperial system. Its hatred of Russia was so profound that it permitted Italy and Germany to run amok in Europe, even adding, by its policy, to the power these could deploy against it. Warned of the implications of German and Italian policy, it was lacking even in the courage to tell its own citizens of the dangers it confronted; the responsibilities of leadership "sealed its lips" against that first obligation of a ruling class, the duty to face the facts. Even when it awoke from its somnolence, it was unable to realize either the scale or the intensity of total war. Not until the very threshold of disaster did it take the people into partnership; and even while it insisted that total war was a revolution in which all citizens must hazard their persons and their property, the overwhelming incidence of its programme was to preserve unchanged the form of its title to power that its full authority might be resumed with victory. It spoke eloquently of equality of sacrifice. But, apart from those who fought in the armed forces— that equality was strictly proportioned to the normal functioning of the property-relation. The main burden of evacuation fell upon the poor; the main educational sacrifices fell upon the children of the poor; in, at any rate, the first two years of war the shortage of food-supplies did not seriously affect the well-to-do; and the main impact of aerial bombardment was far more acute among the poor than among the rich. The latter did not sleep for long months in succession in the tubes and public shelters. They did not participate in the grim nightly trek from Hull and Merseyside to what protection a clump of trees on a country hillside might offer.

I do not for one moment deny that no statesman has ever more fully embodied the will to victory of a united people than Mr. Winston Churchill, or, indeed, more splendidly embodied it. But it is important to remember, first, that the ruling class for eight years rejected with contempt Mr. Churchill's diagnosis of its mistakes and turned to him only when the twelfth hour had almost struck; and it is important, also to remember, that in its acceptance of his leadership was the implied condition that the foundations of capitalist democracy should not be disturbed. He was permitted to put plasters on open wounds—the raising of dependents' allowances in the armed forces, the increase of the old age pension, the advance of agricultural wages, and so on. I do not belittle for one moment the benefits these conferred; I am bound to remark that they left untouched all the vital questions of the relations of production.

And if it be said that this policy was accepted by the leaders of the trade unions and the Labour Party, I am bound, again, to remark that they could not challenge it without risking a breach of that national unity which, as the tragic experience of France had so disastrously shown, was a fundamental condition of victory. The working-class parties were in the dilemma that they must either accept what Mr. Churchill's supporters were prepared to concede or court defeat; and they knew that, with defeat by Hitler, there was no future for the working-class of Britain with which they would need to concern themselves.

That is, I think, the indictment of the ruling class of Britain which is being made to-day by most politically minded workers in Britain. It is true, of course, that most British workers are not politically minded. The things that mainly move them are matters of private, and not public, concern. They have made up their minds to win this war, and there is no sacrifice they will not make to this end. But, in any society, the politically minded are always a minority; their influence depends upon the existence of the conditions which enable them to swing mass-opinion to their side. My point is the very simple one that we shall create the conditions under which the indictment I have described will make a mass-appeal unless we take steps now to prevent their emergence. Without those steps, there will be millions of unemployed, new distressed areas where the vast war-factories have proliferated, sullen anger growing into riots over the problems of demobilization and rehousing. And if we fail to take those steps, our absorption in domestic difficulties will mean a European continent devoid of the leadership essential for its ordered reconstruction. They may mean years of anarchy and chaos, tempered every so often by revolution and counter-revolution. And those years, were that to be their character, would destroy any prospect of recovery in an industrial nation so largely dependent upon the volume of the export trade as ourselves.

If we fail to take those steps; that is the major premiss of this possible future. But it is still possible for us to take them. The public opinion of this country is ready for fundamental change. Its traditional habits have been profoundly disturbed. It is aware that it has lost the security of its insular position. It is aware, too, that it depends for its future upon the maintenance of a peace which it cannot defend alone. Its rulers, however cautiously, have admitted by acceptance of the Atlantic Charter that freedom from want and freedom from fear are the twin pillars of any ordered world. It is beginning to see that the full mobilization of its resources is not available by the dramatic evocation of sudden spurts of energy under the pressure of some sudden crisis, but is a matter of steady and persistent organization which is prepared to transcend both the principles and the pace with which the old order was satisfied. It sees that the full potentialities of our transport system cannot be realized if half a hundred vested interests have to consider not only victory to-day but the interests of their shareholders after victory. What is true of transport is true of every essential element in our resources. Not least is it obvious that, were the war-time controls, especially in finance, to be relaxed after the war, economic disaster would press hard upon the heels of military victory. And there is a wide understanding that, were this to occur, there would be no prospect of social peace in Britain.

To two other things I must draw attention. I have emphasized the failure of the ruling class in this country before the problems of the inter-war years, their immense opportunity in 1918, and the way in which they failed to take advantage of it. The sense of that failure is not confined to the working-class. Something, at least, of its implications has permeated the whole community. That, I think, is the significance of the impression made by Mr. Priestley's early broadcasts upon public opinion; his plea for a wider democracy found a responsive echo in minds far beyond the working-class, driven by the war to a realization that the old routine of thought would no longer do. That is, at least in part, the explanation of the swift hold upon opinion won by Mr. Winant and Mr. Harry Hopkins; they embodied not only the heartening reality of American aid, but, hardly less, of American will to large-scale social experiment. Nor must we omit the achievement of a new level of civic status by the trade unions; the contrast between their position under Mr. Chamberlain and under Mr. Churchill is marked indeed. It is not, I think, an exaggeration to say that, at the least, the mould of traditional thought in Britain has been broken. The fact that men of science have begun to grasp the fact that their laboratories are not ivory towers where they pursue some imaginary abstraction called objective truth, but fortresses which hold or are broken in the degree that there is a social context to their effort is a portent of the first magnitude. The work of men like Sir John Orr in the field of nutrition, of Stapledon and Russell in agriculture, the possibilities of the new discoveries in the field of plastics, these, to take three examples only, suggest that the scientist of our own generation will begin to claim that social and political policy must not frustrate the contribution he can make to the quality of our living. And he will begin to affirm, he has, indeed, already begun to affirm, that his contribution implies a social order in which the present relations of production are radically changed.

The second element of importance, the emergence of Russia as the ally of Britain, I have already emphasized. Its significance, I think, lies in three things. It has bound the prospect of a British victory to that of the Soviet Union; thereby it has made Moscow, inescapably, a fundamental factor in the peace. Since Moscow stands for the idea of planned production for community consumption, since, further, its recovery from the sacrifices of war will lead it to plan on a larger and even more intense scale, the Anglo-Russian partnership will set a perspective to our own tempo of reconstruction to the importance of which no limits can be set. No one, secondly, can fail to see that the idealism of the war effort in this country has, at any rate so far as the workers are concerned, reached a new level because we are in association with Moscow; the hopes of the workers in the original Revolution have revived in a remarkable way. I do not, of course, deny that the revival of these hopes has aroused suspicion among the votaries of the established order; the Moore-Brabazon incident is not without its significance. But it is not, either, without its significance that not even the Churchill government could stand a succession of such incidents; only Mr. Churchill's supreme prestige could have saved a Minister in Colonel Moore-Brabazon's position. And the third point of importance in the emergence of Russia is the large probability that, given the defeat of Hitlerism, the social initiative in France and South-Eastern Europe, perhaps also in Germany and Italy too, will pass rapidly to the extreme left. No stable governments are likely to emerge there save on the basis of the pretty complete destruction of the existing class-relations in those countries. I do not think, given these horizons, that public opinion in Britain is likely to be satisfied unless its rulers embark upon large-scale social experiments. I do not believe they can embark upon these experiments without a vital change in the productive relations of our society.

There is, indeed, another possibility to which, if regretfully, I must draw attention. The defeat of Hitler will, especially if the war be prolonged, leave the United States in a real sense the predominant economic power in the world, especially since her entrance as a combatant has been made necessary. It is possible, given the parallelogram of economic forces in the United States, that her post-war influence will be reactionary rather than progressive. Most American business men, the more fully the more powerful they are, passionately hate the New Deal; they look upon social reform as the antithesis of economic recovery. Mr. Roosevelt ceases to be President in 1944; there are circumstances at least conceivable in which his successor is, like Harding and Coolidge, essentially the representative of the big economic interests in America. And it is then at least possible that the terms on which such an America will aid in rapid European recovery—and such aid will be essential—will be terms which seek to preserve productive relations in Europe compatible with that *laissez-faire* capitalism equated by men like Mr. Joseph P. Kennedy with democracy. Certainly the influence of the United States in the post-war settlement will be overwhelming; and it is too early to predict in what direction it will be exercised.

There is little difficulty in making the prediction in either of two situations. If Hitler is defeated during 1943, all the power and prestige of President Roosevelt will, none can doubt, be directed towards making secure the foundations of a liberal democracy throughout the world. If, again, in the period before the end of the war Britain embarks upon profound social experiments, their repercussion in the United States is likely to exclude a reactionary candidate from the White House even when President Roosevelt's third term is over. In the first situation, American commitments, by 1946, are likely to assure Europe that the influence of the United States will continue to be at once liberal and internationally minded. In the second situation, the same result will follow because our action would galvanize into new authority those forces in the United States upon which the prestige of the New Deal depends. There is a real sense in which its fortunes are interwoven with the principles by which we shape our own future.

From this angle, I suggest, the fate of Europe, in either of these situations, depends upon the survival of New Deal America in power. And, again from this angle, this survival implies once more that now is the appropriate moment to begin the process of fundamental change in Britain. For nothing would be more helpful to our future than a victory won while President Roosevelt is in the White House; and there is no bigger step to that victory than the intensification of our productive effort. But, if we are to intensify it, a change in productive relations is the highroad to that goal. Without it, we shall lack that steady and persistent stroke which it is beyond the power of any vested interest to arrest. If the gap between German power and our own cannot be bridged within such a period, the present time still remains the appropriate moment to embark upon the task of fundamental transformation. For it will present America with the momentous spectacle of a capitalist democracy able, by consent, to create the conditions in which the resumption of expanding welfare is possible. It is difficult to exaggerate the psychological results this would have in the United States. It would create there a demand for parallel experiment of unbreakable power. It would arrest the danger—omnipresent in the United States in existing conditions—that big business will use the war-emergency to stifle the struggle of the New Deal to continue. It would put behind the Anglo-Russian effort all the power and energy of the organized American workers; and it would destroy the propagandist value of the Nazi legend of a British plutocracy masking its true image behind democratic forms. The effect, I think, of such a policy on our part would be to give to the friends of democracy in the United States that fresh lease of power upon which so much of the European future depends.

For it must be clearly understood that while the sentiment of America overwhelmingly favours the defeat of Hitler, the relation of American to European interests is still an issue of doubt and complexity. Much of it depends upon the date of the war's ending; much of it depends, also, upon how deeply, when it ends, the United States are involved in the actual conflict. The longer the struggle persists, the more likely, on the mounting evidence we have, is American big business to exact a high price for the extension of its aid; and the signs multiply that it would use the opportunity of a "shooting war" to repair the losses it has suffered in the period of Mr. Roosevelt's first two terms. It is of considerable importance that the outlook of men like ex-Ambassador Kennedy should be so widespread among the industrial oligarchs of America; and it is important, also, that, from very different motives, the youth of America should have been for so long profoundly averse from any participation in the war. The isolationist temper in America is basically far more profound than a superficial view or propaganda cares to admit.

There are, of course, many reasons why this should be the case. About some of them, the attitude, for example, of American Italians and American Germans to their homeland we can do comparatively little; and the anxiety of those who share Mr. Kennedy's view for a peace of accommodation is only likely to disappear if and when the war beats directly upon the shores of America; until that moment, the temper of "appeasement" is as natural to them as it was to similar interests in Britain until its futility was finally demonstrated by the seizure of Prague in March 1939. What we can do is to influence those sectors of American opinion which are capable by their character of response to a great idea. We shall evoke that response not by the rhetoric of promises of future behaviour but by the actual fulfilment of those promises we undertake now. That is the only real way to appeal to the idealism of American youth; there is no other method by which to free it from the massive heritage of disillusion the last war bequeathed. That is the only real way, also, to appeal to that sector of American opinion which, in Mr. Roosevelt's years of office, has been seeking with all its power to strengthen the foundations of American democracy and has recognized in the four freedoms the sole pathway to that goal. Unless we can win these elements in American opinion to our side we may well find, at victory's end, that we have brought into being a climate of American opinion more disillusioned about its relationship to Europe than the climate created by its last experience of war. I do not need to emphasize the magnitude of such a disaster.

V

All this is to say two things. We cannot, in any ultimate sense, win this war unless we make the idea of a more just society a part of the actual policy by which it is won; and we cannot build a more just society now unless the forces of privilege are willing to co-operate in that task. I do not venture to predict whether such co-operation is possible. I admit fully that it is one of the rarest phenomena of history; and I admit, also, that little has occurred, even since the fall of France to indicate that the ruling class of Britain has recognized the implications of our position. The legislation of the Churchill government has touched no vital spot in the productive relations of our society. No plans for the reconstruction of Britain have been announced by it in which one can trace audacity or courage. In education, in public health, in housing, one sees that old manœuvring for position on the part of the vested interests so typical of experience in 1918–1919. The workers, as in the last war, are asked to contribute the sacrifices; and privilege, as is its wont, is gracious enough to patronize those who, uncomplainingly, bear the burden they impose.

I do not mean for one moment that the ruling class of Great Britain shrinks from its full part in the military obligations of the war; the record of the Royal Air Force alone is eternal testimony to its courage. I mean rather that it cannot conceive of a world in which the title to rule is not naturally vested in that partnership of birth and wealtn which, ever since the Civil Wars of the seventeenth century, has possessed the power to shape British destiny. Its thought is so deeply embedded in the tradition of that power that it seems unable to conceive the need for new foundations. Even Mr. Churchill, in whom the nation's will to conquer has been so superbly embodied, cannot escape from the implications of that tradition. Like a new Marlborough, he "rides in the whirlwind and directs the storm." But he thinks of a great heritage preserved rather than of a new world conquered. He re-fights the ancient battle against the effort of the Grand Monarch to dominate Europe; he does not see in the struggle over which he presides new and immense possibilities which he can harness to the task he has set himself. He can be thrilled by the courage of the common man in Coventry or Merseyside, in the East End of London or the slums of Glasgow. His imagination is caught by the majestic spectacle of a people voluntarily organizing itself for civil defence. He can speak of the epic of the little ships at Dunkirk in phrases that Thucydides would not have disowned. He can be moved by the attack of Hitler against the Soviet Union to transcend all the emotions of his past. Yet he does not glimpse behind all these things the vast impersonal forces which have gone to shape them. He fights the war like a great aristocrat whose honour is involved in victory because the aristocrat accepts the challenge. He does not fight the war like a great statesman who sees beyond victory to the opportunities it might make.

I say this because, of all statesmen whose lives have lain in traditional Britain, none saw more clearly or more courageously in the pre-war years than Mr. Churchill did that Hitler meant war; and none drew more starkly than he the grim consequences which followed for Britain from Hitler's preparations for it. But it is obvious enough that Mr. Churchill has never understood either the economic forces of which Hitler was the representative nor the reasons why the main bulk of his party were "appeasers" until the eleventh hour. That is, I think, the proper inference from the fact that only after the entry of Italy into the war did Mr. Churchill understand that Mussolini represented the same configuration of forces as Hitler. He had grasped the fact, in 1933, that Hitler was a threat to British power; he was unmoved by the implications of Italian Fascism because, except as jackal to Hitler, Mussolini was never a danger to British authority. He wages the war, fearlessly and superbly, to preserve that authority. To maintain it, there is no effort he will spare, no sacrifice he is not prepared to make. The man who in one supreme gesture could offer union to France, who, in another, could wipe out the misunderstandings with Russia of a generation was not lacking in the traditional power of the aristocracy to suit the event to the occasion. I know how deep is the inspiration Mr. Churchill has given to free men not merely in Britain but all over the world. I yield to no one in my admiration of its quality.

Yet I suggest that Mr. Churchill is as blind to the real nature of this war as Burke was blind to the nature of the French Revolution. That is why he seeks to wage total war without adapting the framework of our productive relations to its consequences. That is why he can at once proclaim that we fight for democracy and freedom and leave unresolved the problem of our relations with India. That, also, is why he insists that he is concerned with the maintenance of "traditional" Britain, why, again, he has failed to understand what the amendment of the Trades Disputes Act of 1927—for which his own responsibility is so heavy—would mean to millions of workers. The premisses of Mr. Churchill's thinking are set by the old world that is dying, as Burke's were set in 1789; he is unable to see, as Burke was unable to see, the outlines of the new world that is struggling to be born.

And if Mr. Churchill, with his great gifts of heart and head, his courage in taking risks, his noble inability to accept defeat, thus looks to prescription for the sources of his insight, it is hardly surprising that those whom he leads should rarely see beyond his vision. Lord Halifax speaks in terms of that doctrine of Christian stewardship which the Church has preached for two thousand years without being able to apply it; the significance of a doctrine which has adjusted itself to slavery and feudalism and capitalism does not seem to dawn upon his mind. Mr. Eden renews the ideology of Tory democracy, much in the accents of the Disraeli who wrote *Sybil*; but he does not seem to infer from its postulates the continued existence of a privileged class which, historically, has only felt the claims of *noblesse oblige* when it felt it could afford them without undue sacrifice of what makes for the hold of privilege upon a class. Sir Kingsley Wood, so long and so persistently blind to the implications of Hitlerism, represents the orthodox outlook of the business man's conservatism; the bills must be met because bankruptcy is dishonourable and inflation dangerous; but there has been no word from Sir Kingsley Wood to suggest that we have reached an epoch where new economic and social conceptions are urgent.

The major party in the National Government, in a word, moves to a planned society without any serious effort to formulate to itself the nature or the possibilities of planning; it assumes that somehow, what Mr. Churchill has called a "few practical measures of reconstruction" will meet the case. Yet it is uneasily aware that it in fact faces implications of revolutionary magnitude even while it pursues the historic policy of "muddling through." It is, of course, the fact that it pursues this policy which leads the Communist Party to insist that a violent revolution is inescapable. Unless there is adjustment by consent resort to violence is written in the nature of the things we clearly confront.

The Communist prophecy may well be right; though upon it there are two things of importance to say. There is no reason, in the first place, to assume that the working-class would be successful in a violent revolution unless those conditions existed which made for success. I cannot easily conceive their existence here save after a long experience of tyrannical government; and, of that experience, there is so far no evident sign. The second reason goes to the root of the Communist philosophy of history. That philosophy omits to notice that the triumph of the bourgeoisie over the feudal aristocracy was not won until it had achieved predominant economic power in society and was able, by its experience and capacity, directly to charge itself with the governance of the state. It dominated the property-relations; it had transformed the cultural. It was not until both processes were complete that it was able to conclude the final step of capturing the state-power. The workers in Britain have accomplished neither of these things. Predominant economic power is still, overwhelmingly, in the hands of the middle class; and the culture of our society is only beginning to be affected by the change in the productive forces of our civilization. The danger we confront is that the example of the Soviet Union—an example still solitary in character—should lead to a premature adventurism which invites the suspension of the democratic process from motives similar to those which have led to its overthrow abroad.

I am not denying for one moment the urgency of a profound change in the productive relations of our society; on the contrary, I have argued that it is the necessary condition for the resumption of expanding welfare, the basis, therefore, upon which alone we are likely to maintain democratic government in Britain. But I am arguing, also, that unless this profound change is made with a sufficient volume of consent to make violent resistance seem an illegitimate gamble to the ruling class, it is likely, in our special circumstances, to be an illegitimate gamble on the part of the workers also. From this I draw two inferences. I draw the inference first that the mental climate of profound change is available to us only in the period when the gravity of danger breaks down, over wide areas of opinion, the normal inhibitions of privilege. I draw the inference, second, that if this opportunity, now available to us, is missed the working-class will only be in a position successfully to defend its right to embark upon such changes when it has become, by constitutional means the accepted government of the country.

I have already discussed the first of these inferences; I have explained why the Conservative Party—essentially the political instrument of economic and social privilege in Britain—is unlikely from its constitution to see far enough into the nature of things to abdicate from the possession of power. The second inference assumes that, at the close of this war, there are three possibilities before us. It is possible that the Conservative Party will retain office and approach the task of reconstruction in a spirit which denies the need for profound change. In that event, its inability to create the conditions of expanding welfare will be rapidly demonstrated. It will then either be compelled to give way to the Labour Party, or, in one form or another, to make an end of Parliamentary Democracy in this country. If it gives way to the Labour Party the latter would then have at least the opportunity of initiating fundamental change; and because, by hypothesis, public opinion would be on its side, it would embark upon its experiments in the favourable condition that its opponents were on the defensive and discredited. Or it is possible, in the second place, that the mood of the people at the end of the war will result in a direct victory for the Labour Party. In that event, once more, it will have a constitutional title to embark upon experiment, and the power of its opponents to resist, while far from broken, will be seriously weakened by the strategic position it will occupy.

Both of these possibilities depend, in the context of our power to maintain social peace, upon the quality of the intellectual and spiritual preparation of the Labour Party for its task. It will have to know with precision what it wants to do. It will have to be prepared to do it in a temper of courage and resolution. It will have to be built of the men and women fitted to be the instruments of these great ends. How far can we be sure that the necessary quality will be forthcoming?

It is a difficult question to answer. The achievements of the Labour movement of Great Britain are, on any showing, very great. To have built the co-operative societies and the trade unions in less than a century of effort is an achievement of a high order. In local government, not least in London, it has shown in the last generation a quality at least as great as that of either of its rivals. In certain aspects of its two periods as a government, above all in international affairs, it showed a grasp of realities which, had its term of office not been abruptly terminated in 1931, might well have saved Europe from the present conflict; and it is worth noting that, in the two crises of 1939 and 1940, it gave that lead to the nation upon which, as events have shown, its independence and safety hung. It commands a voluntary devotion and loyalty from its members which no other party in the country can rival.

All this is true, I think, and important on any balanced estimate. But it would be foolish to deny that there are grave weaknesses in the Labour Party which no honest observer can view without alarm. The road to authority in its ranks is hard and long; it tends therefore to be a party leadership in which belongs to men in late middle age when something, at any rate, of the energy and flexibility of mind has gone in all but extraordinary men. Great social changes are usually the work of a young government, especially in a revolutionary time. The weakness of the Labour Party in the years since 1919 has been its inability to adapt its forms to the claims of youth to representation. It has few young men among its members in the House of Commons; proportionately, it has still fewer among its adopted candidates. Its tendency is to regard the safe seat in the House as the proper reward of long trade union service; and not a few of its representatives in Parliament enter it at an age when there is little prospect of a creative political career. Nor can it hope like its rivals, to persuade its older members to retire to a dignified retreat; financial compulsion makes it necessary for most of them to go on until defeat or death. Anyone who knows at first hand something of the economic tragedy that resignation involves in most instances will realize the gravity of this problem. No party, to put it bluntly, can hope to govern this country after the war until it has made room in the House of Commons for a full representation of the generation which will have fought the war. The Labour Party has not yet shown signs of an ability to meet this problem.

This is, no doubt, a weakness that it is possible to correct by suitable procedural changes. But it is important to emphasize that the real need of the Labour Party lies in a different sphere. It requires to recover the faith and enthusiasm of its pioneers; it requires, also, the power to communicate them to an area of the population far wider than the ranks of the trade unions to whom it now predominantly appeals. It has got to make the man of science, the technician, the managerial class, recognize that the kind of society for which it stands offers them an opportunity, a power, and a security, which they cannot attain under the present order. It has got to win for a planned democracy groups that have so far largely failed to recognize its claims, groups, moreover, upon whose contribution the success of a planned democracy in large part depends.

To win those groups, as I think, there is need of something like a spiritual revolution in the Labour Party itself; and one of the gravest issues of this epoch is whether that revolution can be made in the time at our disposal. That spiritual revolution is not easy to define. It means the capacity to train leaders who are able to put the long-term view ahead of the short-term view, who can say with emphasis to their followers that a really adequate educational system is worth more in the end to the workers than half an hour off the day or an extra shilling on the daily wage. It means also the capacity to choose leaders who do not accept the bureaucrat's plea that this innovation is dangerous or that this vested interest is too powerful to offend. It means the willingness, in short, to train leaders who will have the courage to demand from the movement sacrifices of the scale that the building of a planned society will require And I do not think the Labour Party will have, at least in due proportion, leaders of this quality until the working-class movement has the knowledge which an understanding of the issues necessarily exacts from those who propose to embark upon great changes.

Here, as I think, is the grave danger implicit in the class-structure of British society. Its imperial and economic supremacy was for so long unchallenged that not since the seventeenth century has it given to intelligence that place in public affairs to which it is entitled. We are paying now a heavy price for that partnership of gentleman, lawyer and business man to whose hands, for two centuries and a half, our destiny has been confided. They built a dualistic Britain in which there was absent that full interpenetration of mind between classes which we now require. We had two systems of education; we had an army in which, as Mr. Lloyd George has told us, birth and deportment were more important than intelligence; we had a church in which "good form" was more important than either saintliness or learning; we had a diplomacy whose practitioners were hardly even aware of the existence of nine-tenths of the population in the states to which they were accredited. Until the end of the last war, a man had to leave the working-class in order to have an effective place in the government of the country. In the inter-war years it was what Mr. Justice Holmes called the "inarticulate major premiss" of the system that, if Labour was permitted to take office, its leaders should not act upon the postulates of action by the preaching of which they arrived at office. Even the leaders of the trade unions become, in considerable measure, members of the middle class in habit and in standard of life as they arrive at power; and their children become members of the class to which their parents have been promoted.

It is a system which has bred, in almost every walk of life, extraordinary individuals; and, until quite recently, it has had a sense of security which enabled it to display a gracious tolerance hardly known elsewhere. But it is not a system which has deliberately and consciously set itself the purpose of elevating the common man; that has been a casual by-product of its organization. Its cure for poverty has been charitable effort; its cure for ignorance has been an educational system which ended, for the great mass of the people, at the very point where knowledge begins to exercise its fascination. We have lived so long upon the accumulated results of our primacy that we adjust ourselves with difficulty to the idea that the canons of survival are no longer those by which our primacy was won. We have entered a period in which, whatever the value of the extraordinary individual, the future of our society depends upon our power and our willingness to organize the elevation of the common man, if we are to remain a democratic society.

This, it is worth remembering, is the warning that Matthew Arnold gave to the Victorian age; a warning that went in large part unheeded. For it is a fatal indictment of our rulers in the inter-war years that when our economic system bred millions of unemployed their zeal for the privileges they enjoyed should have failed to arouse in them any desire to scrutinize its foundations. A society cannot hope to endure when one-tenth of its adult workers are allowed over years to rot on the dole without creating a sense of personal responsibility in its rulers. A society cannot, either, hope to survive which does not attempt, as in the inter-war years we did not attempt, to make the relations of production proportionate to the forces of production. Nothing, so far, has been said by the representatives of the ruling class during the war which suggests that they see the need to make the attempt. The leaders of the Labour Party have proclaimed the need. But I do not think they will convince the mass of the nation of their own faith in their principles until they are insistent upon their application. One practical example is more exhilarating than a dozen eloquent manifestos.

We have got to build an equal society in the next generation or we must abandon the democratic experiment; that is the stark alternative before us. It is an immense experiment. It has never been successfully attempted even by peaceful means. Were we to embark upon it now there are two reasons why we could reasonably hope to carry it through. The first is the degree to which men's minds are attuned to the temper of innovation; the expectation of great changes is in the mental climate of this war. The second is the degree to which the awareness of our common danger makes for the acceptance of experiment which, three years ago, might well have broken the unity of the nation. Great leadership to-day could plan a revolution by consent it will not be open to us to-morrow to make.

That cannot be said too often, and it cannot be said too insistently. A total war which threatens the national existence calls either for great victories or great measures; no people, as the French example shows, survives a total war on a diet of great rhetoric merely. When we are in the presence of revolutionary forces whose impact touches the foundation of our national life we cannot ignore their existence; and it is the outstanding weakness of our present leadership that it seeks to ignore them. That is why, as I have said, the duty of the leaders of the Labour Party is to insist that the principles for which it stands should receive fulfilment to-day; left as half-promises for the aftermath of victory they will then merely tear asunder what to-day they could aspire to unite. For if it was clear that the revolution by consent was the price of victory, the nation would insist that the revolution be made. It is the supreme inheritance of its traditions that it contemplates no alternative to victory but annihilation.

But exactly as the appropriate moment is now, so, in all likelihood, we shall pay the penalty for allowing it to pass by. In all revolutions there comes a period of inertia when the fatigue of the effort compels a pause in the process of innovation. That period is bound to come with the cessation of hostilities. After a life on the heights the human constitution seems to demand tranquillity and relaxation. To insist, in the period of pause, that we gird up our loins for a new and difficult journey, above all for a journey into the unknown, is to ask the impossible; the great rebellion is followed by the Restoration. When hostilities against Nazism cease, men will want, more than anything, a routine of thought and habit which does not compel the painful adaptation of their minds to disturbing excitement. Thinking government is a specific for the extraordinary time. With normal relations restored thinking government always appears to the vested interests of a society a luxury it cannot afford.

My argument is therefore the obvious one that we must find the plane on which democracy can function after the war during its course, or we are unlikely to find it at all. That lesson seems to me the outstanding inference from the experience of the inter-war years; above all, it is the outstanding inference from the tragic experience of France. In the grim crucible of war, a nation can build that pattern of reform which makes possible recovery after the war; in peace it is compelled, as the New Deal has demonstrated so conclusively in America, to choose between recovery and reform. But we face the issue that recovery upon the basis of the productive relations of the pre-war epoch is no longer compatible with the resumption of expanding welfare. That was already clear before 1939. It explained the growing suspicion of the democratic principle among all those who found in its application a threat to the interests they believed to be jeopardized by that principle. A war for democracy which does not create the conditions in which the democratic principle is viable is no more likely to attain its purpose than was the war of 1914. No one who lived through the days of triumph after November 11, 1918, can doubt the will of men to "make the world safe for democracy." But the conditions of safety had not been created when men were ready to accept them; and a will that functions in the absence of the conditions required for its fulfilment is bound to remain a vain and empty thing. No talk of reconstruction after the war will give it assured foundations. Either we make the revolution during its course, or it will be forced upon us at its conclusion. But, in the latter event, democracy and freedom will be its first victims.

Chapter VI

THE INTERNATIONAL ASPECT

I

AT the end of the last war, hopes were high that the main problems of power-politics had at last been solved. Democratic government seemed everywhere triumphant; the establishment of the League of Nations seemed to provide machinery through which disarmament and the peaceful settlement of international disputes might be expected. The reaction against militarism was profound; and the anxiety of men to turn to tasks of creative reconstruction was one of the obvious features of the political landscape. Even to so cool and detached an observer as Field-Marshal Smuts it seemed clear that we had reached one of those epochs where "humanity had struck its tents and was on the march."

Within a decade of the Peace of Versailles the facts had made havoc of the dream. This was not, I think, because the treaty there made was inherently a bad one; most of its more obvious errors had, in any case, been corrected by 1929. It was rather that the statesmen who presided over it made, so to say, the wrong treaty. They were already confronted by the problems of the twentieth century; they solved the problems they inherited from the nineteenth, and trusted that the League of Nations would answer those with which they omitted to deal. What they forgot was, first, that they had failed to create the conditions under which the League could answer them, and, second, that their multiplication of sovereign states created, as it reaffirmed, a body of vested interests which would be bound, as they gathered momentum, to intensify the disproportion between the problems of the League and its power to solve them.

For the central issue which was already vital at Versailles was the breakdown of the productive relations of capitalist-society, if these were to be set within the framework of democratic institutions—and that breakdown was exacerbated by the American disillusion which resulted in its return to isolationism. The suspension of its welcome to immigrants from Europe, and its adoption of a high-tariff policy, in fact combined to shut off the safety-valve of an economically interdependent world. Once the first glow of post-war emotionalism had passed, it was obvious that the future meant either such an adjustment of productive relations as would enable democracy to survive, or, as the alternative, a struggle for survival between groups of nation-states which would, sooner or later, mean a second world-war.

And, on the international stage, this is the central theme of the inter-war years. It is a contrast between immense potential production and actual widespread poverty. It is a contrast between eager hopes and bitter frustrations. No reader of the literature of these years, above all of its economic literature, can fail to observe the width of the abyss which separated the expectations men had formed, and the capacity of statesmen, within the framework of existing productive relations, to satisfy them. The scene seemed set for an economics of abundance; the vested interests of the productive relations compelled an economics of scarcity. The victorious nations, within that framework, were above all anxious to maintain their inherited advantages; the defeated or disappointed nations were above all anxious to find ways of overcoming their inferior position. The productive relations created, as it were, an upper limit of possible adjustment which was completely inadequate to the problems set for the statesmen of the major powers.

Most of the diagnosis of the issue in these years, especially the academic diagnosis, was beside the point, because it assumed that, given good will, the problem set was soluble within the categories enforced by the existing productive relations. There were thinkers, like Professor Gilbert Murray, who argued that the main need was to abrogate sovereignty; an argument which assumed that the sovereignty of the state is like a tap which can be turned on or off at will, instead of seeing that the sovereignty of the state is an instrument for protecting a given system of productive relations, and that only a revolutionary change in these makes it politically possible to abrogate the sovereignty of the state. Others, like Professor Lionel Robbins, traced the *malaise* to the abandonment of *laissez-faire*, without, seemingly, perceiving that this abandonment had itself been the outcome of the experience of *laissez-faire* in action.

What became, above all, evident in the inter-war years was the dependence of democratic institutions upon an economics of expansion. Once that was unavailable, the contradiction between the implications of capitalism and the implications of democracy could not be overcome. Fear that the Russian experience might be repeated put the beneficiaries of capitalism everywhere on their guard; and where the tradition of democracy was weak, as in Italy and Germany, its overthrow was accomplished with relative ease. But because, as I have sought to show in an earlier chapter, its replacement by Fascism still left the major problems of a contracting capitalism unsolved, the makers of Fascist states were compelled to embark upon an imperialist policy as the price of their internal security. But this they could not do without a threat to their rivals. Mussolini, no doubt, was not powerful enough to challenge alone any of the major powers; he had to content himself with minor loot which whetted, without satisfying, the appetite of his people. Hitler had to spend the first five years of his authority in the concealment of his true purposes while he posed, in his anti-Bolshevist crusade, as the enemy of the enemy of all capitalist interests. He sprang only when he thought, not wholly without justice, that a lightning war would take him directly to his objective. If the West acquiesced in his assault upon Russia, he was the master of Europe, if not of the world. If the West resisted, his speedy triumph over its resistance would put him in a position where his power would be unbreakable.

Once the attack had been launched, the technological foundations of modern warfare made it rapidly assume the character of a world-struggle far more intense, and much wider in its implications, than the war of 1914–18. It has become certain that either Fascism must triumph completely or be defeated completely; between these alternatives there is no middle way. And if we assume the defeat of Fascism, the problem of international relationships at once presses itself upon us as, in substance, the problem left unsolved by the authors of the peace of Versailles—that of the productive relations of the modern world. For let us be clear that the destruction of Fascism does not of itself create the conditions in which democracy and freedom are safe; it merely creates the conditions in which, because their chief enemy is removed, their safety permits of being organized. It still leaves us with the issue of achieving that organization.

Nothing is more dangerous than to underestimate the difficulties of this organization. It is easy to draw up paper Utopias, Anglo-American Union, European Federation, a new League of Nations, and so forth. Our chief concern must be to remember that democracy and freedom flourish when economic systems expand, and not otherwise; and that within the productive relations of the existing order, the principles of no major nation-state, except those of the Soviet Union, permit this expansion. We must set this concern in the background of the realization that the productive capacity of the world, and especially of the United States, will have enormously increased by the end of the war, and that, if the principles of ownership and control remain unchanged, there will be no increase in the effective demand corresponding to that increase in productive capacity. The military defeat of the Fascist powers, this is to say, will leave us confronting, though far more intensely, all the problems that we confronted on November 11, 1918. Only by organizing the conditions in which an economics of expansion again becomes possible have we the hope of solving them.

That means, quite simply, raising the standard of life all over the world, and, particularly, in those areas, China, India, South-Eastern Europe, South America, where it is to-day pitifully low. The secret of peace is the enlargement of effective demand; without that achievement this war will have been fought in vain. But to enlarge it means a planned economy for the many; and a grim historic experience ought to convince us that this is not possible within the present relations of production. Unless, therefore, we can transcend them, the character of the post-war period already defines itself. A boom will be followed by a slump; there will be hurried attempts at some partial and fragmentary "New Deal" expenditure upon which will result in an upward turn of trade. We shall then be warned by business men of the danger of government intervention, and there will develop that clash between progressive governments and the interests of property which defines the age-long antagonism between recovery and reform. An intenser economic nationalism will again emerge while the specialists offer remedies which no government will have the courage, and few will have the power, to attempt. The institutions we shall have constructed to maintain peace will find their authority slowly eroded by their inability to deal with conditions outside their postulates of action. Among the masses there will develop an angry disillusion at the second frustration of the brave new world they were promised; and among the forces of privilege there will develop an angry fear at the inroads upon their privileges the expectations of the masses seem to threaten. To the masses the war for democracy and freedom will appear an empty sham; to the privileged, their expression of anger at the sham will seem a threat to law and order which promises only anarchy and confusion. Once again we shall find that we have not enough in common to decide our differences by consent. We shall move from an age of conflict between nations to an age of conflict between classes; and, where the forces of privilege find a new Hitler as their instrument, the success of counter-revolution in some major state will at least imply, and may well involve, the prospect of a new world-war.

This diagnosis may have more immediacy than we like to admit to ourselves. For, on the assumption of a victory for the United Nations in this war, there are no certain indications that the purposes they hold in common can be maintained. The hate and ruin the war will have imposed are bound to go deep; on no showing will it be easy to transmute them into constructive channels. The policing of Europe and Asia by the victors up to that stage where, in Germany, Italy and Japan, they have stable governments in being to which the normal tasks of statehood can be entrusted raises, at the very outset, an immense question: for what purpose are they to be policed? If, for example, the military defeat of Hitler is followed in Germany by a Communist revolution will its policies be accepted by the other United Nations, apart from Russia? And if the German example were to spread to France, for instance, and to Italy, what, again, would be their attitude? And is it likely that most of the provisional governments now in London can hope, if they return to their native lands, to attain serious relevance to the problems they will confront without undertaking large-scale economic changes which sweep out of existence the prescriptive privileges they now so predominantly express and by which, also, they are predominantly sustained?

We are in a realm, in fact, which goes far deeper than the questions of frontiers, armaments, and minorities by which we were obsessed in the inter-war years. We have got to learn to think of these matters as symptoms of deeper causes we have to tackle. It is the outstanding experience of the Soviet Union that the problem of nationalities is soluble on a plane of economic equality; where this is absent, a frontier is a threat and a minority an almost inevitable source of trouble. It is not enough for the United Nations to agree upon ends which, formally, announce that these issues have been met. It is the rhetoric merely of statesmanship to announce great ends without organizing the conditions which give realistic availability to those ends. These conditions, I suggest, are, overwhelmingly, a question of the relations of production in the post-war era; and upon the nature of those relations none of the United Nations, except Russia, is yet committed. Most of their governments, indeed, have shrunk from facing the question of their nature for fear of the decision's impact upon the unity of its people.

It is, I think, one of the clear lessons of the inter-war years that while the interest of a Communist state, like that of Russia, is peace, since peace is the condition of the success of its experiment, the interest of capitalist states is held to be threatened by its successful development. That is why, as I have already argued, even the statesmen of the capitalist democracies did not, in its early phases, at least, regard the anti-Bolshevik crusade of Hitler as unwelcome. A society of states can permit wide disparities of system in an age of economic expansion; in an age of economic contraction, like our own, a state which destroys privilege is bound to seem a challenge to states which maintain it. Not unless the conditions of expansion are renewed is there the likelihood that they can live together in peace. That is why any profound social revolution, being, in its nature, a doctrinal revolution, puts vested interests all over the world on the defensive. That was the effect of the French and Russian Revolutions; and it is not accident that, in 1848, all the forces of reaction in Europe combined to suppress the rising hopes of the third estate.

From this angle, I see no merit in international programmes of institutional change which do not deal, from the outset, with the relations of production in such a manner as to make possible renewed access to the economics of expansion. The protagonists of Anglo-American union, for example, would not, even if they achieved their aim, do more, granted the persistence of the present relations of production in both states, than strengthen the power of Anglo-American imperialism. It can doubtless be argued that this imperialism has been, on either side, less evil than the alternative imperialisms which are, or have been, its rivals; those of Spain, for example, or Japan, and quite certainly that Hitlerite imperialism with which Britain and America are now locked in deadly combat. An Anglo-American imperialism might be able, for a whole epoch, to keep the peace by the massive power its resources would make possible. But there is no reason to suppose that it would not face the historic dilemma of all imperialisms—either that, in a period of economic contraction, it lived by its power to exploit abroad, or was faced, at home, by the contradiction between capitalism and democracy. Once the productive potentialities of modern industry and agriculture imply an interconnected world-market, Anglo-American unity is, on a capitalist basis, unrelated to the problems of a creative peace.

Nor, as I think, are the proponents of a Federal Europe in better case. For, once more, if its productive relations remain upon the present basis, it confronts two difficulties that it is powerless to solve.

If it is built upon freedom of trade within the European unity so made, it is likely merely to stereotype the existing distribution of economic power within its area; and it becomes a potential threat to American markets in the Far East and South America. In so far as the threat is successful, it then prevents the full use by the United States of its power to produce; so far, it diminishes the power of the United States to increase the standard of life of its citizens. And the idea of a Federal Europe, again upon the present basis of productive relations, raises the problem, so acute between the North and South in the United States, of the free movement of capital within its area to obtain the advantage of cheap labour conditions. In the age of giant industry, the absence of uniform standards in the labour market creates problems of increasing complexity. Is there, for instance, to be compulsory trade unionism in the European mining industry? If not, is the reply of the British coal-owners to a strike of British miners for higher wages to be the introduction, say, of Polish miners into British mines? Is it likely that this could be attempted without violence? If it were successfully attempted would not its result be a general lowering of the miners' standard of life in Britain? Is not the probability, as a matter of psychological fact, that freedom of migration would have to be forbidden in the federation? Is the idea of a European federation real in which a prohibition has to be laid on the free movement of persons? And does not the corporate character of modern private enterprise, especially with its international ramifications, require the establishment of a uniform standard of labour conditions if we are to prevent the exploitation of the backward areas at the expense of the more advanced? Granted, in fact, the general character of the relations of production at the present time, a European federation might well have economic implications that were reactionary rather than progressive.

Nor is it easy to see that a reconstitution of the League of Nations would solve our problems, unless its basis were drastically revised. For the problem of keeping the peace—the main reason for the League's creation—is only in part a matter that depends upon the wills of men. For those wills, after all, are determined by the environment in which they have to function. If they relate to common interests, they can move on common lines; but if the interests are not held in common, the drive of each will becomes different in character. So much of our thought is the product of our situation, that a different situation begets a different pattern of thought, and this, in its turn, leads to purposes not less capable of dividing than of uniting. It is not merely a question, important though this is, of abolishing that rule of unanimity which, between 1919 and 1939, was so grave a hindrance to international legislation. Cosmopolitan law-making becomes a practicable proposition when either the states involved in the process have an approximately equal interest in its results, or are not powerful enough to risk a breach of the law. Where a state is convinced that some proposal is ruinous to its interests, if it is strong enough, it will fight rather than give way.

I do not think it is a sufficient answer to this view to say that, after the experience of this war, we shall organize collective security against aggression. In all probability we shall. But the real question turns upon the durability of the organization we build. Our interest must be not in the pattern of international institutions which within a brief time of victory, it is possible to get accepted; our interest must rather be in the pattern behind which there is likely to be an effective sanction say thirty years from now. Collective security can be organized on a durable foundation if the conditions exist which give the major states of the world a direct and equal interest in applying its authority against a possible or actual aggressor. But anyone who examines either the Sino-Japanese dispute, or the conquest of Abyssinia by Italy, will see that neither good will nor the necessary power is sufficient in the absence of an interest in the full application of the principle. All the smaller European powers disliked German aggression after 1933; but none of them was willing to risk its neutrality in the service of the only principle which could have made that neutrality have meaning.

It must, moreover, be understood that once we create a system of sanctions against the use of war as an instrument of state-policy, we are creating conditions which either stereotype the *status quo* of some given moment, or else compel the abrogation of the sovereignty of the state. The retention of sovereignty in the state stereotypes the *status quo* because no state is prepared peacefully to surrender some interest it deems vital; that is why it retains its character as sovereign. That is why, to take an obvious example, though Great Britain signed, in 1930, the Optional Clause of the Permanent International Court, it reserved from its application certain regions in which it regarded itself as having a special interest; which was, in fact, another way of saying that it would defend this interest by force unless a change in the *status quo* were made with its consent.

But we must be quite clear what is involved in the alternative conclusion that states will agree to the abrogation of their sovereignty.

For all effective purposes, this means the limitation of the power of the great states; the resources required by the technology and scale of modern warfare have already made sovereignty impossible for minor states. To speak of Denmark or of Portugal as sovereign states is to dwell in a purely formal realm. In the world of hard fact, it is, to-day, the United States, the Soviet Union, Great Britain, Germany and Japan that are truly sovereign; to-morrow, perhaps, China and India, and, it may be, France once more. But the essence of sovereignty is, as Bodin said, the power to give orders to all and to receive orders from none; in the international sphere, it is the power, if challenged, to impose its will by the sword. The sovereignty of any state is the supreme coercive power which its government operates against any rival contender for its possession, internal or external. But the character of a government, the ends, therefore, for which, if it can, it will exercise its supreme coercive power, are set by the parallelogram of forces in the society which it controls. The determining factor in that parallelogram is the relations of production in the society. To surrender sovereignty, therefore, is for any state to surrender the power its government exercises of maintaining any given relations of production within the society.

II

Here, as I think, is the real core of the international problem. Unless we learn to see that the political character of a given nation-state is the result of the experience embodied in its particular system of productive relations, that the forms always express the drive of the interests these relations involve, we cannot understand the questions we have to answer. Great Britain is a capitalist democracy because, in the three centuries since the Stuarts began to reign, that was the form of state which best suited the way in which our relations of production developed. The small oligarchy of property-owners, landed and industrial, which limited the power of the Crown in its own interest between 1642 and 1688, gave way to bourgeois democracy after 1832 because the emphasis of the Revolution Settlement no longer suited the requirements of the shape the relations of production had taken by that time. 1832, in substance, was a conquest of Britain by the industrial middle class with the support of the workers; but, once the conquest was, for practical purposes, complete, the industrial middle class joined hands with the landed, mainly aristocratic, Britain it had conquered to exercise the sovereignty of the state for their joint interest; the workers had to fight their way to each item of their share in the new dispensation, and it was only because the new character of the productive relations coincided with an epoch of immense economic expansion that their struggle did not assume, as the Chartist Movement shows it nearly did assume, a revolutionary character. So far, the delicate union which capitalist democracy represents has been successful in Britain because the immense accumulation of wealth achieved by the ruling class in the epoch of expansion enabled it, if with increasing difficulty, to satisfy the established expectations of the workers. The British problem is how to continue that process of satisfaction within the frame of capitalist democracy, as the standard of expectation increases and the period of expansion comes, as within the existing system of productive relations it has clearly come, to a decisive end.

It is worth comparing the British pattern with those of Germany, the United States, and Russia, in broad historical terms. In Germany there was not, as in Britain and France, a middle-class revolution which established a capitalist democracy; particularism prevented German unity until 1870 and the late development of industrialization made the attempt to democratize German institutions in 1848 abortive. When the revolution was effected, after the defeat of 1918, the pattern of the Weimar Republic was already obsolete. Partly, this was because its relations of production were already in contradiction with its forces of production; the epoch in which capitalist democracy could expand peacefully was already over; there was not the leeway, either in time or in accumulated wealth, for the ruling class of Germany to make the concessions to the workers which would satisfy them without a fatal injury to its position as a ruling class. When, to this, are added the grave psychological results of defeat, foreign control, and the destruction of the lower middle-class security by inflation, it was clear that there was no stability in Weimar. It had either to reinforce its democracy by transcending its capitalism; or it had to make its relations of production secure by safeguarding them against the implications of democracy. When it chose the latter, with the masses, perhaps, hardly aware of what had been chosen, it became the inevitable citadel of counter-revolution.

The American experience, though dramatically different in the rhetoric it has employed, is really a variant upon the experience of Great Britain. Its boundless extent and immense resources seemed to safeguard it, almost by nature, from the tragedies of a Europe racked by ancient national antagonisms and deep-class divisions. The United States began without the marks of a feudal inheritance and without the prejudice against social equality which is now part of the pathology of English life. It was able to offer opportunities upon a scale which must have made its horizons seem wider to more millions than have dared to scan them with hope until the outbreak of the Russian Revolution. No modern society, certainly, has been able to offer greater scope to talent, or a more certain refuge from oppression, than did the United States in the century and a half from the Declaration of Independence.

Yet, in essence, the outcome of American history is a capitalist democracy which faces the same problems as Great Britain, even if it has a greater leeway within which to solve them. That this might be the case was, indeed, foreseen with marvellous insight by Tocqueville just over a century ago. He prophesied that if there developed in America an excessive concentration of economic power in a few hands, so that, as he put it, between employers and workers there was a relation but not a partnership, that concentration would beget an industrial feudalism incompatible with democratic principles. While it is untrue to say that this industrial feudalism has arrived—had it done so President Roosevelt would not be in the White House—its arrival is at least threatened. American economic expansion, in the classic sense, is over; the relations of production deny the possibilities of the forces of production in the same way as in Great Britain. The standard of life of the masses does not satisfy their established expectations; the state is everywhere compelled, by the drive of political democracy, to intervene for its protection. But each phase of this intervention is fiercely resented and fiercely resisted by the privileged class; a positive state is denounced as "unamerican"; "true" democracy is equated with *laissez-faire* in every sphere where it seeks to aid the under-privileged. Meanwhile the power of American production increases without any parallel power, within the domestic market, to consume the commodities so made available. There develops the classic need to capture foreign markets to satisfy that profit-making motive which is the drive of capitalist production. But since America, like Europe, has, as the great depression after 1929 made obvious, entered upon the period of economic contraction, its democracy, in its present form, can only survive either by becoming imperialist or by transcending its capitalist relation. If the future of America were to lie in the first direction it could not surrender its sovereignty. For, if its will as a state could be bound by the wills of other states, it would be unable to develop an imperialism. That would force it to choose between capitalism and democracy; and, if it chose the first, America, like Hitlerite Germany, would be driven to aggressive war. That would, of course, involve the resumption of sovereignty by the American state; for a declaration of war is the supreme expression of sovereign power.

I am arguing that the sovereignty of these major states is necessary to the maintenance of the particular configuration of economic interests of which, in final analysis, it is the protective armament, I am suggesting that, historically, the logic of capitalism enables it, in its phase of expansion, to marry with political democracy because it has then the economic elbow-room necessary to satisfy the demand of the masses. But I am arguing, also, that, when the phase of contraction comes, capitalist democracy must, if it is to continue, become imperialist, that this means international tension and conflict, and that, therefore, the logic of its productive relations requires the retention of sovereignty. Since, further, in the epoch of contraction the sovereignty of the state is incompatible with international organization, it follows that the objectives of the United Nations in this war are, in their turn, incompatible with the maintenance of democracy on a capitalist foundation.

The modern history of Russia bears out this analysis. Under the corrupt and inefficient autocracy of the Czars, the backwardness of its economic development was obvious; but it could not create the conditions of economic progress without also creating conditions fatal to the vested interests of that autocracy. When Czarism broke down under the double strain of mismanagement and defeat the Russian bourgeoisie was neither numerous nor experienced enough to establish a capitalist democracy. The hesitations of those who seized power from the feeble hands of Nicholas were fatal to their retention of it. Lenin had the genius to see and the resolution to fulfil the immense possibilities of a combination of the peasantry and the urban proletariat against the indecisions of the Kerensky régime. He established a socialist state which, in its essentials, has been built upon the principle of planned production for community consumption. And, granted the immense resources of the Soviet Union, the absence of the vested claims on production there of a privileged class which builds by the profit-making motive, there is not, nor can there be, a contradiction in the Russian system between the relations of production and the forces of production. Russia, this is to say, does not need to confront the prospect of an epoch when, as with Germany to-day and, it may be, the United States to-morrow, the antithesis between capitalism and democracy means a domestic Fascism which is inherently compelled to foreign conquest. The Russian experiment has, if the United Nations are victorious, and if international security be available to it, all the promise and opportunity of the American age of expansion without the latent contradictions which brought that epoch to a close.

This is why, always granted external security, the Soviet Union does not need sovereignty in the sense in which Great Britain or Germany, the United States or Japan, requires it. In each of these states supreme coercive power is in the hands of a class which controls the government in the interest of its privileges. It cannot surrender its sovereignty without danger to those privileges. The whole shape of its life is geared to the pattern which that class believes to be the safeguard of those interests it regards as fundamental. Any attempt to change the pattern is resisted; the whole purpose of the law is to prevent that change. This is the fundamental fact we have to face when we strip off the massive rationalizations by which a ruling class persuades itself, and, perhaps almost as often, those over whom it rules, that the things it believes to be the safeguard of its privileges are part of the permanent order of nature. Each element in the foreign policy of the capitalist democracies touches the vital nerve-centre of some vested interest; an alteration, therefore, in a tariff-schedule may be the difference between life and death for that vested interest, and, if it be strong enough, it will mobilize all its power to prevent an alteration to its detriment, even if it be to the common interest that the alteration be made. So, to take the supreme instance of our time, in order to prevent the development of a synthetic oil industry outside of Germany and Italy, the Standard Oil Company of New Jersey, during the war itself, gave to the German chemical combine the secret formulae by which the cost of manufacturing synthetic rubber was halved while it denied the use of those formulae to the American and British governments. Standard Oil, indeed, was almost in alliance with interests with which the government of the United States was practically at war.

Sovereignty, in short, is the instrument through which the vested interests in any society wage what Mr. Brailsford has happily termed the war of steel and gold; and, under the cloak of government authority, they invoke the half-rational sentiment of nationalism to maintain their power abroad. In the sense in which there are vested interests in a capitalist society, there are no vested interests in the Soviet Union. There are inequalities, as I think grave inequalities, of reward; but those inequalities do not involve those relations of production which, as with ourselves, are helpless in foreign relations if they may be subjected to a rule of conduct to which they do not consent. The motive to aggression, except on grounds of external security, is ruled out by the nature of the Russian system; in any capitalist society, which has reached the period of contraction, every vested interest must be aggressive if it wishes to maintain its ground. The way to aggression lies through the exercise of sovereignty.

When, therefore, Professor Gilbert Murray calls sovereignty the flaw in the nineteenth-century system, he is right; but the flaw is not removed simply by declaring it abolished. For it reaches down so deep into the roots of capitalist society that, to abolish it effectively, requires a revolution in those relations of production upon which the political superstructure of a society depends. Men can settle their problems by discussion and consent when either they have an equal interest in whatever decision they make, or when they are certain that they will benefit by the result. But they cannot so settle their problems if, in a contracting economic universe the settlement in fact depends on the physical power of the parties. It is this kind of settlement that sovereignty is intended to maintain. It is, so to say, the right, ultimately, to impose its own terms by force if it cannot get them by agreement. It is the threat to use violence if argument is ineffective, in the belief that the violence used will secure the desired end.

It is no use saying that civilized peoples do not permit their governments to act in this way; a large part of history is the record of just such actions. It is the history of African colonization right down to our own day; it is the history of the treatment of Asia by Europe; "dollar diplomacy" in Central America has been marked by just the same features. Capitalist democracy, when it faces economic difficulties at home, is bound to play power-politics abroad on two conditions. It must have the strength to do so, in the first place; and it must have the skill so to play its cards that it does not outrage its domestic critics in the second. On these terms, its vested interests will attract to the exercise of sovereignty all the emotional drive that national feeling can provide. Few people now doubt that the South African war was waged on behalf of a shoddy group of financial adventurers; its wrongs were not righted until the great gesture of 1909. But, at the time, even Fabian socialists like Sidney Webb and Bernard Shaw drew the simple inference that right must be on the side of the big battalions. That the ethics of imperialism have more complex roots does not seem then to have occurred to them.

III

The organization of peace therefore presents us with problems the main emphasis of which is on the economic plane. Peace depends upon the resumption of the conditions of an economics of expansion. That economics is unavailable to us within the framework of the present relations of production. For these make it impossible to push up the volume of effective demand to fit the requirements of our capital structure. The root of economic crises lies in the conflict, which is permanent in any capitalist society, between productive power and consumptive power. Hence arises not only the perpetual tragedies of the trade cycle, but, in the long run, domestic revolution and foreign war. Given a mal-distribution of individual income within a community, and of productive resources in nation-states competing in the world-market, and there is no escape from the ultimate arrival of any capitalist system of production at an epoch of conflict because its contraction of available welfare is bound to breed war and revolution. This has become even more clear, since Marx's day, by the breakdown of the classic theory of an equilibrium supply price of capital. And even if it be true that no alternative theory has yet acquired the same status among economists—most of whom were, until the devastating incursion of Keynes, little more than the ingenious defenders of capitalist society—it is at least certain that within the historic framework of capitalism a stable and peaceful international society cannot be built.

It is, after all, of quite ultimate significance that only twice in our own lifetime have we known a period of full employment, and each was during the course of a world-war. Each was a period of planned production in which the full potentialities of our resources became available in the degree to which, if only for the sake of victory, we transcended the claims of vested interest. And in Britain during each of these periods, it was surely significant, also, that the health of the population was better, its general standards of nutrition more adequate, a larger proportion of its citizens, the armed forces apart, productively employed, than in peace-time. If it be granted, as practically everyone grants, that we shall not return, after the war, to a *laissez-faire* system, that planning, in some form has come to stay, the central question of the peace then becomes quite simply whether we are going to plan for the many or for the few.

The whole future of international organization turns upon our answer to this question. World-peace means widening everywhere the distribution of economic demand. So long as the Indian ryot and the Chinese coolie, the worker in the sulphur-mines of Sicily and the fellaheen of Egypt, are so poor and so ignorant as now, so long, also, as the extension of abundance is a threat to the owners and controllers of the instruments of production, peace is merely a period in which we prepare for new wars. Capitalism in contraction is bound by its nature to be imperialist and militarist, for it is driven to monopoly and thence to restriction. And this is true even if part of the profits of a restrictionist policy are shared, as in the United States and Britain they have been shared, with labour organizations powerful enough to exact concessions from their masters. In any case, this power does not last; for any nation which becomes imperialist and militarist will soon confront needs which drive it to Fascism, and the first steps of a Fascist state are the suppression of those labour organizations which seek to exact concessions from their masters.

To plan the expansion of effective demand is therefore the central issue we confront. In a sense, this planning has two sides, though in life itself they cannot be separated from each other. On the one hand, it means an internal change in the productive relations of each society; on the other, it means joint action by states to develop effective demand in the backward areas of the world. It is with this second aspect that we are here concerned. But we must note that, in any thorough-going way the road to such international development depends upon the ability of the states involved to secure it on a plane which avoids imperialist exploitation. If such international development were the basis upon which the richer nations became, as it were, rentier-parasites upon the poorer nations a stage might easily develop in which the usurer's claim would be repudiated, with a consequent ill-feeling that might easily breed conflict. We must not forget the history of foreign loans to Russia, and the temper bred by the Bolshevist refusal to recognize them. Nor must we forget, either, that if a community attempts, like the Soviet Union, to exploit its potential resources at the cost of present consumption-standards, it may exact a terrible price from one generation for the benefit of another. The Soviet Government was able to impose that price; but no one will ever be able to measure the misery and the suffering it caused.

From this angle, international organization in the post-war period seems to imply, above all, an economic foundation. It argues the need for the planned development of a world regarded as a common pool of wealth to which all nations have access, on terms as nearly equal as we can make them. The administration of the common pool needs common principles of action. Clearly enough, those common principles are the valuations of a new civilization. They require an international legislature in which, on behalf of all the peoples, the representatives of governments can agree upon those valuations and settle the priorities they involve. Below this ultimate task, there is a mass of technical decisions to be taken each general category of which will require the supervision of a functional body. The allocation of raw materials, the organization of stable prices for primary commodities, the planning of means of communication, the control of tariffs and migration, the decision to devote international loans to one purpose rather than to another, the creation of a pool of specialists available for backward areas or for special crises, these are illustrations merely of functions it is important to see in an international context.

The war itself has made the central principle of action an obvious one. It is the principle which underlies President Roosevelt's great conception of the Lend-Lease Act. Like all great conceptions, its essence is a simple one. The United States, out of its abounding resources, aids the United Nations in need as an investment in the victory of freedom. That one transcendent aim governs all the purposes to which the Lend-Lease Act is devoted. It is not the profits of American business men which determines their application; nor is it the extension of the corporate power of the United States. What determines the allocation of priorities under the system is the best judgment the leaders of the United Nations can make of their relevance to victory.

It is this conception, I suggest, that we require for the organization of an economics of expansion in the post-war world. We have to learn to regard it as an investment in the victory of that peace without which there is no freedom. The obvious value, for example, of the rapid industrialization of India and China, the advance in their purchasing power implicit in this effort, does not require emphasis. The interdependence of prosperity is a platitude; what we forget is that we must apply our platitudes if they are to be living truths. Just as a bank is interested in the success of its customers, so is a nation interested in the success of other nations. But we must remember that this reciprocity of interest is true only in an expanding economic universe. Once we are conditioned to scarcity through contraction, each nation seeks to get the most it can for itself of what welfare there is. The supreme example of this practice was the German barter system developed by Schacht after Hitler came to power. It sought to make the economy of South-Eastern Europe so dependent on that of Germany that no other nation could penetrate the markets it thus controlled. Economic penetration led, inescapably, to political domination. To assure its markets Germany had to be the virtual sovereign of that area, and it had to see to it that the forms of economic development there did not interfere with the character of its own manufacturing potentialities. In effect, South-Eastern Europe had to be kept as a source of raw materials for Germany; and that meant the conditioning of its industrial potentialities to German needs. In any fundamental way, none of the states in South-Eastern Europe could escape from the German net without a dislocation of the German economy; granted the character of Hitler Germany that meant the possibility of war.

This dilemma does not obtain in the economics of expansion. British investment made largely possible the development of American railways; but that did not result in the subordination of American economic potentialities to the requirements of the British pattern. Where the economic relations of peoples rest upon the plane of equality, there is a common benefit in the exchange of goods and services; but the equality is fundamental. Without it, the weaker people as inevitably passes into a subordinate position as the superior power of the white man in Africa forces the African native into a position of inferiority. And, without it, the weaker people can only escape from its subordination by challenging the position of the stronger, just as the African native, in Kenya, for example, can, under present conditions, only challenge the privileged interests of the white settler by revolt. The extension I have indicated of the underlying principle of the Lend-Lease Act provides a high road of escape from this dilemma. And, in essence, there is no other way of escape.

For, in essence, the situation by which we shall be confronted at the end of this war offers only the alternatives of organizing expansion or organizing restriction. If we decide upon the latter, we leave in being all the fundamental causes out of which the two world-wars have been born. If we decide upon the former, it becomes essential to change, in all the major states except the Soviet Union, the present relations of production since they have proved themselves incompatible with this decision. We ought not to under-estimate the scale of the choice we have to make. It is as vast in its significance as the change, at the end of the middle ages, from a feudal to a capitalist economy. It involves adjustments in our values not less momentous in character. It denies, for example, the historic validity of the purpose to which, in fact, as distinct from idea, the power of the state has been devoted. It rejects the classic conception of freedom of contract by assuming that its operation is set, not in the context of effective demand, but in the context of needs which an organized international society decides to recognize and to the satisfaction of which it applies its power. It rejects the idea of individual freedom as born of the citizen's right to achieve wealth in a competitive market which is morally neutral; on the contrary, it starts by introducing the idea of moral purpose into the market itself, and submits that the individual must find his freedom in the performance of a function which is born of that moral purpose.

I do not assume that so vast a change in human relations, above all on the economic plane, is one that we are likely to achieve in any rapid way. No one who knows an old society like Britain can fail to see that old habit dies hard, that the sociological adjustment of national *mores* to a new culture is a slow and painful process. I am concerned only to insist that, unless we create the conviction that the adjustment is, in fact, being made, the defeat of the Axis powers will leave us with all the old problems and all the old evils, perhaps, it may be, even in an accentuated form. For, clearly, with that defeat, we shall all suffer from the impact of three unmistakable consequences of these years of war. There will be the deep fatigue which their nervous strain will exact; the temptation of that fatigue will be to postpone experiment until our energies have been renewed. There will be the liberation of the angry nationalisms which the Axis Powers have suppressed and outraged during their period of superiority; the temptation will be great to assume that the satisfaction of this anger by the punishment of the Axis Powers is itself the institution of a new social order. And there will be the need, for at any rate some years, for the United Nations to stand on guard against the danger of a recrudescence of aggression organized by the Axis Powers. Unless we are wiser this time, than we were after 1919, this may easily result in an attempt at a new post-war stabilization of power which is in contradiction with the dynamic of the historical period upon which, with the cessation of hostilities, we shall enter.

Each of these dangers is very real; and each of them is likely to be exploited to the full by the vested interests, both among victors and vanquished, whose privileges are menaced by our movement towards an economics of expansion. That has been evident in their habits since 1939. The history, for example, of the attitude of the great aluminium interests in the United States to the expansion of independent productive capacity; of British rubber interests to the development of synthetic rubber; of British interests to the rapid extension of manufacturing possibilities in India; all of these are a warning. It was significant that, when Mr. Bevin sought power from the House of Commons to introduce a Trade Board into the catering industry he was at once challenged by the employers on the ground that this was not relevant to the war effort; as though it is not elementary that the promise of hope and security to the workers is the safeguard of that morale which is the guarantee of victory. Nor is it without importance that, in the first months after the entry of the United States into the war, the industrial debate seemed to concentrate itself, less on the maximization of production, than on manœuvres for position in the post-war period; an atmosphere rapidly assimilated by a Congress which seemed, from its discussions, to think less of the struggle in which America was engaged than of the impact of their decisions upon their members' fortunes at the November elections. The great purposes announced by the leaders of American opinion, Mr. Roosevelt, for instance, Mr. Henry Wallace, Mr. Milo Perkins, found little equivalent sustaining action to prove their primacy.

IV

Nor must we forget the danger implied in the effort to attribute the habits of Nazi Germany at war to the inner constitution of human nature in Germany. Learned men combined with statesmen to argue that the German mind and character was of a different texture than the mind and character of other peoples, that, when victory had been won, it would require a treatment of some special kind relevant to the difference of that texture. The fault in the German received the most varied explanations. Sometimes his inherent badness was taken back to the beginnings of his written history; sometimes it began with the Great Elector; sometimes it began only with the "blood and iron" of Bismarck. What, in all the discussions, was so tragic was the inability of the exponents of the thesis of a special dose of original sin in the German to see that they were merely supplying the obverse side of the Nazi claim to a racial superiority which gave the Germans rights to which no other people could pretend.

For it is obvious, on any serious analysis, that we are concerned not with the nature of Germans in general but with the behaviour of particular Germans. That this behaviour has been savage and barbarous on a scale to which modern history, at least, knows no parallel is beyond dispute; history will remember the evil deeds of these years as it remembers the massacres of Alva or the sack of Magdeburg. But we must be careful, as we analyse their causes, to retain a sense of proportion. The men who were responsible for Lidice were responsible also for the infamous ill-treatment of the Jews from 1933 to 1939 and for the attack on Guernica; these did not lead many of those who are now foremost in their denunciation of German savagery to a word of protest. "Peace and justice," said Sir Thomas Moore, the Conservative member for Ayr Burghs, "are the keywords of his (Hitler's) policy." The late Sir Arnold Wilson, the Conservative member for Hitchin, was able to satisfy himself not only that there was no "militarism" in Nazi Germany, but, also, that there was no great power with which Great Britain was less likely to be involved in war. Anyone who studies the list of members of the Anglo-German Fellowship—a body created to organize good relations between Britain and Nazi Germany—will almost be led to believe that he is reading a special edition of Debrett's Peerage and the Directory of Directors.

The barbarism of Nazi Germany was fully exhibited in its treatment of its German opponents between 1933 and 1939; after the declaration of war that barbarism was extended to its external opponents. Few leading statesmen—President Roosevelt, Mr. Churchill, and Mr. Stalin are honourable exceptions—felt that it was barbarism until after the outbreak of war. Not only, indeed, is that the case; but many of the patrons of friendship between Britain and Nazi Germany were ready to denounce Mr. Churchill as a "warmonger" when he drew attention to the plain implications of Hitlerite policy. And the same people who were enthusiastic about friendship with Nazi Germany—in whose savageries they found no obstacle to an alliance—were ruthless in their denunciations of the unspeakable atrocities of the Soviet régime which they did not hesitate to attribute, until June 22, 1941, to the uncivilized character of Russian human nature.

The only sensible approach to what is without doubt a very grave problem is the historical one. German behaviour is conditioned by the German situation. Lidice is as ghastly an expression of what it is capable, under Nazi leadership, as Amritsar is an expression of what British rule in India was capable under the leadership of General Dyer. American lynchings of Negroes in the Southern States express an important aspect of American behaviour as conditioned by the situation there. So, also, of the Portuguese in Angola, of the Belgians in the Congo, of the French who, under Thiers, massacred so relentlessly the Communards of 1871. Human nature, rationally speaking, is born of the historic environment in which it is found; it adapts itself to that environment; and the way to change its expression in behaviour is to change the environment to which it is adapted.

We gain nothing, this is to say, by thinking of the post-war international problem in terms of a fixed German "national character" the traits in which are excessive aggressiveness, excessive arrogance, and an excessive obedience to the orders which are imposed upon it. These are no more inherent in the German than snobbishness is inherent in the Englishman, or pioneering in the American, or clarity in the Frenchman. Everyone knows that, before the Civil Wars of the seventeenth century, the English were a profoundly musical nation, and that the influence of Puritanism on the decline of that characteristic was profound. Everyone knows, too, how different was the French judgment of the English national character before and after the Revocation of the Edict of Nantes. No Englishman to-day attributes aggressive ambitions to the French people. Yet it is hardly seventy years since the historian Stubbs could ask why the English and the Germans have always been the peace-loving nations of history, and answer his own question by affirming that it was "because France shows herself to-day what she has been throughout the course of a thousand years—aggressive, unscrupulous, false." Our own generation finds it difficult to recognize in the practical, hard-working and scientific-minded Russians of to-day, the mystic, dreamy and lazy Slavs whose stereotype was constructed for us out of the experience of Czarist Russia in decay in 1904.

I do not, of course, for a moment mean that German behaviour under Nazi control has not created problems of urgency and seriousness for the post-war period. Quite obviously it has. Quite obviously the imposition of punishment on Hitler and his accomplices is as necessary in the interest of the world as the punishment of Alf Capone and his fellow-gangsters; nor can the defects in international law be permitted to enable them to escape the just penalty for their crimes. The scale of this aggression has made it necessary to demonstrate in a decisive way that men cannot be permitted to organize and order the infamies that they have organized and ordered without a penalty that will deter others, in Germany or elsewhere, from following their example.

But the punishment of the Nazi leaders, and their accomplices, does not mean that we are entitled to avenge ourselves on the German people, still less that we shall do ourselves any good by such vengeance. Clearly, we are entitled to safeguards against a third attempt by the rulers of Germany to attempt world-domination. That means the disarmament of Germany, and the organization of such controls over its political and economic life as will make that disarmament effective. But we shall have learned nothing from the grim lessons of the inter-war years unless we realize two things. First, no prolonged control of a major power like Germany is possible without transforming nationalism into chauvinism, and thus preparing the ground in which portents like Hitler grow. Except, this is to say, by methods which are fatal to those who employ them the relations between a victorious and a defeated power must rapidly become those of genuine friendship if the psychological condition of the defeated power is not to become diseased. And, second, unless, with a defeated major power, there is a rapid recovery of self-respect, the danger is real that the internal relations will lack the stability necessary to give it an ordered place in the life of the international community. This again, will operate to prepare the ground foı the advent of men like Hitler.

It is not, I think, a valid answer to this argument to say that it proves that the Treaty of Versailles, so far from being too severe, was not severe enough. There are those who urge that the real safety of the world from German aggression lies in the break-up of Germany into a number of small states; it is, they say, the strength of its concentrated unity that makes it a source of danger. Others, again, visualize a Germany of which Austria may well be a part, but from which Prussia is separated. Others, once more, while prepared to maintain the territorial unity of Germany, visualize some system of international ownership and control for the heavy industries of the Ruhr. It is in their relevance to militarism that the real danger lies; and such international ownership and control would enable us to by-pass that danger.

I do not believe that there is a remedy in any of these views. To break up Germany into a number of small states is to denature the form that history has given, piece by piece, to the German nation; and the only result, I think, of any such effort would be to create an overwhelming determination in Germans to build together what the compulsion of foreign defeat had torn asunder; and only potential or actual war could prevent the fulfilment of that determination. Nor do I think there is any virtue in the separation of Prussia from the rest of Germany; that is only to create the same problem in a different form. The problem of Prussia, historically, is set less by any innate habits in its people than by the social relationships built by its junkers which, both internally and externally, have required a policy of "blood and iron" that they might be maintained.

It must be remembered that any great power is a menace to the peace of the world if it has ambitions it cannot fulfil except by the making of war. That was once true of Spain; it was once true of France; it is true in our own day of Germany and Japan. But we have to remember that, in the next age, it may be true of the United States if the character of its economic system pushes it, as may well be the case, to imperialism. But no one would seriously argue that the possibility of this danger makes it desirable to break-up the unity of the United States. The problem we confront will not, on the historic experience we have, be met in any serious degree merely by multiplying the number of small states. Balkanizing the world will not secure the peace of the world.

Superficially, at least, there is more attractiveness in the idea of the international ownership and control of the heavy industries of the Ruhr. No one can seriously deny that a gigantic firm like Krupps' has been a "sinister interest," in Bentham's sense, in the life of the modern world. But what is true of Krupps' is not less true of their opposite numbers in other countries; the private manufacture of armaments is, on massively documented evidence, a contributory factor of importance to war. It is, therefore, difficult to see how the proposal of the international ownership and control of the Ruhr industries is a real solution of the problem unless, at the same time, their potential productivity can be turned to objectives not connected with war. That will, given the present economic system, only be the case if post-war Germany does not need to think in terms of war as the means of fulfilling its wants; for, given the need of war, the fact of international ownership and control only means a delay, after its outbreak, in the devotion of the machinery and manpower of the Ruhr to munitions. The state-power transcends the character of ownership whenever, in its view, its existence depends upon that transcendence. If the majority of shares in a Birmingham engineering firm were held abroad by enemy aliens, that would not prevent its machines being used, after appropriate adaptation for the war effort to-day; and a failure on the part of the executive personnel to comply with the orders of the government would merely mean that its members were replaced. This remedy, therefore, seems to me merely to deal with a symptom in the deeper *malaise* of which this war is the outcome. It does not reach down to its causes.

Nor do I think there is substance in the view which affirms that German militarism is the result of the over-industrialization of Germany, especially in the heavy industries; and that what we require is to organize a better proportion between the resources by which post-war Germany is to live. So long, it is said, as this over-industrialization obtains, so long Germany is bound to prevent the adequate economic progress of South-Eastern Europe and even parts of South America; for, partly, they cannot compete with its industries on technical grounds, and they are driven to remain countries of primary products, with a low standard of life, by reason of that incapacity.

Over-industrialization is as vague a concept as "optimum" population. It is clearly referable to a whole host of variables none of which has been carefully defined by those who seek to lessen the industrial potential of Germany. None of us is really able to answer the question of the unit in relation to which Germany is over-industrialized. Are we referring to the internal structure of her economy? If so, by what test do we decide when optimum industrialization has been achieved? Is it the ability of Germany to feed itself? Is it the resultant average standard of life for each German family? Is it the volume of the reserve army of unemployed that the level of industrialization entails? Is it continuing capacity to attract capital for investment? Or is the test, in fact, not economic at all, but social in character? Is it the militarist implications of the industrial potential to which we refer? Or is the unit of reference not Germany alone, but Germany and her neighbours? Or must we extend the unit, granted the conditions of the modern market and make the whole world the unit to which we refer?

Quite obviously, an answer to any of these questions which seeks to give a fixed character to the elements in German economy is already assuming some kind of planned world. And, once this is the case, the criterion by which the plan is judged becomes of decisive importance. If the purpose of plan is simply to deprive Germany of the power of potential aggressiveness in the future, the obvious way to that purpose is to dismantle all German factories which may be used for armament purposes, actually or potentially, and to transfer the machinery to other countries. The result would be a catastrophic fall in the German standard of living without any equivalent gain in well-being unless the new labour-force operating the transferred plant had at least a skill in its operation and development equal to what Germans have brought to these. It would be, in fact, a fantastic operation which would seek to impose a kind of permanent peonage on Germans. It would be very unlikely, in any case, to succeed; and it would repeat, if in a different way, the worst follies of the Treaty of Versailles. We must not forget the degree in which Hitlerite Germany is, even if unconsciously, the product of those follies. We must not, either, forget that not only does this impose on Hitlerite Germany the economy which, to our horror, the Nazis are seeking to impose on occupied Europe, but also that its underlying assumption is the theory of a double dose of original sin in German nature against which there must be permanent safeguards. I have already argued that the evidence for this view is, in fact, quite without foundation.

The alternative is to think of a planned economy in which the full use of Germany's industrial potential is part of an effort to raise the general world-standard of life, including that of Germany itself, and so to use it that the heavy industries of Germany are deliberately geared to pacific purposes. When we begin to approach the problem in this way, it seems to me clear that, in the German context, there are two stages, each different from the other though in point of time they may well overlap. The first stage is one of European relief. Granted the destruction wrought by German aggression to the industrial structure of Russia and Poland, Holland, and Norway, Greece and Jugoslavia, I see no reason why, for a period, the resources of German manpower and machines should not be employed in helping to repair the damage. I see no reason for example, why the great Dnieper dam should not be rebuilt by German labour, with German materials, under Russian control. I see no reason why, again for a period, German labour, with German materials, under Dutch control should not be devoted to the rebuilding of Rotterdam. There is an important psychological lesson for this generation of Germans in learning that the compulsory labour they imposed upon their victims can be imposed, also, upon themselves. That would set free Russian and Dutch energy for other tasks of reconstruction during the first period of recovery; and it would drive home to the German mind the important fact that the world does not propose to permit aggression to pay.

Assuming that a defeated Germany is prohibited from building up a conscript army, it seems to me reasonable to organize from among its people a civilian reconstruction corps for purposes of this kind.

But it is, of course, important that such a corps should not be so operated as to frustrate once more the recovery by Germans of their self-respect. Any such effort would not only need to be seriously limited in time; the members of the reconstruction corps, also, would have to be away from Germany only for a period comparable with their normal term of military service. They would then return to Germany and take up again the normal life of a German civilian. This apart, it seems to me that the main need we have in thinking of the German problem is that of fitting German economic capacity into schemes for the raising of effective demand throughout the world. No sane person can deliberately condemn so highly developed a nation as Germany to a permanently inferior place in the international economy. Our need is to occupy her industrial capacity with tasks directly relevant to the needs of peace instead of to the needs of war. German factories must have their share in the rapid mechanization of world agriculture. They must aid in the universal development of electric power. German engineers and German geologists must play their part in the development of the unexploited industrial resources, for example, of China. Given the power on our part as victors to organize an economics of expansion, and the chances are not only that we can use the full possibilities of German machinery, but that we can subdue the German habit, so active since the time of Bismarck, of fighting to win its place in the sun by conquest, to that temper of peaceful co-operation which has distinguished so much of Anglo-American economic relations.

Given, I say, the organization of an economics of expansion. It is worth noting that where the German settles down into an environment of this character, his civic virtues are very great. German settlers in the United States, especially after 1848, brought qualities of high value to American civilization; America has been enriched by men like Carl Schurz and Louis Brandeis, by settlements like those made by the German emigrants to Pennsylvania and Wisconsin. The same is true of those Germans who, in the second third of the nineteenth century, settled in Lancashire, and especially in Manchester. They became by their skill and energy not only a very valuable element in the economic life of Britain, in the development, for instance, of its cotton trade for export. They brought with them, also, intellectual habits which did much, in music, for example, to raise the level of the culture in which they found themselves. There was nothing in them of that parvenu quality the arrogant aggressiveness of which was so much the keynote of German habits in Germany after the arrival of Bismarck at power. They were sober, industrious, and, as names like Bessemer and Schuster, like Sir John Simon in sanitary science, and like G. J. Goschen in industry and politics, make evident, able to adapt themselves to the nature of their environment. An expanding Britain whose main object was peace used their qualities as easily and as valuably as it used the Fleming in the fourteenth century, the Huguenot in the eighteenth, and the Jew in the nineteenth, centuries.

This, surely, suggests that the problem of Germany is a problem of Germans whose behaviour was conditioned by the peculiar characteristics of German historical-economic conditions in the latter half of the nineteenth century. The slow recovery from the Thirty Years' War is the first great clue. It resulted in the retardation of German economic development for nearly a century. When the Enlightenment began to prepare the way for the rise of a German middle class, the impact of the French Revolution made the growth of that class to power the victim of Napoleonic adventurism. German nationalism was associated with changes promoted by the soldier and the administrator from above; the cameralism of the seventeenth and eighteenth centuries was prolonged, if in a different guise, well into the nineteenth century. The defeats of Germany in the Thirty Years' War, on the one hand, and the Napoleonic wars, on the other, made the industrial evolution of Germany a growth late in time, without the constitutional changes which accompanied it in France and Britain and the United States, and promoted by an alliance between a state-power essentially conceived in military terms and a bourgeoisie which, though it made an effort in 1848, had no serious working-class support and no independent experience of exercising political power. Bismarckian Germany became a great power because its great leader used numbers to support the policy of "blood and iron"; when, in 1918, the hollowness of that policy was exposed, the German bourgeoisie was already, as a governing class, seeking to build its authority in peaceful foundations, an economic anachronism, and the German proletariat was not yet ready to take its place. It could threaten its masters, but it could not displace them. The result was that German industry, unable to stand alone, accepted the alliance of German militarism as the only way to maintain its claims; and both, in the fear of Bolshevism, which united them as Napoleon had previously done, accepted the partnership with Hitler that they might defeat and destroy the rising claims of their own working-class. But to do so, at the historical stage in which they were involved, they had to destroy the institutions which the working-class of Germany had developed for their protection. They could not destroy them without the provision of some means of satisfying working-class aspirations. They had no means of doing this, granted the disproportion between the relations of production and the forces of production in Germany, save by the attainment, of an economic predominance which they could only win by war. Hitlerism, in all its aspects, was the great gamble of that alliance between militarism and large-scale economic organization which the late development of German economic power rendered necessary. And it became possible, as a gamble, because, when the previous defeat was inflicted on the alliance in 1918, the peace which followed it dealt with the problems the world in general, and Germany in particular, had confronted in the nineteenth century. It did not deal with the problems by which they were confronted, had the victorious statesmen been aware of it, in the twentieth. It was, in essence, that failure which led directly to the second world war.

I note this, not to excuse the aggressiveness of Hitlerite Germany, but to explain it. And I infer from the explanation that the basis of the settlement, this time, must be related to the major issues we confront and not with the minor issues. For compared with coal and oil, iron and steel, food products and their transport, the problems with which the statesmen dealt at Versailles, frontiers, minorities, and the rest, were minor issues because their future status depended upon what was done with the ownership and control of productive power. "To what a different future Europe might have looked forward," wrote Lord Keynes,[1] with prophetic insight, in 1919, "if either Mr. Lloyd George or Mr. Wilson had apprehended that the most serious of the problems which claimed their attention were not political or territorial, but financial and economic, and that the perils of the future lay not in frontiers and in sovereignties, but in food, coal and transport." It may be true that the boundaries of states were made more coincident with the boundaries of nationality than at any previous period; Mr. Herbert Fisher has told us that only three per cent of the citizens of Europe were left under alien rule. But the makers of Versailles were legislating for an age that was already gone.

[1] *The Economic Consequences of the Peace.*

V

"You cannot create a large number of new states," said Stresemann,[1] "and wholly neglect to adapt them to the European system." But to-day, when New York is within ten hours' flying time of London, the rights of the modern state must be adapted to the technological conditions of an economic system as wide as the whole world. In these circumstances two things are surely clear. First, it is obvious that, in a military sense, the independence and neutrality of the small state is quite devoid of meaning; the code of rules by which they are protected in international law will be observed just so long as the great state decides, in a period of conflict, that it is to its interest to observe the code. And, secondly, it is obvious that the exercise of sovereign rights in the economic sphere by a mass of petty states is as harmful to the best working of the productive forces as was the system of internal customs duties in France under the ancien régime. The unified control of those things the material nature of which seems to call for unified control has claims before which no concept of sovereignty is likely for long to remain real.

The step from this conclusion which a number of thinkers have judged it wise to take is the building of a European federation, or, more often, of a number of federations. I do not share this view. The problems that we confront seem to me to call not for the total correlation of areas, but for the partial correlation of functions. I take that view on a number of grounds. First, on all experience, the rigidity of a federal structure does not easily lend itself, without the support of a strong historical tradition, to the management of a multinational state; at this stage, as Dr. Beneš and General Sikorski have wisely seen in the Czech-Polish Agreement, the confederative principle is probably, for a long time to come, the margin of safe adventure. Secondly, I think there is much to be said for the preservation of cultural nationalisms within the larger framework of what economic unity we can safely build. Thirdly, there is the danger that the division of the world into a system of separate federations may, unless their creation is coincident with a great increase of economic welfare, sharpen the thrust to autarchy which has been characteristic of our time, and, thereby, increase rather than diminish, the dangers of militarism. A world divided into some ten or twelve great federal systems, each concerned, for example, to keep its prosperity for its own citizens by methods like the Hawley-

[1] *Diaries* (edited by E. Sutton), III, 619.

Smoot Tariff, or limitations upon freedom of migration, would not inherently be a better world than the one in which Hitler grew to power.

It seems to me, therefore, that the material nature of each given factor ought to be the decisive element in settling the unit of governance. It will, if we are wise, be one area for one function, and one area for another. Aviation, for example, hardly permits of effective organization except in world terms; hardly less is it obvious that the railways of Europe require a single planned control; and the development of road transport seems to call for a single European commission concerned to plan, to build, and to maintain, a great network of mainroads linking the great cities together. I think it probable, moreover, that the unification of high tension electricity supply in Europe, for public and industrial use, is both feasible and desirable. On a smaller scale, the Tennessee Valley Authority offers us an important model of governance for adaptation. And it is grimly clear that the inherent nature of the problems involved in stabilizing the post-war currencies will require a world federal reserve system. Nothing would be more disastrous to post-war international relations than the attempt on the part of states to enable producers to capture markets by the competitive debasement of their currencies. Unified regulation of the amount of currency each state may issue, of re-discount rates, and of the volume of bank credits are matters too important, now that the epoch of the gold standard is over, to be left to the sovereign discretion of a particular government.

I have chosen examples in which the nature of the function involved seems to make the appropriate unit of governance either as large as all Europe, or, as with aviation and currency, the whole world. It is not less clear that there are other functions, education, medical service in the advanced communities, wireless, in which it is neither desirable nor probable that the unit of governance would transcend the boundaries of the national state. In neither case, of course, does unified governance prevent the largest possible measure of decentralized administration; it is highly likely, for instance, that a European high-tension electricity supply commission would devolve the task of distribution upon a great mass of lesser bodies; just as a world reserve bank would have the relation to national banking systems of the type that the American Federal Reserve Board at Washington has come to have to its regional boards. Decentralization is of the essence of successful administration; for in no other fashion can the necessary flexibility be attained.

In my own judgment, this is to say, the problems of international government exist on two levels—that of decisions the application of which will be made by states directly, and those which will involve direct government either by the society of states or by some group within the society. I envisage, therefore, the creation, with the achievement of some real stability after victory, the recognition of the need for four general organs of international government. There will be an international court, and no small measure of its effectiveness will depend on our agreement that there are in truth no non-justiciable disputes between states. There will be an international legislature in which all states will be entitled to representation on equal terms. No one can, I think, prophesy with any assurance the range of its powers. But it will have, on past experience, to avoid the Scylla of unanimous consent, on the one hand, without rushing into the Charybdis of legislation by simple majority-rule on the other. For these are matters upon which the coercion of a state against its will, of the Soviet Union, for example, by the votes of Finland, say, and Ecuador, and Denmark, is a less helpful procedure than its persuasion. I do not think, for instance, that the principle of separation between the state and church in a particular national society ought to be made a general rule to which England, for example, is ordered to conform; it is better for the achievement of the very purposes which those who hold this separation to be desirable that English opinion should come of itself to this principle. I do not think, either, that a given national society should be ordered to accept unlimited migration, especially where the racial question is likely to cause special tension, save where the majority for making the rules regulating movement is an emphatic one both in its quality and quantity.

The society of nations, moreover, will require an executive body. It is inevitable that its members should be representatives of the governments of the great states as a permanent category, together with representatives of the lesser states chosen by election; and I think it probable that it will be wise to insist that the elected representatives are not immediately re-eligible in order that a process of rotation may increase responsibility and interest. The executive body will probably require a considerable ordinance-making power within the framework of the general principles upon which the society of nations is based.

Obviously, also, it will require a permanent civil service of its own. And it is important to emphasize at once that, whatever the failures of the Geneva experiment, in no field was it more outstandingly successful than in that of administration. Until some such period as the general deterioration which set in with the great depression of 1929, it established a remarkable tradition among its officials of an international loyalty which transcended the limitations of national origin and training. Men and women of diverse cultures found that they could build high common standards of co-operation and performance. The work of the Health and Economic Sections of the League, the aid given, for instance, to China in the one field and to Austria in the other, was an achievement of great importance. So, too, was the work of the International Labour Office; and it is safe prophecy to insist that the success of a new experiment in international government will, in considerable measure depend upon the extension of the scope of the Labour Office's powers and the drive put behind the effort it can make to diminish the distance between the standards of mass welfare in the advanced and backward nations.

I assume that a new society of nations will, within the framework of its general principles, encourage the formation of special organizations to deal regionally with the local problems of regions. The adaptation to its needs of the idea which underlies the Pan-American Union can add enormously to its effectiveness; and it is through organs of this character that it can best direct developments like the European Railway Union and the European Electricity Union which, as I have suggested, are experiments implied in the technological character of the next age. And there are, I think, three areas of authority in which the larger the competence of the new society, the deeper and more unbreakable will be the faith and loyalty it can evoke. Its permission should be necessary for all loans made to the governments of particular states, and where wholesale barter-transactions are proposed between states, no effect should be given to them until, upon the expert examination of its officials, the Executive body has approved them in the light of their bearing upon the general raw materials position. It is, moreover, of the first importance that the new Society shall be able, not merely at periods of crisis, to operate, by supervision, a continuous programme of international public works. Nothing is more likely than the operation of such a programme to make international government a living reality to ordinary men and women.

Two other functions require some special emphasis. A new Society of Nations must devote a large-scale effort to the modernization of the backward areas of the world. It must be in a position to supply technical assistance in economic surveys, in medical and educational development, in industrial and administrative training. What, for example, on a small scale, Yale-in-China has accomplished for medical science there, the Society of Nations must strive to perform everywhere that its services are required and in all fields of effort. It must become as natural for the geologist to search for oil in China, as an international official, as it has been for him in the past to search for it on behalf of the great oil companies. It must become as much a matter of course for a free India to seek the services of the new Society of Nations in planning, for example, its hydroelectric development, or the remaking of its fantastically antiquated system of land tenure. For it is urgent to remember that only as this development proceeds does the capacity of the market begin to bear its due proportion to productive power. The pace at which this backwardness is transcended will measure the rate at which we can overcome the vicious circle of depression that has brought this system to catastrophe.

The second function is the liquidation of imperialism, alike in its political and economic aspects. Here, if we have the will, we start with knowledge that gives us two immense advantages over our position in 1919. We know, at least, from the swiftness with which the European empires in the East collapsed, and the inert acceptance of their new masters by the native populations, how fragile was their real hold there, how morally rotten the foundations upon which they had been built. We know, further, from American abandonment of political imperialism in the Philippines, and from the immense Russian experiments with its backward peoples, that self-government and the serious search for economic and educational opportunity offer prospects of rapid advance far beyond anything previously conceived; the Russians, for example, have done more for the education of peoples in the Arctic Circle and the Caucasus who, in 1917, had not even a written language, in a quarter of a century than we have done for India in an occupation of nearly two hundred years. The colonies of Africa and the West Indies remain as a challenge to us, the former set in the perspective of a South African doctrine of white domination which spreads grimly northwards, and is not easy to distinguish from that Nazi racialism we have denounced with such indignation. Nor must we forget that as Americans have occupied their leased bases in the Caribbean there have been ominous signs that they have brought with them an exacerbation of the evil implications of the colour-bar as well as a safeguard against external aggression.

I do not myself believe that imperialist exploitation, political or economic, will easily end, so long as the exploitation pays, and there is behind it the backing of a major power. But I do think that we can greatly accelerate the ending of its ugliness if, first, we not only formally announce that "the interests of the native are paramount," but make the organization of the results of that paramountcy a matter upon which the final judgment is in the hands of the new Society of Nations. No state which dominates the life of an alien people is fit to be the judge in its own cause. It may have moments of passionate moralism about its obligations. Britain had one of those moments in the movement which led to the abolition of slavery and the suppression of the traffic in slaves. There are wholesome signs that the grim reports of enquiries, usually, it is worth remarking, themselves made as the result of labour riots, are evoking a serious attempt to clean up some of the worst features in the slums of empire. But I do not think it can be honestly said that to take two examples, there was any serious public opinion in France concerned about the standards of native welfare in French Indo-China, or that there is to-day in Britain the sense of responsibility there ought to be for our standards of colonial administration beyond a fairly narrow professional circle. It was, at any rate, not without significance that when, in the summer of 1942, the under-secretary for the Colonies reported on his department's estimates for the year, the press frankly admitted that he spoke to an almost empty House of Commons. Nor is it, I think, irresponsible to suggest that the Parliamentary obligation to the native peoples in the Colonies and Protectorates is unlikely to be adequately fulfilled, if the examination of its results is normally confined to one day's debate in the year. Here, indeed, it is legitimate to adapt the famous maxim and insist, first, that the colony is neglected which has no Parliamentary history, and, second, that it only attains a Parliamentary history if it attempts a violent protest against that negligence.

I think it probable that to confer upon the new Society of Nations the obligation to be responsible for the standards of native welfare in all colonial territories, and to start by fixing minimum standards of achievement in labour conditions, public health, housing, and education, with a technique of public examination of the results obtained by the administering power, cannot fail to do real good; even the Belgium of King Leopold II disliked a public humiliation. But I do not think an annual report to a Colonial Commission, modelled on the old Mandates Commission, even accompanied by a day in court for the colony, is enough, I think it is important that the Colonial Commission should possess its own independent staff of resident officials and travelling inspectors, who own no national allegiance to the administering power, and are not concerned in their reports to put the best face on its achievements. I suggest that such a Colonial Commission should, in an occurrence like the riots in Trinidad, or the violence which accompanied the strike in the Northern Rhodesian copper belt, prosecute its own enquiries on the spot; to an administering power an educated native, still more an uneducated native, with a keen sense of the elements of social justice, seems only too often to appear to his white employer in the guise of a riotous agitator, not seldom infected from Moscow. The power to make public enquiries would itself be a healthy beginning if only because it would go far towards preventing the sacrifice of officials who are keen on their job to pressure from powerful economic interests at the Colonial Office. I do not suggest that it would end imperial exploitation; but it would do a great deal to temper the wind to the shorn lamb.

We cannot, indeed, end imperial exploitation under any system where the main economic power belongs to white interests, often absentee interests, and where the colour bar operates to impose a permanent subordination, economic, educational, social, upon the coloured peoples. The evidence is clear that, in these circumstances, the administering power, be it British or French, Dutch or Belgian, will think first of the public constituency it must satisfy at home and of the interests of the coloured peoples a long way afterwards. That was convincingly demonstrated when, on top of Lord Passfield's decision to maintain native paramountcy in Kenya, gold was discovered there; the relevant land was at once sold for exploitation to the white interests.[1] It was, indeed, already sufficiently evident in investigations like those of Morel in the Congo,[2] of Nevinson in Portuguese Angola,[3] of Casement in Putumayo[4]; and the accounts of colonial evolution by investigators like Woolf and Macmillan tell their own irrefutable tale, largely from official documents.[5] A bad riot cleans the Augean stables, at any rate for a time; and the creation of a check upon the exercise of power in the manner I have suggested will, on experience, domesticate in the administering

[1] Not, however, I am glad to note, without an impressive protest in Parliament.

[2] *Red Rubber* (1901); and cf. Casement's report, *Parliamentary Papers* (1904), vol. 62, p. 357.

[3] *A Modern Slavery* (1904).

[4] *Parliamentary Papers* (1912–13), vol. 68, p. 819.

[5] L. S. Woolf, *Empire and Commerce in Africa* (1929); W. M. Macmillan, *Warning from the West Indies* (1936).

power a far keener sense of responsibility above all because it will give the fair-minded official independent support against the threat of vested interest to his career; that has induced many otherwise honourable men to keep silent until they had reached retirement. But I do not pretend that it will do more than mitigate the worst excesses of the system. Only reforms as drastic as the Russians have had the courage to attempt will really strike at the root of a system in which exploitation is, by its very nature, endemic.

VI

The main preoccupation of the peoples all over the world during the inter-war years was the achievement of an enduring peace; yet no record is more dismal than the failure of their leaders to accomplish it. Disarmament conferences were held in 1921, 1927, 1930, and 1932; but they revealed rather the degree to which the contradictions of capitalism in its imperialist phase required war as an expression of their implications than any possibility of serious agreement. After Hitler's accession to power, and, especially after his remilitarization of the Rhineland in 1936, there could be no question of disarmament in Europe, while the Japanese seizure of Manchuria in 1932 was obviously the beginning of conflict in the Pacific. For nearly ten years, in short, before the outbreak of the Second World War in 1939, the only question was the shape that it would take and the forces that would stand together, in the East and in the West, against the states that were preparing for aggression.

In the event, it became clear that no common insurance against aggression—the so-called policy of collective security—was possible. No state, except the Soviet Union, was ready to take the risks involved in agreeing, before the aggressors struck, to meet force with force; each vaguely hoped that, by some stroke of fortune, it would manage to escape its impact. The result was twofold. First, the aggressors had several years' start in armaments upon the states which were anxious to keep the peace, and, second, there was no common plan of action against aggression. Indeed it is true to say that even as late as the autumn of 1942 there was no common plan, in the strict sense of the term, between the major partners of the United Nations. Priorities, both in strategy and in materials, had to be worked out as each phase of the conflict proceeded. There was no common high command in any of the three services; there was no common general staff; there was no common intelligence service; each of the partners had even its own principles of publicity and propaganda. Airmen, sailors, soldiers, the organizers of war production, all co-operated with one another; all the governments were committed to a refusal of a separate peace; all of them, in the Declaration of Saint James's Palace, in the spring of 1942, accepted a body of large, and rather vague, general principles as the aims to be achieved with victory. But none of this was built upon an agreed strategy made in common. There was continuous consultation; there was not co-ordination for unified action.

The problem will arise at the end of this war, as it arose at the end of the last, of the methods by which collective action can be taken against a state which seeks some given end by methods which endanger peace. We are offered a number of specifics. There must be an international force; there must be an international air force exclusively at the disposal of an international organization, it being assumed that national air forces are abolished; or it is argued that. with the disarmament of the Axis powers after defeat, a strong Anglo-American alliance will be able to police the world, much as the British navy successfully policed the seas until the rise of German naval power. Or we are to hope, after a suitable interval in which there grow up in the Axis countries governments upon whose pacifism we may generally rely, for all-round disarmament in which, the international force perhaps apart, the defence establishments of states, will be rather local militia for internal police purposes than the immense and costly structures we have known. Perhaps, also, the abolition of the private manufacture of armaments, and a stringent system of international inspection, will combine, it is suggested, to make the *blitzkrieg* and a treachery like Pearl Harbour, with the immense initial advantage they give to the aggressor, impossible in the future.

One other thing in preamble must be said. It is clear that air-power, especially as based upon the aircraft carrier, has transformed entirely the whole character of war. Technologically, it has made the small state which is geographically useful to the aggressor, a base and not an obstacle; and it has meant transcontinental inter-dependence, as between the United States and Australia, for example, upon a scale previously undreamed of; while it has made every island with a landing-ground capable of effective development of strategic significance once it is near either to useful territory or the possible sea routes along which supplies may pass. Nor must we forget that, as the development of air-transport develops, it is already obvious that it will play an increasing part not only in the movement of men and materials, but, also, in giving the element of surprise a vital part in strategy.

The inference from all this is, I think, the necessary and growing dependence of the small state upon the large state if it is to be defended against the kind of attack made by Germany in 1940 against Norway, Denmark, and the Low Countries. Just as Britain occupied Iceland, Madagascar, and after a struggle, Iraq and Syria as insurance, and as Britain and Russia established a military condominium over Persia for the war period; just as, also, Britain has leased bases in the West Indies to the United States, as an element in a policy of mutual insurance; so it seems to me inevitable, in the future, that vital strategic points in the smaller states will need, no doubt by international agreement, to be used and developed by the great states, if the former are not to be the foundation upon which attack by an aggressor is attempted. If France, for example, were permanently to disappear from the ranks of the major powers after the war, the United States is bound, in the light of possible developments of air power, to seek assurances that Dakar cannot be used as a base from which to attack its Atlantic seaboard; and the obvious way to safeguard itself against that danger is provided by the model of the leases granted by Great Britain in the Caribbean. It is difficult to see how Russia can leave Finland open to possible use by Germany again; and the need for full assurances against Japanese aggression a second time in Malaya, the Dutch East Indies, and the islands of the Pacific, including Australia, now needs no emphasis. Pretty obviously, the organization, after his war, of collective security against aggression will not, on any showing, be a simple matter.

Its principle is a choice between two immense alternatives; and I do not think we gain anything by concealing from ourselves that this is in fact the only choice. Collective security may come because some state, or enduring alliance of states, is so powerful for so long a period, that it can deny effectively the necessary instruments of war, if necessary by making war, to any rival or potential alliance of rivals. Or the new international organization may itself, on behalf of its members, be able to maintain and operate so massive a power that no contingent aggressor will dare to gamble on defiance of its authority.

That the second of these choices is the only rational safeguard against the use of war as an instrument of national policy does not seem to me to admit of dispute. Granted a victory of the united nations, the first choice means either an immediate American, or

Anglo-American, domination of the world which other powers will only accept as long as they are compelled to accept it. It seems to me, also a domination which, in the very nature of things, is bound to be abused. For in order to make it an authority beyond challenge, the United States, or the Anglo-American alliance, whichever it be, is bound to shape the economic life of any other community, or group of communities, from which that challenge might come. This is, in fact, the making of a new Roman *imperium* in which the growth of all states is subordinated to the primary demands of a peace the conditions for which they will not themselves be able to determine. It is quite unlikely that such a position would long remain stable; Russia, for example, would, pretty certainly, view it with suspicion from the outset, unless there was a far greater approximation than now exists to an identity of social purpose. The very attempt, indeed, at the imposition of this *imperium* would lead to organized, if secret, efforts to subvert it. To maintain itself against the prospect of effective challenge it would be driven to much the same type of exploitation as has marked the history of the Axis Powers in recent years.

It seems to me inevitable, therefore, that we should look for the maintenance of peace to an organization like the new Society of Nations of which I have spoken. From this, it follows that, in the first stages, its character will be primarily set by the wills of the Great Powers among the United Nations; for a period of some years, at least, is likely to pass before Germany and Japan are admitted to a full share in the duties of keeping the peace. The reasonable way of evolution is to remember that the circumstances of this war have brought into being at least the basis upon which permanent co-operation for defence can be built. The Royal Air Force is an international air force in composition; so, if in less degree, are the Royal Navy and the British Army, each of which enjoys the assistance of important foreign contingents. If we could maintain this basis after the cessation of hostilities, it is at least conceivable that it might grow into that international defence force which could act as the sword of a new Covenant.

But there are two indispensable conditions to that growth, neither of which, perhaps, is properly separable from the other. The maintenance of this form of collective security will depend, as, indeed, everything progressive depends, upon our ability to resume a world in which there is economic expansion after the war. A common prosperity begets a common trust; and in an environment of common trust a serious attempt at disarmament—itself a condition of improved standards of welfare—might be made. But we ought to be quite clear that the resumption of economic expansion is fundamental.

We ought to be quite clear, further, that this is not an automatic process. It has not only to be planned, we have to agree upon the character of the plans before we go into the post-war period if they are to have any chance of success. We have to agree, for instance, that we shall not this time, as in 1919, end at a stroke all the existing arrangements for the pooling of economic resources, in food, in shipping, in the stabilization of currencies, in raw materials, and so on. We have, on the contrary to maintain them as the moulds out of which the planned economy of the next age will take shape. We have to use the years of transition to some kind of definite stability at the end of which alone can we hope to give a final outline to the peace, experimentally to extend their authority into a framework of permanent institutions. We have to do this realizing that it is highly unlikely that our civilization can afford a third breakdown.

This means, I say, an agreement about the post-war world before we enter into its hazards. For the evidence is pretty plain that without this agreement the power behind the centrifugal forces will be very great. There will not only have ended, with victory, the pull of the common purpose which now enables us to transcend our differences. There will not only be fear, alert and anxious of an American isolationism that may easily be aided by the knowledge of America's predominant strength. There will be the feverish nationalism of the liberated countries. There will be the revolutionary urge of millions of repressed workers intensified by the inspiration of Russian achievement. And over against that temper must be put the fatigue, the inertia, the craving, especially among the propertied classes, for a period of relief from the tensions of the unknown and the insecure. To preserve a system of common purposes in a world in which the achievement of the transcendent aim will engender, in most of our rulers, a yearning for the right to relax will be more difficult than the hour of crisis permits us to realize.

To preserve a system of common purposes, let us remember, among states which were themselves deeply divided until the war compelled them to put aside their differences; to reconcile New Deal America with that America which, at any rate up to Pearl Harbour, was not quite certain whether Franklin Roosevelt or Adolph Hitler was its chief enemy; to heal the scars of a France with no element of its destiny predictable save the ruin of Vichyism;

to safeguard a Britain which, in the face of its massive uncertainties, must find remedies against mass-unemployment among its demobilized millions; to find what will be little less than the basis of a new world in the Far East; and, alongside of all this, to find terms of common living with a Russia whose socialist faith will have been strengthened both as experiment and as inspiration by victory; these major issues among the United Nations only, raise their heads as things about which we have to be clear as we confront the grave complexities involved in restoring the peoples of the Axis countries to habits of civilized living. None of these matters, let us be certain, is seriously met even by the most solemn incantations of the Atlantic Charter. To lay the foundations of collective security needs more than the rhetoric of statesmen. In the kind of world this war is calling into being it is the deed that is the word.

I do not doubt the ease with which one can draw up on paper the draft constitution of an international society; wiser than in 1919, we may even omit from its clauses any reference to the sovereignty of the state. Eager prophets, like Mr. H. G. Wells, may give us a twentieth-century version of the Rights of Man. We may solemnly swear a new Pact of Paris outlawing the use of war. The new Rumania, the new Hungary, the new Poland may pledge anew their determination to respect the rights of national or religious minorities. General Franco's Spain may again be transformed from a prison into a civilization. The claims of the worker to a decent standard of life may be embodied in a new international charter. On the morrow of the Armistice there may be no man or woman amongst us not vowed to the dream that it shall not happen a third time.

"Desires without deeds," wrote Blake, in one of his supreme moments of insight, "breed no more than pestilence." I do not for one moment underestimate the power of high intentions; the capacity of great purposes to steel men to great acts has been shown constantly in history. I am making the different point that unless we give to our high intentions the environment in which they can flourish, they are bound to fail. We know that the pre-war system bred the tragedy of this war. We know, also, that, unchanged in its essentials, it is bound to lead remorselessly to its repetition. For men have to work with the materials they are given; it is folly to expect that they can achieve results with them that the materials do not permit. It is not a matter of learning from experience; there is not a statesman living to-day who is not aware of its lessons. Our problem is not even the discovery of common ends; in a broad way, there is agreement about those ends. Our problem is that, at every step, the methods those ends require are in conflict with powerful vested interests which do not easily consent to abdicate. There are times when the pressure of opinion makes abdication inevitable; so it was, for example, on August 4, 1789. But these times are of extreme rarity, and, if the favourable moment is missed, it is unlikely to recur. And when it is thus missed, there are few powerful vested interests which are prepared to surrender without a conflict.

My argument is built on the view that this is the favourable moment, and that, if we let it pass, all effective plans for the organizing of that economics of expansion which is the condition of an enduring peace will fail. It is when men are conscious, as they are now conscious, of a transcendent end which overrides all lesser claims that the mood exists in which great experiment is possible. It is then, and only then, that we can mobilize the will to peaceful change on the scale and with the intensity that our situation requires. It is then, and only then, that the dynamic of events makes the opponents of change incapable of resistance to its demands. The power to recognize the favourable moment gives to the statesman the capacity to effect by consent and swiftly what, at other times he can do only at a slow pace and, too often, only by compulsion. For at such a moment, the transcendent purpose seems to sweep men beyond themselves. The big thing seems the right thing; the big thing seems the reasonable thing. The greatness of the challenge permits, even exacts, the greatness of the response. So it was, for example, in the workshops of Britain after Dunkirk; so it was, also, in those days when our fighter pilots drove the German Air Force from British skies; so, also, was it in Russia when what seemed the irresistible German drive on Moscow was halted.

But the mood of exaltation does not last; no nation can live for long upon the heights. If the favourable moment is allowed to pass unused, old habits resume their former sway. And with that resumption, the sense of transcendent aims disappears. We seem in the presence not of Reason itself, which exacts a unified allegiance without compulsion, but of a hundred competing reasons, each of which presents itself in some guise which interest, prescription, custom, tradition, all seem to support. It is then that we begin to be conscious of our differences, differences within nations, and differences between them, and to forget the identities which enabled us to transcend them. It is then, too, that the historic emotion which surrounds those differences seems to clothe them with an urgency that, at the favourable moment, we had forgotten they possessed. Compare the quality of the world's response to Woodrow Wilson's principles before the Armistice of November 11, 1918, and after the peace conference had begun at Paris. Compare the atmosphere in Washington in the first hundred days of the New Deal with the atmosphere after big business had discovered that the crisis was past. Compare what the makers of the Weimar Republic could have achieved in the first electric days of the Revolution—which was not a Revolution—with what they did achieve when they called in the interests of the old world to redress the balance of the new.

That is why, in my judgment, the favourable moment is now and no other moment. The kind of temper its use requires cannot be improvised; that is made clear by every day, almost, of the inter-war years. Those who do not act on the new faith they proclaim when they have the power to act do not maintain acceptance of their faith; all they do is to arouse scepticism among their supporters and hope among their enemies. That is why, to take an obvious example, the first two British Labour Governments failed. They lacked the courage and the insight to seize upon their favourable moments. Instead of showing that they held the faith their members had so long professed, they seemed to set themselves to prove that from socialist principles they arrived at much the same conclusions as those opponents whom they had so fiercely denounced for their policies. They were defeated, less because the electorate had made up its mind to reject socialist principles in action—it had never seen them tried—than because, with obvious common sense, the electorate decided that if Conservative principles of governance were to be applied, it was only reasonable to authorize their application by those who believed in their validity.

So it is, I suggest, with ourselves in this grave hour. We shall gain nothing but disillusion merely by preaching the new world; we must begin to lay its foundations if we want to see it built. That economics of expansion which offers us the prospect of a peace that can endure is not something we can suddenly improvise when the whole current of events runs against it. For a brief time, the vested interests of the United Nations are on the defensive. A government which announced that the requirements of the war impelled it, for example, to retain the control of all capital investment after the war might encounter angry criticism; but it is, I think, quite certain that it would have overwhelming popular support so long as it convinced the people that it believed in its own proposals. When, without any public preparation, and in circumstances of terrible necessity, Mr. Churchill made his offer of union with France to its government, he strengthened his position by showing that he was capable of audacious action proportionate to the danger. The statesmen who fail are those who, in an hour of crisis, think that we can totter on with the kind of measures of which that crisis is itself a condemnation.

On the international plane, therefore, my argument resolves itself into a twofold plea. On the one hand, I am urging that we must organize without delay a realm in which there is unified action between states which liberates the forces of production in the world; on the other hand, I am urging that unified action between states is in some realms impossible, and in most realms unlikely, unless we alter within states the relations of production that this liberation may be real and swift and effective. I am arguing that if we enter the post-war world without having begun the process of reconstruction, we shall find that the dynamic of peaceful change is simply not open to us. We shall enter upon an epoch in which the hopes the effort for victory will have aroused will fall so far below the realities we can make available that conflict within each community is more likely than agreement. Such conflict may have one of two issues. In nations either defeated or exhausted, it will take the form of popular upheaval; in nations in which, like the United States, the productive forces are largely unimpaired, but the productive relations practically unchanged, it will take the form, either of an attack from above on the maintenance of capitalism in a democratic context, or the purchase of a new, though dubious and uncertain, lease of life for that democratic context by a movement towards economic, perhaps even territorial imperialism.

Let us make no mistake about the meaning of these probabilities. They mean the defeat of Hitler; but they do not mean the defeat of the conditions which made Hitler possible. And because they do not mean the defeat of those conditions, they mean that in some other nation, at some later time, a new Hitler will make a new challenge to the freedom we shall have maintained at so bitter a cost. We gain nothing by the refusal steadily to confront the prospect that this situation may well be ours. On the contrary, it is perhaps only by the steady contemplation of this prospect that we shall learn how urgent is the need for action now. For the tragedy of these years has been wholly in vain unless from it we have learned two things. We ought, in the first place, to have seen that power which is not the instrument of justice is altogether terrible and repulsive, that it builds a tyranny far more terrible than any the past has known because its ability to destroy is so much more efficient and so much more organized. And we ought, in the second place, to have seen that a society in which acquisitiveness is the root of power becomes the enemy of reason itself because it makes of reason the slave of the blind impulse to power. "The lust of government," wrote Harrington, "is the greatest lust." It can provoke the basest, as well as the noblest, of ambitions. Its ability to degrade is not less profound than its ability to elevate. I know no moment when its ability to degrade is more complete than when the leaders of a people postpone the fulfilment of the pledges they make to a period in which all history makes it probable that the conditions of fulfilment will no longer be available. That is the supreme danger before us; and unless we tackle it while it can still be overcome, the high purposes we seek to serve are being built upon foundations of sand.

The betrayal of a civilization is always a long process; in the end, it is always a fatal one. And the surest way to its betrayal is to allow the abyss to widen between the values men praise and the values they permit to operate. For when this occurs, there ceases to be a scheme of values by which men can live. Age becomes cynical; youth is deprived of hope. The world becomes a theatre in which an indifferent audience watches without concern the drama of a struggle for power by whose outcome it is unaffected. We have, as a race, passed through epochs of this kind before. We have seen conscienceless ambition hack its way to power in defiance of all the principles which give to human life the quality of a dignified self-respect. For those epochs bring out in the habits of men all the impulses which proclaim their animal origin; they kill in them pity and benevolence, charity and love. That is the kind of epoch into which we may move unless we put behind the principles we proclaim the passion which gives them life. And the period which separates us from the coming of such a disaster is shorter than most of us care to admit, even in our moments of deepest pessimism.

That is why I have made the emphasis of this chapter less the description of a possible pattern of international government than the analysis of the central conditions without which, as I think, the idea of international government is no more than a conceptual toy with which men may play. I have urged that its availability depends, above all, upon two conditions; upon the resumption, first, of an economics of plenty, and the use, secondly, of the favourable moment to begin the process of its organization: upon these two conditions being successfully fulfilled, everything else depends. To begin fulfilment is to engender hope, and only hope that feels itself the mistress of time has the power to create faith. Without some such essay as this in fulfilment now, it is, I have argued, probable that we shall enter the post-war world still prisoners of a tradition fatal to the very ends we seek to attain. Without it, all the seeds of conflict, economic, national, social, religious, will remain in the soil of our civilization, forgotten, it may be, in the momentary triumph of victory, but certain to grow again when its first spring of ecstasy has died away.

If it be said that it is too much to ask of leaders driven so relentlessly by the pressure of the immense responsibilities of war to give their minds to the problems of peace, there are, as I conceive, two quite decisive answers. The first is that in totalitarian war, measures of reconstruction are an integral part of its vital strategy, since upon their impact depends that morale which is the key to victory The second is that the separation of victory in the field from the building of the conditions which enable the victory to be used is an artificial and static conception of totalitarian war which mistakes altogether its inherent nature. To build our policy upon the assumption that the separation is real is to repeat the cardinal error of 1919; it is to make it certain that our statesmen will write the wrong peace.

If, finally, it be said that man, after all, is a thinking animal, and that, in the light of the massive evidence which indicates awareness of our position, we have the right to be optimistic, there are, I think, again two decisive answers. The first is that the thinking self reaches, in all of us, but a little way; and that it is a self which transcends the power of passion only when we have consciously organized the conditions of its mastery. The second is the answer that Bagehot gave less, I suspect, in mockery than in sadness, when he said that "one of the greatest pains to human nature is the pain of a new idea." It is a new idea that we are seeking to domesticate in persuading men to make power the servant of peace instead of war. It is a revolutionary idea which will not easily come to terms with our traditional ways of life. We live in a moment when a treaty between the present and the future is available to us; and it is in such moments that the thinking self can obtain the upper hand. But it is imperative for us to remember that such moments do not last, and that, when they have passed, nothing is more capable of driving us to battle than the reason which does not command our allegiance.

Chapter VII

THE THREAT OF COUNTER-REVOLUTION

I

THE central argument of this book is, in essence, an extremely simple one. We shall not understand the nature of the war in which we are engaged unless we recognize that we are fighting the forces of the counter-revolution. It is to this basic fact that our whole outlook and strategy must be adjusted. We fight, no doubt, that we may survive as free peoples. We seek to punish the ruthless cruelty of our enemies. We propose, if we can, to make impossible, in the future, the baseness and treachery of their methods. We are concerned to root out their crude worship of power for its own sake. But unless our effort is adjusted to the fact that we are fighting the counter-revolution we shall fail to mobilize on our side the resources that are necessary to victory.

We are fighting the counter-revolution. What do we mean by this term? That we are fighting the exponents of an idea. That we are fighting men who are seeking to revolutionize the society in which we live in order to adjust those of its principles and institutions which are in decay to the new conditions of our time. The counter-revolutionists are not simple reactionaries. They have no nostalgia for ancient forms. They are not less aware than we are of the impossibility of a return to *laissez-faire*, or an aristocracy of birth, or the simple, and largely self-sufficient society which enabled Jefferson, for instance, to formulate his ideal of agrarian democracy. The counter-revolutionaries are not conservative. They have not an atom of Burke's respect for tradition and prescription. They have no admiration for the old merely because it is old; on the contrary, they are prepared to use all the latest techniques of modern science, all the experimental potentialities of our institutional system, to attain their purpose. That purpose is to adapt capitalist society to the conditions of modern technology, of a world-market, of a division of labour which has made the collectivist organization of social relationships inevitable. Fascism is capitalism rejecting its liberal origins in order to adapt its relations of production to a situation in which the liberal idea, politically, economically, and socially, would be fatal to the capitalist idea. It uses all the forces that it can, above all the idea of nationalism, in order to breathe new life into the capitalist idea at a moment when the peaceful evolution of its relations would exhibit the fatality of the contradictions in which it is involved. It is revolutionary in the sense that it is bound to break in pieces all the organizations it encounters which interfere with its objective; that is why it is driven by its own logic to assume the form of totalitarian dictatorship. But, unlike a true revolution, that of England, for instance, in the seventeenth century, of France in 1789, of Russia in 1917, it does not seek to enlarge the boundary of power for the benefit of a class or classes previously excluded from that benefit. On the contrary, it seeks to continue the confinement of privilege to those who were its possessors before it seized the state-power. To be successful in that effort, it is compelled to suppress political parties, churches, trade-unions, and any other organizations which may stand in its way. It is an attempt to transform a whole society to its purpose. It must therefore, quite logically, destroy in that society, persons, ideas, organizations, procedures, which might hinder the work of transformation.

The counter-revolution is bound to be anti-democratic. For the purpose of democracy is to enlarge the number of those who share in the benefits of available welfare by enlarging the number of those to whom the rulers of a society are responsible. It is bound to be anti-democratic, because it comes upon the historical scene when the relations of production it is defending are in decisive contradiction with the forces of production. Because it is anti-democratic, it is bound to be ultimately and inherently hostile to all that capitalist relations of production could permit democracy to be when those relations were capable of an expanding exploitation of the forces of production. A democratic society seeks for peace; the counter-revolution is bound to make war. A democratic society is rational, constitutional, pushed, by its inner logic, to set freedom in the context of equality; the counter-revolution is anti-rational, anti-constitutional, the enemy of all egalitarianism lest this destroy the claim of the oligarchy it defends to its monopoly of freedom in an age of economic contraction. Hitler is doing for German capitalism in its decline what the Ironsides of Cromwell did for the English middle class in its rise, what Richelieu and Colbert did when they buried the last efforts of aristocratic feudalism in France and created the necessary conditions for the rise of the French bourgeoisie. Just as war and revolution mark the death of feudalism and the rise of capitalist relations, so do war and revolution mark the effort of those to whom those relations mean a special privilege to maintain them when they are no longer capable of remaining on the world-stage except by violence.

It is characteristic of a counter-revolution such as we are fighting that it should evoke an *élan* in those who lead it which can easily be mistaken for the dynamic of a revolution. We are horrified by the blunt avowal of their purposes by Hitler and Mussolini and the leaders of Japanese militarism; they seem to us an outrage upon the decent instincts of mankind. They are for force against persuasion, for the few against the many, for slavery against freedom, for ignorance against knowledge, for authority against unfettered enquiry, for unreason against reason. That is why they elevate the claims of race against the demands of mankind. That is why they are compelled to bar the gates of knowledge against all who reject their dogmas. That is why they reject the objective findings of science, with their international validity, in favour of some narrow tribal insights which, even a decade ago, they could not have found one learned man to defend. That is why, above all, they deny the experience of the masses, and the claims built upon that experience, and seek to make of ordinary men and women the dumb slaves of a charismatic leader whose will they may not dare to explore. Their pattern of authority is that of an oligarchy, drunk with unlimited power, to whose purposes the common man is no more than an instrument. He is denied the right to share in the definition of those purposes. He may not conceive of himself as an end; for him, thought is a forbidden luxury, and scepticism a crime. Their pattern of international order is that of a conquering race which imposes its will upon the world. It recognizes no sin save weakness; and it admits no rights save those which power can exact. It sees conflict as the parent of all human virtues; and it regards the qualities which we regard as the marks of a civilized man, justice, mercy, tolerance, imagination, as the signs of that weakness which provokes defeat.

Granted the end the counter-revolution has in view there ought to be no surprise either at the habits or the ideas of which they make use. They are the technique of which a decaying system always disposes when it seeks to reassert its authority. So, for example, the opponents of the English Revolution sought to breathe new life into the doctrine of the divine right of Kings; so, also, Gregory XVI and Pius IX denounced the mental climate of the world which had rejected their claims. And anyone who analyses in all its details the long struggle in seventeenth-century France between Jesuit and Jansenist will, I suggest, see in the effort of the latter an attempt to maintain the ethic of a Church habituated to a feudal society against the ethic of a militant and far-seeing body of theological janissaries who had already realized that they could not maintain the authority of that Papacy to whose service they were vowed unless they persuaded it to come to terms with a new social order it was too late to defeat on the old basis. From this angle, the famous polemic of Pascal falls into its place as part of the effort, however unconscious, of the old order in France to arrest the adaptation of ecclesiastical sanctions of conduct to the world which the eclipse of feudalism was shaping.

The counter-revolution has to impose the habits of tyranny upon the world for the simple reason that it cannot look for consent to its purposes. It is irrelevant that it presents itself in the guise of a "new order"; it is irrelevant, also, that, here and there, it should have been able to persuade philosophers and learned men to prostitute their knowledge to its service. The significant index to the nature of the counter-revolution is the methods by which, and by which alone, its exponents can extend their authority. Internally, they coerce; externally, they make war. They have abandoned, that is, the hope of persuasion; they take refuge in their power to make men afraid. It is not, therefore, accident that the executioner and the concentration-camp are the symbols of their régime, nor that, wherever they set their feet, their first victims have been those who have sought to extend the boundaries of human knowledge. They recognize that thought itself is their chief enemy; that is why it is their ambition to impose an orthodoxy from whose rigors there is no escape. The barbarian of the fifth century had at least the humility to venerate the Rome he looted; the barbarian of the twentieth century is incapable of either humility or of veneration. Whatever is different from the pattern he desires to impose, he must seek to blot out from the memory of mankind.

There are those who argue that the next generation will deeply concern itself to discover why three great nations should have challenged the world on behalf of the counter-revolution. Men, they say, do not easily lend themselves to the service of the tyrant, above all, when he brings terrorism and war in his train. A Germany in the tradition of which there was not only a Reformation, but also an Enlightenment; an Italy which knew not only a Renaissance, but also a Risorgimento; from, at least, the Western nations which gave birth to Goethe and Marx, to Galileo and Vico, the acceptance of counter-revolution is held to be astounding. They are tempted to argue that something in their national character must have disposed them to love their chains. I have already rejected this view. I have already pointed out that we know far too little about national character to dogmatize about it with confidence; and, apart from the fact that, at some time, the acceptance of tyranny is a habit that every nation has displayed, just as every nation, at some time, has proved itself capable of striking a blow for freedom, it is with national behaviour that we have to concern ourselves. Nations are what their circumstances make them; and if, at some given time, a nation sets its feet on the path of counter-revolution that is a problem to solve rather than a sin to denounce.

Counter-revolution is a principle to which the masses of a nation do not submit with ease. For it is the nature of man to affirm his own essence; and this requires a capacity for continuous expansion with which the principle of counter-revolution is in direct contradiction. For to affirm one's own essence is to declare that one stands by the meaning one finds oneself in life; and counter-revolution is nothing so much as the demial of the ordinary man's right to express that meaning. It is the imposition of alien experience upon one's own, the enforcement of a dogma from without upon a faith that has grown from within. It is the arrest of the movement of mind and conscience in the individual in favour of dogmatic commands which he must accept even to his own frustration. It is the denial that spontaneity is valid, the insistence, accordingly, that we are instruments and not ends. Yet because, at some point, man is not merely nature's rebel, but authority's rebel, also, he refuses to accept a position of permanent subordination. At some point he insists that his insights must be his own. At some point, he refuses to give his allegiance except upon the condition that he freely chooses to give his allegiance. In every age, there have been men who would rather die than surrender their right to their own insights. In every age, also, there has been a point beyond which the rulers of a society must yield to their subjects or be broken by them.

Counter-revolution succeeds when a quite special set of historical circumstances have taken a deep hold of a people. Its established expectations are disappointed; its sense of failure is profound; it has ceased to be at unity with itself, and has lost, thereby, the capacity to respect its traditional political institutions. When these three conditions co-exist, the prospect of a counter-revolution is profound; when the second is absent, a revolutionary situation is emerging. It was in the three conditions I have described that Mussolini and Hitler arrived at power. In each case, the nation they came to control did not know what the morrow might bring forth. In each case, its inner security was gone; fear was the prevalent disposition. In each case, also, the nation had been deeply injured in its self-respect; none of those who mainly shaped the climate of its opinion deemed its place in the world adequate to its claims. In each case, again, internal antagonisms had reached a point where men could not tolerate the results implied in difference of opinion with their neighbours. As always, intensity of difference bred fear, and fear, in its turn, intensified insecurity. Where men feel insecure, they look to the traditional state-wisdom for assurance, much as a child in distress turns to its mother for comfort. If, at the moment when assurance is required, it fails them, the institutional system is inevitably in danger. For the habit of routine is not less essential to men's comfort than the capacity for adaptation; the success of a state lies in its power to maintain a due proportion between these. When the proportion is unavailable in some particular political system, its utility is exhausted. Men will no longer give loyalty to a state which cannot get its orders obeyed.

The new political order is, in such conditions, imposed by the men who have the resolution to plan, and the capacity to execute, the manœuvres necessary for the seizure of power. I have discussed that seizure in Germany and Italy in an earlier chapter. The reasons for its success are clear. The counter-revolutionaries were united and determined; their opponents were divided and uncertain. And these opponents relied upon a programme the first results of which would clearly have been to intensify the disunity and insecurity of each nation; the counter-revolutionaries made it the supreme virtue of their platform that it had the magic power to dissipate these. Socialists and Communists dwelt on the tawdriness of those traditions with which history had associated the past glories of each nation; the counter-revolutionaries affirmed their splendour. And while the opponents of counter-revolution frankly insisted that their sufferings were, at least in part, their own misfortune, the counter-revolutionaries built up the comforting myth that the nation had been the victim of its enemies, domestic and external. The call to socialism meant a long epoch of material adjustment and spiritual renovation; the leaders of the counter-revolution offered an immediate renaissance in which the lost faith would be swiftly rewon. To peoples, in short, angry with humiliation, and fatigued with the labour of constant adaptation, socialism seemed to offer a future in which humiliation was at least possible once more, and fatigue quite certain. But the counter-revolutionaries promised a future in which there would be an instant renewal of strength and a routine which would save them from the pain of thought.

It is not difficult to understand either victory in the conditions in which it was attained. Revolution or counter-revolution was the immense alternative without the fact being plain to the masses that this was in fact the choice they had to make. Behind the votaries of revolution they saw neither unity of aim nor of method; to achieve it meant certainly a breach with their own past, and perhaps a European war in which aid was doubtful. Behind the counter-revolutionaries, there were massed immense forces with a single purpose, the creation of the conditions of order; and they could count upon at least the sympathy of all who feared a departure from the traditional system. Counter-revolution was built upon a coalition of forces each of which not only had a special interest in its success, but a secret hope that in the final co-ordination achieved it might become the dominant authority; and each of them realized that only by the overthrow of democratic institutions could its special privileges be maintained as legal rights. Economic power, military authority, aristocratic tradition, the dynastic principle, all these united with the *déclassé* adventurers whom Hitler and Mussolini led in the hope of protection from the organized rise of mass-assault upon their privilege.

The business man saw in the overthrow of democracy an end to the power of the working-class, through its political and economic organizations, to set limits to his authority. The soldier was satisfied that new empires were to be won once the destruction of democracy restored the historic status of war. The aristocrat believed that he need no longer fear the claim of talent to share in careers in which, in the pre-democratic age, he had possessed a virtual monopoly. The monarchist hoped that the restoration or strengthening of the throne would follow upon the eclipse of a democracy inherently hostile to the *mystique* by which he lived. To outlaws like Hitler or Mussolini and their followers, the counter-revolution was the one opportunity of obtaining power, and the prizes of power, without the obligation to pay respect to principle. None of the traditional classes which allied itself with the outlaws had in fact taken their measure. For none of them understood that, in the classic sense, a state based upon the rule of law could not be built under the patronage of outlaws, since law would drive them back to that twilight world to which, in an ordered society, they were normally confined. None of these traditional classes understood that it is the outlaw who gives its character to a counter-revolutionary, as distinct from a reactionary, state. They could not rid themselves of the outlaws because it was to these, and not to the men of the old order, that the support of the masses was given. This was the natural result of the fact that only the outlaws could promise to make all things new; unlike his traditionalist allies, the outlaw was bound by no conventions, respected no ties, and was ruthless in a degree of which a group inheriting a tradition was incapable. The traditional groups did not desire to do more than limit the power of democracy to challenge their privileges; but they found that, in the historic position they occupied, an alliance with the outlaws meant the destruction of the very bases of democracy, and that this pushed them beyond reaction to a counter-revolution they could not hope to dominate.

II

It is not difficult, I think, to explain why this is the case. The interest of the masses is in security, freedom, equality, knowledge and peace. These are the conditions of their self-realization. These are the environment the masses require if the masses are to have the opportunity of expanding welfare. For where knowledge is the monopoly of a few, the ignorance of the masses limits their access to welfare. Where there is war, the masses are its primary victims. Where there is inequality, the masses are excluded from the area of benefit, just as a denial of freedom is always the exclusion of the masses from some field of opportunity.

So that the masses in every society have always remained the supreme revolutionary force; it is to them that king, aristocracy, middle-class, have appealed in their upward march to power. Historically, each of them has used the masses as an ally, and then broken the partnership when its power was established. The masses were too ignorant or too poor to be trusted to shape their own destiny. It is not, indeed, until after the American and French Revolutions gave the principle of popular sovereignty its letters of credit, that the idea of democracy began slowly to secure the status of respectability; how slowly can be seen in a speech like that of Macaulay on the Chartist petition,[1] or in the writings in which Guizot so brilliantly defended the theory of the *juste milieu*.[2] But it

[1] Macaulay, *Speeches* (World's Classics Edition), p. 184 f.

[2] *Mémoires* (1875), *Des Moyens d'Opposition* (1821).

was still more slowly that it began to be insisted that the well-being of the masses ought to be the primary object of the state-power; and it was even more rare for the statesmen who insisted that this was so actually to take steps to make it the case. That it was the business of a government to satisfy demand on the largest possible scale was a conception always set in the context that the claims of prescription must be met before this could legitimately be attempted.

This was the natural outcome of an economy of scarcity in a society where either demand was satisfied because, in the technical sense, it was "effective," or because it evoked the emotions which are satisfied by charity. The masses, in an economy of scarcity, are the residuary legatees whose claims are met after "effective" demands are met. The true purpose of the state-power was always to put the force of law, the coercive authority of the society, at the disposal of those who possessed "effective" demand, those, that is to say, who owned or controlled the instruments of production in a given society. The degree in which this fact was apparent depended on whether the society was more or less prosperous. In "good" times, there was more to distribute, and the state-power was less nakedly in evidence; in "bad times" the maintenance of "law and order" was its primary function. If, indeed, the threat of the masses in "bad times" to law and order went deep enough to endanger their stability, experiments in concession, the Speenhamland system, for instance, might be attempted to bribe them into acquiescence in the fundamental equations maintained by the state-power. The extension of the right to vote carried with it only formally the right to disturb this essential equilibrium.

Even the Christian Churches, which had made their way by the affirmation of the great principle that equal need establishes equal claim, and had been deeply critical of the effect of great wealth upon the human soul, were bribed by endowment into partnership with privilege; and they became, through the centuries, one of the main weapons in the grim task of persuading the masses to accept their misfortunes. They cried down secular knowledge; they made obedience to magistrates a condition of salvation; their chiliastic principle was used to console men into tolerance of material suffering. They were even prepared, as the history of groups like the Waldenses and the Spiritual Franciscans makes clear, to outlaw the men who strove to recall them to their original purposes. By making themselves the mediator of salvation between an unknown God and the masses for whose ignorance the Churches conspired, they made themselves, through the centuries, the agents of a social order whose inner and immanent principle has been to confine the main goods of this world to the few at the expense of the many. It is not accident that the Roman Church has been the main prop of both monarchism and Fascism in Spain, or that the Russian Orthodox Church accommodated itself to the evil premisses of Czarist autocracy. Nor was it accident that no influence was more persuasive than that of Wesley in inducing the masses in England to accept the grim discipline of the new factories in return for the dubious consolation of an unproved and unprovable eternal bliss.

Yet every counter-revolution has to take account, at least while the civilization in which it operates is able to endure, of two clear principles. No social order that it builds is able to last if it fails to give the masses a sense of expanding horizons; it must so order its arrangements that access to social benefit is not permanently denied save to those for whom it is made. No doubt there is ebb and flow; for in politics, as in nature, action and reaction are equal. If 1789 produces 1815, 1815 also produces 1848. And, increasingly since the Reformation, and at an even greater tempo in our own day, the forces of production make for a world in which the claims of privilege are dependent upon the co-operation of the masses; and a higher price has continually to be paid if the masses are to be persuaded to co-operate. The Fascist form of counter-revolution is, in its very suppression of the masses, paying tribute to the fear they inspire in its leaders. They may nullify the effect of universal suffrage; they may drive back the workers' organizations to the status of illegal conspiracies; they may hope for the advance of industrial technology without the development of popular education. But they are still faced by the need to give men the vital nourishment of hope; and the very character of their propaganda is the recognition that, unless men are given hope, they turn inevitably to remake the foundations of the state-power that they may attain it.

The counter-revolution, this is to say, denies the validity of an historical movement the implications of which have gone deep into the consciousness not merely of Western man, but also, as events have shown, that Far East he has so largely subjugated to his purposes. From about 1800 onwards, the drive to exploit more fully the forces of production required the free mind; and experience has shown, even if in pain and suffering, that power cannot ultimately set limits to the horizons the free mind will seek to scan. From, further, about the settlement of the American colonies, the idea of a more equal opportunity in life began to seek the verification of experiment from men who were oppressed, men who were persecuted, men whose sense of justice was outraged by a society in which the well-being of the few was increasingly seen to be purchased at the expense of the many. We cannot exaggerate the impact of America upon our civilization.

For it gave something like the status of unbreakable law to the notion that no man is the permanent victim of a fixed destiny. From the *voyages imaginaires* of the seventeenth century we can trace how America has domesticated the ideas of liberty and equality in the mind of the common man. From the travellers of the eighteenth century we can learn how it broke routines which had been held a part of the order of nature. The American War of Independence acted on the age it illuminated with something like the force of a new gospel; it gave to the basic ideas of democracy a status to which, despite themselves, the leaders of the counter-revolution are forced to pay homage. Since Washington was transformed from a rebel into an immortal, there has been no privilege anywhere that has felt complete assurance about its foundations. Not only had the right of rebellion been accorded a vindication which has permanently altered the pattern of men's thoughts; it was given a vindication which has built itself, however imperfect the realization, upon the premiss that men were created free and equal. That was declared a self-evident truth; and there is a vital sense in which all later history has been an attempt to discover the institutions through which that premiss may be expressed.

A century and a half have passed since Washington assumed the Presidency of the United States. In that period, the most important change that has occurred in men's minds is their transfer of emphasis from form to substance. Their passions, from political, have become social. They see no more validity in the present distribution of welfare than their ancestors saw in seventeenth-century England or in eighteenth-century France in schemes they believed they had the power and the right to transcend. They are no more willing to accept our social diseases as inevitable than their ancestors were prepared to accept the ancien régime as a final form of government.

A revolution has already shaped itself in men's minds which makes them judge the states under whose authority they live by their power to offer the masses economic security upon the basis of expanding welfare. That, in our time, has become the meaning of freedom to the masses all over the world. It is held in India and in China, as well as in Britain and in the United States. In its name, an upheaval at least as profound as that of 1789 in France has changed the whole way of life of the Russian people and has set new currents stirring in every quarter of the globe.

It is in this perspective that the counter-revolution must be set. This perspective, like all changes in the fundamental pattern of social life, has come very slowly to maturity. We catch a glimpse of its influence in the Anabaptists of Munster; it is present again in the passionate debates of the Army Council in the English civil wars; it is the motive which, after the fall of Robespierre, gave birth to the conspiracy of Babeuf; and, thenceforward, brought to maturity by increasing industrialization and urban life, it develops from a half-hidden insight, which men hardly dare avow to themselves, into a conscious principle of action for which its votaries are willing to die.

In the first instance, the revolution which Hitler and his associates seek to destroy was mostly content to operate upon the purely political plane. It believed that the wider the basis of the franchise, the more certain was the citizen of access to welfare. It transformed all political institutions, the legislature, the executive, the judiciary, the bureaucracy, in an increasingly democratic direction. But it began, also, slowly to discover either that these changes made an improvement in its situation far below what it had been led to expect, or that the improvement was so slow that it failed to make a decisive alteration in man's fate. So that, presently, it rediscovered the central truth that always comes into the foreground when political changes fail to satisfy: it discovered that the root of its misfortunes lay in the relations of production. It then insists that the laws of property shall become the central matter for political consideration. It asks, that is, for the remaking of the foundations of state-power.

Whenever the rights of property become the fundamental matter of debate in a community, privilege and prescription are called into question; and it is the clear evidence of history that men whose position is the outcome of either will defend themselves by whatever expedients they can. Because we live in an age in which the foundations are in question, those whose interest it is to refuse to adapt the relations of production to the new claims made upon them are bound to attack every principle and institution those claims can mobilize in their support. The idea of democracy, the humanitarian impulse, the craving for equality, the passion for freedom, all these they must deny. Because scientific discovery and philosophic insight advance the expectations men form of their rights, counter-revolutionaries are driven into hostility against any science and any philosophy which appear to lend colour to these expectations.

But that hostility is bound to take the counter-revolutionaries further. It leads them into an attack upon all speculation the relevance of which is unfavourable to the relations they wish to maintain. And as with principles, so with institutions. The masses have built in their forward movement above all three types of defensive association—the trade union, the co-operative society, and the socialist party. The counter-revolutionaries are bound to exact their suppression. To succeed in this, they must destroy the democratic environment which secures to these associations the right to live. For this purpose, they must reject the process of self-government since it is inseparably related to democracy. And once they reject self-government they must, by a dreadful logic, deny the legitimacy of any power they do not themselves authorize; opposition to their purposes thus becomes, in the instant, treason. In a collectivist society based upon the world-market, the totalitarian state is the inevitable instrument of the counter-revolution.

Its makers chose a favourable moment for their enterprise. None of the traditional sources of reaction, the Army, for instance, or Big Business, could have hoped to organize a movement of the masses. They required the services of a demagogue of genius who could bring them that mass-support without which their fight for power would have been at best a dubious gamble. They bought those services; they built the totalitarian state. But, when they had constructed it, they still found themselves confronted by the problem it is the aim of the counter-revolution to suppress as a living issue: how to satisfy the expectations of the masses. Within a totalitarian Italy or Germany there was no way to solve it except by a fundamental alteration in the relations of production, which, by depriving privilege of its claims, would render abortive the whole aim of counter-revolution. They thus confronted a position in which, as the German massacre of June 30, 1934, made clear, they must always face the prospect of rebellion. They then realized, what, indeed, it is probable that the German general staff had recognized from the outset, that they could not maintain their power so long as the rest of Europe was independent of their influence.

When the last internal enemy had been crushed, external relations still remained as a source of potential disaster. The world could not remain for them half-slave, half-free; its conquest was the necessary condition of their survival. From the outset, they therefore prepared for that conquest. Savage repression at home, brutal conquest abroad, they offered this, with a share to their domestic victims in the spoils of conquest, in return for the acceptance of the counter-revolution. The outlaws who enforced this programme were no more concerned at the price their method exacted than the Renaissance bravo who sold his private army to the highest bidder. They took the only means available in the historic period at which we have arrived forcibly to maintain the relations of production as a system of privileges which, by limiting the development of the forces of production, denied the masses access to a rising standard of welfare. If this meant an attempt to impose the counter-revolution upon the world, that attempt became a necessary sacrifice upon the altar of the only religion in which they believed —the sacred right of their class to its prescriptive privileges.

III

This is the counter-revolution with which we are at war; and it is vital that we should understand it for what it is. But before I turn to the implications of its principles, there are two things relevant to it which must be emphasized. The first is the falsity of the argument which seeks to make of Fascism, in its various national forms, and Bolshevism, twin aspects of the same principle. It is false for a number of reasons. First, it confounds the superficial with the fundamental. Because both Fascism and Bolshevism grow out of a situation in which the rise of mass-claims is the central phenomenon, that does not build identity between them. Bolshevism, no doubt, has been cruel; and many of its methods of propaganda have been adapted to Fascist purposes. It is even true that something of the idealism in the early Bolshevik movement has been lost as it has been applied to a semi-Oriental civilization, barely literate, surrounded by enemies, and requiring for self-protection a rapid industrialization which would enable it to defend itself. The discipline involved in this process was bound to be hard, even ruthless. But we fail to judge it rationally unless we remember that, without this discipline, Russia to-day would be the *latifundia* of the counter-revolution, and that it would then be well on the road to that world-dominion at which it aims.

The difference is the vital one that there is nothing in the nature of the Bolshevik state which is alien from the democratic ideal. Its realization has halted, in the main, because its experiment, as I have pointed out, has never been conducted in an atmosphere of security. It is only as the tensions which have so far surrounded it are broken down that its true character as a genuine search for democracy and freedom, a search, be it noted, upon terms that are new in the history of the world, can verify itself in experience.

The other thing that is important is our need to realize that the counter-revolution was never capable of being contained within the countries of its origin. There are statesmen and publicists who have argued that it concerned only those peoples over whom it obtained the mastery so long as it did not become an article for export; even Mr. Churchill has heaped eulogies on Mussolini. When the international relations of the counter-revolution became threatening, democratic statesmen exhausted themselves in attempting its appeasement; few things now seem more ironical than Mr. Chamberlain's announcement, after Munich, that he had found the formula for "peace in our time." The fact was, of course, not only that the principle of counter-revolution requires war as the law of its being, and that no state, therefore, can be indifferent to it. The fact was, also, that, because counter-revolution waxes and wanes in a world unified by the nature of the international market, its life depends, in the period while it is preparing for war, on the trade-relations it can organize.

Japanese aggression in China was fed for years by the main democratic powers; thereby they gave vitality to a principle of social organization they professed to abhor. German rearmament, the dangers of which were an obvious commonplace, was partly financed, and wholly made possible, by the assistance of those it was set upon destroying. Even after Hitler had struck his felon's blow at Czechoslovakia, Mr. Montagu Norman, with the assent of Viscount Simon, completed the obsequies of the Czech state by handing over to him its gold deposit in the Bank of International Settlements. Mr. Anthony Eden connived at the hypocrisy of non-intervention in Spain at a time when he must have been fully aware that Hitler and Mussolini were making the Civil War a dress rehearsal for the larger drama they proposed to stage; and, as late as January 5, 1942, in commenting upon his visit to the Soviet Union, he said with emphasis that he would not have been concerned with the destruction of Nazism if Hitler had confined his operations to the German people. Surely by this time, the principle of counter-revolution has been applied upon a wide enough scale for its meaning to be clear to the Foreign Secretary in Mr. Churchill's government?

The truth is that the principle of counter-revolution is bound to appeal to any class in the situation of those responsible for experimenting with it. Partly, that is clearly seen in the emergence of Fascist groups in almost every country. Partly, also, it is seen in the methods, for example, of some of the great employers in the United States, with their private armies, their bombs and tear-gas, their professional thuggery, under-cover agents in the trade unions. Men like Governor Talmadge in Georgia, or Mayor Hague in Jersey City, are already, no doubt on a small scale, seeking Fascist ends by Fascist methods. Most striking of all is the fact that, in June 1940, the defeated French government chose the principle of counter-revolution rather than experiment with the dynamic of democracy; and it is significant that the choice was made by the collaboration of Big Business, and the Service Chiefs, with Laval as the prospective, if pinchbeck, Hitler, weaving from the background the sinister threads of this tragic conspiracy.

The drive to reaction, in short, becomes counter-revolution when an economic system is in the final phase of its decay. It requires two conditions for its emergence. It must find a situation, first, in which the traditional rulers are convinced that their vital privileges are in danger; and it must find one, second, in which there is no clear lead from those who challenged the existing order to which, in the given circumstances, the masses feel able to respond. Where these conditions obtain, men like Mussolini and Hitler will be able to cement an alliance with the forces of privilege while they speak to the confused masses in the accents of freedom. The effect of the alliance is to give them direct access to the state-power; while the absence of a clear lead means that the parties of the Left are separated from the masses, upon whom they rely for support, long before they are aware that their authority is undermined. Dr. Brüning's use, for example, of Article 48 of the Weimar Constitution had prepared the way for Hitler's advent to power long before either the Socialists or the Communists in Germany had grasped the fatality of their position.

No doubt, in a high degree, the emergence of these conditions upon the psychological atmosphere which military defeat or frustration engenders; the traditional rulers of Italy and Germany were discredited by failure. Their alliance with the outlaws enabled the counter-revolution to masquerade as revolution until its purposes were secure. It even enables the new régime to continue to speak in the accents of revolution without producing a general understanding of the deception it has practised. For though, once it is safely in possession of the state-power, Fascism does not even attempt to change the class-relations of society, the large-scale introduction of its legionaries into positions of authority gives the superficial appearance of the career open to the talents; and the realignment of economic forces it is compelled to undertake to complete its consolidation of power—for Fascism lives by the public works programme of rearmament until it is ready for war—gives, again, the superficial appearance of a control of privilege which is easily represented, especially abroad, as revolutionary innovation. It is not until the consolidation is complete that capitalism, in its Fascist phase, stands fully revealed as counter-revolution.

That full revelation is accomplished when the power of the state has been reorganized as monolithic. It remakes the foundations of order to retain the claims of privilege. To do so, obviously, it must subordinate the entrepreneur-function to the needs of order; for the characteristic of capitalism in its Fascist phase is that its growingly monopolistic character makes risk, experiment, freedom, the enemies of its central principle. This is the first great subordination it achieves; and it is worth noting that one of its effects is to disguise the inherently capitalist character of Fascism by the depth to which it relies upon state-action. For here we are largely deceived by the obsolete stereotype of capitalism which persists in our minds. We think of the concepts which shape its character in terms of categories which belong to its epoch of expansion, the impersonality of its institutions has, even yet, become so small a part of our mental climate that the economics of imperfect competition are still in their infancy, and we adjust ourselves only with an effort to the realization that freedom of contract can no longer operate in the conditions which produced the decision in the *Mogul Steamship case* in England[1] or *Adair* v. *United States*[2] in America.

The monolithic character of power is necessary, further, to prevent the rise of the masses against the discovery that the counter-revolution has, in fact, no revolutionary prospects in offer them; it requires, that is, a plan through the authority of which it has the power to crush all resistance to itself. The plan cannot be anything other than preparation for war, and, eventually, war itself; the hope, that is to say, of regaining by victory for the new leaders of the old social forces the credit lost by the old leaders. And this plan, of course, has, for the new leaders, the immense merit of keeping the society they control in that state of tense emergency where, in any field directly relevant to their interests, the idea of the rule of law is inadmissible; for tense emergency can only be met by the application of extraordinary measures.

[1] (1892) A.C. 25.

[2] 208 U.S. 161.

One other aspect of this monolithic power deserves a word. It is driven, I have argued, by its inner necessities to plan for war; it therefore assumes a quasi-collectivist character in which the state-power determines the ends to which the instruments of production are devoted. The essential status of privilege is unchanged; but the habits of accumulation, which were previously determined by innumerable private decisions become a matter of state determination. The rate of interest and profit, the direction of investment, the channels of commercial intercourse, the character of consumption—guns instead of butter—are all controlled by the state in the name of the overriding plan. It adapts capitalism, this is to say, to the conditions which safeguard the forces of privilege against revolt from within. It is true that this safeguard is purchased by the necessity of external war. It is true, also, that defeat in that war is bound to bring the whole edifice crashing in ruins. But, up to the moment of defeat, what Fascism achieves for capitalism which is threatened by social revolution is the organization of the conditions which delay its advent. More than this. The fact that technological conditions make the modern world-war totalitarian unites the inert mass to the conquerors by their dread of the price of defeat. No doubt the achievement is a gamble. I do not think anyone who has lived through the years since 1939 is likely to underestimate the degree to which it has approached success.

IV

The theory, therefore, which underlies the Fascist assault upon civilization is a simple one. The outlaws seek to maintain the framework of a decaying society by the transference of wealth from other nations to themselves; and they assume that victory in the war will give them a monopoly of armed power against those whom they thus reduce to economic peonage, and moral and intellectual slavery. There is no *a priori* reason to suppose that victory would not give them this power; the condition to which they have reduced nations like the Czechs, the Poles and the French, is sufficient evidence of it. There have been dark ages before in history; there is no logical reason why there should not be dark ages again.

A system that is found wanting at a great crisis can always adapt itself to the needs of that crisis if its enemies are divided and it is reckless of the price it pays. The Roman Catholic Church met the challenge of the Reformation very much in this way. The Counter-Reformation was nothing so much as the successful adjustment of those elements in Roman principles and organization without the sacrifice of which it would have been overwhelmed. Rome adapted itself to the demands of the new economic order of the sixteenth and seventeenth centuries slowly, no doubt, and painfully; the wars of religion, controversies like those between Jesuit and Jansenist in France, like that over religious toleration in England, are sufficient evidence of that. But it adjusted itself. And the method of adjustment was to give up what it was impossible to retain while concentrating all its strength on the organization of the positions it was still possible to defend. Nor must we fail to note the degree to which its survival was due to the divisions among its enemies.

The defeat of the Axis powers is a vital and essential stage in the defeat of the counter-revolution; it does not, of itself, automatically assure the fulfilment of the ends for which the common people in the United Nations have been asked to fight. This defeat is the provision of an opportunity; it is not an assurance that it will be used. And until we have given that assurance the form of an effective organization, the defeat of the Axis powers is a stage only in the defeat of the counter-revolution. It destroys an evil expression of its principles. It does not root out the principles themselves.

This can, I think, be seen in two ways. It can be seen, first, by examining the special post-war situation in which, to take two examples only, Great Britain and the United States will find themselves; and it can be seen by looking at the implications of the international scene which will confront us after the war.

The relation of capitalism to democracy will be as certainly the outstanding problems in post-war Britain and the United States as they were in the Germany of the Weimar Republic. The victory, no doubt, will give a formal status of immense value to the Four Freedoms. But, over against the power of that formal status, the drive of other, and not less important, factors must be remembered.

There is, first of all, the distribution of the incidence of the cost of victory, and the demand of the masses for a freedom that they see, above everything, in terms of economic security, and a greater equality in material welfare. There is, secondly, the intensification which war-production has involved, of the tendency to concentrate ever greater economic control in a few hands; economic structures tend to beget their own political systems, and private monopoly tends rapidly to create that economics of scarcity which destroys the availability of political democracy. There is, thirdly, the growth of the centrifugal forces in the Imperial system, the emancipation of Australia, New Zealand, and, in a still greater degree, Canada, from dependence upon the London money market, the exhibition of empire in decay in Malaya, Burma, and the West Indies, the necessity, however unpalatable, to recognize that India, in the post-war world, must be either free or ungovernable. Africa, no doubt, will, for a considerable period, provide the basis for secure investment and unchallengeable control; but even in Africa there are immense stirrings.

Nor must we forget that the very narrow gap which, in 1940, separated Britain from a defeat akin to that of France, has done much to break the faith of the masses in the traditional claims of the ruling class. Their scepticism has been strongly reinforced by the contrast between its massive errors and the not less massive successes of the Soviet Union. Psychologically, the inherent principle of the Russian Revolution—planned production for community consumption—has been domesticated in the British worker's mind, and, significantly, in the mind of the rank and file of the armed forces, by the harsh impact of war with a swiftness that is remarkable. The need is obvious for the renovation of basic British institutions, the Army, the Civil Service, the educational system, industrial leadership, Parliament and local government. No one can honestly say that they have shown either the foresight or the flexibility which the crisis has demanded. This absence of foresight and flexibility raises the question, which is fundamental for any régime, of whether the scale of the renovation required is within the capacity of the system in the light of the economic foundations to which it is geared. For each of the institutions the renovation of which is called for is at the heart of the system of privileges we maintain, It is difficult to see how the renovation can be achieved without the surrender, at least in large part, of the basis upon which that system of privileges rests.

For that surrender implies a change of heart in the ruling class of Britain which is one of the rarest qualities a ruling class is ready to display. Such a change of heart is associated, historically, with the expansion of an economic system which has followed on the rise of a new class to power. Capitalist democracy in Britain has no longer, in its present form, the prospect of discovering those conditions. It has therefore either rapidly to reorganize its relations of production in order to resume expansion, or to confront the growth of those conditions which lead to the rise of counter-revolution. So far, no steps have been taken towards that reorganization. Though the degree of state-intervention is profound, it has left wholly unresolved, indeed largely undiscussed, the supreme issues of whether it is to continue into the peace, and, if it is to continue, to what ends it will be devoted. All the essential instruments of production remain in private hands; the whole system is still based upon the principle of production for private profit; and, if anything, monopolistic enterprise will be in a stronger position after the war than before it. The question whether, once the Axis Powers have been defeated, the forces of privilege in Britain will co-operate with the workers by hand and brain sufficiently to enable the great ends of life to be held in common permits of no assured reply. And that question will have to be answered at a time when the removal of the direct threat of external danger will not only, on all experience, erode the high mood of exaltation and sacrifice which it bred, but tend to make the treasured securities of the past, rather than the unknown risks of the future, the source in which the governing class of Britain will seek its principles for the new epoch.

"Traditional" Britain passed into history on September 3, 1939. To transform it so that it does not involve profound frustration for the masses means, I repeat, not only large-scale reforms in almost every department of the national life, but, also, the sacrifice of vested interests which were the spinal-column of "traditional" Britain. It is possible to imagine arrival at terms of accommodation with those interests if advantage were taken of the mood of experiment the war has bred in so many people in so many classes. We might then see the provision, before the war is over, of some at least of the bridgeheads we shall require to reach the new Britain. That is how a nation wins hope, for, with hope, it buys time.

But it is not the policy of Mr. Churchill and his colleagues to provide those bridgeheads. On the contrary, it rather seems to envisage the conscious postponement of any issue deemed "controversial" until victory is won; and a "controversial" issue is held to be any issue by which parties were deeply divided before the war. This means, if this policy be maintained, that the relations of production are to remain unchanged until peace comes, and that accordingly, one of the instruments required for social change on a large scale, will be at the national disposal for agreed purposes. With the main drive to unity of outlook and interest withdrawn we shall then have to find, if we can, the means to agreement about fundamental differences in the realm where such differences most easily oreed conflict.

Frankly, I do not find it easy to believe that, in such circumstances, the means to agreement will be readily forthcoming. I know that the roots of our democratic tradition lie deep. I am aware that no nation has a longer capacity than ours for compromise. I admit that the British impulse for "fair play" has, with us, something like the status of a moral principle, and that we shall approach the search for agreement with victory behind us. But the abyss to be bridged between classes will be wider than at any time since the Chartist Movement. It is not an abyss that can be spanned by a bridge of great perorations. It will not be conjured away by rhetorical appeals for the maintenance of unity in the face of grave problems, for, with peace, the drive of our political system is bound to be towards emphasis on the differences between men's interests, and not on their identities; that is the normal purpose of our political system in its classic shape. Each group in the community will remember the sacrifices it made for victory; and each will view with intense resentment the plea for further sacrifices behind which there is none of the dramatic compulsion of the period of danger. Each will begin to examine with suspicion and disfavour the expectations of the others, the postulates of action upon which those expectations are based. The difficulties inherent in the transition to a peace-economy, the problems of demobilization, of the return from evacuation, of the principles upon which Britain is to be rebuilt, will be exacerbated; and because we shall not have laid the foundations of hope, time will not be a weapon we can command. The fear of insecurity will be the main shadow over everyone's life. Where the source of insecurity in a nation is internal, and not external, a privileged class approaches that frontier where fear and blind anger begin to play with the idea of counter-revolution.

Our duty, at any rate, is to face the fact that this is the kind of situation when social peace hangs by a very slender thread. We gain nothing by urging that such a mood is unthinkable in this country. The triumph of 1918 provoked the massive disillusion of the inter-war years; and, if we are honest, we must admit that it bred among considerable numbers of the governing class that sympathy for the counter-revolution which received continuous and significant expression in the years of appeasement. It is at least possible that a refusal on the part of the Churchill government to find the new basis upon which, when peace comes, expanding welfare can be organized means a drift more rapid and more widespread than we can now imagine away from the acceptance of democratic procedures as normal.

Constitutionalism, after all, is a doctrine of which we ought to have learned the inherent fragility; its preservation depends very largely upon the ability of men to agree upon its objectives. A situation may easily arise when, for example, the forces of the under-privileged are not powerful enough, or united enough, to secure the control of the state, but when their purposes differ so widely from ends that the forces of privilege can approve that neither is prepared to accept the measures of the other. Or a Left government in office may discover that social reform can only be purchased, given the present relations of production, at the expense of the confidence of those who guard the inner citadel of economic power. Or a Right government in office may, as in 1928, pursue a deflationary policy in that national interest which it is so easily tempted to identify with its ability to command the applause of the rentier class. Any of these is a situation in which the impulse to counter-revolution becomes strong. The fears of the propertied class, angry disillusion in the trade unions, the presence amongst us of a large middle class with no clear political convictions, these are the elements which, in an epoch of frustration, make for the emergence of the idea of counter-revolution. Like its prototypes on the Continent, it will find no difficulty in building private relations which contradict its public professions. Like them, also, whatever those professions, its real purpose will be to destroy political democracy in the interest of a capitalism no longer able to expand.

My argument does not presuppose either the success or failure of a counter-revolution in Britain, it assumes only that if we allow the conditions to develop in which there is no other way in which privilege can protect its interests, the drift to counter-revolution will be inevitable. It may well be that the British Labour movement will prove tougher than its neighbours in Italy and Germany. It may even be that the power of Fascist principles over middle opinion in Britain will prove smaller than it did in those countries. Neither fact alters the position that when the interests of capitalism contradict the interests of the masses, the natural evil of counter-revolution is prepared, and that, historically, the seed which finds its natural soil tends to spring into life. What we have to remember is that once a counter-revolutionary movement has assumed serious proportions, it becomes impossible to maintain the classic democratic procedures. That is the unmistakable lesson of Italy and Germany.

For democratic procedures are built upon the existence not only of the right of opposition, but of the right of those in opposition peacefully to become the government. That right is only maintained by the power of men to hold the great ends of life in common And the very emergence of a Fascist party means the decay of that power. It proves the existence of crisis and emergency; it means that the traditional hold of unity and order is going. And if unity and order are threatened in their democratic context—which is what Fascism really means—then we are left with the choice of remaking them either by revolution or by counter-revolution. We are faced, in short, by the prospect of a violent upheaval which may well render abortive the victory we shall have won. For violent upheaval is bound to deny freedom and democracy until the rulers of society judge that they may safely transform the processes of coercion into processes of consent. Where the counter-revolutionaries succeed, that transformation is, *a priori* ruled out, because it would be fatal to the principle by which they live; that has been the experience of every counter-revolution. Nor is it easy even when the revolutionaries are successful. It is worth remembering that, despite its immense achievements, a whole generation has not sufficed for the Soviet Union to complete the transition from the one to the other.

It is worth while to remind ourselves, from this angle, of the internal situation which the United States will confront at the end of this war. Its ruling class is not only more powerful, it is, also, more hostile to fundamental change, than any other in the Western democracies. With victory, the productive capacity of the United States will be greater than at any previous period; but only a profound change in the relations of production will enable that productive capacity to be used for the common benefit. Even the immense demands of a war economy still leaves America with some millions of migratory labourers on its hands to whom the Four Freedoms are largely devoid of meaning.[1] The history of the New Deal up to 1940 was already an ominous indication that the forces of privilege in America were prepared tenaciously to defend every position they occupied; there were many Americans who, up to Pearl Harbour itself, were uncertain whether Mr. Roosevelt or Adolf Hitler was their major enemy. Even after American entrance into the war, the history of aluminium, of synthetic rubber, of the revelations of Mr. Thurman Arnold, the Assistant Attorney-General of the United States, of the practices of great corporations like, for example, the General Electric Company,[2] the effort of Mr. Ford to prevent the development of an adequate housing policy in the Detroit area, showed that the power of what Bentham called

[1] *America's Own Refugees*. By H. H. Collins (1942).

[2] The columns of the *New Republic* and the *Nation* during the first six months of 1942 provide an interesting commentary on this experience.

"sinister interest" remained impressive. The suffrages of ordinary people might keep Mr. Roosevelt in the White House; but it is not an exaggeration to say that his ability to carry out the economic programme victory required depended upon the co-operation of forces profoundly hostile to the main social purposes for which he stood. Very largely, he had to secure co-operation on their terms, and these meant, to put it bluntly, that New Deal principles went into cold storage for the duration of the war.

The American situation is, no doubt, complicated by the fact that the emergence of the positive state is so new in its history. The social consciousness of many of its most powerful elements has not yet adapted itself to the logic of the positive state. Its political leaders, Mr. Hoover, for example, and its industrial leaders, labour hardly less than in finance and manufacturing, still think in terms of the frontier civilization which ended at least by the beginning of this century. It is not, indeed, an exaggeration to say that it is the main assumption of the most powerful interests in the United States that, as President Hadley once put it, "the forces of democracy, on one side, divided between the executive and the legislature, are set over against the forces of democracy on the other side, with the judiciary as arbiter between them. . . . It has allowed the experiment of universal suffrage to be tried under conditions essentially different from those which led to its ruin in Athens and Rome, The voter was omnipotent—within a limited area. He could make what laws he pleased, as long as those laws did not trench upon property-right. He could elect what officers he pleased, as long as those officers did not try to do certain duties confided by the Constitution to the property-holders."

This is, in effect, the Hamiltonian theory of the American constitution. Underlying it is an assumed equation between wealth and political power. Madison never concealed his view that the basis of authority ought to be a stake in the country; and his whole scheme of thought implied an economics of permanent scarcity. "It is a lot of humanity," he wrote, "that of this surplus [the landless labourers] a large proportion is necessarily reduced by a competition for employment to wages which afford them the bare necessaries of life. The proportion being without property, or the hope of acquiring it, cannot be expected to sympathize sufficiently with its rights to be safe depositaries of power over them." The inference from Madison's argument was drawn by Webster a generation later. Where property is concentrated in a few hands, he thought, and the masses are poor and dependent, "popular power must break in upon the rights of property, or else the influence of property must limit and control the exercise of popular power. . . . The holders of estates would be obliged in such case, either in some way to restrain the right of suffrage, or else such right of suffrage would ere long divide the property."

This is still, in effect, the mental climate in which privileged America has faith. No doubt it has always encountered the great Jeffersonian tradition which, in their different ways, men like Channing and Emerson, Lincoln and Franklin Roosevelt have sought to maintain. But, so far, only the emotion of great crisis has made possible any considerable period of office for that Jeffersonian tradition, and it has come to terms with the Hamiltonian view because of the power of America to overcome depression. The period from 1933 is the first in which it became obvious that this power no longer possessed its former elasticity. After seven years of the New Deal, with its great experiments, and immense public expenditures, there were still millions of unemployed in the United States, the concentration of economic control proceeded rapidly, alike in industry and agriculture, and a great proportion of American productive capacity remained unused for lack of effective demand. With victory, each of these problems will impose itself with new intensity. America will confront a choice between imperialism, that Caesarism Webster foresaw as the outcome of the clash between property and suffrage, and a renovation of its democratic tradition which will depend upon the organization of profound changes in its relations of production. I must add that, if its choice be Caesarism —a pseudonym for counter-revolution—the movement towards imperialist habits in America will be swift. A population, like that of the United States, will only accept the discipline counter-revolution requires if it can show a speedy result in terms of expanding welfare.

All this may be put in general terms before we turn to its international implications. The Soviet Union apart, the capitalist foundation of our society is practically, though at different levels, a universal phenomenon. That foundation is no longer able to supply the expanding welfare its democratic context involves. The danger is therefore great that it will seek to destroy its democratic context, for there is no capitalist society in which the material is not present capable of being organized for counter-revolution. The present war has suspended that capacity mainly because it has directed men's minds to the things they have in common and away from the things by which they are divided. When the national existence is threatened by a common enemy, the hold of the things a nation has in common is always, in the absence of defeat, temporarily more powerful than any other factor.

But it must be noted that the war suspends the capacity; it does not solve the problems it implies. On the contrary, in the absence of foresight, it may give that capacity new energy if it is released by the coming of peace. For war enormously enlarges the authority and ambit of the state-power; and it is this enlarged power that the forces of counter-revolution require in order to fulfil themselves. Crisis government, whether in peace or war, changes the balance of authority in a democratic system from the electorate and the legislature to the executive; where the forces of counter-revolution are strong and determined, executive direction becomes, with unhappy facility, the prelude to Fascism; that is the lesson, above all, of the transition from Brüning to Hitler. And nothing so tends to destroy the democratic controls which permit the strong executive power to be compatible with freedom as the situation where men of property are in a panic. Nothing, moreover, so tends to throw them into a panic as the need to improvise hastily great measures of change which they are not prepared to sanction as necessary, above all when such measures seem to them unrelated to a great purpose. At this stage, anyone who promises order to them on the old terms seems something like a saviour. This is the moment when the outlaw, like Hitler or Mussolini, has his opportunity. It is, therefore, a necessary part of the task of winning the war to obviate, if we can, the need for such improvisation. It is the essential safeguard against the grave danger that we win only to put in hazard all the possible benefits of victory.

V

Nowhere is this more plain than in the international relations of Britain and the U.S.S.R. The problem of each government is not merely to co-operate with one another, and with their allies, in the period of common danger; it is also to build the permanent basis for co-operation at the moment when the transcendent aim which unites them gives to that task a proportionate emotional support. The emotional support does not last; that is painfully clear from the proceedings at Versailles in 1919. Permanent co-operation depends upon an equal interest in its results. Unless we begin to build the conditions which make for that equal interest, it will not be easy to secure permanent co-operation.

It may be said that the Anglo-Russian treaty is valid for twenty years after the victory. But it is no use concealing from ourselves the fact that those twenty years will see great changes, and that the wills of the signatories will adapt themselves to what effect those changes have upon their interests. A Britain which can afford friendship with Russia will honour the terms of the treaty, as a Russia will do which does not feel that British foreign policy jeopardizes her security. But otherwise? It is, after all, the primary lesson of the years of appeasement that we interpret our obligations in terms of our interests, as we see them at the moment when the obligation falls due. The meaning of a treaty is not something static and objective; it is the whole dynamic which gives that moment its character that will determine then what the treaty means, on both sides. If Russia then seems by its habits as great a challenge to interests which Britain proposes to maintain, we shall find ways out of the clauses of the Treaty, as we found ways out of fulfilling our international obligations to the constitutional government of Spain during its Civil War. And the same is true on the Russian side. Interest enabled the Soviet Union to take one view of the government of Finland in 1936 and a very different view in 1939. There is no reason to suppose that the Anglo-Russian treaty of 1942 will have a history set by other considerations.

Even more is this likely to be the case in Russo-American relations. It is significant that recognition, even, was not accorded the Bolshevik state until the crisis of the Depression brought a New Deal President into office. Though the Anglo-Russian Treaty has the warm approval of President Roosevelt, it is not flanked by a Russo-American Treaty mainly because American distrust of communism makes it at least uncertain whether the necessary majority for its confirmation could be obtained in the Senate. Even the trade unions in the United States share this distrust; the American Federation of Labour has refused to join the Anglo-Russian Trade Union Council. It is, I think, legitimate to conclude that an America which continues progressive in policy will find it relatively easy to continue collaboration with Bolshevik Russia. But an America which returned to the atmosphere of action in which, as under Harding and Coolidge, the White House was an annexe of Wall Street would find that collaboration difficult in the degree that the socialist experiment in Russia was successful. For exactly as, before the war, Bolshevism was regarded as a challenge to the capitalist way of life, so it will be regarded as a challenge after the war against which the interests which feel themselves threatened will take precautions. The same, no doubt, will be true from the Russian side also; the German attack is, after all, the drive of counter-revolution to destroy the chief source of revolutionary ideas. With the defeat of Hitler, an America dominated by Big Business would rapidly become the chief patron of counter-revolution, and, thereby, the author of a policy necessarily hostile to the world-objectives it must be the purpose of a socialist Russia to promote.

Security, in a word, is possible as between great nations that are like-minded in aim; but there can be no like-mindedness of aim between great nations which seek antithetic economic ends. This is the more certainly the case because the habits of capitalism in contraction are bound, as we have seen in the last generation, to become increasingly imperialist. To safeguard themselves they are bound, where they have the power, to bring under their influence the smaller peoples who cannot stand alone. For those peoples are, as it were, the psychological frontiers which they seek to interpose between their own power to maintain themselves and the challenge to which a system in expansion exposes them. The notion that effective and continuous co-operation is possible on these terms is as foolish as to expect it between the Roman Catholic Church and the Nonconformist Churches. Even where they use a similar language, it will be found, on a close scrutiny, that they attach different meanings to the words.

And already, before the issue of victory has been decided, one can see in the stresses and strains of policy among the United Nations the manœuvres within each of them of the different interests for position in the post-war world. That emerges with striking clarity in the confusion which surrounds our propaganda both to enemy and occupied countries, as well as to the few remaining neutrals. We want to incite the people of the Axis Powers to revolt against their governments; but we do not want the revolt to assume a communist shape. We want them to revolt, but, military defeat apart, the main incitement to revolt depends upon our ability to pledge them a future less grim, after defeat, than they have been led by their rulers to expect from us. But to make that pledge which, if it is to be believed, must be authoritative and specific, there must be agreement upon the policy of which it is the expression; and there is no such agreement because the vested interests within, and between, each of the United Nations prevent it from being made. We cannot speak, for instance, of the future of the Baltic States, since Russia has a view of that future which the American government has not accepted. We know that a free Poland will be brought into being; but of its relations to the corridor, to Hungary, and to Russia we can be neither authoritative nor specific. Russia urges sabotage and guerilla warfare upon Czechoslovakia at the same time as we advise the Czechs not to act until the word is given. The implications of our propaganda to Spain are rarely on all fours with that to France; since the Germans point out the discrepancies to the Spaniards it is we who suffer from the difference.

It seems tautologous to say that propaganda depends upon who are the propagandists; yet this is a matter of real importance. What we say, for instance, to Germans in our effort to provoke resistance to Hitlerism amongst them depends, in large measure, upon the view we hold of the nature of this war, on the one hand, and our judgment of German behaviour and its possibilities on the other. If, as I have argued in this book, we believe Hitlerism to be counter-revolution, then our propagandist methods must be, above all, an appeal to the forces in Germany which, at the appropriate moment, are capable of revolutionary action. Those forces are the working-class forces, in particular; the time for a middle-class revolution in Germany has passed away. But if we are to appeal to the German workers, the best form that appeal can take is the proof, in our own society, of our capacity to do justice to the interests of our own workers. That proof lies in the statute and not in the promise; as Mr. Howard Smith has said,[1] a deed, like the nationalization of the armaments industry, is worth a hundred speeches, even from the most eminent of statesmen, on the need to substitute butter for guns in the future. But, if we do not believe that Hitlerism is counter-revolution, and regard this war as simply a phase in the history of the struggle for the balance of power, propaganda for revolution in Germany has little meaning. What produces, quite certainly, the minimum effect is propaganda which reveals that we have no clear view of the nature of this war.

And it is certainly of very little use to appeal to Germans if our view of their behaviour is built upon the doctrine that has come to be known as "Vansittartism." For, obviously, if we assume that all Germans are Nazis, are, therefore, brutal, corrupt, and amoral, the same type as the outlaws who have become their leaders; if, further, we think that ordinary Germans accept as legitimate the German Army's behaviour, for example, to Czechoslovakia and Poland, that all Germans have an inexhaustible lust for world-dominion, that they believe in the ignorant and arrogant racialism of Hitler and Rosenberg, it is surely evident that no propaganda to Germany is

[1] *Last Train from Berlin* (1942), especially the last chapter.

likely to have any effect save that built upon our ability to strike terror into them. And this means that, after their defeat, we must impose the terror we threaten, for nothing could be worse in its ultimate results than to threaten a nation made up of Nazis by nature with penalties we lack the courage to impose. This policy confronts the three difficulties, first, that the terrorization, over any considerable period, of eighty million people is a fairly large undertaking; second, that the policy is contradicted by the main assumptions which underlie Russian propaganda to Germans; and, third, that a government which practises a policy of terror abroad creates thereby the habit of mind which is ready to practise the same policy at home.

It surely becomes evident, as this situation is analysed in all its implications that the use to which we put our victory is conditioned by the philosophy for which we wage the war. If we wage it without a philosophy, as simply a threatened group of nations resisting slavery, the conflict of interests within the group means that its unity is unlikely to persist after the threat has been overcome. If we seek to wage it as a war of ideas, then the purpose of victory must be such a pattern of international relations as will enable unity for survival to be extended into unity for peace. The only philosophy which seems to offer the prospect that this unity will endure is one that, translated into action, creates the necessary conditions for international economic expansion. Such a philosophy is bound to be revolutionary in character. Its central problem then becomes that of the methods and speed with which it is given application.

VI

We can fight the counter-revolution successfully if we fight it with a revolutionary idea; but nothing less than this idea will suffice if our victory is to be a creative one. No doubt those peoples which have already known freedom will resist with all their power the assault of Nazism. That has been demonstrated beyond the need for discussion not only by ourselves and the Russians; it has been proved by the inability of Hitler and his allies to secure the effective co-operation of any European people. In one sense, perhaps, it has been proved most strikingly by the Filipinos, for, with them, the promise of freedom was enough to evoke courage and endurance in the face of power that might well have intimidated men who did not know the significance of freedom.

But there is evidence that we have not yet learned the significance of the revolutionary idea as the vital weapon in our armoury. That evidence comes from two sources. In part, it is an obvious inference from the British collapse in the Far East; in part it is a conclusion which may, I think, be legitimately derived from the ebb and flow of our own war-effort.

The evidence is overwhelming that, in the Far East, the native populations watched the defeat of the British with something like indifference; and it is impossible not to contrast their attitude with that of the Filipinos to the United States. In India there is the grave spectacle of men like Jawarnahal Nehru, whose hatred of Fascism requires no proof, willing to take steps of which the logical outcome might well be a Fascist victory. It is impossible not to explain this indifference in terms of the failure of British imperialism to see that it had outlived its claims. It was associated in the minds of those in whom it produced this indifference with a racial arrogance which they did not distinguish from that of its enemies, and an economic exploitation which, whatever the rationalizations by which it was explained, still, at the end, remained exploitation. Whether in Malaya or Burma or India, British statesmen handled the problems they confronted with a wooden unimaginativeness for which no condemnation can be too strong.

For, I repeat, there, as in Europe, they were fighting the counter-revolution; and they lacked the insight to understand that they needed the formula of freedom to fight it on equal terms. They did not seek the aid of the Chinese in Singapore until the Japanese assault was almost launched. When they refused the Burmese request for Dominion status after the war they were bound to create the conviction that they proposed to retain in their own hands the effective reality of power. And even if one grants the complexity of the Indian issue, their approach to its handling had about it a massive futility which gave good reason to their critics for doubt of whether they understood the nature of the war in which they were involved. They gave too little; what little they gave, they offered too late; and when their offer failed to elicit the enthusiasm to which they felt themselves entitled, they took their stand upon a dead prestige with a self-righteous alacrity which made it at least open to suspicion whether they were not relieved at their failure.

Let us remember that they took India into the war without even the pretence of consultation and by a unilateral act from Whitehall. The resignation of the Congress Party governments in the Provinces produced, no doubt, a series of petty concessions the futile character of which evoked continuous protest from the Labour Party. There was no really profound effort, until the actual entrance of Japan into the war, either effectively to mobilize for the war-effort the resources of India in men and in material, or to awaken the faith of the Indian masses in the good faith behind the British cause. Indians were admitted to the ante-rooms of power, as when the Viceroy's Council was enlarged, and an advisory body on defence created; an effective share in the reality of power was withheld All the old arguments were trotted out. Indians were not united, the Congress Party was not representative, constitutional change was impossible in wartime. The British government even had the bad taste to congratulate itself on the loyalty and generosity of the Indian princes; though there can hardly have been a Minister who was not aware that not half a dozen of the princes were fit to occupy their thrones, that few of them were safe but for the support of the British Government, and that most of their generosity was paid for from the pockets of their subjects. Until Sir Stafford Cripps took out his offer to India in the spring of 1942, it is impossible to feel that any serious effort had been made in Britain to reach an accommodation with India. And it is impossible not to feel that the impulse to the Cripps mission derived less from an inherent belief in its desirability than from the proximity of the Japanese threat, on the one hand, and the criticism of British allies, especially in the United States, on the other.

The failure of the Cripps mission is one of the major tragedies of this war, the more so because there were clearly moments when it was on the very edge of success. What, I think, is significant in its failure has two sides to it, though perhaps both of them are referable to the same principle. The first side is the inability of the British Government to realize that only a truly national government in India could mobilize the necessary depth of popular conviction that the defeat of Japan was necessary to India not less than to Britain, and that the ersatz-national character of a Viceroy's Council whose members, however distinguished, were, with one exception, officials who symbolized nothing in the national life, could not evoke the temper appropriate to the emergency. The second side was the absence of any serious effort on the part of the British Government to overcome the consequences of Sir Stafford Cripps' failure. One may feel, as I do, that the Congress Party's threat of civil disobedience was a grave error incapable of justification while remaining convinced that the speed with which the repression of the Congress Party was undertaken, without even an attempt to explore the meaning of the Congress demands, was evidence of a certain relief in Whitehall that the historic outlines of Indian administration remained unchanged. Certainly the statement of Mr. Churchill on the Indian situation on September 10, 1942, was above all remarkable for the eagerness with which he widened the abyss between the Congress Party and the British Government at a moment when almost every non-Congress Indian outside the leadership of the Moslem league was seeking to bridge that abyss.

Two reflections upon the British position in India are inescapable. The first is that, in both the material and in the intellectual realms, Indians have made less progress in a century and a half of British rule than the one-time subject nationalities of the Soviet Union have made in twenty-five years. The second is that at a time when the peoples of the Far East, above all the Chinese people, have made it evident that the terms of their relations with Europe and America must be those of equal collaboration and not of subordination, it is pitiful to see that the British Government remains unable to adjust itself to this position. For that is the real meaning of its acceptance of Sir Stafford Cripps' failure. It has lacked the audacity to force upon the Indian communities the experiment for which the times have called aloud when that audacity was its supreme weapon against its enemies. The blindness of prestige, the arrogance of a ruling race, the fear of economic loss, all these have played their part in that acceptance. For even if one grants the reality of the divisions in Indian life, it remains true that great statesmanship could have compelled their transcendence, and that they have been consistently envisaged in exaggerated proportions by interests which did not in their inner hearts desire that they should be overcome. Mr. Churchill congratulates himself on the failure of the Congress Party's demands to influence the attitude of the "martial" races; but that only reveals Mr. Churchill's ignorance of the fact that the division of India into the so-called "martial" and "non-martial" races is the outcome of a deliberate British policy adopted, after the Mutiny of 1857, to secure the foundations of British power. He speaks of the Congress Party as the creature of Indian business interests; yet no one knows better than he that this description is no more valid in relation to its leadership, to Mr. Gandhi, or Pandit Nehru, or Dr. Azad, than it is of his own leadership in the Conservative Party. His government approaches one of the supreme psychological issues of the war in a temper which largely fails to grasp either its nature or the opportunity it presents.

For it is certain that a free India which took its full place, of its own choice, among the United Nations would bring a strength to their cause which nothing can make available while a Britain which fights for freedom and democracy keeps Gandhi and Nehru in jail.

Counter-revolution can only be fought with revolutionary means; it is never destroyed by a policy which is excessively tender to tradition. The result of our policy in the Far East is not a doubtful one. A revolution is in progress there which we may well delay but are powerless to prevent. It is an essential element in that world-movement of which this war itself is one expression. To seek, as we are doing, to arrest its fulfilment is to put ourselves, in this theatre of operations, on the side of counter-revolution. We are then in the contradictory position of fighting a counter-revolution in Europe the interests of which we are objectively promoting in Asia. That contradiction not merely weakens our power to win in Europe. It has the not less disastrous result of making it certain that, when Hitlerism is overthrown, we shall be pursuing an Indian policy which appears counter-revolutionary to those upon whom, mainly, it is imposed. We shall be the exponents of a "law and order" hostile to the expansion of which Asiatic economic life stands in such grave need; and our exposition will involve us at least in Amritsars, and, conceivably, in tragedies even worse than Amritsar. That will be because we shall not have made the choice, which is even yet open to us, of co-operating with a future from whose implications we cannot escape while the chance of co-operation is given to us.

It is not an answer to say either that the demands we confront are impossible or that they are made at an impossible time. For their essence is a claim to self-government the principle of which we have conceded; and we are ourselves largely responsible for the difficulty of the time at which it has been made. For in the inter-war years the drive behind the Indian nationalist movement ought to have made it clear to every liberal mind that no policy could hope for permanence which sought to retain the keys of Indian power in London. Our attempts in these years at a partial solution never convinced those to whom they were offered; on the contrary, they succeeded only in persuading them that we would not, if we could, surrender the substance of authority. Anyone who examines the Government of India Act of 1935, and the discussions which accompanied its passage in Britain and India, can have no real doubt upon this head; it is we, and not the Indians, who emphasized the generosity of its terms. We noted the large powers it granted; Indians noted the still larger powers it withheld. We remarked upon the magnitude of the experiment it initiated; politically conscious Indians remarked upon the disproportion between their expectation and our response.

When the war came in 1939 we were, for all effective purposes, a counter-revolutionary power in the Far East. Setting out, as we did, to destroy the Counter-Revolution in Europe, there was an acid test of our ability to embark with full sincerity upon that task; that test was our capacity to win the co-operation of India for our cause by its free choice. Partly, the test was one of form; the choice of war or peace ought to have been left to the unfettered discretion of the Central Legislature in India. Instead, by a piece of graceless clumsiness which revealed the incapacity of our rulers to set the war in its true context, the choice was made for India without consultation by British decision. I do not need to emphasize the folly of that procedure; it is set out in a document of the Congress Party—it is said from the hand of Pandit Nehru—which is likely to remain one of the historic pronouncements of this war.[1]

But we were given, as nations are rarely given, a second chance. If we committed a bad blunder in method, at least we could correct that blunder in substance. We could show the whole world, our enemies not less than our friends, that we understood the nature of this war, as its drama began to unfold itself, by arriving at a settlement with India which set us by our deliberate choice on the side of the future. From 1939 to the spring of 1942, we offered a series of niggardly concessions which did not command any general approval even from our own citizens. When, at long last, circumstances compelled the British Government to face the Indian problem at a new level, there was missing from its attitude that grasp of the psychological background in which the evolving dynamic of history had set it. Sir Stafford Cripps made a brave effort to succeed. But he was handicapped by three things. The time-factor was against him; the rigidity of his instructions prevented that elasticity of manœuvre which a negotiator in his position required while it safeguarded every vested interest, both in India and Britain, which feared a change in the traditional relations; and he was acting in collaboration with colleagues some of whom, at least, were afraid of the consequences of his success. The high hopes his mission had aroused served only to embitter the situation created by his failure. By the autumn of 1942 it looked as though Great Britain would be defending against Japanese aggression an

[1] Printed in 1939 by the India League of London as a pamphlet.

India which doubted the good faith of that defence. We had the right, I think, to affirm that some part, at least, of that doubt was of deliberate Indian manufacture. But we had not the right to deny that, in major part, it was due to a lack in ourselves of the courage and the energy of mind which the problem called for. That lack maintained us in a relation to the forces of freedom in India which struck at the root of our declared purposes in this war. Thereby, it is bound to endanger, if it continues, not only the ends we ourselves seek to serve, but the whole pattern of freedom in the post-war world. For there is no lesson in history more clear than the lesson that a nation cannot serve the cause of freedom with its whole heart if it denies that cause out of a fear of the risks that freedom involves.

VII

The vital need, in fact, in any conflict like that in which we fight is to be certain that its central idea penetrates every nook and cranny of our war-effort. Faith in the claims of freedom must have something like a religious intensity not only in the minds of our leaders, but in the minds, too, of those whom they lead. Men cannot destroy the counter-revolution if some part of them gives allegiance to its principles. Our gravest danger is the very real one that in the name of democracy and freedom we destroy democracy and freedom. For its enemies are not only those who, like Hitler and Mussolini, set out with the deliberate end of destroying them. Its enemies are also, and perhaps not less, those who are unaware of the conditions upon which they can be preserved. It is by the exploitation of mass-ignorance that Hitler and Mussolini made themselves the indispensable agents of counter-revolution.

It is the danger that mass-ignorance may be exploited by the demagogue which makes the grasp of the social forces in play by the individual citizen an indispensable instrument of democratic safety. Unless we are assured that he will not be deceived by the easy slogan, the fallacies which, as Bentham showed a hundred and fifty years ago, are part of the permanent armoury of irrational privilege, the possibility is always real that counter-revolution may succeed by masking itself in the guise of revolution. This is the more fundamental in an age in which, as in our own, a traditional culture is entering upon a new phase. Our intellectual problem is the urgent one that the main values we have been taught to recognize as valid are those which belong to that epoch of economic liberalism of which the day is definitely over. In a general way, we are all aware of this. We all say that it will be a new world after the victory has been won. We all insist that the planned society has come to stay, even though our rulers are anxious that we shall not discuss the purposes for which it is to be planned. We all, too, agree that the educational system in the democracies of the inter-war years was inadequate, not least in Britain, to training the citizen for the kind of world in which he had to dwell.

In its British expression, the difficulties of our educational system were obvious enough. For all but a small section of the population education ended at the point where knowledge begins to exercise its fascination; and no small part of that section which had larger opportunities was chosen less on the ground of natural ability than of parental income. Our system suffered, further, from certain other characteristics none of which was rationally defensible. Its division into private schools, almost wholly attended by the middle and upper class children, and public schools almost wholly attended by the children of the workers, meant the absence in our society of a genuinely common culture, and the creation, for those who attended a small number of famous private schools, of special avenues of opportunity in the after-school period; it was difficult, for instance, for the ordinary observer to believe that fifty per cent of the natural diplomatic talent in Great Britain was sent by a mysterious dispensation of Providence to the single school of Eton.

A further division complicated matters. A national system of elementary education, for which the taxpayer was responsible, only dated from 1870; before that date a variety of religious denominations had built schools in the interests of their different sects which enabled them to control, even when they were aided by government grants, no small part both of the curriculum and the standard of teaching. Each of these sects had a vested interest to protect so that most attempts at educational development suffered from the assumption that their placation was the price to be paid for advance; and all political parties conspired to accept the ecclesiastical claim that religious instruction had a healthy effect upon "character" of which the community would be deprived at its peril. That the evidence for this claim disappeared under sober scrutiny was not deemed relevant; the vital fact was that, despite the declining hold of all supernatural dogmas on the population, politicians, with hardly an important exception, agreed to accept this curious piece of mythology. At the Trades Union Congress of 1942, a Roman Catholic member of the Transport and General Workers' Union warned the

Congress that his co-religionists would, under all circumstances, fight for their right to separate schools, aided, of course, by public funds, for the members of their denomination.[1] This meant, of course, also, that the choice of teachers, and, to a considerable extent, the content and standard of the curriculum in such schools, would be in clerical hands.

Two other matters require some emphasis. After the last war, and largely in obedience to its stimulus, an eager debate had taken place upon the purpose education must seek to fulfil. After almost twenty years of controversy a committee of the Board of Education, of which the chairman was the eminent and profoundly Conservative head of a Cambridge College, Mr. W. Spens, had agreed that the aim of the school should be "the highest degree of individual development" in each of its pupils. By the outbreak of war, that is to say, it had become the defined objective of official policy that the child should be regarded as an end, and that education should seek to give him, boy or girl, the chance of the fullest self-discovery as a person who, though in and of society, was to bring to its shaping an experience he alone could know and for which, as he knew it, he was trained to seek verification in adult life.

The other matter was not less fundamental. Education was, it was agreed, to build a citizen who could think for himself, who brought to life a meaning he had himself discovered in a journey the plans for which he had the right to help in making. He was not simply a soldier schooled to discipline in an army the strategy of whose high command was permanently beyond his ken. That made the idea of citizenship one that it was important to regard in a positive and active way. It was imperative, if the procedure of democracy was to be real, that the part of the citizen in the state must be something more than putting a cross on a ballot-paper in a local or national election once every three or four years. He had to be able to see his life shaping the decisions which determined the character of the community to which he belonged. Politics was not to be for him a process outside himself, about which he mainly felt aloof; and politicians mysterious, not seldom malignant, beings whose habits he did not understand, about which, indeed, he felt for the most part indifferent compared to the interest he took in his favourite film star or football team, or to the zest with which he put his sixpence for the "pools" in the post or tried to solve the cross-word puzzle as he went to and from his work. The salvation of a democratic way of life depended upon his sense that it was

[1] *Daily Herald*, September 10, 1942.

important for him to have the opportunity of continuous initiative in the significant matters of the time; and, hardly less, it depended upon the willingness of those who had the central decisions of state in their hands to recognize that this continuous initiative of his was important.

It was this which was slowly shaping a new status for adult education in the inter-war years. Painfully, perhaps, but I think surely, we were coming to see the importance of democratizing our cultural heritage. No nation could preserve the quality of its civilized life if the intellectual and material forces which shaped its character were unknown to those masses who were reaching out for predominant power. They lacked even that hold on values which had been provided for them when religious belief was still a vital factor in our lives. Once it degenerated into a social routine, with little influence on behaviour, even that access to a great literature which a knowledge of the Bible had provided was denied to them. Neither the meaning of great literature nor the meaning of scientific discovery penetrated far beyond a small élite in society. Yet without their creative influence a large part of the quality of civilization had little or no meaning for most citizens. Anyone who thinks of the small part played by books in the household of an average Englishman even of comfortable means must realize how many of the gates of civilization were closed to them. The sense that thought was an urgent matter had characterized, in the main, four periods only in British history. It was true from the opening of the seventeenth century until the Restoration; it was true, a second time, in that brief epoch between the outbreak of the French Revolution and the reaction of panic against all ideas and experiment which made the distribution of Paine's *Rights of Man* an act of treason; it was true a third time in that period of protest against the new industrialism which gave birth to our trade-unions, to the consumers' co-operative movement, and, at a lower level of influence, the socialist phase in Chartism; and it was true, I think, a fourth time in the last two years of the first World War, mainly through the immense hopes and emotions aroused by the Russian Revolution.

The impulse of this fourth period lingered on during the inter-war years without attaining the level of influence the situation required. Men were rather uneasily aware that thought was urgent, that a wider and deeper knowledge was the clue to the capacity to understand their situation, than active in securing for it the status it required. A number of factors operated against the recognition that such activity was vital. The press became a department of big business; in the hands of men like Lord Northcliffe it deliberately stripped itself of its main educational function. If we have learned nothing in the last generation at least the lesson has been massively provided of the degree to which freedom depends upon supply of truthful news. A second factor was the immense externalization of pleasure—the cinema, sport, and the dance-hall became both cheap and easy ways in which our generation found escape from the pain of thought. And to these, I think, must be added a certain disillusion born of the abyss between the hopes with which men entered the post-Versailles world and the frustration of those hopes with which reality presented them. I suspect, too, that something is due to the fatigue of the effort involved in the war of 1914–18. Men are rarely aware of the strain of great effort while they are making it; and when its tension is relaxed only great leadership can renovate the energies of a people.

In the inter-war years Britain never had that leadership. The Conservative governments in office were above all anxious to prevent any scrutiny into the foundations of the state; and the two Labour governments, if their periods of office were relatively brief, spent their main energies in proving that their opponents need not expect any fundamental changes from them. After 1931, and particularly after 1933, the main efforts of successive Prime Ministers seemed to be devoted to obscuring from public opinion the gravity of the situation; nothing else can adequately explain the "sealed lips" of Lord Baldwin, or Mr. Neville Chamberlain's indifference to the tragic fate of Czechoslovakia. But, after Munich, it was no longer possible to conceal even from those who wished to be blind that we confronted nothing less than a crisis of our civilization. Thenceforward there was apparent that traditional capacity of the British people to look danger squarely in the face. And the more desperate the position grew, after the actual outbreak of war, the greater was the anxiety of the masses to understand the crisis in which they were involved. Not, I think, since the seventeenth century has there been in Britain a deeper anxiety to probe into the roots of its problems, a greater willingness to experiment on a scale proportionate to their intensity.

I draw this inference from a number of obvious facts. It is, I think, clear in the welcome given to Mr. Churchill when he replaced Mr. Chamberlain as Prime Minister; no leader of our people has been given a confidence more profound or a power more ample. It is clear, again, in the enthusiasm which greeted Mr. Attlee's announcement, as France was falling, that the Government took powers to use all persons and all property for the service of the community; at that moment, there was no sacrifice of vested interest for which a government with imagination could not have secured approval. It is clear, thirdly, in the depth of the demand for clear blue-prints of the post-war world, in the eager applause which greeted the efforts of President Roosevelt and Vice-President Wallace to find the way to the conditions in which what the latter termed "the century of the common man" could secure its chance. It is clear, fourthly, in the width of popular interest in the Russian experiment; the breach in the *cordon sanitaire* which, ever since 1917, vested interests had thrown around its ideas was both decisive and final. It is clear, fifthly, in the wellnigh universal demand that, before this war ends, we shall have prepared the ground for massive educational reconstruction. And I think myself, finally, that this inference may be drawn from the inability of the hate-mongers in this war, so differently from our experience in 1914–18, to infect the masses with their poison. British public opinion had learned that the crisis was too serious for those fantastic theories which seek, whether with or without the panoply of scholarship, to draw up an indictment against a whole people; and few things in British history are likely to win greater honour than the fact that it was public opinion which, in 1940, compelled the Government to revise its policy of general internment for all aliens of enemy origin.

The first three years of this second world-war had, I suggest, taught the mass of the British people that the answer to the counter-revolution was to widen and strengthen the foundations of the democratic way of life, and that a vital high-road to that end was educational action so planned as to give intellectual reality to individual citizenship. Measured by the scale of our past efforts, that is a revolutionary idea. It means, in the long run, that what is to count in our community is the citizen's mind, the interpretation that mind operating as an active social factor, gives to his or her experience; the citizen is not to count in terms of the effective demand his ownership or control of property represents. That is, I say, a revolutionary idea, for to make the citizen count in this way is to remake the fundamental pattern of traditional Britain. It means the use of the state-power not to protect an existing pattern of vested interests but to adapt it to needs the priorities of which the masses, so instructed, will ultimately decide.

Because, as I say, this is a revolutionary idea it is important to examine its reception by the Conservative Party, since that is the body which, politically, represents the claims of traditional Britain.

This reception is available to us in the First Interim Report of the Conservative Sub-Committee on Education, a disquisition on educational aims published by the Conservative Party's General Committee on Post-War Reconstruction.[1]

The whole document is of extraordinary interest and importance. It disagrees with the Spens Committee's definition of the school's aim as the promotion of "the highest degree of individual development"; it suggests, indeed, that the main trends of contemporary thought on education are "in stern need of connection." For what end are they to be corrected? "It must be a primary duty of national education," says the Report, "to develop a strong sense of national obligation in the individual citizen, to encourage in him an ardent understanding of the State's need, and to render him capable of serving those needs." Already, that is to say, the individual is the instrument, the State is the end; and it is in enabling the individual to serve the end of the State that education performs its primary duty." So did Krieck, perhaps the ablest exponent of Nazi philosophy, define its outlook. The idea of "the highest individual development" has ceased to be relevant to the problems of the counter-revolution. "Private religion, a private world-outlook," he has written,[2] "in a word, all forms of private existence have ceased to have meaning. We stand with our personal life in service and responsibility to the totality of the community (völkisch) life whose members we are." So, also, the well-known Italian exponent of Fascism rejects the aim defined in the Spens report. "The liberation," Rocco writes,[3] "of the individual from the State which was carried out during the eighteenth century, will be followed in the twentieth century by the rescue of the State from the individual."

To most of us the content of that "strong sense of national obligation" which the Conservative Report demands, depends, in large measure, upon the nature of the experience in which each of us is involved; clearly that content is one thing in Mr. Churchill; and it is a very different thing in its expression in Mr. Harry Pollitt. Our agreement, too, upon what constitutes "an ardent understanding of the state's needs" is likely to be coloured by the principles of action inherent in our experience; and the life of a democratic community is marked by the assumption that no special experience is *a priori* valid. It is, we have been led to believe, by the intellectual clash of

[1] "*Looking Ahead.*" *Educational Aims.* Published by the General Committee on Post-War Reconstruction set up by the Conservative and Unionist Party Organization. London. September, 1942.

[2] Ernst Krieck, *Wissenschaft, Weltanschauung, Hochschulereform* (1934).

[3] A. Rocco, *The Political Doctrine of Fascism. International Conciliation* (1926).

argument about experience in the market-place of ideas that some given view of action is translated from the idea to the deed. Without this free play of ideas, the very essence of freedom is in jeopardy.

The Conservative Report rejects this view. It does not seem to imagine that differences in political outlook go very deep, or that the citizen-body, as a whole, attaches great importance to what is done in its name. "The core of the nation," the Committee writes, "consists of a large central mass which desires, above all things, what it has never been given or been able to command—continuity, consistency and positive certainty in national policy." It is this core, we are told, which is the "ultimately dominant part of the nation." At what does it aim? Not, the Report assures us, at "an ideal of conquest or self-profit. It implies notions superior to these—notions which any good teacher should have no difficulty in making real to the average child. The character of the strong, wise and unselfish leader is one of the easiest characters to present in popular literature; because that is what all men want their leaders to be, and what all children want to imagine their parents to be. *To translate this simple and right wish into a national ideal—into the ideal of the nation as a leader among the nations—with which every child can identify his own future, is the necessary first task of national education in the United Kingdom.*[1]

It is essential to be clear upon the implications of this view. It is set out unmistakably in the speeches of Hitler in which he has discussed the idea of leadership. "To lead a nation which longs for clear and capable political leadership," he has said,[2] "can always only be the task of a leading minority. He who puts in the foreground this conception of an organic selection of leaders is thinking historically. When we acted in this way we were not keeping in view merely the present; our aim was that posterity should be forced to admit that the men of our day had created foundations which would guarantee for centuries the life of successive generations." He has explained that this ideal cannot be achieved if parliamentary democracy survives, if there is a right of free criticism, if there are independent trade-unions. Not least important he has emphasized that "revolutions in the past have with very few exceptions failed because their leaders had not realized that the essential thing was not the assumption of power but the education of men." It is to achieve this education that the process of *Gleichschaltung* has been carried out.[3] That was why Hans Frank could

[1] The italics are those of the Report from which I am quoting.
[2] *Hitler's Speeches* (ed. Baynes), I, 483.
[3] *Ibid.*, I, 236 ff. Cf. especially pp. 261–3.

say that he supports "complete intellectual liberty and liberty of teaching—on the basis of National Socialism. . . . It must be, however, maintained beyond all challenge that the unity of our *Weltanschauung* as a basis shall be put in question by no one";[1] and Broemser explains that the "genuine scholar . . . will acknowledge the superiority of the political leadership and will not seek to discredit it through any petty criticism."[2] Is it accident that, in a similar way, Mussolini has said that the main task of the intellectual is pitilessly to criticize, from a Fascist point of view, socialism, liberalism, and democracy?[3]

It is difficult not to see a direct connection between the view of educational purpose the counter-revolutionists proclaim and the recognition, in the Conservative Report, that its ideal neither will nor can be met "without a more thorough-going overhaul of the whole educational system than appears yet to have been anywhere envisaged." Explicitly, indeed, the Report repudiates the "mistranslation" of its theory into the "totalitarian heresy" that the individual is of no account; but there are fifty passages in which Hitler has repudiated the same "mistranslation" of Nazism. To avoid this mistranslation the Report then insists upon the vital importance of religious education in schools, and sets a series of administrative proposals the purpose of which is to "*succeed in quickening the child's religious consciousness*."[4] "A great effort needs to be made," says the Report, "for a new, positive and generally sympathetic attitude towards religion. *Religion in the United Kingdom needs to be conceived, politically and administratively, in general terms as a basic and vital element in the national life, to be deliberately encouraged and fostered*."[5]

Why is this? The Report has at least the merit of giving a completely frank answer to this question. "The present war," it says, "is putting the social compromise to a very dangerous strain endeed, and the influence of the Russian system upon our own cannot be sensibly ignored. (We are thinking of the emotional, quasi-religious influence and not of "economic" influences.) There is an evident possibility that the Russian example will seem to great numbers of people in this country an example to be followed here. Upon those who are not aware of the vast differences between the two countries, and who are not sustained by belief in a supra-temporal order, this idea is capable of exerting an extremely powerful attraction. We do

[1] Quoted by N. H. Baynes, *Intellectual Liberty and Totalitarian Claims* (1942), p. 27. [2] *Ibid.*, p. 30. [3] *Ibid.*, p. 34.
[4] Italics in original. [5] Italics in original.

not mean to suggest that there is, or should be, any opposition between the ideal of social progress and religious belief. . . . But we do suggest that decay of religious belief exposes a people, thereby deprived of respect for its own past, to the temptation of violent and ill-considered social experiment. It would appear, then, that if the State is rightfully concerned for its own future development (as we conceive it to be) it must also be concerned for the presence of religion among its citizens." To this must be added that, in the view of the authors of the Report, our failure to meet the crisis of the war "is indicated by the excessive emphasis placed in our present educational system (as in our social life) upon the ideal aim of individual happiness." We are reminded that because "disease, disablement, pain, death; inherited defects; limited capacities; misfortune, unhappiness, and the sense of guilt or sin—all these are a necessary part of every man's life," education must set out to make men "tough." It must breed "the bold qualities of adventurousness, initiative, enjoyment of difficulty and danger, in a word, grit." And we are warned that other necessary qualities have "been steadily losing ground, the will to work, pride in occupation, regardless of its social or monetary reward, the self-discipline acquired through submission to discipline, and the desire to find salvation from selfishness in service. Finally, the Report emphasizes the "special contribution" made by the public and preparatory schools to the "education of talent and the development of leadership," a contribution which would be "jeopardized" if they lost their independence by becoming part of the state system of education.

The simple comment that I want to make upon this doctrine is that it is a recommendation to the Government of Great Britain to adopt both in spirit and in principle the full gospel of the Counter-Revolution. The praise of "toughness," the enthusiasm for submission to discipline, the emphasis upon work without thought of personal reward as a civic duty which the humblest workers must display, the refusal to permit the public schools to become a part of the national education system on the ground that they have a special contribution to make to leadership—each of these can be quite precisely duplicated from the pronouncements of Nazi leaders.[1]

Yet perhaps the most significant part of the Report goes back beyond the decisive epoch in which we live to that period, a century and a half ago, when the French Revolution struck panic into the

[1] Cf. *Hitler's Speeches* (ed. Baynes), I, 534 ff., especially pp. 543 f.

mind of the governing class, and made them seek in the discipline of a religious faith the specific by which privilege is safeguarded from invasion. In a well-known chapter of their *Town Labourer*,[1] Mr. and Mrs. Hammond have summarized the famous work of Wilberforce, the *Practical View of the System of Christianity*,[2] in which the friend of Pitt explained the function of religion in society. "There he explains," write Mr. and Mrs. Hammond, "that Christianity makes the inequalities of the social scale less galling to the lower orders, that it teaches them to be diligent, humble, patient, that it reminds them 'that their more lowly path has been allotted to them by the hand of God; that it is their part faithfully to discharge its duties, and contentedly to bear its inconveniences; that the present state of things is very short; that the objects about which worldly men conflict so eagerly are not worth the contest; that the peace of mind which Religion offers indiscriminately to all ranks, affords more true satisfaction than all the expensive pleasures which are beyond the poor man's reach; that in this view the poor have the advantage; that, if their superiors enjoy more abundant comforts, they are also exposed to many temptations from which the inferior classes are happily exempted; that 'having food and raiment, they should be therewith content,' since their situation in life, with all its evils, is better than they have deserved at the hand of God; and, finally, that all human distinctions will soon be done away, and the true followers of Christ will all, as children of the same Father, be alike admitted to the possession of the same heavenly inheritance. Such are the blessed effects of Christianity on the temporal well-being of political communities." And Mr. and Mrs. Hammond point out that Wilberforce drew Pitt's attention to this chapter of his book as the "basis of all politics."[3]

In its warning against the dangers of Russian infection, and in its reliance upon the state support of religious teaching against its risks, it is difficult not to see in the exhortations of the Conservative Party Committee's Report the same "basis of all politics" as that which appealed to Wilberforce. The kindred conditions of the two periods are remarkable in their resemblance; perhaps, too, the authors of the Report fear, as did Wilberforce and his friends when they founded, in 1802, "The Society for the Suppression of Vice and the Encouragement of Religion and Virtue throughout the United Kingdom," "the late usurpation of Reason over Revelation" with its encouragement—a notable combination—of "infidelity

[1] Chap. xi, pp. 221 f.

[2] First published in 1798.

[3] *Op. cit.*, pp. 231–2.

and insubordination." One catches, certainly, in its pages the echo of the sentiment of the Society's secretary Prichard, who told a Committee of the House of Commons in 1817 that "the influences of religious obligation seem much on the decline among the lower orders of society, to which is probably attributable much of that impatience under civil restraint which is the characteristic feature of the times.[1]

Man's reason, uncontrolled by the influence of religion, seeks for large changes in the foundations of society; it is desirable, therefore, to prevent "impatience under civil restraint" on the part of the masses for the state to give religion power to control the unfettered exercise of reason. That was the inference drawn by the ruling classes at the time of the French Revolution; the Russian Revolution leads their successors to no different conclusion. The approach, no doubt, is more indirect and more sophisticated; its underlying principle is identical. And it is important to recognize that this fear of reason has always been the inner essence of the counter-revolutionary spirit; for the one thing that endangers a system of privilege which has outlived its usefulness is its critical examination by reason. "He who frees criticism," said Hitler,[2] "from the moral duty of placing itself in the service of a general, recognized, and pursued life-task is treading the path which leads to Nihilism and Anarchy." For Hitler criticism is subordinated to Nazi objectives; for the authors of the Conservative Report it is subordinated to the task of preserving amongst us that "respect for the past" which prevents "violent and ill-considered social experiment." The language is different; the purposes are common. Each is protecting privilege in decay from being revealed as obsolete to the masses. And it is not less true of the *Report* I have examined than it is of Hitlerism that as a method of social action it is ultimately bound to suppress the ideas it is unable to refute.

That is why, perhaps only half-consciously, it emphasizes as virtues the things against which, at any rate since the French Revolution, the principle of democracy has been a protest. Submission for the many, and leadership for the few; the recognition that material suffering is man's inevitable lot; the insistence that the masses are indifferent to political matters; the denial that large social changes are wise or justified; the deep fear of innovation; the feverish search for some mystic safeguard against the will of the masses for great social experiment; the demand that the educa-

[1] Quoted by W. H. Wickwar, *The Struggle for the Freedom of the Press*, 1819–1832 (1928), pp. 36–7.

[2] *Hitler's Speeches* (ed. Baynes), I, 500.

tional institutions of the privileged be left undisturbed, the depreciation of the training of the mind in favour of toughness—"our men," promised Hitler,[1] "will be trained to become a hard breed"; the plea that men accept their lot in life without repining, that the duties of their allotted station shall be their reward; no one can, I think, examine this Report at all rigorously without seeing that it is already a full-scale plea for the counter-revolution with which we are at war. What is the lesson to be drawn from the fact that men fighting the counter-revolution can yet accept its basic assumptions as their own?

VIII

It is the lesson, surely, that the ruling class in Britain, for all its deep anxiety to defeat Hitlerism, is yet profoundly anxious to organize that defeat on its own terms. It is uneasily aware that grave issues are in dispute; but it is determined, if it can, to define the principles by which those issues shall be solved. That is why the war has seen no great experiment with measures or with men; either would reveal the fact that the traditional foundations of our society are not its necessary foundations. To obscure that revelation from the view of the masses is a preoccupation of Conservatism hardly less great than its sense of the urgency of victory. For its leaders are not willing, even when the national existence is at stake, to experiment with the dynamic of democracy. That is true in the relations of production at home; it is true in the consideration of empire abroad. The breakdown of democracy in France is only the final term in a series of social equations which we shall not have solved, either in Britain or America, merely by the achievement of victory.

If it is said that Mr. Churchill leads the forces of Conservatism and that, as Prime Minister, he has supremely shown that there is no price he would not pay for victory, there are, I think, certain important reservations to be made. It is urgent, first, to realize that there was undeclared war in Europe at least from the period when Hitler remilitarized the Rhineland; for some years after that time, the forces of Conservatism resented alike his diagnosis and his remedies. Not until the major part of Western Europe lay prostrate under Hitler did they reconcile themselves to his leadership. It is, I think, true to say that the creation of the Churchill government was the work of the nation, and imposed by public opinion on a

[1] *Op. cit.*, I, 533.

Conservative Party which was for long resentful of its possible implications.

The first year of Mr. Churchill's administration will, on any showing, give him a great place in the British political tradition. In the face of overwhelming danger, he symbolized, in a remarkable way, the will of the nation to survive. Courage, inflexible resolution, the power to maintain the people's faith in itself, the unconquerable pride which can never admit defeat, these qualities he displayed in a degree unsurpassed in our history. But it must be noted that these are, above all, the aristocrat's virtues. They reveal the man who inherits the great imperial tradition which he is determined to safeguard; they find their roots in the habits of past achievement rather than in adaptation to an emerging future. There was no audacity in Mr. Churchill's policy in the sense that he displayed any capacity for innovation proportionate to the emergency; on the contrary, the very basis of his policy was the demand that no issue be discussed which might be the subject of controversy. It became, in fact, increasingly clear that Mr. Churchill viewed this war as no different in essence from the great wars of the past; he was Marlborough fighting Louis XIV, or Pitt fighting Napoleon. He was uninterested in the social implications of the struggle; that was an aspect of its nature foreign to his genius or his character. What progressiveness of outlook he had was the outcome of the aristocrat's impulse to generosity; he could be magnanimous where he was visually affected by the tragedies of war—as when he saw the effects of air bombardment—but he had no philosophy of the conflict which made his imagination see new perspectives to the endless adventure of politics. He did not, therefore, ask the forces of Conservatism to wage the war on terms which might have compelled them to consider the fundamental alteration of the basis of social power.

Maybe, he would have been compelled to do so had the Labour Party demanded that alteration. Two things prevented the Labour Party from making that demand. The first is the fact—which does it great credit—that in the months of acute danger after it took office, it thought of nothing save the survival of the nation; when Britain no longer found itself alone the moment had passed when great changes could be had for the asking. The second is the fact that, within a few weeks of taking office, Mr. Churchill had built himself a moral ascendancy over the Labour leaders so complete that they were not prepared to seek for changes which might have created difficulties for him with his Conservative followers. So that though the Labour Party put forward a programme which insisted that fundamental alterations must be made as part of the war effort itself if the victory over Hitlerism was not to be thrown away, its leaders tamely accepted Mr. Churchill's rejection of that programme on the ground that controversy in wartime might endanger the unity of the nation. This tameness not only left the vital initiative in defining war policies in Mr. Churchill's hands; it meant, also, that the war would be won, as Pitt won the war against Napoleon, without touching the basis of social power. Britain, this is to say, would debate the issues about which the war would be fought after, and not before, victory.

As soon as this is understood, certain things of major importance become clear. First, the British ruling class would be able to defend its privileges without the embarrassment of a powerful external enemy compelling it to make concessions of principle to the masses whose co-operation was essential for victory. Second, the failure in wartime to associate parliamentary democracy with great measures of social change made by consent was bound to weaken its authority over public opinion in the post-war period; to weaken it, I must add, in its creative status abroad hardly less than at home. This failure emphasizes a distinction which English writers have too rarely made since 1848, the distinction between representative government and popular government. The first is not the second unless it recognizes that justice is impossible between men where their claims to welfare are set by their ownership and control of property. Thirdly, it is evident that the socialist basis of the Labour Party was formal rather than substantial. That is evident from the fact that it permitted its leaders to accept from Mr. Churchill a series of minor social reforms all of which assumed not merely that expanding welfare was possible in a permanent way in the period of capitalist contraction—the typical assumption of a trade union party whose principles were shaped by the experience of daily experience rather than by the analysis of a secular historic development—but assumed, also, that respect for constitutional procedures is a permanent habit of the British governing class.

This attitude, on the part of the Labour Party, revealed two great weaknesses. It assumes an insularity of outlook before the operation of great world-forces in which Britain is now not less involved than any of its neighbours, a naïve belief that, in the light of the period since 1660, we can somehow contract out of that counter-revolution the power of which has proved so immense elsewhere. And it defends that insularity at a time when, everywhere, the quickening tempo of social change calls for a rapidity of adjustment of which Parliamentary Democracy has never in the past proved capable. This attitude overlooks the fact that the economic leeway which enabled Britain to overcome its crises in the past has, in large degree, disappeared. It omits to notice that the classic formulae of parliamentarism were valid in a period the conditions of which no longer obtain. Its pride in the continuance of the historic ritual of parliamentary procedure fails to notice that this has been able to continue because it has not been applied to the seminal questions of the time; or, rather, there has been an agreement between the political parties that those questions shall not be raised lest they disturb that unity upon fundamentals upon which the success of the parliamentary system depends.

This poses a question to which only future experience in Britain can give an answer. It raises the issue of whether the success of parliamentary government in Britain is not the outcome of a special set of historical circumstances which represent a comparatively brief period in British history, unique in their character, and unlikely to be repeated. The pre-war years make it obvious enough that the climate of counter-revolution was deeply pervasive of the whole atmosphere which surrounded our ruling class. The war years suggested that socialism could be professed by a great political party only because its leaders did not seek the practical expression of their principles. When the last word has been said in favour of the time-honoured British genius for compromise, the decision that no vital question should be raised in wartime leaves it at least an open question what will happen when, in the post-war epoch, that genius is put to a test likely to be more severe than any it has previously known at least since Chartism, and, perhaps, since the reign of Charles I. And this, in its turn, has to be set in the background of the realization that, once again as after the Napoleonic wars, the ability of Britain to save itself by its energy will have a considerable influence in settling its influence in Europe by the force of its example. A Britain whose hands are largely free from the intricacies of domestic controversy can no doubt do much to provide the model basis of change upon the European continent. But a Britain which finds, as the facts suggest that we may easily find, that the depth of our domestic preoccupations compels us to devote our main attention to those issues of principle which we postponed in the period of war, has already gone far to depriving itself of that power to aid as arbiter in Europe and Asia upon which so much of their freedom in the next generation will depend. The time to destroy the roots of counter-revolution is when we fight it. We have refused to use that time for its destruction; and the agreement to overcome it has yet to be made. It is at least an open question whether the agreement can be achieved by consent when the main psychological impulse to agreement no longer has the dramatic validity that common danger imposes.

Chapter VIII

FREEDOM IN A PLANNED DEMOCRACY

I

WE are in the midst of the profoundest crisis our civilization has known, at least since the Reformation, and perhaps since the fall of the Roman Empire. On our ability to act upon an understanding of what the crisis is may well depend the peace and the well-being of the human race for centuries to come.

It is not a crisis which any simple or single remedy can resolve. For there are in dispute amongst us not only the ultimate character of the relationships of men but also the faith, or system of values, to which those relationships give birth. There is no plane of thought or of action that is exempt from the influence of the crisis. Religion, politics, economics, science, culture, these in the massive totality of their interaction upon one another are all deeply affected by it. Old nations, like China, are destined to renovation as it proceeds; old classes, the Prussian junkers, for instance, are destined to see their historic function destroyed. The strategic implications of the war this crisis has brought in its train will alter the habits of communication even more profoundly than the geographical discoveries of the Renaissance. Its character in the Far East is certain, in the long run, especially as the results of the Soviet experiment become more widely known, to put the relation of the white peoples to those of different colour upon a wholly new footing. The application of science to social problems is likely to be, as the single field of nutrition already makes evident, qualitatively different from anything we have known in the past. The age of Grotius has drawn to its close; for it has become clear beyond dispute that a world so unified and interdependent as ours cannot afford to run the risks imposed by the continued existence of the national sovereign state. That is bound, again in the long run, to mean the emergence of a truly international law, and it is probable that in the great society of the future the main significance of nationality will be in the cultural, rather than in the political or the economic, field. We seem likely, moreover, to be moving to a plane of social action where it becomes possible to transcend that economics of scarcity by which all past human behaviour has been rigorously conditioned.

Given the victory of the United Nations, the overthrow, that is, of those forces in the world which have deliberately made war in the interest of counter-revolution, the individualist capitalism of the classical economists is bound to be revealed as obsolete. It has, indeed, long been known as an anachronism by all who have watched the growth of industrial combination, on the one hand, and the emergence of a caste of economic directors, mainly remarkable for their skill in financial manipulation, who are the masters alike of their shareholders and of the consumer, and are not seldom in a position to hold even states to ransom. Their power is as massive in volume as it has largely been irresponsible in operation. We have reached a stage in historical evolution where either their power must be subordinated to the interest of the community or the interest of the community will be a tragic pseudonym for their power. Precisely as in the nineteenth century, the irresponsible privilege of rentier and aristocrat was broken by the development of democracy in the political field, so, in the twentieth century, we have to break the irresponsible privilege of rentier and plutocrat by the development of democracy in the economic field. Power in society is destructive of society unless the purpose it fulfils and the terms upon which it is held are matters controlled by citizens who are recognized to have an equal claim for equal needs upon the common stock of well-being. Any other conception of the responsibilities of power corrupts alike those who possess it and those over whom it is exercised.

It is for the democratization of economic power upon these terms that, in the last analysis, this war is being fought. We must avoid the easy illusion that this end will be attained simply by the defeat of Hitler and his allies. That defeat creates the opportunities required for the democratization of economic power; it is far from an assurance that they will be wisely used. As I have sought to show in this book, there are few among the United Nations in which there are not present, often in a dangerous degree, the elements which made a successful counter-revolution in Italy and Germany, which were willing, as in France, to betray its people into slavery in the hope of winning the patronage of their Nazi conqueror for their special privilege. The same elements exist among ourselves and the American people. The victory, let us be quite certain, that ends the danger of Hitlerism may well be the prelude to the continuation of the conflict he provoked in a different sphere.

For what is certain is that we shall have moved, by the end of this war, into the era of the planned society; what is quite uncertain is the purpose for which we can plan. The counter-revolution has shown, above all in its Nazi setting, that planning can be attempted in the interest of the few, and that the techniques of modern armament and administration enable those few to be the complete masters of the many. It is, indeed, unlikely that this mastery will have permanence about it since it depends, in the long run, upon a totalitarianism at war with the free mind which is essential to the highest forms of scientific discovery. Here we must remember that there has been nothing original in Nazism save the massive scale of the deception it has practised and the cruelties it has inflicted. Its science is simply the legacy of the past; its military genius is simply the great Prussian tradition furnished with munitions purchased by the sacrifice of mass-welfare; its organization is, mostly, the adaptation of Bolshevik methods to the climate of counter-revolution. The real lesson of Nazi planning for ourselves is, first, that it means war, and, second, that it abridges the personality of the individual citizen as a necessary part of its effort to safeguard, regardless of the cost, the privileges of its ruling class.

We cannot hope to achieve the democratization of economic power if those who own and control property, especially in the era of the giant corporation, are in a position thereby either to acquire special privilege or to act in an arbitrary way. It is difficult to see how we can prevent the growth of these habits unless the vital instruments of production are owned and controlled by the community as a whole directly in its own interest. For there is no other way in which we can end that economics of scarcity which is inescapably involved in the psychology of large-scale capitalism, especially where its basis is monopolistic.[1]

I do not think this means the necessity of taking over all industry and agriculture by the State. Rather, I think, it means that the fundamental bases of economic power shall be in the hands of the community; once they are assured to the interest of the many, instead of the few, the economic future can develop within the framework defined by the possession of these fundamental bases by the historic methods of parliamentary democracy. There are four of these bases. The most vital is the control of the supply of capital and credit. This means the nationalization of the Bank of England, of the joint stock banks, of the insurance companies, and of the building societies. There is no other way to be sure that

[1] On this see two able articles in the London *Times*, September 18–19, 1942.

investment is directly and continuously related to public need and not to private profit. We have to think of this investment as the conscious instrument of an economic plan which aims at re-equipping the nation to play its part in the post-war world. This means, quite obviously, a system of priorities in the granting of commercial loans which will depend upon the importance on the economic plan of the objective the promoters have in view. Houses for the poor are more important than luxury-flats for the rich; schools are more important than cinemas; loans to assist agricultural improvement are more important than loans to promote the manufacture and sale of a new cosmetic or a new patent medicine.

The state must own and control the land. That is essential for three purposes. It is essential to the proper planning of towns, especially the blitzed areas. It is essential to secure for agriculture the proper place in our national economy. It is essential to secure both the proper location of industry and the preservation of the aesthetic amenities of Britain.

There must be state control of the import and export trade. This control is obviously vital to any planned production which has the interest of the consumer in view. It follows logically from the state control of capital and credit. Without it, clearly, we cannot hope to fit our national economy into that international control of the exchanges which is now inevitable. Only in this way, moreover, can the bulk purchase of raw materials and the bulk marketing of our exports, with the great economics both made possible, be organized in the national interest. That is the plain lesson of Russian experience; and it is a lesson of which the significance has been given decisive emphasis by our own experience during the war.

There must, further, be state ownership and control of transport, fuel and power. I will not here elaborate again the argument for regarding them as fundamental to democratic planning. But certain simple things deserve a word of comment. Each of them is, in its present form, a source of waste. Without the nationalization of shipping we cannot relate that service to the best results obtainable by state control of imports and exports. Without the nationalization of railways and road transport there is not only unnecessary duplication and competition; as their historic relations have shown, the possibilities of road transport, especially for short journeys, are sacrificed to the political pressure the railways can exert. To leave aviation in private hands, after our wartime experience, is obviously impossible; indeed the problem it raises is whether anything less than a full international control is advisable. The alternative is, almost certainly, a vast system of subsidies and rate-wars with undesirable, even dangerous, repercussion. The nationalization of the coal mines is a psychological ncesssity in the light of the miners' attitude to the owners; it offers an immense opportunity for economies, especially in the marketing of coal; and, on experience, it is the only way in which the scientific exploitation of coal by-products can be attempted on an adequate scale. The case for the national ownership of electric power is the simple one that, already, the superiority of the municipal to the private unit of supply has been demonstrated, and that, without the unification which national ownership will bring, rural electricity, so urgent in the rural areas, and for agricultural development, will remain impossible without large subsidies to a mass of separate companies. The same is true of gas and water supplies; in the rural areas, especially, only unification under state ownership will bring their conveniences to the numberless households which now lack them.

Upon this basis, it would be possible seriously to begin the process of democratizing economic power. Much, obviously, would depend upon the personnel of the controls this system envisages. Many of these must clearly be business men with a direct and intimate knowledge of the industry involved; whatever other experience we use, without this experience we cannot do. But, obviously, also, the war-time controls in their present form are, in the main, a grave public menace. It is impossible to entrust functions of this importance to men who, like so many of the controllers of to-day, have a direct interest in both the present and the future of the industries they control. In the new system, the sole allegiance of the controller must be to the state he serves.

I cannot attempt here to discuss the forms either of nationalized industries or of the controls which will operate over those which remain in private hands. In any case, in my own view, it is at least doubtful if they will conform to any single pattern; they are, I think, likely to be adapted with considerable flexibility to the shape of the particular industry to which they are related.

More important is the question of their relationship to Parliament. That will, as I conceive, be effected through the Cabinet; and I believe that the Cabinet, in its turn, will find it necessary to set up a Committee of Ministers whose work is relevant to the field of production. This Committee will need an expert staff, much like Gosplan in the Soviet Union, whose business it will be to prepare for it the material upon which it makes its final submissions to the Cabinet which will, in its turn, obtain for them the general approval of Parliament. For reasons I have discussed elsewhere,[1] I see no reason for the creation of an Economic General Staff in addition to these bodies; a new tier in the hierarchy of controls would detract from, rather than add to, its clarity and have the certain effect of delaying decisions which require speed not seldom as of their essence. The general layout of the plan, in a system of parliamentary democracy, is the clear responsibility of Ministers; and that responsibility is weakened, and not strengthened, by a conception like that of Sir William Beveridge, in which an Economic General Staff meditates generally upon planning without the power to decide upon the applicability of its meditations. The more clear the line of responsibility for decisions, the more direct is likely to be the judgment of their worth.

Quite obviously these proposals do not assume the establishment of a socialist state at the end of the war; they are a foundation only upon which, if the electorate should so decide in the future, a socialist state could be built. Their purpose is the different, though related, one, of safeguarding our political democracy against those forces of counter-revolution which are present among ourselves, and were growing in authority and determination before the outbreak of war. It is, indeed, evident, as I have argued in this book, that in the absence of these safeguards the growth of monopoly-capitalism which the necessities of the war-effort have fostered may well, even if half-consciously, renew the authority and determination of those forces. I believe, therefore, that unless some such programme as this is brought into effective operation with victory, the chance of our being able to democratize economic power in Britain is very small; and the same principle applies to the other partners among the United Nations, especially to the United States of America. Either political democracy must be the master of economic monopoly or economic monopoly will be the master of political democracy.

The reason for this is very simple. Economic forms tend to beget the political structure most suited to their purpose; our experience has shown quite unmistakably, that the restrictionist economics of monopoly capitalism are only with supreme difficulty adjusted to the expansionist politics which a democratic society requires. The way in which the rising middle class, after the Reformation, enforced the adaptation of all social institutions to the economic power they acquired is only the most dramatic recent expression of this tendency. We have reached a phase in our civilization where, once

[1] "Government in War Time" in *Dare We Look Ahead?* (1941).

again, fundamental renovation is required. The war provides us with an opportunity to attempt it without going through one of those bitter internal conflicts which emerge when men refuse to look their problems starkly in the face, and act while there is time to agree upon the means of their peaceful resolution.

But it is unlikely that the opportunity will outlast the duration of hostilities. The dramatic atmosphere of sacrifice will fade; fatigue will take the place of exhilaration; and policy will tend to grow out of differences men wish either to preserve or overcome rather than from common objectives they wish to attain. That is surely already clear in the relations of the major political parties both in Britain and in the United States; the abyss, for example, which separates the Labour Party's conception of post-war education from that of the Conservative Party is not greater than the abyss between the New Dealers' conception of property-rights and that of "economic royalists" like Mr. Henry Ford or Mr. Tom Girdler. But it is not less true on the international plane than on the domestic. The power-relations between the great states, especially between Great Britain and the United States, on the one hand, and Russia on the other, are bound to be set by the internal relations of production which they maintain. If these internal relations look to expansion as their end, we shall find that peace is the natural outcome of expansion; but if they still are, as now, relations which imply restriction, the forces in play will as inevitably lead to war as in the inter-war years. We are in a position where the needs of victory coincide with the opportunities renovation requires. The mood is present, as it is so rarely present, when no sectional interest could prevail against the national interest. But the mood will not outlive the war; and the leadership which fails to utilize its possibilities will, thereby, frustrate the very purposes it is seeking to fulfil.

II

The planned society, it is said, is the very negation of freedom. It is destructive of man's personality as an individual and unique human being. It means an autocratic state. It invólves the regimentation of us all by great hordes of officials. We can see, we are told, in Nazi Germany and Fascist Italy and Bolshevik Russia the price of the planned society. Its very essence is dictatorship. Our task is to recover the terms upon which the impartial and impersonal mechanism of the market, maintained by the rule of law, is the frame within which each of us pursues his life's adventure. We need anew that "invisible hand" of Adam Smith's famous euolgy in which, by that miracle never fully explained to the common man, self-love and social good were somehow united in a majestic harmony.[1]

Quite obviously such a view has many problems to explain. It has to show why the mechanism of the free market was increasingly replaced by those vast combinations which became almost empires which it was difficult not to confuse with the state-power itself. It has to demonstrate that liberty of contract can be given any meaning in the absence of equality of bargaining power; it has, indeed, to demonstrate why, in the full tide of the system, it meant all over the world that freedom had little or no meaning, as it has little or no meaning to-day, except for the owners of property. It has to justify a system which has rarely consented to any social reform until the postponement of its acquiescence has deprived the consent of any magnanimity of temper. Above all, it has to produce the proof that a state-power in which the instruments of production are privately owned is capable of maintaining an impartial rule of law. Certainly it was not so capable either in the United States or in Great Britain at the height of *laissez-faire's* success. The warnings of Emerson and Channing, the denunciations of Carlyle and Dickens and Ruskin, are, all of them, nothing so much as a massive commentary on the degradation of the common man which was the result of a society built upon a profound faith in the impersonal mechanism of the free market.[2]

At the end of all its achievements, it still left the division between the few rich and the many poor the fundamental division in civilization. It still placed formidable barriers in the way of access by the masses to our intellectual heritage. It still did not dare to risk what Mr. Lippmann himself[3] regarded as an indispensable condition of freedom—a supply of truthful news. It still exploited every

[1] This is the thesis, presented with characteristic eloquence by Mr. Walter Lippmann in his *Good Society* (1937). He there accepts the view that only the free play of the market can safeguard liberty. This leads him to reject all forms of collectivist planning on the ground that they ultimately involve the rejection of the free market and therefore *pro tanto* the denial of as much freedom. Mr. Lippmann relies on the "rule of law"—a revived or revised law of nature—to maintain the necessary rules of the game he thinks that society ought to play. The main enthusiasts for his views in the United States were the members of the Liberty League.

[2] For the history of this liberal doctrine which Mr. Lippmann, and others of his way of thought, are anxious to revive, see my *Rise of European Liberalism* (1936).

[3] See his *Liberty and the News* (1928).

prejudice of colour and race and creed in its search to safeguard the principle of acquisitiveness upon which it was built. It still, in considerable degree, made longevity, health, security, leisure, dependent upon the ownership of property. The rulers of its imperial domains bought legislatures and corrupted judges and officials with no sense of guilt unless their actions were found out. The armed forces of the state were still an instrument whereby, whatever the social consequences, its right to its privileges were forcibly maintained; the sit-down strikes of 1937 in the United States were the first industrial conflicts since the Civil War in which the President did not, in the name of law and order, intervene on behalf of the owners of property once the dispute had reached important proportions. It still made the social sciences, at least in their academic expression, operate overwhelmingly within a framework which assumed that no one was really fit for an academic post who questioned the title of the owners of property to their privileges. In Britain, it was notable that, during the century after the Reform Bill of 1832, the Conservative Party could find not a dozen workingmen whom it would choose to represent it in Parliament, even though, in that period, working men built up great organizations like the trade unions, the friendly societies, and the co-operative movement, all of them evidence of at least average political and economic ability. In all capitalist democracies the so-called "impartial" men who presided over social and economic enquiries undertaken by the government were always chosen from professions dependent, like the legal profession, in a large degree on the owners of private property; and if, like Lord Sankey in 1919, they surprisingly reported that the private ownership of a fundamental commodity like coal could no longer work satisfactorily for the nation, they were treated like men who had betrayed a trust.

The inherent weakness of the society built upon the mechanism of the free market was, as Carlyle saw, that it built the essential relations between men on the basis of the cash-nexus merely. When it broke down the principle of birth as the foundation of privilege and replaced it with the principle of wealth, it secreted a fatal poison in the very roots of its soil. That poison was the establishment of the idea that the acquisition of property as the main source of power was the true end of man. Not holiness, not culture, not fellowship, were vital articles of the faith. Social life was, in Sir Henry Maine's phrase, a "beneficent private war" in which, because the fittest survived, the fate of the individual was a matter of indifference to the cosmos; it was rarely seen that, given the postulates, fitness for survival tested only the acquisitiveness which was the energizing principle of social organization. It was an acquisitiveness which was always being compelled to pay a ransom it resented if the society was to be maintained as a going concern. It was always trying to extend its authority to spheres, religion, for example, or the arts, which it felt, rather than knew, to be a threat to its claims. It was always bound to press its criteria of value upon material to which they had no application; and, because the life of man is short, it was always bound to think of the immediate return rather than the long end. Anyone who has seen the abandoned settlements in the timber regions of the North-West Pacific States can see something, in the physical sense, of the price society has paid for the elevation of acquisitiveness to the place of the main dogma in our secular religion. If it has promoted the development of science, it has been not less successful in its frustration. If it has assisted the growth of literacy, it has consistently argued that there can be too much education, and it has, thereby, gone far towards separating the masses from that share in the achievements of the creative imagination the enjoyment of which is the real fulfilment of their humanity. The ultimate condemnation of the acquisitive society is its relegation of the artist to the periphery of its life so that he has become not the proof of its greatness but the plaything of its leisure. And, even as plaything, it is of profound significance that, with the painter, for example, the estimate of his work is set not by the beauty it embodies, but by the price the fashion of the moment will compel a rich man to pay who, mainly out of vanity, desires a reputation as a patron of the arts.

I am not for one moment arguing either that acquisitiveness is a new thing—obviously it is as old as the world—or that we lack the men and women to protest against its authority. I am arguing only that, as the central principle of social organization, it was bound to lead to a tragedy like the present war. An immense indictment could, no doubt, be drawn up against the civilization of ancient Athens; yet if one compares the defence of it, at its best, which Thucydides put into the mouth of Pericles, with Macaulay's famous eulogy of the acquisitive society in its first and ardent dawn,[1] it is not easy to say that the verdict must go against ancient Athens. And Macaulay, we must remember, was speaking of a society which still had before it something like half a century of dramatic expansion. Our problem is the far graver one that when a society built upon the acquisitive principle passes into its phase of contraction,

[1] Speech of July 8, 1831, *Speeches* (World's Classics Edition), p. 27.

it entrusts its defence of the principle to men like Hitler and Mussolini and Laval. They can only continue to impose it by war without and dictatorship within; for it has reached the stage where it is in necessary antagonism to all which gives dignity to the human spirit.

All government, in fact, which represents the interests of property is bound, if those interests are built upon an acquisitive system in decay, to be corrupt. Fascism has revealed to us that business men reject the claims of democracy as soon as these are seriously put forward as a way of life and not as a formal political procedure; more, than even in wartime, when the national existence is at stake, business men are afraid of the dynamic of democracy. Men of property, no doubt, will always announce their anxiety to be generous when crisis makes them dependent upon the co-operation of the masses; but it is the grim habit of war to reveal the depth of corruption behind the rhetoric of their promises since it exhibits their fear lest they be taken at their word.

Wherever men of property in an acquisitive society that is in its phase of contraction are challenged, it becomes apparent that justice is impossible between nations and individuals whose claims on welfare are not recognized as equal. For such a challenge always breeds fear; and this infects every nook and cranny in the community. The official class is anxious at all costs to avoid mistakes; it refuses to see that when men are always afraid of making mistakes, they are likely to accomplish nothing at all. Too many of them will take refuge in the pathetic fallacy that the multiplication of papers is the proof of fruitful energy. They will insist upon a fictitious impartiality of outlook; thereby they become blind to the fact that men who have no point of view can never put philosophy into their actions. They refuse to risk that extension of the limits of the practicable which a great war always makes possible lest they lose their reputation for soundness. They fail to understand that, in a decaying system, war reopens grievances that had been thought forgotten as it creates potentialities which had not been previously suspected. When this timidity on the part of property-owners is combined with caution in the official class, it is difficult for a government to seize or to maintain the initiative in action; for this initiative is always born of that audacity in ideas which, by winning the imagination of the masses, creates the environment in which great leadership secures a full and free response. The power of a nation to engage all its energies in war depends, in a democracy, on the willingness of its rulers to embark upon great reforms; in their absence, only rapid and overwhelming success will maintain confidence in a faith the purpose of which becomes increasingly alien from the experience the masses are seeking to affirm.

Those thinkers, therefore, who, like Mr. Lippmann, regard all forms of collectivism as a threat to freedom have, I suggest, forgotten two things. They have forgotten, first, that the substance of freedom requires redefinition in every new set of historical circumstances, for these give a different emphasis to the impact it makes. The consumer's freedom of choice among a large variety of goods seems far more important to the liberty of a distinguished journalist who has never felt the pinch of poverty than it does to a migratory labourer wondering if he will find a job as he "hitch hikes" from the cotton-fields of Georgia to the vast fruit farms of San Joaquin valley. The danger of bureaucracy implicit in state-ownership will impress Mr. Ford far more than it is likely to impress one of Mr. Ford's employees who is seeking to escape victimization because one of Mr. Ford's industrial spies has reported that the employee has joined a union. The absence of equality and security from the context of freedom as the masses experience it means that the judgment of its reality is made on quite different premisses by an unskilled labourer and a successful man of letters. They dwell in realms the contact between which is too fragmentary in character for a common interpretation of freedom to be normally valid for both.

The second thing, I think, which men like Mr. Lippmann forget, is not less important. The rule of law under whose operation freedom is to achieve its reality is, after all, a principle with a fairly long history behind it. And if the burden of that history has one outstanding lesson it is that, over the social process as a whole, the rule of law is only equally applied as between persons, whether individual citizens, or corporate bodies, whose claim on the state-power is broadly recognized as equal. First of all, it is invariably subject to suspension in an emergency where the executive deems a certain result of vital importance; even Lincoln suspended the writ of habeas corpus during the Civil War. Secondly, the rule of law is not an automatic principle of action which operates indifferently as to time and place and the persons to whom, as judges, its application is entrusted. It is very likely to be one thing for a Negro in Georgia and another thing for a white man in Georgia; and then, again, pretty much the same thing for Negro and white man in Massachusetts. The history of the use of the injunction by American courts in labour disputes; of the widely divergent interpretations of which the Fourteenth Amendment was capable in the hands of

Mr. Justice Holmes and Mr. Justice McReynolds; of the practically irreconcilable premisses upon which, in England, Lord Haldane and Lord Sumner approached the examination of judicial authority entrusted to executive hands; of the doctrine of "public policy" in such a case as *Osborne* v. *Amalgamated Society of Railway Servants*,[1] or of the canons of statutory interpretation invoked by the judges in such a case as *Roberts* v. *Hopwood*[2]; of the elasticity of concepts like "sedition" and "seditious conspiracy" which varies with the era in which the alleged offence is committed, the opinions of the judge presiding over the trial, and, not at all improbably, with the social composition of the jury trying the case; the clear implications of the relation of the rule of law to politics in such famous trials as those of Dreyfus, of Mooney and Billings, and of Sacco and Vanzetti; all these ought to warn us that if, as Mr. Lippmann argues, the rule of law reflects a law of nature within the protective envelope of which freedom is to be found, it is a law of nature the content of which has never an unchanging and equal application. No small part of the discredit into which the Weimar Republic fell was the outcome of the fact that its judges applied one standard of evidence and sentence to Nazi offenders gainst the law, and another and much severer standard to offenders with socialist or communist convictions.[3]

The fact simply is that the content of the rule of law is set by that sanctioned usage which the play of social forces tends to make predominant in some given time and place; and the history of the relations of production proves incontrovertibly that they play by all odds the most vital part in determining what usage will be sanctioned. In a society like ours, committed, almost, to the religion of inequality, it will vary in its application from class to class. To see in its operations, therefore, a permanent safeguard of that equality before the law which is of the inner essence of the democratic idea of freedom is to make at least the abstraction, if not, in truth, real nonsense, of a good deal of legal history. Law is that body of rules behind which the state places the authority of its supreme coercive power. Those rules are not made in the service of abstract concepts, however noble in appeal. They are made because those who made them were, no doubt, convinced that they were wise and just. But that conviction, in its turn, is born of the interests the government of a state decides that it must protect; and a close examination of

[1] (1910) A.C. 87. [2] (1925) A.C. 578.

[3] R. T. Clark, *The Fall of the German Republic* (London: George Allen & Unwin Ltd., 1936), is much the best account in English of these years.

most of its decisions will show that they are intelligible, like Lord Abinger's rule in *Priestley* v. *Fowler*,[1] only in the context of the relations of production.

Mr. Lippmann, in short, and those who think with him, have still to make the discovery which transformed Jeremy Bentham from a benevolent Tory into a radical reformer—the discovery that the law can easily be bent to the service of what Bentham called "sinister interest," and that those who so bend it may quite sincerely believe that this "sinister interest" is, in fact, identical with the well-being of the community. And the more unequal the society, the more likely is this identification. The conquerors in an acquisitive society have rarely the imagination to see its problems from the angle of vision of the conquered. In judging the idea of freedom not as concept but in application, it is important to remember that the analysis and history have mostly been written by the conquerors or their dependents. Freedom in the capitalist democracy in which the middle-class established, first, its right to freedom from state interference, and, when its security was in hazard, its equal right to protection by the state from those who, externally, threatened that security, is one thing when its history is written by Macaulay or Guizot; it is a very different thing when it is written by a Catholic who believes in monarchy like Mr. Belloc, or a socialist of Jacobin origins like Louis Blanc. No doubt every society contains men and women who can transcend the limitations of their private interest, and perceive the national validity of the case for its sacrifice; and the debt we owe to them when they refuse to accept the conventional standards of their time is immeasurable. But, as a general rule, the social philosophy of an age is an attempt to justify, with the appropriate apparatus of learning, the way of life of those who succeed in that age. We all remember Locke; the very powerful critics who attacked his work gather dust upon the shelves, and only the occasional antiquarian disturbs their peaceful obsolescence. Few people paid any attention to that remarkable school of early English socialists, men like Hall and Thompson and Bray, until the evolution of social forces had made trade unionism a vital historical force and men like Marx and Engels had provided it with a flaming indictment of its opponents by which it was persuaded to believe that the future was on its side.

The case against a planned democracy, or, rather, the case that planning is incompatible with democracy, that Mr. Lippmann has sought to make must, above all, be read in this background. It has,

[1] (1837) 3, *M. & W.*, 1, 7.

like the work of Mieses and Professor Robbins, all the historical characteristics which mark the defence of a system which is nearing its close. It renews, as at such a period there is always renewed, the eager claims made for the system in its first creative epoch. Its early power to liberate men by the expansion it has made possible is discussed with zest as though it was a contemporary feature of the system. Its quintessence, in its epoch of outstanding achievement, is extracted from the disfigurements it has accreted about it as it moved into its phase of contraction, and these are explained away as irrelevant to the thing-in-itself. We are then urged to recreate the conditions of its dawn; and we are warned that this is the only condition upon which we can avoid disaster.

But in actual history there is never recreation of this kind. Adam Smith's "simple system of natural liberty" which Mr. Lippmann and Professor Robbins desire so ardently to rebuild was no more than a generalization, like all social theories, from the specific conditions of his day. It was, of course, a remarkable generalization, massively conceived and stoutly supported by a brilliantly selected body of testimony. As its main outlines were applied, it gave, at any rate to Britain, many of the benefits Adam Smith claimed that it would bestow. It gave them, indeed, for special reasons very partially valid elsewhere, least of all valid in a new country like the United States, or an old country which, like Germany, had not found, and until Bismarck did not find, the conditions of effective economic unity. Its intellectual hold was, even in the first half of the nineteenth century, far more limited than the more enthusiastic of its devotees were willing to admit; for the alternative generalization of Alexander Hamilton, which List imported into Europe, fitted the climate of a deepening nationalism more aptly, if less productively. Adam Smith's ideas were well suited to the "nation of shopkeepers" whose customers were the whole world. But it is not difficult to understand why a Jugoslav delegate could insist to the League Economic Conference of 1927 that the postulates upon which the system was based could only be afforded by a powerful economic nation whose industries were strong enough to stand the pressure of world competition without aid from the state.

The truth is that the "simple system of natural liberty" ceased to be workable in the middle part of the nineteenth century; it was slain by the growth of the limited liability company, the growth of technological invention, and the discovery, by the upper and middle classes in alliance in the old world, and the men of property in the new, that they could use the state-power, both internally and externally, to protect their privileges from invasion. The system, as in Dickens's day, was strong enough to admit recruits from below as the British aristocracy had always done in the hey-day of its power; but it is evident in the later work of Dickens that the self-confidence is already beginning to fade. The system has already to be safeguarded by an increasing degree of state-intervention. Public health, public education, factory conditions, the rights of labour all require the increasing repudiation of *laissez-faire*. And in the United States, where national self-confidence was born only after the Civil War, it becomes obvious within little more than twenty years that the state-power must intervene to set limits to what Theodore Roosevelt called the practices of "malefactors of great wealth. "My faith in the people governing," said Dickens in 1869, "is, on the whole, infinitesimal; my faith in the people governed is, on the whole, illimitable." That was because Dickens felt that the "people governing" were an essentially "sinister interest" in society, tempered only by the achievements of benevolent men of the type of Oastler and Shaftesbury.

As early as 1843 Dickens had ceased to have any faith in the ruling class of Britain. "The necessity of a mighty change," he wrote to the Benthamite reformer Southwood Smith, "I clearly see." That insight did not become general until, with the first world-war, it became ever more clear that the central economic and social problems of our civilization were not compatible with the continued existence of capitalist democracy. The masses were no longer willing anywhere, at its close, to admit the claim of Lord Salisbury that "the affluence of the rich is necessary for the amelioration of the condition of the poor."[1] What Lord Salisbury was probably seeking to say was that a country must produce more than it consumed if it was to be able to develop its estate. What he did not seem to understand was that capital accumulation for such development could, as the experience of Russia made evident, be a deliberate and planned act of state-policy as it had previously been the by-product of a sum of individual efforts. Nor did he realize, any more than Mr. Lippmann realized, that the admission, in a capitalist democracy, of a limited area in which state-action was desirable still assumed the neutral character of the state-power and concealed the fact that the operations of that state-power were in the hands of men whose authority depended upon the goodwill of the owners of property.

The unconscious *agenda* of capitalist democracy, in short, as this

[1] *Post-War Conservative Policy* (London, 1942), p. 5.

is conceived by the opponents of planning, is really built on two unexplored assumptions. The first is that because the main modern states are built upon universal suffrage, each citizen, in fact, counts for one and not more than one in the making of political decisions; and the second is that citizens generally, and the members of a government in particular, can rise above the implications of their private experience to that vantage ground where the effective considerations which weigh with them disregard the limitations of that experience.

Neither of these assumptions, of course, is true; and neither is made true by the fact that every society offers remarkable instances of people who can transcend the limitations of private experience. The truth is that the individual citizen is helpless in a modern democracy unless he has extraordinary powers or the special position which birth or wealth bestows; without one of these, the measure of his influence in the thing for which he is anxious is the strength of the combination of like-minded persons with whom, in this context, he is in alliance. And since few men have extraordinary powers, or the special position which great wealth or birth bestows, the working of a democratic system depends upon the degree to which the second of these assumptions is valid. Even if we grant that most members of most democratic governments sincerely seek to do their best, the historic evidence that this best does not go far enough to make what Mr. Lippmann calls the "good society" good for the large mass of its members is overwhelming.

John Stuart Mill has told us, in a moving page of his *Autobiography*, how he and his friends "while fully recognizing the superior excellence of unselfish benevolence and love of justice, . . . did not expect the regeneration of mankind from any direct action on those sentiments, but from the effect of educated intellect, enlightening the selfish feelings."[1] But there are two comments upon this view which must be made. The first is the grim pessimism with which the economists of the post-Napoleonic epoch confronted the future of mankind. "No one," wrote Cairnes,[2] "can have studied political economy in the works of its earlier cultivators without being struck with the dreariness of the outlook which, in the main, it discloses for the human race. It seems to have been Ricardo's deliberate opinion that a substantial improvement in the condition of the mass of mankind was impossible." This view, the joint outcome of

[1] *Autobiography* (World's Classics Edition), p. 94.

[2] Appendix to A. Bain, *J. S. Mill* (1882), p. 197.

Malthus's principle of population and the iron law of wages, was given additional emphasis by the grave inadequacy of British administration, and, indeed, of any civil service save that, perhaps, of Prussia, before 1870 or thereabouts; it was the general climate of opinion to assume that the economists had proved the folly, in almost all cases, of positive action by the state. The best that could be hoped for was either the revival of that *noblesse oblige* which Disraeli so curiously compounded from the *Patriot King* and Burke, or else that survival of the fittest which would ensue when the imprudent and the thriftless had gone to the wall. Dickens was not far wrong when, behind the stout fortress of Manchesterism, he discerned the oily complacency of Mr. Podsnap.

But the second comment relates to our own day. We can study the "effect of educated intellect" in the conquerors of the richest civilization the world has so far known in the massive body of enquiries which followed upon the accession of President Roosevelt to office in 1933. No one would seriously suggest that the revelations of the Senate investigation of Wall Street,[1] suggested that "the selfish feelings" had been "enlightened" there. The simple truth is that, in a capitalist democracy, those who own or control the capital have different premisses of action from those who have nothing but their labour-power to sell; and when these latter send a reforming President to the White House the former either become altogether uncertain about the validity of democratic principles or insist that departures from the principles of *laissez-faire* are the denial of democracy. When ex-Ambassador Kennedy, on his return from London to the United States in the autumn of 1940 said, in a famous interview, that "democracy is finished in England," he meant, like Mr. Lippmann, to say that democracy was the "simple system of natural liberty"[2] in which successful men could take full advantage of the mechanism of the free market. And what that full advantage involved Judge Pecora had decisively demonstrated as he examined witness after witness from Wall Street before the Black Committee of the Senate.

Those, therefore, who seek to maintain the mechanism of the free market, upon the basis of private ownership of the means of production, and argue, like Mr. Lippmann, that the alternative is dictatorship, are really asking for other things obscured by the character of their argument. They are asking us to restore the

[1] Cf. Ferdinand Pecora, *Wall Street on Oath* (1934).

[2] Cf. my article in *Harper's Magazine*, November, 1940.

capitalist democracy that existed in the days before the advent of giant industry. Very largely, their anxiety for this restoration is a nostalgia for the security it seemed to offer, and the relative simplicity with which it was able to impose its discipline. A distinguished intellectual, like Mr. Lipmann, a successful speculator like Mr. Kennedy, felt free when that security was available and its appropriate discipline raised no problems they could not face. But they had never really investigated the price that was paid for their freedom. They saw only that there was no interference with their activities by the state-power. They noted that where, in other countries, there was such interference, the kind of freedom they enjoyed was not available to men of their type. They therefore inferred that the wider the area of intervention by the state-power, the smaller was bound to be the degree of civic freedom.

This is why the despotism of the business man can appear to him as freedom, and why he can be quite genuinely amazed that it does not appear in this light to his dependents. That is the reason which enables him, in some mysterious fashion, to convince himself that, say, the private ownership of the American Telephone Company is democracy at work, but that the public ownership of the Tennessee Valley Authority is communism, and, therefore, contrary to sound "American" principles. Mr. Thurman Arnold has quoted the illuminating evidence of Mr. J. E. Edgerton, a former President of the National Manufacturers' Association at the hearings of the Senate Committee on the Black-Connery Bill for the regulation of wages and hours of labour in American industry. Mr. Edgerton explained that "he never thought of paying men on a basis of what they need . . . he paid men for efficiency. Personally, he attended to all those other things, social welfare stuff, in his church work. . . . That's the feeling side of life, church contributions and church work. That's not business."[1] Mr. Edgerton takes the view that Burke took when he wrote that "politics and the pulpit are terms that have little agreement." He assumes that when the needs of the working man begin to affect the habits of business enterprise the logic of democracy is in danger. It does not occur to him that the working-man may think a system in which his needs are satisfied has a vital relation to freedom and democracy.

The position we have reached is the simple one in which the

[1] Quoted by Mr. Thurman Arnold in his *Folklore of Capitalism* (1937), p. 361, from the *Washington Post* of June 12, 1937.

philosophy of the system under which we live makes it impossible for us to satisfy the needs that we encounter. And our position is the more difficult because not only does that philosophy enable the needs of the most powerful interests to be satisfied, but it is supported by profound traditional emotions which regard with horror the prospect of its replacement; and those emotions are so deeply embedded in those who accept them that any change in the social values they represent seems like an attack upon the inherent order of nature. That is why Mr. Lippmann takes the American way of life he happens to like and identifies it with democracy and freedom. He then sets against it the counter-revolutionary societies of Italy and Germany, and that Soviet Union which had hardly emerged from chaos and civil war to the grim insecurities of the inter-war years over which, as we can now see, the shadow of the second world-conflict was already looming, and declares that a planned society is incompatible with freedom and democracy.

But he does not, of course, draw attention to what is omitted from his argument. He has, in fact, assumed that the conceptual pattern of the "good society" is realized, in a general way, in the societies in which we live; and his emotional attachment to the principles of that pattern enables him to disregard or to minimize what they mean for those men to whom Mr. Edgerton paid sixteen dollars a week for an average of forty-two weeks in the year because it was their "efficiency" as a source of profit and not their "needs" as human beings which seemed to him important. Mr. Lippmann, moreover, assumes the identity of association with causation. The main planned societies we have known in recent years have been dictatorships; from this he infers that we can only plan in dictatorial terms. The importance of the historical context in which the dictators rose to power is left out of sight; we are asked to believe that it was the decision to plan which led to the destruction of freedom. And, all the time, Mr. Lippmann, and those who belong to his school of thought, are building their "simple system of natural liberty" upon the basis that the state-power is a neutral force making objective laws which, by an unexplained but mysterious magic, affect men equally whose claims upon the common welfare are not recognized as equal.

It is, of course, inevitable, when a social system is drawing to its close, that men should seek to recommend the principles by which it achieved its victories. For, first, our fear of the unknown, our distaste for the risk of large-scale experiment, always gives the past a glamour which a hazardous future can scarcely claim; and since most social philosophies are a rationalization of the claims that have won rather than the claims which seek for victory, they are more likely to be written from the angle of the holders of power as their justification than from that of their opponents who seek to destroy what those holders have so laboriously built up. That is why the growth in the number of officials in the positive state seems so much more dangerous an attack upon freedom to successful men who, the armed forces, the police and the postman apart, have little need of the state, than it does to the working-man who has begun to find in the National Labour Relations Board that the right of recognized combination can set liberty of contract in the context of a more equal bargaining power. That is why, also, it is far easier to convince a member of the New York Stock Exchange that the Tennessee Valley Authority puts his historic liberties in danger than the resident of the area it serves who enjoys, for the first time, equal access to cheap electric power and water-supply. That is why the impersonal mechanism of the market, in an unequal society, increases the authority of the powerful at the expense of the weak and leaves the latter with a sense of frustration and impotence for which the sense of freedom and ease in the powerful is in truth no compensation. There could hardly, I think, be a grimmer comment on that strategy of freedom Mr. Lippmann recommends than the fact that, in a period of war like our own, it makes administratively impossible any real attempt at equality of sacrifice.

But the fatal case against the "simple system of natural liberty" on the terms upon which Mr. Lippmann and others recommend it is, I think, twofold. First, it involves an historical regression in the institutional forms of industry which either, as in the Sherman Act, never adequately attain their purpose of restoring "healthy" competition, or results in an attack upon vested interests which, given their relation to government in a capitalist democracy, the state-power is rarely in a position to sustain. From this angle, anyone who measures the disproportion between the effort of Mr. Thurman Arnold, the Assistant Attorney-General, to break up monopolies in the United States, and the results he has been able to attain even with a vast army of officials (whose growth seems to this school a threat to freedom) will, I suggest, be tempted to conclude that as fast as the government discovers devices to restore competition, so fast, also, will the ingenuity of lawyers find ways around those devices; the scale of the problem is beyond the power of a government that is subject to the normal pressure-politics of capitalist democracy.[1] And it is not less vital to understand that the consumer's sovereignty which the "good society" is to afford us, if it is not protected by state-planning on a democratic basis, in matters of fundamental concern, will, in fact, encounter capitalist planning which, both in production and in distribution, creates mechanisms for the exploitation of the consumer which go far to destroying any prospect of that sovereignty by the creation of private empires which effectively challenge it. "What is notable among British consolidations and associations," wrote the Committee on Trusts in 1919, "is not their rarity or weakness so much as their unobtrusiveness. There is not much display in the window but there is a good selection inside." That is an understatement a quarter of a century later. And to their influence must be added the increasing power of the retail trade associations which extends from the protection of coffee-stall keepers to the defence of the interests of undertakers.[2] Not the least interesting aspect of this latter development is the growing institution among these associations of what they tend to call "codes of ethics" which, when their panoply of rhetoric is stripped away, usually turn out to be variations upon the theme of the ancient adage that dog does not eat dog.

But the other aspect is not less important. An unplanned society means an unequal society; and an unequal society may still be not unfairly divided into Matthew Arnold's three broad categories of "barbarians, philistines, populace." Its tragedy is that its dependence upon the possession of "effective demand" in the economists' sense, makes its central principle acquisitiveness; and to this principle all other aspects of life become subordinated. The influence of this principle is written painfully over the history of English education; it has had a baneful effect upon the place of scientific research in the national life; it has limited the power both of the central government and of local authorities to recognize their duty to promote the fine arts, the drama, and learning and literature. By making the man who was successful in acquisition the object of its main admiration, it has never been able to escape from the

[1] It is interesting to compare Mr. Arnold's views of the limits of possible achievement in this field before his appointment as Assistant Attorney-General with his views after his appointment. Cf. *The Folklore of Capitalism* (1937), chap. ix, with his *Bottlenecks of Capitalism* (1940).

[2] Cf. Professor Hermann Levy's *Retail Trade Associations* (1942). It is interesting to note that in the last chapter of his book Professor Levy concludes in favour of reversing the attitude of freedom which the Common Law has taken and suggests the creation of a new government department with "a staff of well-trained . . . civil servants" to deal with them.

belief that poverty is, somehow, the evidence not merely of failure but even of sin; and the result of that outlook is that the poor man is still regarded, especially when he is unemployed, as morally inferior to the man in steady work. Even when, with the coming of social insurance in its different forms, that charity which, in the days of Dickens and Carlyle was largely a nauseating safeguard of property against revolution, was replaced by the idea that maintenance was a right, it still retained the idea, as W. R. Greg put it in his criticism of Young England, "of benefits to an inferior not . . . justice to a fellow man."[1] We still live in the shadow of that grim pessimism by which Malthus and Ricardo seemed to make the imposition of a rigorous discipline upon the poor a part of the law of nature. It is better administered because so largely professionalized; but the distinction between the "deserving" and "undeserving" poor still lies at the base of all our remedial arrangements. Since "deserving" is a moral category, that is perhaps why Mr. Edgerton thinks that "social welfare" is a matter that he must consider not as an employer, but as a Churchman; and Mr. Edgerton is not alone in drawing that distinction.[2]

Here, as I think, is the ultimate weakness of the social system which is drawing to its close. By building itself around the idea of acquisition, it degraded the dignity of human nature in the masses; and by the very fact of that degradation it separated its successful men from its unsuccessful by the abyss of fear. It knew no way of bridging that abyss save charity, and its rulers were always uneasily conscious that charity which, in a just society, could be one of the most gracious of the virtues, in an acquisitive society bore all the marks of that ransom which injustice pays to fear. Once it had made the power to acquire the normal criterion of success, it lost its main hold upon a system of values capable of rational defence. Its standard at the top was, as Veblen so remarkably showed,[3] the ability of the successful to prove their success by their capacity to waste conspicuously. And because power was so predominantly a function of property there was no aspect of the social fabric which could escape this economic permeation; those who operated it dared not experiment with the possibilities of a faith which denied its central theme. Good, on their view, consisted of the solid, material

[1] *Westminster Review*, June 1845. I owe the quotation to the admirable and illuminating book of Mr. Humphrey House, *The Dickens World* (1941).

[2] Cf. letters in the *Times* of October 1, 1942, from Dean Inge, the ex-Dean of St. Paul's, and Mr. C. K. Allen, the Warden of Rhodes House, Oxford.

[3] *The Theory of the Leisure Class* (London: George Allen & Unwin Ltd., 1904).

things that are capable of purchase and sale; and, quite obviously, the more costly they were the more of goodness they contained.

Set, as this philosophy was set, in the background of an economics of scarcity, it was only capable in two conditions of binding men together in the unity of fellowship. It could do in its period of expansion, since it then made real for the masses the hope that they, too, could share in well-being. It could do so in a period of crisis, a catastrophe, for instance, like an earthquake or a war, when the depth of the dangers men share in common enable them to find the realities of one another in a purpose which transcends its normal scale of values; for it is above all in the common experience of a transcendent purpose that men discover that the true goods cannot be bought and sold.

But there is a fatal flaw where the first condition operates. The price that is paid for the inherent logic of an acquisitive society is the heavy one that its rulers mistake security for freedom. They do not oppress the masses so long as they feel safe; but they only feel safe so long as they are certain that the power of the armed forces and the police is sufficient to safeguard their privileges from attack, and that certainty is only rarely available and then only for brief periods. In times of crisis, the sense of fellowship lasts only while the danger endures; when it has passed, as the last war showed, the abyss of fear again separates men from one another. Security may re-emerge, as it re-emerged in 1794 after Thermidor, after the June days of 1848, after the suppression of the Commune in the spring of 1871, after the defeat of the Russian Revolution in 1905; but such security lacks altogether the power to satisfy that hunger for creative adventure which is central to the climate of freedom.

What is, in fact, fatal to the plea that the good society can be unplanned and acquisitive is, from one angle, that behind the forms of capitalist democracy it always, in sober truth, becomes a plutocracy; while, from another angle, it always ultimately is hostile to any purpose which seeks to make impalpable values like goodness and beauty and truth more desirable than material wealth. That is shown by the historical evidence that whoever defends a purpose of this kind endangers the security of an unplanned society; that is why most movements which seek to realize the Christianity of the Gospels are driven, like the early Quakers, to come to terms with the world they set out to change, or, like the Spiritual Franciscans, are broken on the wheel of material power.

For we never sufficiently remember how fragile is the hold of our acquisitive society upon the great mass of its members, how deep are the resentments beneath the formal appearance of submission to its habits. Yet that is the truth we have to re-learn in each revolutionary epoch of history. It is of decisive importance that the first phase in such epochs is always a period of exhilaration, not seldom, even, when the splendour of the ideal of fraternity is re-emphasized. The one gospel that always brings a sense of hope is the gospel that all things must be made new. No doubt it is a dangerous doctrine. But men feel a real liberation in the effort to overcome its dangers, partly because the adventure itself is freedom, and partly because the conquest of fear is the true fulfilment of self. The security which our present system affords to the few by its endowment of ownership with religious value, means, for the overwhelming majority of men a drab routine with only an occasional moment of escape. It condemns the masses to insignificance because it fears the effect upon them of the call to fulfilment; for it is convinced that the response to that call means the end of its security. Yet it is not in fact surprising that a society which thus dwarfs the personality of its members should fail to evoke the emotions out of which a system builds the power to endure.

This is the main reason, it may be added in parenthesis, why the counter-revolution, in its initial stages, could make an appeal to many of the men whose interests as a class it had come to destroy. They were frustrated and disillusioned; the counter-revolution presented itself as adventure and danger and hope. They responded to its call because it seemed to offer an escape from the insignificance to which they felt themselves condemned by capitalist democracy in decay. No doubt the counter-revolutionary leaders were false Messiahs who preached a false gospel. But the disillusioned masses who heard them were more moved by the fact that it was a gospel than by the fact that it was false.

Here, as I see it, is the fatal error of those who seek to defeat the counter-revolution in the name of our traditional institutions; they forget that it is the character of our traditional institutions which has provoked the counter-revolution. The savage barbarities of Hitlerism may give enough power to them to enable the challenge to be overcome. But the loyalty evoked by that power will not last. It is the loyalty of a negative indignation, not the loyalty of a positive conviction. All over the world, the masses are increasingly aware of the hollowness of the faith, the emptiness of the values, traditional institutions have been able to impose. That is the meaning of the restless spirit of our times; and it is strengthened by its alliance with the Russian Revolution. It may well be—though even this is doubtful—that victory over Hitlerism will give the old order a temporary respite. But neither the prestige of victory nor the emotion of ecclesiastical organization will be able for any serious length of time to give the stability of renewed faith to that order. The society of the future must make up its mind to pursue its search for freedom in the context of equality if it desires to avoid the tragedy of a revolutionary war without being followed by a revolutionary war within. To achieve that context while there is time, it must build the foundations of a planned democracy.

III

It requires no elaborate argument to prove that a planned society imposed by the state-power after society has been bitterly rent in pieces by civil war is not likely, for a long period, to admit the climate of freedom, even where, as in Russia, the purpose of the plan is to benefit the community as a whole. Ancient habits persist; historic suspicions linger; and if Napoleon from his tomb could set his nephew upon the throne of France, it is not surprising that, down to the very outbreak of the war, the makers of the Soviet Union found it hard to admit the right of opposition. Even after twenty-five years, only one party in Russia has the legal right to existence. In the light of the traditional political habits of capitalist democracy, it is not, perhaps, surprising that the critics of planning should see in freedom its antithesis.

Yet we must be careful to avoid some obvious fallacies of perspective. That freedom and a planned society are contradictory terms would not be a legitimate inference from the experience of building up the Soviet Union in a hostile world, after crushing defeat in war, after four years of civil struggle and foreign intervention, with a population overwhelmingly illiterate and with but little experience of the disciplined precision in work which is exacted by the technology of the machine. It would not be legitimate, either, to conclude that what the ruling class in capitalist democracy agrees to recognize as freedom is the only valid way in which we can regard it. To argue, as the critics of planned democracy argue, that its ultimate decisions are *a priori* authoritarian, and, therefore, incompatible with freedom, is merely skilful fencing which bypasses all the vital factors in the problem. To insist, as the critics do, that a planned democracy means a society overwhelmed with officials, and, therefore, permeated by a bureaucratic temper from which the mood of freedom is alien, is either a species of that anarchism which, as Mr. Shaw once said, regards the policeman as a standing defiance of personal liberty, or wholly to mistake the endless habituation to an imposed routine within which all but a small proportion of our own society is committed. To compare the relative poverty in the supply of consumers' goods in a co-operative store in Moscow or Tashkent with the massive richness of choice in Fifth Avenue or Bond Street is to forget, first, the grave alternatives between which the Soviet Union has to choose—as well as to be ungrateful for the result on ourselves of the choice it made—and, second, the small number of those in either the United States or Britain to whom that massive richness of choice is in fact available. To urge, as the critics of planning urge, that it destroys the great chance of the free and varied career our own system offers must appear curiously ironical to, say, a retired miner in South Wales as he contrasts the opportunities he enjoyed with those that the planned society has opened since 1917 to any man or woman of energy and character in Russia; and the contrast, I venture to think, must seem even more striking to a peasant's son, like Timoshenko, when he reflects upon what his history might have been if the Revolution of October had not been triumphant.

But economics, we are told,[1] involves making decisions between the alternative uses of scarce means, and there must be a loss of freedom if, with the abandonment of the impersonal mechanism of the market, with objective price as the measure of supply and demand, political authority intervenes to decide what shall be made and the price at which it is to be sold. And there are, it is insisted, two further dangers. Men, it is said, who are disposing of capital that is not their own lack the incentives to efficiency and inventiveness which, whatever its defects, the profit-making motive supplies; and there is the risk that the governing group may take advantage of their position to acquire privileges for themselves which are not proportionate to the function they perform but to the power of which they dispose. And there is the danger, even beyond these, that the "pull" on politics of the producer may unfairly tilt the democratic equilibrium towards the group or groups in a strategically pivotal position.

The first of these arguments refuses to confront the central issue that it raises. Political authority is not, in fact, neutral in the market-mechanism; it has already decided in favour of the persons who, in an economic sense, can make their demand effective. The rules that authority makes do not, except in times of crisis, seek so to

[1] L. C. Robbins, *The Nature and Significance of Economic Science* (1932), p. 15.

dispose of scarce means as to make them supply urgent social needs; it has, as it were, already intervened before use is determined to assure that effective demand is satisfied whenever the entrepreneur believes that he can make a profit out of that satisfaction. In the state of capitalist democracy the main purpose of the rulers is to protect the owners of property. It is to their interest that the scarce means are mainly devoted. If political authority intervenes, as with rationing in war time, that is not necessarily a loss of freedom unless we define this to mean the right of the owners of property to use their economic power in any way they please.

To the second of these arguments there is the reply both of theory and experience. In fact, the argument, originally produced with triumph by Professor von Mieses,[1] and since then enthusiastically repeated by a host of disciples,[2] has been shown to rest upon a fallacy;[3] and the socialist economy of the Soviet Union uses a price-mechanism just as effectively as the capitalist economy of Great Britain or the United States.[4] The theory that public ownership, with management in the hands of salaried officials, is bound to be inferior to a system based on the private ownership of capital is, quite obviously, a compound of a particular theory of human nature and of the propaganda which an acquisitive society requires to protect itself from invasion by the principle of public ownership. A really able man will clearly run his private business better than a second-rate man will run a public concern; but that is not the issue. The real question is whether the service of the public will, in a planned society, provide an incentive to effort as effective as that which service for private profit will evoke.

The answer, of course, is that it depends partly on the character of the men concerned and partly on the status the society attaches to men in such positions. Given reasonable remuneration, there is not, historically, an atom of evidence to suggest that men work less eagerly in public than in private employment, granted that the work interests them and that an equal esteem is attached to its performance. If, in a given society, the man who can acquire most is most highly regarded, it is very probable that ambitious and able

[1] *Socialism*, by L. von Mieses (1936); and see F. von Hayek (ed.), *The Economics of Planning* (1935).

[2] E.g. Mr. Lippmann in the United States, Professors Robbins, Plant and Hayek in Britain. For its most extravagant expression see W. H. Hutt, *Economists and the Public* (1936).

[3] O. Lange and F. M. Taylor, *The Economic Theory of Socialism* (1938).

[4] M. H. Dobb, *Political Economy and Capitalism* (1940); and note the acceptance of socialist planning by Professor Pigou, *Socialism Versus Capitalism* (1937).

men will drift into the most lucrative occupations. And if, as with ourselves, the defence of the power and privilege which attach to wealth is an urgent preoccupation of the ruling class in society, they will, of course, see to it that everything possible is done to cry down principles of social action which threaten their power and privilege. It is even reasonable to expect, where men are measured by their wealth, and they can look for higher rewards in private industry than in public employment, to assume that the standard of performance in the first will generally be higher than the standard of performance in the second since it will be more likely, other things being equal, to recruit ability. But where the standard of public judgment is not set by the power to acquire wealth merely, there is not an iota of serious evidence to support this argument. Here, at least, the experience of the Soviet Union is conclusive.

That a governing class may use its position to acquire privileges by which it is differentiated from the rest of the citizen body is, of course, a danger as old as history itself; there is no power in which there is not the risk of corruption. It is also obvious that in all nations where the counter-revolutionary principle has triumphed the officials who organize the planning there have used its opportunities, at least with rare exceptions, to build up their private fortunes; we have ample testimony upon this point. But this is not a field in which the protagonists of capitalism can afford to take an attitude of superiority. After all, the history of the great fortunes in the United States and Canada, the technique of the "two hundred families" in France, adventurism like that of Kreuger in Sweden and of Juan March in Spain, are a grim record of the corruption of legislators and officials in the interest of wealthy privilege. Since some such time as the Chartist Movement, open corruption of this kind has been rare in the central government of Britain, though it has been more frequent than we like to admit among local authorities. But even in Britain we must not forget the significance of the Honours List as the main source from which the historic political parties have drawn their financial support; and no small part of their policies has been shaped by the character of this source.

It is at least an encouraging fact that, so far in the history of the Soviet Union, not only has this form of corruption been rare, not only has it, on discovery, been ruthlessly punished, but the higher up we go in the hierarchy of its officials, the more austere has been the standard of life with which they have been satisfied. The stamp of Lenin's simplicity has gone deep into the habits of the régime; generally, it may be claimed that to whatever forms of corruption its planned use of power is open, from this form, at least, above all in comparison with capitalist societies, it has been honourably and remarkably free.

The critics' claim that a planned democracy gives the strong producers' interest an advantage over the weaker by the exercise, I suppose, alike of its industrial and political power seems to me very largely unreal—a bogey to frighten children rather than an argument rooted in solid historic experience. For, first, let us note that few things have been more rare in the history of the modern state than a corporate attempt by its officials, administrative or industrial, to exploit their position; the economic conditions of the British and American civil services is a proof of that. The same can be said of the police forces; where, as in Boston in 1919, there has been a strike, it was the outcome of many years of grievance which the government had persistently neglected to remedy, and, in the Boston strike, as in that in Britain in the same year, with a little wisdom in those who handled it, there is every reason to doubt whether it would have occurred. And it is of the first importance that, where the armed forces of the state have intervened in politics, except in actual circumstances of revolution, usually, as in Leningrad in 1917 and Kiel in 1918, after military defeat, the impulse to intervention has come from the officer class, as in the Ulster incident of 1914 and subsequent Fascist developments, and not from the rank and file; even then the interest the intervention sought to further was general in character and not specifically related to their separate economic welfare.

The more usual situation in the experience of capitalist democracies is when a group seeks to secure a special protection from the government; the farmers in England, in the Derating Act of 1929, Labour in post-war America over the immigration laws, are instances of this type of action. But in any examination of this experience it is important to remember that special protection has usually been conceded not to the power of numbers but to the ability of the group concerned to assist or hinder political parties in their fulfilment of wider ends than the group itself has in view. The tenderness of British Conservatism to the farming interest is closely bound up with the general relation of the Conservative Party to the landowning class which enables it still so largely to dominate the rural constituencies in Britain. It may be doubted whether the American trade unions, after the last war, would have secured the drastic limitations upon the European immigrant that they did had their demand not coincided, first, with a general desire for isolation from Europe, and, second, with the suspicion that the European immigrant was the bearer of revolutionary infections about which, largely on account of the Russian Revolution, the United States was at the moment hysterical. And, as a rule, the safeguard a special economic interest secures is an index to a general climate of opinion for which the government affording it believes there is approval. The very small number of English banks have been able to stop the development of municipal banking in this country not in terms of principle—that was conceded almost a generation ago in the case of the strikingly successful Birmingham bank—but because it was felt by business men generally that any great extension of municipal banking might form the basis of an ultimately irresistible claim for a socialized system of credit in general. Every enquiry into the British coal industry since 1919 has revealed the waste and inefficiency and ill-will endemic in the present system of ownership; but, even in war time, nationalization has been refused because interests far beyond the coal industry believe that no gains that might result from it would compensate for the loss represented by the admission of the thin end of the wedge. The dramatic legislation forced upon Congress by President Roosevelt in the creative period of the New Deal was less a direct tribute to the power of Labour in American politics—though this was, of course, a factor of importance—than it was the penalty exacted by the little man in America for his conviction that the unregulated leadership of big business had failed him badly in the Great Depression. Measures like the Securities and Exchange Act, the Act creating the Tennessee Valley Authority, and the Wagner Act, were the safeguards the little man sought against a return to the risks of "rugged individualism."

There is, of course, a special reason why Russian experience throws only a partial light upon this problem. The fundamental power has remained throughout in the hands of the Bolshevik Party, and, though there has been a complex system of consultation with non-party opinion, especially in industrial matters, the decisions have been party-decisions for the reversal of which there existed no organized machinery. The balance of interests has been maintained in terms of what the party thought effective, and the history of the purges in the party make it obvious that it has never been easy to strike the balance. But I see no reason to suppose that the experience of planning in Russia justifies the inference that it is incompatible with either freedom or democracy; it proves only that in the quite exceptional circumstances out of which the Revolution developed the objectives set for the plan by the Communist Party could not have been fulfilled within the framework of opposition that parliamentary government has permitted in Great Britain.

But this leads to a view of the limits of opposition in a society which is fundamental to the understanding of freedom. "Freedom," said Marx, "is the recognition of necessity." Every society is built upon a system of postulates the continuing life of which its members must agree to respect; and their freedom is only available within the limits of that respect. Great Britain, for example, is a constitutional monarchy; its life would be inconceivable if the turn of electoral fortunes could, every so often, make it into a republic. And, in the same way, the acceptance of a planned economy involves the necessity to think of freedom in terms of the assumption that the decision to plan is broadly respected. The relationships of a community could not be worked out in a rational way if, let us say, private persons took over the Tennessee Valley Authority whenever the Republican Party was in power, and, on a victory of the Democratic Party, it was returned again to government ownership. The right of opposition in any society is only effective so long as it respects the fundamental principles of the society. A change in these is only possible where there is general consent to its being made, or where the power of those who dissent is not strong enough to gamble upon its prevention by force; a change, that is which permits the continuance of democratic processes. Where either general consent is absent, or the dissenters are prepared to fight against it, neither freedom nor democracy is available to a society.

On this basis, I think it is clear that two conclusions follow. The first is that if the introduction of planning into a capitalist democracy is to be compatible with the maintenance of freedom it must have behind it the general consent of citizens; freedom will not be maintained if there is room for doubt whether the decision to plan as an essential element in its life is likely to be reversed by some chance hazard of electoral fortunes. The essence of freedom is the ability to exercise continuous initiative, and that continuity is not available in the absence of agreement on fundamentals in the society. Where this agreement is absent the drift to open conflict permeates all political and economic relations and means, inevitably, that certain types of initiative will have to be restrained or suppressed. We can see this without difficulty in a period of external war; the overriding purpose of victory sets limits, defined pretty well by the gravity of the danger, to the limits of opposition that will be permitted.

And that leads me to the second conclusion. When a society accepts the decision to plan it is, thereby, providing itself with an overriding purpose to the general principles of which the mass of citizens must conform. Their freedom becomes a function of its necessities; the limits of their permissible initiative are set by the logic it implies. Planning, obviously, means priorities; the decision is taken that this thing is more important than that, that the resources of the society must be used for it before they are used for its alternative. And, once there are priorities, freedom, obviously again, has a context different from that of an unplanned society in which the use of resources is determined by supply and demand in the market. The citizen with capital to invest, for instance, will not make up his mind between the pedestrian safety of government bonds and the tempting risk of a South American silver mine. The public control of the whole credit mechanism in society is the necessary basis upon which priorities can be planned; the investor's freedom, in the classic sense that capitalism has known, is bound to disappear. In the same way, again, there will be areas of economic activity which will be monopolized by public ownership in its various forms; the citizen will not be free to enter that area except as a servant of the public concern which occupies it. How far the public areas of activity in the economic field will extend it is, of course, futile to prophesy; though, as I have pointed out in the previous chapter, the conception of planning for mass-welfare makes the occupation of certain vital areas essential.

On this basis, the compatibility of planning with freedom is, in the first instance, a question of the psychology of politics. It means the transfer from private to public ownership of what, as I have argued, are the central keys of economic power. It means that private persons can no longer use those keys to open the doors which lead to areas of privilege. Can that be done with general consent?

My own answer, frankly, is that I do not know. It depends a good deal upon the time at which it is attempted, and it depends a good deal, also, upon the way in which it is attempted. I have argued in this book that if the change is to be made with the highest prospect of success the present is the most appropriate time. I have suggested that this is so because the impact of the war has created a mood in which there is widespread readiness to accept great change. But I have pointed out that, on all historic experience, this mood is very unlikely to last beyond the war, that, accordingly, to attempt it when there is no longer the exaltation of spirit provoked by profound danger, is to miss the favourable moment for action. For, with victory, the relief from strain makes men search again for that rhythm of life to which experience has adapted them. At the time between Dunkirk and the end of the Battle of Britain I doubt whether any vested interest could have opposed its claims to a demand from the War Cabinet for such a scale of change as I have urged as a means to the control of the future; had it done so, an indignant public opinion would have swept its opposition on one side. But each month since the Battle of Britain has given the vested interests involved increased power to resist change. If we follow to its logical conclusion Mr. Churchill's policy of refusing to discuss "controversial questions" during the war, lest, as he suggests, the national unity be disturbed, I should have thought the natural psychology of those in occupation of the area to be transferred would be to say that if so great a sacrifice was unnecessary when the national existence was at stake, it is far less necessary when the threat of Hitlerism has been overcome. In such a situation, the temptation of the vested interests to defend the existing social order is, I think, bound to be great; and there is no sort of assurance that they will not yield to the temptation.

On this view, a good deal will depend upon a number of factors each of which has an influence at present beyond our power of measurement. The attitude of America, with the immense authority it will have, to the post-war world; the manner of the Axis defeat and, involved in this, the degree to which revolutionary passions are loosed in Europe and Asia; the strength, military and economic, of Russia at the close of hostilities, and the degree of which its rulers will use its strength to support revolutionary passions; the impact of all these upon the Labour Party in Britain, and the problem, still concealed from us except as a problem, of whether it will have learned that, without a planned society, its power to meet the main post-war issues will be so small that it may well rapidly cease to command an electorate it cannot satisfy; all these, I say, are factors beyond our present power to estimate. I record only my own conviction that, granted the forces which this war expresses, for it is as much their result as their cause, if we have failed, by the Armistice, to lay the foundations of a revolution by consent, we shall pass rapidly to a position where, because men no longer hold the great ends of life in common, they will be unable to agree upon the methods of social change. In that event, the reorganization of our basic principles will not be capable of accomplishment by peaceful means; and the final disposition of forces will be determined not by discussion but by violence. That this outcome will mean, whichever side is successful, the end of freedom and democracy for a period all previous precedent makes clear beyond dispute. In modern times, only the Spanish Republic put confidence in the good faith of its enemies. Its example is unlikely to encourage those who settle the character of the post-war epoch.

I have put the problem in British terms, because they are the terms with which I am most familiar. They are the setting, also, in which the past relationships of social forces gives the best opportunity available of building a planned democracy by agreement. I have said that, as well as the time, the methods also are important; and these require some general consideration because of the perspective in which the experience of Russia enables us to set them. I note, at the outset, that, for the overwhelming majority of our citizens, the fact that the claims of property must be, to some extent, subdued to the transcendent purpose of victory, does not generally result in the frustration of our personalities as citizens. We seek more rationing, not less. Proportionately, the evasion of the obligations the government thinks it right to impose, is relatively small. I speak, I think, for most Englishmen when I say that war brings a sense of fulfilment in the degree that it enables us to find significant service. More: I suspect that in these terrible years more men and women have found a genuine liberation in fulfilment than was the case in the years of doubt and disillusion between 1919 and 1939. The nation as a whole has discovered that it is most free when it is most committed to the performance of duties which, five years ago, it would have bitterly denounced as an unwarrantable invasion of its liberties. War is a hateful thing, ugly, brutal, cruel; yet, being all these, if it is the means to fulfilling a great end, its service, seen in right perspective, can bring both dignity and exhilaration.

What is the secret which lies beneath this paradox? It lies, I suggest, in the fact that citizens who participate in a great end about which they are agreed find a freedom in its service which makes right and duty reciprocal terms. The presence of this great end as the supreme social purpose enables a system of priorities to be constructed which determines the frame of individual action. The mechanism of the free market is suspended; an approach, at least, to a planned society takes its place. And it is of the utmost importance that the scale of priorities we have had to construct to enable that purpose to be fulfilled has results which, in things like food and clothing, appear less arbitrary than in the non-authoritarian market of a *laissez-faire* world. I agree, of course, that the planning is incomplete. Obviously, it encounters frictions, above all the friction which it inherits from the psychological habits of the pre-war world, which make it fragmentary, interstitial, lacking in comprehensiveness. But I think it is relevant to emphasize that where supply of goods is short a government decision that the basis of acquisition shall be the fact of personality and not the merely economic principle of effective demand has unquestionably operated to social benefit.

A simple analogy will perhaps emphasize my point. The operation of priorities has involved a large element of planning in our life; and that, in its turn, has meant reduction in the differences between individual claims on the common welfare. It is as though from a system in which our income determines the number of votes we can cast, we move to a system in which the margins at each end of the scale, though still wide, have come much closer together. We have recognized that free consumers' choice would frustrate the overriding end we have in view; we have defined an area in which it ceases to operate. I do not think that, in any real sense, the element of equality imposed by the state-power has been widely felt as a loss of freedom.

There are, to put the issue in general terms, at least three aspects in which there is no necessary relation between the free market, as that is recommended to us by the critics of planned democracy, and the good of the community. The primary step in the free market is taken by the producer; the consumer's choice operates only on the alternatives before him. And this producer's initiative is accounted successful by a commercial criterion only. A miner in a South Wales mining village did not indicate, until schemes of municipal housing began, the kind of house he wanted; he had to take his choice between one house and another neither of which we think to-day should ever have been built at all. Or the consumer buys amid a range of commodities many of which, like patent medicines, he would not purchase at all if he had any specialist knowledge about them. The pathos which surrounds the parent who thinks that he is purchasing social advancement for his children when he sends them to the kind of private school at which Mr. Lewisham is an assistant master instead of to the council school where they will mingle with "common" boys and girls is a pathos which needs protection from better-informed authority.

Even the critics of a planned democracy admit that there are services which the community as a whole must undertake, without regard to the free market. Public health, education, the prevention of crime, protection against fire, are obvious examples. Upon the extent of those services, no doubt, there may be both spatial as well as temporal differences. Free secondary education seems natural to most of us in 1942; it did not seem so forty years ago. Every municipality in England thinks a public library service an indispensable social service; but there are still rural areas where it is regarded as an unamiable waste of the ratepayers' money. It is clear, moreover, that this genus includes a category in which the individual is compelled, in the public interest, to make his purchase conform to certain regulations; he must have the plans for his house approved by the local authority, and he must fit a silencer to his motor-car.

The third type of case is of a different order. It relates to those commodities where the sheer range of variation provided involves a higher price than would be charged for commodities of a more standardized form. Here the presumption that it is the consumer's choice which dictates the profusion assumes optimum satisfaction without regard to the waste that is often involved; and, not seldom, that profusion is nothing more than an unnecessary response to what Veblen calls "conspicuous consumption." A good example of what I mean is the normal menu provided for a first-class passenger in peace-time on a Translantic liner. To Mr. Lippmann the range of this *à la carte* fare may represent a freedom which a more restricted *table d'hôte* meal would destroy. The range of food, in fact, bears no resemblance to the normal habits of the traveller; it is simply an index to a standard of luxury demanded by a society in which the power to waste is taken as the proof that one is a successful man. There are many instances of this kind, especially in the luxury trades like, for example, the cosmetic industry, where standardization releases productive capital, at one end, and, by the cheapness it permits, extends the market at the other.

The characteristic of a planned democracy, in a word, will be the subordination of the market to a purpose or system of values upon which its members have agreed. But because it is a democracy that is to be planned, the purpose, or system of values, is decided by men and women as citizens, and not, in the economists' sense, as bundles of "effective" demand. The degree to which the democratic character of a planned system is capable of permeating it, and giving to its members the sense of freedom which, in a general view, it is historically accurate to say that only a minority of persons has been able to enjoy continuously will depend very largely upon the way in which planning originates, the manner in which it is able to sccure the full co-operation of all classes of citizens in its application.

Quite obviously, if planning is not based upon consent, if, even, as a planned system is brought into being, it lives in the shadow of threat from within, whether direct, like that of Hitlerism to the Weimar régime, or of the more subtle, but persistent sabotage by vested interests which has haunted the New Deal in America ever since its first dramatic honeymoon was over, the likelihood of its inception, at least, being democratic is small. No government will permit a challenge, open or secret, to the imperatives behind which it places the fundamental authority of the state-power; if it does, the historical evidence is massive that it will not long remain a government. Men who have the responsibility for ultimate social decisions will only tolerate criticism of those decisions so long as the critics do not seriously threaten the agreed values upon which those decisions are based. That, quite frankly, is why, so far, the existence of socialist parties in capitalist democracies has been permitted. The battles those parties fought, as distinct from the ideas they sought to spread, was a battle for a certain quantum of social reform which, in fact, their opponents could accept without the sense that the vital principle they existed to maintain was in danger. Once they had that sense, as in the last years of the third French Republic, the ability to accept the purpose of socialist parties rapidly declined; and, in periods of panic, as in the months of the "red hysteria" in the United States in 1919, that ability suffers rapid decline also.

There is no reason to suppose that a government built on the principle of planning will differ, in this regard, from a government committed, in the main, to the *laissez-faire* principle. On the other hand, I see no evidence to suppose that the transition from capitalist democracy to planned democracy involves any temporary or permanent loss of freedom. But the defence of this hypothesis requires precise analysis of the content of freedom. I have already quoted the profound aphorism of Marx that freedom is the recognition of necessity. There is no point in crying for the moon unless we live on the moon. There are facts in the world about us to the inescapable consequence of which we must adjust our minds, like death and the need to buy, often with pain, the experience which gives its character of uniqueness to human personality. The essence of freedom, given the framework of necessity within which each of us must discover it, is, I think, to be found in what I have called the sense of continuous initiative, the conviction that each of us, even if involved in a social purpose which transcends our private purpose, can yet contribute to its definition some emphasis which is our own. Freedom, in short, is the knowledge that each of us counts as end, as well as instrument, that there is elbow-room in the society which gives us power to make our own choices, to experiment with ourselves. So that our freedom comes of a sense of spacious horizons we are empowered to scan, of opportunities unbarred in which we can find significance. A man is free in society when the operation of its institutions gives him that mood of creative hope which spurs him on to achieve a fulfilment in which he finds significance and exhilaration.

This is the explanation, I think, of why, despite the massive prohibitions its rulers have felt bound to impose, there is, nevertheless, in the Soviet Union a real freedom in the sense I have given to the term. If the Russian worker may not criticize Stalin, as the British worker can criticize Mr. Churchill or President Roosevelt, he can criticize his foreman or the manager of his factory in a way that is not easily open to the British worker. If his means are narrow, his housing poor, his career is not limited by his birth, he has no fear of unemployment, or of old age. His health is a national concern; the well-being of his children is the first care of the state; and the labour-power he puts at the service of society confers upon him dignity because it has ceased, in the capitalist sense, to be a commodity that is bought and sold. He has felt, for a generation, the zest of great adventure, the exhilaration that comes to most of us when we feel that we are part of an historic experiment that is big with fate. And what is true of the working-man is even more true of women. Communist dictatorship may plan the growth of the individuality of the citizens; and it may punish with harshness those who seek to escape from the fundamental rules of the plan. But that the communist dictatorship has in fact achieved for millions the sense of a capacity for growth seems to be beyond the possibility of serious denial. That sense of a capacity for growth, which enables its possessor to affirm his or her personality, is the very secret of freedom.

Here it becomes important to note that the adoption by a society of a planned system is based upon the common ownership of the instruments of production. If the purpose of the system is, as in Russia, community consumption, and if this is seen in terms of economic security, not for a small class of owners, as in capitalist democracy, where their privileges are limited only by a humanitarianism that is rarely widespread, on the one hand, and the power of the democracy to extract concessions from that class as the price of its safety, on the other, this purpose is bound to effect a pretty thoroughgoing trans-valuation of values which opens new individual and institutional perspectives for the idea of freedom. Because they are new, we must be careful to analyse them in terms of the premisses upon which they are built and not to assume that their effect is a denial of freedom.

Perhaps the simplest illustration of this trans-valuation emerges in the contrast between the functions of a trade union in a planned society of this kind and the methods of trade unionism in the capitalist democracies we know. The great British and American trade unions seek the protection of their members' interests by methods that are conditioned by the character of private ownership in an unplanned society in which profit-making by the owner is the main incentive to production. The result is that, first, no union can consider the effect of improvements it secures for its members, in wages, or in the hours of labour, either upon the general wage-structure of the society or in their reflection upon the general standards of consumption. The trade union which, like the United Garment Workers of America, deliberately interests itself in the efficiency of the employees in the industry with which it is concerned is rare. The trade union which can seriously enter the field with which management concerns itself is still more rare. Mainly, it requires a social consideration over and above the normal economic relationship of employer and workman, to make the trade union concern itself with advancing either the skill or the output of its members. The British or American trade union is engaged in a process which is concerned almost entirely, first, to safeguard the worker in his job, and, second, to secure for him the maximum material benefit out of its performance. The employer, at the same time, is mainly concerned only to purchase that supply of labour-power which he can use profitably, and, second, to admit only those conditions of material benefit to his workers which, granted their organized power, he is bound to admit; the limits of his admission being, once more, his ability to continue to earn a profit when he does so. The final weapon in the bargain on either side is the strike or the lock-out; and the bitterness these may engender, especially in the United States, has not seldom become a threat to social peace which compels the intervention of the state-power. And, in the last resort, since the purpose of the state-power in capitalist democracy is the preservation of the ultimate thesis of private ownership, that is, the making of profit for the owning class, it is rare for such intervention to assume the form of organized assistance to the trade unions. On the contrary, the very premisses of thought of those who operate the power of the state point in the opposite direction.

Now I do not think it can be denied that the benefits trade unionism has secured for its members in Britain and America have been very great and socially of vital importance. But I do not think it can be denied, either, that these benefits are not proportionate either to the social importance of any given industry in the national economy, or to the performance of any individual member in a particular union. Our economic system makes the process of collective bargaining imperative; but the interest of the community in its result is indirect rather than direct. The state-power which, from 1926 to 1939, stood idly by while hundreds of thousands of skilled workers in industries like mining, shipbuilding, or engineering, watched their craftsmanship rot slowly away, or sought to transfer from the job of a Welsh miner to that of a waiter in a London restaurant, paid the penalty for its faith in the uncontrolled higgling of the market for which it paid a grim price when it met the challenge of counter-revolution.

I certainly should not argue for a moment that the Russian experiment has solved in a really satisfactory way the place of trade unionism in the planned society. The Russian trade unionist can only bargain within limits about the wages he receives; for all practical purposes the strike-weapon is incapable of use; and so friendly an observer as Sir John Maynard has recorded his conviction that "the trade union movement in the U.S.S.R. does not defend the individual against overwork.[1] It is, I think, necessary to conclude that the main function of the Russian trade unions is more the increase of output than the defence of their members' interests. There are, no doubt reasons why special factors in the Soviet Union made this the position, above all the great race against time in the defence industries of the country; and it is clear that the place of the Communist Party in the trade union leadership means that the wage-earner's conditions are in large part settled upon a single plane of argument. The decisive factor is the Politbureau's view of what is desirable from the angle of the state's requirements after it has considered what it regards as the necessary volume of relevant evidence. The trade unions function in the

[1] *The Russian Peasant, and Other Studies* (1942), p. 341. I should like generally to express my debt to Sir John Maynard's remarkable book, the most profound and fair study of the Russian experiment known to me.

capacity of advisers who see that the implications of the evidence are made fully available. They have no sanction they can bring into play to compel a change in the ultimate decision.

Yet, granted that this is the case, I think it is probable that the Russian theory of the trade union function is more likely to be valid in a planned democracy than the theories to which either British or American experience have given rise. Once we agree that planned production for community consumption is the basic social principle in the economic life of the community, it seems to follow logically that an organization which exists to protect the interest of the workers must be directly and deeply interested in maximum output; for the level of that output will obviously determine the remuneration of the workers. It is, of course, not less clear that this interest involves a further interest in the technical and administrative efficiency of industry, and the safeguarding of those conditions of sanitation and safety upon which the workers' health depends.

But it is, I think, important to note that most of the restrictive devices of trade unionism in a capitalist society are built upon the assumption of an economics of scarcity with that reserve army of unemployed which the system involves, and upon the notion that the conditions attained by the workers in one field of industry may be legitimately settled by the strength of their bargaining power in that field without regard to the conditions attained by the workers in another field. The society which depends upon the mechanism of the free market, with its initial hypothesis of perfect competition and perfect mobility of labour, has had, save at brief moments and in particular places, very little relation to reality. Those hypotheses were the basis of that freedom of contract between an individual employer and an individual workman the unhappy results of which led to the growth of trade unions and their attempt to mitigate those results by the device of the common rate. The power of combination was invoked with results measured only by the comparative strength on either side—of which the strike or the lock-out was the ultimate test—and with but little relevance to the idea of a social purpose which gave the necessary perspective to economic conditions. It is worth remembering that, apart from relatively small experiments in New Zealand and Australia—the concept of a legal minimum imposed upon the employer by the state in "sweated" industries is so predominantly a twentieth-century conception, and largely the response to universal suffrage, that it is only with difficulty that it has won its way to constitutional acceptance by the Supreme Court in the America of the New Deal. It would not be true to say that the unions of one industry felt no responsibility for the standard of life of men and women working in another industry; the sympathetic strike alone is the proof that this is not so. But it is true to say that, on the economic plane, the system of the free market made that responsibility interstitial in space and occasional in time; it was as a voter seeking to reshape the state-purpose rather than as a trade unionist concerned with the implications of his place in industry, that the worker gave attention to the civic factors in economic organization. How slowly he developed the sense of those civic factors can be seen from the fact that, even in Britain, it took three-quarters of a century from the repeal of the Combination Acts for the political consciousness of the workers to recognize that the older political parties virtually assumed that the recognition of those civic factors by the state was a departure from, and not a recognition of, the norm; and that consciousness, in any wholesale way, has not yet developed in the United States.

It is important to emphasize all this because it reveals how deeply trade union organization has been unconsciously permeated by the individualism of the capitalist society to which it has been conditioned. The impossibly low wages of the girls in the department stores of New York would engage the attention of a civic organization, mainly middle-class in composition, like the Consumers' League; the organizations of the aristocracy of American Labour, the four Railroad Brotherhoods, for example, felt no concern for them. And it is national necessity rather than trade union action which, over a century after the Tolpuddle martyrs, has raised the minimum wage of agricultural workers to three pounds a week. The strategy of organization in trade unionism is still, historically for reasons that are quite natural, set by the forces which, in an unplanned society, divide the workers from one another rather than by the things which unite them. In the autumn of 1942 the British Trades Union Congress rejected a resolution to permit its General Council to enquire into the adequacy of its structure to the problems that it confronts; too many powerful unions feared the results of such an enquiry into the vested interests they fear to endanger. In 1942, also, one group of railway workers rejected the overtures of another group to form a single organization for the protection of their common interests; the first group held that the grades then represented would be better safeguarded by the maintenance of an independent union. Even the Mineworkers' Federation of Great Britain, which has behind it a great tradition of common action in the coalfields, still possesses an executive whose meetings resemble a congress of quasi-independent ambassadors from the different districts rather than the unified cabinet of a single industry which realizes that an injury to one is an injury to all.[1] The latent individualism of the trade union structure in capitalist democracies is revealed in the urgency with which they defend the individual sovereignty of the constituent units even when they face the same need for collective security as the nations which, one by one, Hitlerism was able to destroy. Nothing shows more decisively the implications of this attitude than their inability, during the present war, to agree upon common principles in the determination of wage-policy, and their failure to insist upon representation in the controls of industry at that level where decisions vital to their own future are being made.

I believe, for these reasons, that the process of collective bargaining in a planned democracy will result in a different content in the idea of the workers' freedom in industry than is involved in the habits of trade unionism in a capitalist democracy, and my own view is that it will move far nearer to the Russian model than its leaders in Britain or America are now prepared to imagine. The fact that the democracy is planned makes a difference; the fact that the planning is for the whole community and not in terms of the effective demand of a privileged few makes a difference; and the fact that these changes make possible the movement from an economics of scarcity to an economics of abundance makes a difference also. The trade union in a capitalist society is essentially a weapon of defence against an owning class which not only normally possesses, save in the most exceptional periods of boom, the initiative in financial power as well as the initiative in technique and management since it makes both of these its dependants; it is also a weapon of defence against an owning class the authority of which is such as to enable it, again save in the most exceptional times, to control that state-power which organizes those relations of production required to maintain its supremacy. The freedom of the worker, in a capitalist society, is therefore essentially a negative conception. It seeks, as it were, to safeguard for him a proportion in a total the size of which it is hardly able to determine in any important way; and that proportion, in its turn, is for all workers save a small

[1] Though it should be noted that the annual Conference of 1942 expressed approval of the plan for forming a unified, rather than a federal, trade union in the British mining industry. The negotiations for this plan have still to be seriously begun.

aristocracy of highly skilled men, largely based upon customary modes of living which leaves them no large margin above the sheer physical costs of living. That is why, as Mr. Bevin has pointed out,[1] as soon as a group of workers find it possible, in an emergency like war, to rise considerably beyond that margin, there is an immediate demand from employers that the state-power should intervene to stabilize wages. That reinforces each union in its determination to resist the emergence of a general wage-policy and emphasizes again the negative element in its attitude to freedom.

In a planned democracy, on the other hand, the concept of freedom becomes a positive one. The trade union, so to say, is assisting in the development of an estate no longer subject to the claims of vested interest. The relations of production have been adjusted proportionately to the forces of production. That adjustment makes it possible to transcend the old class-character of the society, and, as it is transcended, there emerges a new psychology of consumption. We can see that emergence, in the past, with the change in the habits of the rising bourgeoisie; it refuses to accept any longer the traditions in dress, in housing, in furniture, in food, to which it was confined in the epoch of feudalism. The writer, the artist, the schoolmaster, even the churches begin to adapt their ways of behaviour to the claims of the new consumers; Lillo, Hogarth, the dissenting academics, the Wesleyan movement, are all the response to a new mental climate in England which can only yearn for expression in contemporary France and remain half-underground; we must never forget that, until 1789, every critic of the ancien régime lived in the shadow of the Bastille, and that a peasant with enough property to be comfortable was, as Rousseau discovered,[2] desperately anxious to conceal its possession from public knowlege.

A planned democracy, as even Russia with limited capital, inferior technical skills, and the need of dictatorship imposed by civil war and external war, makes clear, develops a new psychology of consumption as it frees itself from its old class-character. With all the limitations which the shadow of constant fear has cast over the régime, with all the compulsions it has been found necessary to introduce in order to attain the objectives of revolutionary industrialization, and the end of small-scale agriculture, it is impossible not to notice in the Russian worker a pride in initiative, a sense of new horizons of opportunity, a refusal to be confined to ancient standards, which has made Russian freedom in industry on balance positive and not negative. The trade union has become a partner

[1] Parliamentary Debates cited above. [2] *Confessions* (ed. Hachette), p. 150.

with the state-power in promoting the productivity and the efficiency of the worker. Sir John Maynard has put the result in a sentence upon which too much emphasis cannot be laid. "An honourable status," he writes,[1] "satisfactory to the sense of human dignity has been secured by the Revolution to the Russian worker in virtue of his work. No one would deny an honourable status to the British worker—*if he touches his cap*." Granted that there are wide differences of remuneration; granted, also, that there is a good deal of bureaucratic deformation; granted, finally that the average Russian standard of living was far lower than that of the British worker, still more, that of the American, and that Hitler's aggression has increased the difference; he still has no fear of unemployment, no fear of ill health, and no fear of old age. He knows that his children have access to the best education available. He himself gets holidays with pay; he is ardently encouraged to find the meaning of that cultural heritage knowledge of which in a British worker still leads either to the patronage of his "betters," or to the risk that it may make him regarded as an agitator; and he does not suffer from the sense that there is a social and material world where living standards are qualitatively different from his own, and from which he is permanently separated. He feels that the present is his; given victory, he has a greater assurance than the citizen of any other society at present constituted, that, with the organization of an enduring peace, the future is his also. He has, in fact, the right to that self-respect which comes to a citizen who feels that his fulfilment is written into the foundations of the social purpose. Materially poor, on these prospects he is spiritually rich because there are no boundaries to his hope save those which he chooses to impose, above all, no boundaries of status because he is a member of the working class. All this is the outcome of the planned society—not yet a democracy—to which he belongs. When I compare the implications of this atmosphere with that of the capitalist democracies of Western Europe and America, it seems to me fantastic to deny it the achievement of an emancipation which the mass of men have never known in any other society. For he has, always given victory over Hitlerism and the prospect of enduring peace, the knowledge that the progress of his world is his progress too. Given this acceptance of the chance to assist in that progress, he has, as no other citizen in the masses of any other society, that right to make his destiny an element in the fulfilment of the common destiny which makes him significant to himself.

[1] *Op. cit.*, p. 343. The italics in the text are those of Sir John Maynard.

Over the endless years he has something creative to fulfil; over the endless years he need not, either, fear unemployment. He has status, therefore, and security. Both of these are positive goods; both of these depend upon the adaptation of social institutions to a transcendent aim which calls for an endless succession of pioneers in an adventure that has no end; neither of these is available to man or woman in the unplanned society which lives by the impersonal mechanism of the market in the capitalist democracies we know. That is why I call it a positive freedom which, so far in history, the vast majority of human beings have hardly even known they might dare to claim.

IV

I think it likely, as I have said, that, in the economic sphere, planned democracy will set a new context for freedom. As men are liberated from the fear of want and insecurity, they are set free for ends in which, as in our own society, so large a part of human personality is subordinated to the effort involved in conquering those fears. In the degree that this liberation is achieved, it is, I think, evident that the institutions which, like employers' associations, or the trusts, or the trade unions, have been so predominantly concerned with safeguarding their members from the consequences of that subordination, will operate in a new perspective and be adapted to the performance of new functions. Bodies, for example, like the Bar Council and the British Medical Association will find that their protective function becomes far less important than the contribution they can make to the improvement of the standards of legal and medical practice. A trade union like the Miners' Federation may well become not merely an organization seeking to protect its members from the grim price they have paid for private capitalism in the mining industry, but a body not less concerned to see that those who organize it in the interest of the community adopt the latest inventions and push forward scientific research in the utilization of its by-products. It may begin, too, to play a positive part of its own both in the development of mining engineering and fuel chemistry, and in the only half-developed area in which the problems of what education a miner needs to assure that his technique as a miner related to his social heritage as a citizen begin to be seriously studied. An economics of scarcity will only rarely think in these terms because, by its very nature, it conditions the men and the institutions who live under it to thinking almost wholly of how they can be free from this fear or that limitation. It is only as we move into the economics of abundance that the conquest of insecurity and poverty enables men to think of the positive ends to which freedom can be devoted. And only at the point where a positive freedom, in this sense, is possible can society provide with safety to itself for the expression of the whole individuality of man. Until arrival at that point becomes a conscious social purpose, which men are deliberately setting themselves, this expression is always purchased by some at the expense of others. Athenian democracy demands its slaves; the riches of the Roman aristocracy are built on the plundering of its conquered provinces; the luxury of the American millionaire does not, even when he has reached the level where convention demands philanthropy, conceal the broken lives of the steel worker in Pittsburgh or textile operative in Lowell. Fear is the price that freedom pays whenever its relations depend upon the security which private ownership is alone able to confer.

And just as a planned democracy will mean large changes in the context of economic freedom, so, also, it is bound to mean large changes in the context of political freedom, in both its individual and its institutional aspects. I cannot, of course, attempt here any detailed analysis, still less, venture a prophecy, of their character. I can make only one general observation, and offer two tentative illustrations of my meaning. The general observation is that the political institutions of capitalist democracy, whether in their parliamentary form, as in Britain and its Dominions, or in their Congressional form, as in the United States, are likely to undergo, if we succeed in establishing a planned democracy as the main type of society in the next phase of our civilization, radical changes in their very basis. For any historical study of their operation in action reveals the fact that they are, inherently, the institutions of a negative freedom. Their function has been, first, to protect the rights of a special class of property-owners, and their dependents, from invasion by the masses whose rights were not rooted in the ownership of property; this they effected by making the spinal column of legal ideas the notion that rights were a function of property. No one can scrutinize the principles of the Anglo-American Common Law, especially as the individualist armoury from which the judge draws his weapons to limit undue social presumptiveness in a legislature,[1] or the differential weight attached by the Code

[1] Cf. Pollock, *Essays in Jurisprudence* (1882), p. 85.

Napoléon to the claims of employer and worker,[1] without seeing that this is the case. And the second function of these political institutions has been to gauge the limits beyond which a refusal of concessions to the masses might jeopardize the whole system on which private property is the fundamental source of social power.

Nothing has more decisively exhibited the negative character of freedom in capitalist democracies than the slowness with which their political institutions have moved in the realm of education; and this has been largely the case because the owning class has never been able fully to make up its mind between its fear of popular knowledge, on the one hand, and its hope that its refining influence might mitigate the dangers of mobocracy, on the other. The result has been a compromise everywhere in which, though illiteracy has been largely overcome in the advanced countries of Western Civilization, there is still an overwhelming majority almost predestined, by reason of the stage at which their education ends, to become the victims of a kind of Gresham's law in that area of understanding where knowledge alone makes possible an effective citizenship. The vital fact, of course, is that the purpose of any educational system is necessarily set by the rôle that the citizen is intended later to play in the society; and a capitalist democracy has never been able to overcome, in its educational programme, the initial paradox that the drive of capitalist aims is in inherent contradiction with the drive of democratic aims. Our political institutions enable us to delay confronting the paradox by making now the one, and now the other, of those drives, the controlling factor in educational activity.

The same emphasis upon the negative side of freedom is obvious in the democratic system of political parties. They begin as groups of men almost wholly drawn either directly from the owning class, or from a profession, like that of the lawyers, dependent upon it; and the constituency they have constitutionally to satisfy only broadened slowly, except in the United States, to include the mass of the population. Two conclusions may, I think, be fairly drawn from the history of political parties everywhere: they could only operate capitalist democracy successfully so long as they did not shake the confidence of the owners of property. Once that confidence was shaken, as over slavery in the United States, or over the fear of socialism in France in the months between February and June of 1848, and, again, after the advent of the Blum Government to office in 1936, the effectiveness of the system was paralysed because

[1] Cf. my *Rise of European Liberalism* (1936), pp. 226–30.

those in power and those out of it did not speak a common language. When the system was effective, the difference between parties was always, in the field of action, a difference upon matters of detail and not upon matters of major principle. That really meant that no principle, under the party system, was ever translated into statute until its acceptance left the owners of property convinced that it would not harm them. So it took forty years of agitation to get the beginnings of a decent system of factory inspection, and sixty years' agitation to get a national system of elementary education established in Britain. The triumph of what we call "public opinion," in these and similar cases, means in fact that, at long last, the owning class deems it wise or unimportant to yield to the demand.

That this agreement upon fundamentals, as Lord Balfour termed it, is of the heart of the party system is borne out by the experience of socialist parties in the capitalist democracies. They raise no problem so long as their programme in action is merely a more emphatic version of that proposed by the parties which represent the claims of the owning class; but as soon as they move to act upon socialist principles, they throw the owning class into a panic, and the shadows of social conflict grow ominously dark. This position is interestingly illustrated by the situation of the British Labour Party in 1943. Doctrinally, it is committed to securing great changes in the ownership of the means of production before the close of the war; for it has insisted that, without those changes, the defeat of the counter-revolution which Hitler is seeking to achieve, will be a vain and empty sacrifice. Its leaders make large promises about the building of a new world in which the workers shall enjoy that economic security and the standard of life which, as it claims, would follow upon the great changes. But the representatives of the Labour Party in Mr. Churchill's government do not ask for any of the changes to which they are, like their followers, committed. They do not do so because they believe that Mr. Churchill and his Conservatist colleagues would reject their demands.

The leaders of the Labour Party are thus led to acquiesce in a policy which refuses to their doctrines the status of "fundamentals"; and they accept, as a result, methods of social organization incompatible with the kind of society to which they are committed. They defend their attitude in different ways. "National unity" must not be disturbed, in the interest of victory. The "nation"—which has never been consulted—would never forgive them if they shirked their "responsibilities"; their "responsibilities" being thus interpreted to mean the waging of the war on terms approved by the Conservative Party. At the end of the war, they say, the nation can choose between Conservative policy and Socialist policy, though this view omits the vital fact that, at the end of the war, the impulse that gives agreement and consent their atmosphere of urgency will have largely become inoperative.

Or they urge that an attitude of "give and take" is the implied condition of coalition government; and they point to a long list of social reforms, the "guaranteed week," the increase in old age pensions, the virtual abolition of the means test, and so forth, which, in the absence of coalition, it would, in their judgment, have taken long years to achieve.

But if we seriously examine the character of the social reforms the Labour leaders have secured, it is clear that none of them presupposes any change in the relations of production while the Coalition Government lasts; and it is the central thesis of the Labour Party's doctrine that, in the absence of such changes before the end of the war, the fruits of victory will have been thrown away. There is, therefore, a decisive contradiction between the acts of the Labour leaders and the principles of their party. The Labour leaders assist in the application of a policy which destroys the hope of achieving the ends to which they are formally committed.

The reason for this contradiction is, I think, an obvious one. The vital source of social power is the character of productive relations; it is these that the state exists above all to protect. Political institutions must accommodate themselves to that character; and a political party which seeks to change it is dependent on the agreement of the ruling class (which possesses the vital social power) to the change it proposes. The Labour leaders have been unable to secure that agreement; and they must therefore either accept, in a general way, the *status quo*, getting out of it the best they can, or fight to change it. The latter, of course, involves going out of the Coalition Government. Since this is a risk the Labour leaders do not dare to take, they are compelled to fight the war, for all effective purposes, on the terms which the ruling class approves.

This is to say, in fact, that, whatever the party divisions in a society, the character of a state will set the limits of peaceful action within a framework compelled by its relations of production. There will be, no doubt, some elasticity of movement; differences about the level of taxation, the respective places of industry and agriculture, the quantum of social services, the amount of free education, all these are permissible so long as the boundaries of the framework are not overpassed except with the consent of those who set them. What is vital is that party action is conditioned to that consent by the nature of the parliamentary system in a capitalist democracy. The differences between parties is always a matter of degree and not of kind in the field of action as distinct from the field of ideas. That is why Sir John Simon[1] can fit without difficulty into governments headed by men with political philosophies so formally different as those of Mr. Asquith, Mr. MacDonald, Mr. Baldwin, and Mr. Chamberlain. As soon as the field of action is entered, what is selected, so to say, from the philosophy for the statute-book are those elements only which fall within the framework to which I have referred.

It is, I think, obvious that this will also be true in a planned democracy. Once the character of its state-power is set by the fact that the vital instruments of production are publicly, and not privately owned, the field of party action, as distinct from the philosophies of parties, must be related to the consequences inherent in that principle. A Conservative Party is, formally, conceivable in a socialist democracy which urges the abandonment of socialism and a return to what it recommends as the superior advantages of private enterprise; but its actual measures will always be essentially related to the framework of action implied in the socialist character of the state-power. Its ideas, in short, will operate in the society very much as the ideas of the Communist Party operate in a capitalist democracy. They will be tolerated so long as they are not regarded as a danger; they will be persecuted immediately they seem to threaten its foundations.

For political parties in a planned democracy revolve around a central principle of freedom fundamentally different from that of a capitalist democracy. In the latter, the idea of freedom is negative; set in the context of the private ownership of the means of production, it must at all vital points save the rights of owners from invasion, since, otherwise, it ceases to be a capitalist democracy. Its immanent logic is, therefore, freedom from interference by the state-power with the use to which the owning class puts its property; and the condition which justifies interference is that minor concessions are made for the overriding and ultimate concern. But, in a planned democracy, the idea of freedom is positive; set as it is in the context of the public ownership of the means of production, it

[1] In the Churchill Government, of course, Viscount Simon, and Lord Chancellor.

seeks freedom for the fullest development of the public estate. In a planned democracy, so to say, the more the individual citizen can give, the more, also, he can receive, since the larger the volume of production the higher is the standard of life. The business of government in a planned democracy is thus set in the context of the understanding that the more fully it enables the citizen to give of his best, the more, also it is making available for the well-being of other citizens. Political parties in a planned democracy are, therefore, likely to differ from one another in the respective views they hold of the best way to develop the public estate from the angle of the values they accept.

It is easy, for example, to see that one group of citizens may take the view that it is worth having a higher standard of material comfort in return for some sacrifice of leisure. It is probable, especially if we have the good fortune to pass from the economics of scarcity to the economics of abundance without paying the price of a destructive revolution, that one group of citizens may prefer an earlier age of retirement from the routine work of industry or agriculture. It is conceivable, again, that the difference may be centred upon the age at which the youth of a nation begins to earn its living. Granted, in short, the positive character of freedom the function of a political party seems to me more likely to be particular than general. They will not, as it were, be a method, like the party-conflict in a capitalist democracy, of making war without resort to violence, requiring, therefore, organizations of a permanent character, which organize continuously for battle in the knowledge that to the victor belongs the spoils.

The importance of this implication in the idea of a positive freedom requires little emphasis. Anyone who examines the alternative result in the unplanned society of capitalist democracy will see at once that the negative freedom round which the party struggles of the latter revolve means a twofold struggle. On the one hand, it is a struggle to protect the owners of property against the claims of the propertyless masses; on the other, it is a struggle within the propertied class to tilt the balance of state-power towards one interest rather than towards another. This is seen in the evolution of the state's attitude to the poor, the way in which, with the growth of a capitalist production for the market, they were slowly but relentlessly schooled to the discipline which the factory system required, and the slow recognition by the law that a combination of the poor for self-protection must not be regarded as a conspiracy in restraint of trade, or in measuring the relative importance the law has attached to offences against the rights of property in contrast with offences against the rights of persons.

The second type is illustrated by the history of such controversies as those over the tariff, with its respective incidence upon the interest of agriculture and industry; it is the tariff which enabled the junker of East Prussia to maintain his hold on German sovereignty against the rising power of the German middle class. It is seen again in the history of the grant to corporations of such franchises as those upon which the transport systems of the United States have depended.

The politics of negative freedom, in a word, are, both internally and externally, power-politics. It is the safeguarding by force, whether open or implied, of a privilege which some secure to the exclusion of others. The essence of negative freedom, in fact, is the compulsory maintenance of as much inequality as will not prevent the society from functioning as a going concern. This, of course, is why, when capitalism can no longer fulfil itself in democratic terms, it moves, quite logically, to counter-revolution.

The central purpose of a positive freedom looks to quite different ends. It seeks to organize opportunities which harmonize the individual purpose and the social purpose. It is thus seeking to create the environment in which the emergence of an integrated personality becomes possible for the mass of citizens. That integration cannot be attained in an economics of scarcity; the society it dominates is bound to confine that possibility, save in the case of very exceptional persons, to those who have rights because they have the property which is the basis of rights. In a society built upon the economics of scarcity the lot of most people is bound to be insecurity, poverty, and submission; and this condition means that for these the gate to freedom is barred unless they can enter the class of property-owners. This implies, if we are frank about it, that the frustration of personality is the normal condition of most persons; for the law, at bottom, gives them the choice between submission and defiance. Whichever they choose, fulfilment is not open to them in a way lifely to create an harmonious personality.

It therefore follows that the condition upon which capitalism can serve the masses is its movement from the plane of negative to the plane of positive freedom. To do so, it must be capable of relating the rights it safeguards to personality as such and not to property; and this relation is incompatible with capitalism. For, at bottom capitalism makes the masses dependent on the impersonal laws of the market in the economic field, and upon the values, outside it, which the character of capitalism requires. And those values will not express the experience of the masses themselves; they will express the experience of that owning class which dominates a capitalist society. The masses, therefore, are bound, as individuals, to feel their insignificance; they cannot affirm themselves without challenging the institutions of which they are instruments merely. That is why, as Graham Wallas has shown,[1] so small a proportion of the workers find happiness in their employment. That is why, also, the worker who announces his dissatisfaction with his work risks the security of his job. The conditions of the market exclude this right to affirm himself from the terms of his employment; what is bought is not his personality, but his labour-power, and he must adjust the habits of his personality to the terms upon which that labour-power is regarded as worth purchasing by his employer. Even the attempt by trade unions to mitigate the impact of those terms still means that the overwhelming majority of the workers must find their main means of self-expression outside the economic function they perform. And to this must be added the fact that, in the acquisitive society, only a small proportion of the workers have either the means or the training to make their leisure significant.

It is important to the argument I am making to realize that, even amid the immense difficulties it has confronted, and despite the massive repressions its rulers have felt compelled to impose, the psychological result of social ownership in Russia has been the growing emergence of a positive freedom. Sir John Maynard has remarked how frequently observers have noted the sense in the workers that the factories are theirs, the exhilaration in the atmosphere, the importance for personality of the fact that function, and not spending-power, is the source of social distinction. There is not, as with ourselves, a class-character in education or culture or amusement. To be "somebody" means doing something, not having something. The worker's initiative is valuable to the society; it is not, as in capitalist democracy, a possible threat to the principle of its security. There are wide and important inequalities—in wages, in housing, to take the main examples. But these inequalities, if I may use a paradox, do not destroy the wholesale permeation of Soviet society by the egalitarian idea. Its citizens are, in the main, better able to find public significance for individual personality than in any other society of the present day. With all its limitations, in its phase of dictatorship, it genuinely seeks to exalt, and does in fact exalt, the stature of its citizens. Their fulfilment aids the reali-

[1] *The Great Society* (1914), p. 341 f.

zation of its central purpose, and does not threaten it. Where this situation exists, freedom in society has begun to operate on a positive plane.

This conclusion is, of course, abhorrent to those who accept the desirability of a capitalist society. They point to the limitations on free utterance, the purges, the restrictions on freedom of movement, the low standard of living compared with advanced capitalist countries, the fear of the stranger. Follies like the criticism of music as "bourgeois," or that period in which the man of letters was asked by the writers' organization to conform to standards which suggested that every novel must be a Communist tract and every poem an ode to Stalin's achievements, are contrasted with the uninhibited Paris of the Third Republic, or the London in which Marx and Lenin could discover the materials for the indictment of capitalist civilization. To see in contemporary Russia the emergence of positive freedom seems to such critics a contradiction in terms. And their view is obviously shared by socialist critics of the Right who find in the life of a Soviet citizen of to-day a grim contradiction of the socialist ideal.[1]

I think this view a wholly mistaken one because I think it is unhistorical. What has been taking place in the Soviet Union, amid pain and strife and anger, is a transvaluation of all values, the birth of a new civilization. The change has been effected by violent revolution and not by peaceful consent; it is not, therefore, surprising that it should be marked by follies and blunders and crimes. But the critics are no more justified in identifying these with the whole life of the Soviet Union than they would be in identifying the whole life of the French Revolution with the Terror. It is unhistorical because of its failure to realize that when massive transvaluations of this kind take place the criteria of the past must be adapted to the new principles if they are to be relevant. It is obvious that, in the change from feudal to capitalist society at the time of the Reformation, a change akin to that of the Russian Revolution took place; and it is clear that the impact of the change seemed outrageous to those critics whose criteria were the ethical values of the medieval church. The Wars of Religion and the Puritan Rebellion are evidence enough that the differences of the sixteenth and seventeenth centuries were conflicts about the ultimate matters of social constitution. The men of that age fought bitterly over matters we have hardly the patience to examine. It may seem

[1] For example, my friend and colleague, Mr. E. F. M. Durbin, in his *Politics of Democratic Socialism* (1940).

to us inexplicable that a great Parliamentarian like Sir John Eliot could persuade the House of Commons to resolve, in 1628, that any who sought to "extend or introduce" Arminianism should be "reputed a capital enemy to this Kingdom and commonwealth."[1] The reason, of course, was the intelligible one that it was because religions then formed the basis of defence by which one set of interests and principles rather than another set determined the purpose of the state-power. "These men," wrote Wentworth, of Prynne and Bastwick and Burton, "do but begin with the Church that they might have free access to the State"[2]; it was for this reason that he approved the penalties imposed upon them for religious teachings hostile to the accepted doctrine of the Church of England as Laud persuaded the High Commission to interpret it. The conflicts which tore Europe in pieces between 1500 and 1648 were conflicts about the ultimate values which are to be imposed by the state. That is what Professor Tawney means by saying that Calvin did for the middle class in the sixteenth century what Marx did for the working-class in the nineteenth.[3] The new society which Calvin's doctrines made possible did not seem less outrageous at Rome or Vienna or Madrid than the new society which the doctrines of Marx and Lenin helped to make seems outrageous in Lombard Street or Wall Street. That is because the premisses upon which it is deemed outrageous refuse to take account of the transvaluation it is making.

What the critics of the Soviet Union do in fact, when they deny the emergence there of these new values, is to compare the first phase of a new civilization with the mature achievements of an older civilization; or alternatively, they compare a conceptual capitalism in which competition is perfect and labour infinitely mobile with the actuality of a society which had only begun to recover from the hideous wounds of domestic tyranny, foreign attack, and violent revolution. They naturally award their votes against the idea that planned democracy is compatible with freedom. But they achieve this result first by concealing the fact that the freedom they eulogize is, in fact, enjoyed only by a small proportion of citizens in capitalist democracy, and, second, by refusing to admit that their picture of capitalism *in abstracto* has little serious relation

[1] But cf. the admirable remarks of Mr. Trevor in the introduction to his *Life* of Archbishop Laud (1940); and see Gardiner, *History of England*, vii, 75.

[2] Strafford *Letters*, II, 99.

[3] *Religion and the Rise of Capitalism* (1926), p. 111; but cf. my *Rise of European Liberalism* (1936), p. 29 f.

to an economic scene in which the growth of vast monopolies not only leaves the individual helpless in a world they dominate, but an economic scene, also, a serious protest against which may evoke from his masters that counter-revolution which employs the outlaws like Hitler and Mussolini to add the destruction of his hope to the loss of his security.

Whether we take the manual worker or the clerical worker in capitalist society, even in its democratic forms, what is obvious to any honourable observer is the loss of its *élan* and its elasticity. In the hours of toil, it can find significance only for a small proportion of the great army of workers; and even the land of promise, as in America, is limiting the chance of attaining that significance by the increasing stratification which its economic habits involve. In the hours of leisure, it must seek to impose conventions and conformities which safeguard it against the risk of dangerous thoughts among its dependents. So that its educational systems, its forms of amusement, its press, are all vast mechanisms of propaganda seeking to condition the workers and their children to the acceptance of the vital postulate that no affirmations of democracy are valid if they disturb the confidence of the employers in the security of their power. Man who has mastered the forces of nature is reduced to impotence and insignificance by a system of values which bids him be free at his peril. At the best, he finds escape in that proud challenge which makes him a rebel against the prison in which he is enclosed; at the worst, like Dostoievski's tragic creation, he has "no need more urgent than the one to find someone to whom he can surrender, as quickly as possible, the gift of that freedom with which, unhappy creature, he was born."

This is the reality for the mass of mankind which our present social order bids the common people accept as freedom; and even this reality must be defended by war against a nightmare even more hideous. The power of the rulers in our civilization to deceive their subjects is, no doubt, profound; but it is not a limitless power. I think there is reason to suppose that its authority now approaches its final phase.

V

The economic philosophy which has been the main clue to social action in the last hundred years was very largely the outcome of generalizations, both sociological and psychological, built upon the habits of the middle classes in Western Europe and the United

States; and, in a considerable degree, upon observations of the Protestant peoples who, after the Reformation, increasingly dominated the commercial intercourse of nations. Its principles were vitally affected, therefore, by three factors. There was, first, the assumption that commercial activity, as such, is the index to an advancing civilization; this led to the belief not only that the business man is its central figure, but, also, to a conviction from which we are only beginning to escape, that legislation which impeded the success of the business man was a hindrance to progress. It is this conviction which explains why men of the moral insight of John Bright could oppose the Factory Acts, and why even so passionate a defender of democratic government as Lincoln should believe that a free society was one in which the energetic workingman could hope to move upwards until he himself became an independent employer of labour.[1]

The second factor was its assumption, natural enough in the technological conditions under which it originated, that, whatever the degree of our exertions, the inherent niggardliness of nature meant a low level of material well-being for the mass of mankind. The economic philosopher rarely examined the changing technological horizons; and the very character of the legal system made him view most attempts to transcend the individualist scheme he was unconsciously justifying as an attack on security which would, of itself, be fatal even to the low level attained by men. That is why the nineteenth century is haunted by the idea of revolution; few of its thinkers ever really escaped from the glimpse, as they deemed it, into the abysses of 1789 and 1848. That is why, also, they tend to make the poor a moral, rather than a social category; and they deal with them in terms of a charity which never fully separates itself from religious effort into secular administration. The necessity of mass-poverty is one of the pillars of the middle-class creed; and that pessimistic fatalism is unquestioned by either serious thinkers like Ricardo or men of the type immortalized by Dickens and Balzac. To question the dogma was to embrace a heresy which either put one out of court as a scientific observer or made one a rebel who threatened the security which had been so painfully attained. The angry fears which the First International aroused all over Europe are perhaps less significant in this regard than the panic into which propertied America was thrown by the Haymarket riots; for, in Europe, there were, in the 'sixties and 'seventies, large areas in which the bourgeoisie still lived in the shadow of feudal

[1] *Writings of Abraham Lincoln* (Modern Library), pp. 560 f.

claims to power, while the bourgeoisie of America had no rivals to contest its supremacy.

Reason, in the economic philosophy which shaped the horizons of the state-power, was no more detached from the historic conditions which gave that philosophy birth, than it had been in previous periods. It performed its traditional function of clothing with respectability the title of men to power who actually held power, and deploying the whole army of fallacies which, over a century ago, Bentham remorselessly exposed for what they were, as though, in the new garments in which successive generations reclothed them, they were the soldiers of eternal truth. So, when the socialists turned the labour theory of value against those in whose interest it was originally made, the marginal theory of value emerged as the protective armament of the existing order; and when there grew up a generation unable to perceive good cause for the simple ecstasy with which John Bates Clark, for example, identified the existing property-system with the inherent pattern of the universe, the whole edifice of political economy was abandoned, in its historic form, for a "pure" science of economics which almost resented as intrusion into the perfection of its logical structure the real universe of living men and women whose emotions and ideas made them useless as chessmen in the game economists were playing with one another. It was, perhaps, as much for the perception he emphasized so strongly of the need for economics to confront the facts of life, as for his insistence that the economists could not obtain the right answers because they were not asking the right questions, which has made Lord Keynes seem—what in fact he has never been—a revolutionary figure to the schoolmen of this generation.

The third factor which vitally affected our social philosophy was the nightmare Malthus summoned to haunt the dreams of those in whom the French Revolution had aroused an optimism of outlook. No doubt there are societies, China, for example, and India, in which, given the present level of production, the size of the population bordered upon the means of subsistence. But it is also true that, first, there was no relation between misery and density of population before the Industrial Revolution, and that, since the end of the eighteenth century, an increase in population, both in Europe and America, has been mostly accompanied by an increase in material well-being. Until the war of 1914 Western civilization, from such a period as the age of Charles the Great, has not seriously felt circumstances which could make the warnings of Malthus relevant.

Bourgeois civilization was able to maintain its values as predominant over all competing values so long as three conditions existed. It required the power to expand markets; it had to be able to improve its standards of technology; and it needed continents which, like America, it could populate and bring into use. It began to break down when the legal relations upon which it was built made the first and third of these conditions decreasingly available to it. Granted those relations, and the power-politics which were their outcome, it was bound to lead, as past civilizations similarly situated have led, to war and revolution, and that the more inescapably because the religious sanction it had been able to employ in its rise had so largely lost its hold over men. The purpose of any scheme of values in a society is to promote the habits among its citizens which permit of expanding welfare.

These values can be imposed in either of two ways—by force or by persuasion. But in so complex and delicate an organization as modern society the attempt, over any long period, to impose a scheme of values by force can never be successful since, on the one hand, it contradicts the implications of the technological position—which requires peace if these are to be progressive—and, on the other, it imposes hardships on the masses which breaks their allegiance to their rulers and results in social upheaval. At the point where breakdown occurs, therefore, it becomes necessary to find new values in the imposition of which the conditions of expanding welfare can be re-discovered.

It is this necessity which we confront to-day; and it is the argument of this book that it is a revolutionary necessity. Or, rather, it is a revolutionary necessity if we assume that the purpose of a social order is to widen the area within which the values of civilization, truth and peace, beauty and love and experiment with one's self, are capable of realization in individual men and women. For to achieve that realization we require security, and a civilization, and the societies within it, has the conviction of security only when it feels that the means of peaceful growth are available to it. And it is precisely this conviction that contemporary civilization has lost.

That is why, in nations like Italy and Germany, men of the type of Hitler and Mussolini have arisen. It is evident that if the values I have called civilized are to regain their persuasive power, there is no alternative to the utter defeat of the systems they symbolize since the destruction of those values is, with them, a policy of calculated necessity. But it is less easy to see that the mere fact of their defeat does not restore their past authority to civilized values.

The fallacy of that view lies in the static approach it makes to our problems. All living is process, and all process is by its nature dynamic. We cannot seek, with any hope of success, to recapture a moment in past time. We have to adjust ourselves, first, to the understanding that the effort itself to recapture that moment in which Hitler and Mussolini rose to power will merely give birth to new men of similar mould; and we have to adjust ourselves, second, to the understanding that, in organizing their defeat, we have moved out of the categories, both institutional and intellectual, to which we were conditioned by bourgeois civilization.

Our position is as simple as it is decisive. The technological conditions are present for a wider satisfaction of human demands than at any previous period of man's history; but our power to use those conditions is frustrated and inhibited by a state-purpose which denies their implications. Either we use the period in which, as now, the need to defeat our enemies enables us by common consent to redefine the state-purpose, or, after victory, we shall find ourselves still facing a need we are too divided to meet by persuasion instead of force. There is profound evidence on all sides, and in all countries, of a will to attempt the task of re-definition, of the mood which recognizes in the character of our danger the obligation to great audacity. Totalitarian war compels men to live on the heights; as they stand upon that eminence they can see vistas which become obscure once more when, as the challenge is overcome, they descend again into the valley. To overcome the challenge men and women give of their best, in mind and heart and spirit, straining all their energy of soul and body to defeat the dark forces by which they are surrounded.

Great leadership would take advantage of that mood; and great leaders would be aware that a failure to take advantage of it will appear as cowardice unforgivable to posterity. There are two reasons for this. The great mood when crisis challenges a generation to transcend its recognized past purposes is always followed by a period of fatigue; in that aftermath, the leaders who call for a further effort find only too often that the strength to respond has gone. It is in such an aftermath that the disproportion between what the time needs and what the outworn order permits in response evokes the anger and the disillusion which wreck stability in a social order. The wise statesman, therefore, is the man who asks the most of his fellow-citizens in the hour when they are most eager to give most. That is the one sure way to fulfil hope; it is the one sure way, also, thereby to avoid catastrophe. For no age is more prone to violence than one in which the daily experience of citizens is of a life disappointed by the denial to them of dreams they were invited to dream.

The other reason is simple enough. Twice in a lifetime now the youth of the world has been sent to die in battle in the passionate assurance that thereby they secure the promise of a richer life to those who survived; and twice youth has gone to the abyss in the faith that the richer life would be forthcoming. No one who remembers the millions to whom the first world-war was a high adventure doomed to a frustration which made the inter-war years mean and cold and empty can bear even to suspect that the faith of youth can be cheated a second time. No statesman dare ask that sacrifice unless he builds upon its exaction an achievement the dead would not think unworthy of their death. "I must confess," wrote Fuller three hundred years ago,[1] "I must confess I ever prized Peace for a pearl, but we never did or could set the true estimate and value upon it till this interruption and suspension of it. *Now* we know, being taught by dear experience, that peace is a beautiful blessing." Now, indeed, we know; but we shall never be forgiven unless we make our knowledge a living part of the world that knowledge can shape.

[1] Thomas Fuller, Sermon preached at the Savoy Chapel, December 28, 1642.